POPULATION AND HEALTH IN DEVELOPING COUNTRIES

VOLUME 1

POPULATION AND HEALTH IN DEVELOPING COUNTRIES

VOLUME 1

Population, Health, and Survival at INDEPTH Sites

Samuel J Clark

INTERNATIONAL DEVELOPMENT RESEARCH CENTRE
Ottawa • Cairo • Dakar • Montevideo • Nairobi • New Delhi • Singapore

2002

Published by the
International Development Research Centre
PO Box 8500, Ottawa, ON, Canada K1G 3H9
http://www.idrc.ca

© INDEPTH Network 2002

National Library of Canada cataloguing in publication data

Main entry under title :
Population and health in developing countries. Volume 1. Population, health, and survival at
INDEPTH sites

Includes bibliographical references.
INDEPTH : International Network for the continuous Demographic Evaluation of
Populations and their Health.
ISBN 0-88936-948-8

1. Public health surveillance — Developing countries.
2. Public health surveillance — Africa.
3. Health planning — Developing countries.
4. Public health — Developing countries — Statistics.
5. Public health — Africa — Statistics.
6. Developing countries — Population — Statistics.
7. Health status indicators.
I. INDEPTH Network.
II. International Development Research Centre (Canada)

RA652.2.P82.P66 2001   614.4'22724   C2001-980345-1

IDRC Books endeavours to produce environmentally friendly publications. All paper used is recycled as well
as recyclable. All inks and coatings are vegetable-based products. The full catalogue of IDRC Books is available
at http://www.idrc.ca/booktique.

CONTENTS

PART I. DSS CONCEPTS AND METHODS

Chapter 1. Core Concepts of DSS

Chapter 2. DSS-generated Mortality Rates and Measures

Chapter 3. DSS Methods of Data Collection

Chapter 4. Processing DSS Data

Chapter 5. Assessing the Quality of DSS Data

PART II. MORTALITY AT INDEPTH SITES

Chapter 6. Comparing Mortality Patterns at INDEPTH Sites

Chapter 7. INDEPTH Mortality Patterns for Africa

PART III. INDEPTH DSS SITE PROFILES

Appendix 1. Working Examples of DSS Forms

Appendix 2. Acronyms and Abbreviations

Appendix 3. Glossary

Appendix 4. Bibliography

FOREWORD

Traditional sources of health information collected from health facilities often serve as the basis for health-services planning and allocation of resources in many parts of the developing world. Yet, health-facility-based data provide only fragmentary and biased information. Not all population groups have geographic or economic access to health facilities. Those that do have such access are usually self-selected and are often those who visit health-care centres only when they suffer from a serious illness. A great majority of poor people may have less access to health-care facilities than those who are better off, and poor people often treat themselves or use nontraditional health care. Women may suffer gender disparities as well, with time and cultural constraints on the use of health-care facilities, particularly in rural settings. Services for children are also severely constrained. Thus, health-facility-based data are not representative of the health problems of all rural and urban communities and do not therefore reflect their health status.

This void of valid health information for a large segment of the world's population makes it difficult for policymakers to formulate rational health policies to improve the health of these people. As the authors of this book argue, "the need to establish a reliable information base to support health development has never been greater" (INDEPTH Coordinating Committee, this volume, p. 1). Ideally, reliable health information should be population and community based, inclusive of all groups, and collected prospectively and continuously. Such an ideal is best met through demographic and health surveillance systems collecting demographic and health data on selected population samples. Often, randomly selected cross-sectional household surveys every few years complement these methods of research.

Demographic and health surveillance systems serve a number of functions:

- They provide health information that more accurately reflects the prevailing disease burden of populations;

- They assist in monitoring and tracking new health threats, such as emerging and reemerging infectious disease and drug resistance, and alert the health community to prepare a response; and

- They can serve as a platform for action-oriented research to test and evaluate health interventions, such as new vaccines or drugs, health-education messages, and the cost-effectiveness of initiatives.

The premier example of such a system is the Health and Demographic Surveillance System (formerly known as the Demographic Surveillance System) of Matlab, Bangladesh, which started operations in 1963 as a major component of the field research program of the International Centre for Diarrhoeal Disease Research, Bangladesh. It is recognized as the largest and longest sustained prospective longitudinal demographic and health surveillance of any population in the world. It has made significant contributions to health development in both Bangladesh and the rest of the world. The high cost of running such a system has delayed replication in other parts of the developing world. However, thanks to the fast-paced development of user-friendly computers, this constraint has been partially overcome.

Over the last decade, a growing number of community-based field stations have evolved in Asia and sub-Saharan Africa and started to generate reliable longitudinal population-based health and demographic data. This bodes well for countries with such stations, as it marks the first step toward rational health planning and meaningful health programs for the people of these countries. Recently, these stations joined to form a network called the International Network for the continuous Demographic Evaluation of Populations and Their Health in developing countries (INDEPTH), creating "a trans-continental resource of robust, longitudinal, health and demographic data in some of the most information deprived settings in the world" (INDEPTH Founding Document; http://www.indepth-network.org). In the span of a few years, INDEPTH has matured rapidly, succeeding in strengthening the capabilities of member sites and developing strategies to harness their potential to redress long-standing inequities in health. This development has been possible because of the dedication and hard work of a few individuals, and this monograph is clearly an indication of the high quality of the network's work.

The emergence of INDEPTH should be welcome news to the donor community, where people often, and rightly, complain that the programs they fund in low-income countries are not usually based on the real needs of the people. By the same token, donors should come out strongly in support of INDEPTH, because they will be investing in an initiative that directly addresses one of the major constraints of development assistance. Researchers in program countries should also take advantage of the INDEPTH sites to promote essential national health research. The domination of health-facility-based biomedical research should give way to policy-relevant research with the likelihood of a more immediate effect on the health of the people in the countries in the program.

Demissie Habte
World Bank
Washington, DC
1 June 2001

PREFACE

This monograph is the first in a series from the International Network for the continuous Demographic Evaluation of Populations and Their Health in developing countries (INDEPTH). It seeks to do several things. First, it seeks to compile, for both easy reference and comparative purposes, and in detailed and summary formats, the essential characteristics of each participating demographic surveillance system (DSS) site. Second, it seeks to present, for the first time, the mortality structure of each of these sites in a coherent and comparative format. Third, based on a network-wide analysis of the African site data, it proposes a methodology to generate, again for the first time, African model life tables that are based on objective empirical data.

The focus of this volume is the structures of populations at INDEPTH sites and the characteristics of their health and survival. The monograph is divided into three parts: Part I discusses core concepts and methods used in DSSs; Part II provides a comparison of mortality patterns in INDEPTH sites; and Part III presents profiles of INDEPTH sites.

As this is the first publication of its kind on DSSs in Africa and Asia, we thought it would be expedient to discuss core concepts and methods commonly used in most of the sites. Among the concepts discussed in Chapter 1 are the DSS area, longitudinality, DSS subjects, residency and membership, and core DSS events. Rates and measures generated using DSS are discussed in Chapter 2, with specific emphasis on the use of person–years lived in calculating rates. Chapter 3 discusses the DSS methods of data collection, starting with the initial census to establish the DSS population. This chapter discusses initial censuses, update rounds, and the vital events-registration system. It also puts emphasis on mortality monitoring and the tracking of migrants. The processing of DSS data is the main focus of Chapter 4. This chapter treats the important issues of quality assurance and control at the data-processing level. In Chapter 5, Part I ends with a discussion of the quality of DSS data, both in the field and at the data centre. This chapter then provides a detailed discussion of statistical and demographic techniques for analysis of DSS data.

Part II presents a comparison of mortality patterns of INDEPTH sites for the 1995–99 period. Chapter 6 starts with a discussion of crude overall mortality at INDEPTH sites. This chapter presents an INDEPTH population-age standard for sub-Saharan Africa (SSA) for the standardization of mortality rates, and it gives the reason for using this new standard instead of the United Nations models.

The INDEPTH age standard for SSA typifies the population in developing countries, with its very young age structure. INDEPTH sites have used this standard to compare mortality in SSA. This comparison highlights age-specific mortality, considering mortality in infancy, childhood, and adulthood. This discussion compares the INDEPTH standard for SSA with the Segi population and the new World Health

Organization standard population. The chapter ends with a presentation of basic life-table indicators for INDEPTH sites, based on their age-specific mortality rates over the 1995–99 period. Part II ends with Chapter 7, which analyzes more than 6.4 million person–years of observation at the African INDEPTH sites to identify mortality patterns. The emergent patterns are demonstrated to be substantially different from conventionally used model mortality patterns applied in Africa.

Part III presents profiles of 22 INDEPTH sites. The profiles are listed in alphabetical order, first according to region, and then according to country. These profiles are expected to stand for some time as the main reference source for basic details about INDEPTH sites and their DSS operations. Based on a structured template, each profile provides a site description, including the physical geography and population characteristics. It discusses DSS procedures at the site, including data collection and processing. Finally, each profile presents basic outputs, including demographic indicators. A summary matrix of all the DSS sites, presented in the introduction to Part III, provides the core details for each site.

INDEPTH monograph editorial team for Volume 1:

Osman A. Sankoh (University of Heidelberg, Germany, and Nouna DSS, Burkina Faso)

Kathleen Kahn (Agincourt DSS, South Africa)

Eleuther Mwageni (Rufiji DSS, Tanzania)

Pierre Ngom (Nairobi DSS, Kenya)

Philomena Nyarko (Navrongo DSS, Ghana)

1 June 2001

ACKNOWLEDGMENTS

This volume is an outgrowth of the efforts of many people, both INDEPTH members and its collaborators, who gave of their time and expertise to writing these chapters. We would like to particularly thank the following for their invaluable contributions to the corresponding chapters:

- Pierre Ngom, Justus Benzler, Geoff Solarsh, and Vicky Hosegood (Chapter 1);

- Rose Nathan, Heiko Becher, and Abdur Razzaque (Chapter 2);

- Eleuther Mwageni and Robert Mswia (Chapter 3);

- Peter Wontuo, Noah Kiwanuka, and Jim Phillips (Chapter 4)[1];

- Philomena Nyarko, Fred Binka, and Mark Collinson (Chapter 5);

- Sam Clark and Pierre Ngom (Chapter 6);

- Sam Clark (Chapter 7); and

- DSS site teams (Chapters 8–29).

We would also like to thank INDEPTH site members, whose names are mentioned in the site profiles, for coordinating the writing of their site's profile. Special thanks go to Rose Lusinde and Don de Savigny for producing the map panels for the site locations and particularly to Kathleen Kahn and Don de Savigny for coordinating the formatting and editing of the 22 site-profile chapters making up Part III of the monograph.

The INDEPTH coordinators would like to express their gratitude to the INDEPTH editorial committee, led by Osman A. Sankoh, for its outstanding work in compiling this first monograph. We acknowledge with pleasure the willingness of individual site teams and their leaders to collaborate in sharing such rich data sets and experiences. We also recognize the contributions of all our investment partners — local communities, public-sector services, academic and research institutions, and donors — all of whom, often over prolonged periods, continue to support and sustain our efforts. We express particular thanks and appreciation to the many sponsors of INDEPTH, including the Rockefeller Foundation, the Navrongo Health Research Centre, the Population Council, the World Health Organization, and the Andrew W.

[1] Based on Benzler, J.; Herbst, A.J.; MacLeod, B. (in alphabetical order): A reference data model for demographic surveillance systems. INDEPTH 1999, http://www.indepth-network.org.

Mellon Foundation, for providing the funds needed to enable INDEPTH networking activities to function. We look forward to attracting new partners to join with us in advancing our mission, goals, activities, and products.

Finally, we thank internal and external reviewers for their invaluable comments, which increased the validity and clarity of many sections of the monograph.

INDEPTH Coordinating Committee

Fred Binka, Chair (Ghana, 1998–2001)
Steve Tollman, Deputy Chair (South Africa, 1998–2001)
Pedro Alonso, Member (Mozambique, 1998–2000)
Yemane Berhane, Member (Ethiopia, 1998–2001)
Chuc N.T.K., Member (Viet Nam, 2000–)
Don de Savigny, Member (Tanzania, 1998–2001)
Bocar Kouyaté, Member (Burkina Faso, 2000–)
Boubakar Sow, Member (Mali, 1998–1999)
Siswanto Wilopo, Member (Indonesia, 1998–2001)

1 June 2001

INTRODUCTION

As we enter the new millennium, with the revolution of the information age still gaining speed, it seems inconceivable that large parts of the Earth's population remain devoid of vital health information. For 1 billion people living in the world's poorest countries, where the burden of disease is highest, no one registers those who are born or who die or ascertains the causes of their deaths. From the limited data available, the health profile of these populations can be likened to an iceberg: the bulk of reliable data on trends in age, gender, geographic variations, and burden of disease remains hidden. This great void in population-based information constitutes a major and long-standing constraint on the articulation of effective policies and programs to improve the health of the poor and thus perpetuates profound inequities in health. The need to establish a reliable information base to support health development has never been greater.

Recently, experience has emerged from a growing number of community-based field stations that have continuous monitoring systems for geographically defined populations. These field stations generate high-quality, population-based, longitudinal health and demographic data with the potential to fill this information void in the developing world. Since 1997 a number of organizations have made a systematic effort to harness and make more readily available the products of these disparate initiatives. A series of meetings were convened by the University of Witwatersrand (South Africa) (Agincourt Health and Population Programme); Department of Tropical Hygiene and Public Health, University of Heidelberg (Germany); the Rockefeller Foundation (Bellagio, Italy); and the Ministry of Health (Navrongo, Ghana) to examine the potential for harnessing these sites through a network. These activities culminated in a meeting convened in Dar es Salaam, Tanzania, 9–12 November 1998, to establish such a network.

Seventeen field sites drawn from 13 countries in Africa and Asia participated in this founding meeting. The name adopted for the network was the International Network for the continuous Demographic Evaluation of Populations and Their Health in developing countries (INDEPTH). Network membership has increased steadily since then and currently stands at 29 health and demographic evaluation sites in 16 countries (the 13 countries whose sites are profiled in this volume are shown in Figure I.1). The network's founding document and constitution are available on the INDEPTH website (www.INDEPTH-network.org).

Figure I.1 Countries with DSS field sites participating in the INDEPTH network.

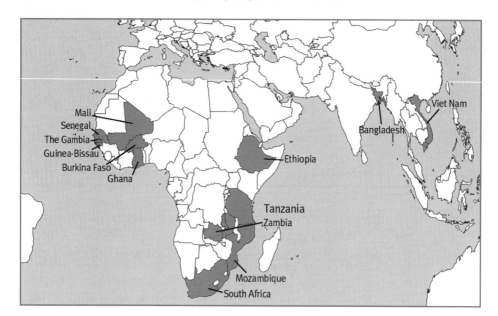

The defining characteristics of an INDEPTH field site are the following:

• A geographically defined population is under continuous demographic monitoring, with timely production of data on all births, deaths, and migrations — sometimes called a demographic surveillance system (DSS); and

• This monitoring system provides a platform for a wide range of health-system innovations, as well as social, economic, behavioural, and health interventions, all closely associated with research activities.

The vision and goals of the network are

• To enhance substantially the capabilities of INDEPTH sites through technical strengthening, methodological development, widened applications to policy and practice, and increased interaction of site leaders, researchers, and managers; and thus

• To realize their potential to generate the information needed to
  – Set health priorities,
  – Allocate resources more efficiently and equitably,
  – Inform the development, implementation, and evaluation of health interventions and other social-sector programs,
  – Strengthen the decision-making capability of information systems,
  – Define a highly relevant research and development agenda,
  – Augment national research capacity, and thereby
  – Fulfill developing-country potential to redress long-standing inequities in health.

To achieve these goals and facilitate the effective interaction of INDEPTH sites, the network has identified the concept of flexible working groups focused on specific scientific issues or topics as a key mechanism. Seven working groups were initially established, with a focus on

- Comparative assessments of mortality;

- Analysis and capacity-strengthening;

- Technical support for field sites;

- Reproductive health;

- Malaria;

- Information and publications; or

- Applications to policy and practice.

Two further working groups have since been formed, focusing on *adult health* and *ethical practice.* Thus, through active and concerted efforts, the network is encompassing a critical agenda founded on traditional strengths in research on infectious diseases and nutrition, with a growing emphasis on reproductive health, and the network is extending this emphasis to chronic disease, injury, and related social phenomena such as rapid urbanization. A central objective is to use network sites to train local scientists in research and research management.

This monograph is the foundation for an INDEPTH series on various themes, including model life tables for Africa and Asia; cause-specific mortality in developing countries; migration patterns; trends in fertility; reproductive health (including HIV–AIDS); and health equity.

INDEPTH Coordinating Committee
Accra, Ghana
June 2001

PART I

DSS CONCEPTS AND METHODS

Chapter 1

CORE CONCEPTS OF DSS

Introduction

During the past 30 years, demographic surveillance systems (DSSs) have been established in a number of field research sites in various parts of the developing world where routine vital-registration systems were poorly developed or nonexistent. Although these systems may have been developed differently in terms of their initial rationale, they are all required to track a limited and common set of key variables determining population dynamics and demographic trends. DSSs have similar approaches to defining key variables and their relationships and to developing systems for collection, storage, and analysis of these data. The core concepts presented here draw directly from the ideas and experiences emerging from INDEPTH DSS sites in Africa and Asia. It should be emphasized, however, that even though an effort has been made to standardize the definitions, many DSS sites still define some of the concepts differently.

Demographic surveillance systems

A DSS is a set of field and computing operations to handle the longitudinal follow-up of well-defined entities or primary subjects (individuals, households, and residential units) and all related demographic and health outcomes within a clearly circumscribed geographic area. Unlike a cohort study, a DSS follows up the entire population of such a geographic area.

In such a system, an initial census defines and registers the target population. Regular subsequent rounds of data collection at prescribed intervals make it possible to register all new individuals, households, and residential units and to update key variables and attributes of existing subjects. The core system provides for monitoring of population dynamics through routine collection and processing of information on births, deaths, and migrations — the only demographic events leading to any change in the initial size of the resident population. This core system is often complemented by various other data sets that provide important social and economic correlates of population and health dynamics. These may include information on events such as household formation and dissolution, acquisition and loss of economic assets, and growth or depletion of income.

In many population sites, the DSS may also provide a platform for other studies within the same geographic area. This support varies from one study to another and may include the provision of an initial sampling frame, adjustment for confounding variables, provision of additional explanatory variables, and measurement of the demographic impact of interventions.

Demographic surveillance area

The demographic surveillance area (DSA) is an area with clearly and fairly permanent delineated boundaries, preferably recognizable on the ground (for example, rivers, roads, and clearly demarcated administrative boundaries). The clear delineation of boundaries enables an unambiguous distinction to be made between individuals, households, and residential units to include in the DSS and those to exclude.

The area of a DSS site depends mainly on the size of the population required for demographic surveillance and related research activities (for a typical example, see "Establishing the monitored population" in Chapter 3). The size is also influenced by pragmatic considerations, such as the cost to the research centre and its capacity to manage the associated logistics and human resources. The DSA may expand or shrink over time in response to changing research needs or sources of funding. These changes usually introduce additional complexity, as they alter eligibility criteria and may make it difficult to maintain consistent definitions of internal and external migrations over the period of transition.

Longitudinality

Longitudinal measurement of demographic and health variables is one of the key characteristics of a DSS. This is achieved through repeated visits at more or less regular intervals to all residential units in the DSA to collect a prescribed set of attribute data on registered subjects, who are consistently and uniquely identified. This and recording events affecting these subjects during the interval between visits allow one to construct their history and differentiate DSS data from data collected in multiround surveys and other prospective studies that allow comparison over time only on an aggregated level.

Visits

DSSs collect data during rounds, or cycles, of visits to registered residential units in the DSA. The interval between visits depends on the frequency of the changes in the phenomena under study and on the length of recall intervals for the collected data, and thus on the research focus of each field site. However, like the size of the DSA and observed population, it also depends on funding and logistics. This interval varies from one site to another, ranging from 1 week to 1 year. However, for the majority of DSSs, observations are made at 3- or 4-month intervals. This is widely considered an appropriate interval to ensure comprehensive recording of births, deaths, and migrations, which is the minimum requirement for maintaining the coherence of any DSS .

When intervals between visits are long (a year or more), researchers commonly ignore migration events and instead conduct a full census at each new round. In- and out-migration flows are then inferred through reconciliation of unlinked census records after account is taken of births and deaths between censuses.

Data collected during each fieldwork round are not restricted to key demographic events but may also include the various attributes of the primary subjects. These attributes may be fixed (for example, ethnicity, gender) or changing over time (for example, marital or residential status).

Unique identifiers

Unique identifiers for primary subjects are an indispensable element of DSSs. All systems invariably formulate rules for assigning unique identifiers at the start of the DSS, but their methods for assigning these identifiers to DSS subjects may vary from one site to another. There are two main approaches. One common strategy is to transparently link the subjects in a single residential unit through a hierarchical system of unique numbers. These are built up from a unique number for the residential unit, followed by serial numbers for each of the households within it (where the notion of households applies) and then for each of the enumerated individuals within each household. In this system, the unique number for each individual in the DSS is a composite of the numbers for the residential unit, household, and household member. This may involve creating complex hierarchies, in which the unique number of the residential unit itself is a composite reflecting allocation to regions, areas, and villages (where they exist). This system requires thorough mapping of the DSA before enumeration. It also requires proper training of enumerators to avoid confusion in assigning identifiers. When mapping of the DSA is coupled with georeferencing of residential units, using geographic information system (GIS) technology, global positioning system (GPS) coordinates are assigned as location attributes of the residential units within the database.

The other strategy for assigning identifiers to individuals is to avoid any fixed link to residential units and households. In this system, identifiers for each subject are simply serial numbers incremented each time a new DSS subject is registered. This system requires providing field staff with block allocations of ID numbers with enough latitude to register new subjects. This approach should be coupled with computer generation of the identifiers to safeguard against the assignment of the same ID to multiple subjects on the ground. This strategy helps to preserve people's anonymity outside their residential units, or when their attribute data are accessed through the database.

Primary DSS subjects

DSSs are typically structured around three main subjects (Figure 1.1) within the DSA. These subjects have both a conceptual and a logistical rationale. From a logistical point of view, it is not feasible to interview all individuals directly, and for this reason individuals are put in groups with physical and social meaning, and information is collected from credible and informed respondents within these groups. The reasons to distinguish between these subjects from a conceptual point of view will be dealt with in greater detail in the following subsections. The three main subjects are (Figure 1.1) as follows:

Figure 1.1. The three main DSS subjects.

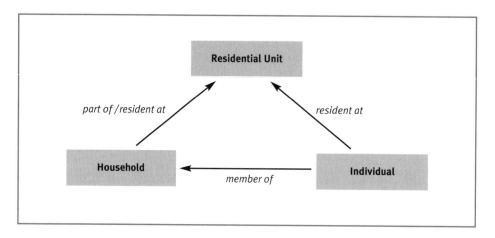

- *Residential units* — These are the places where individuals live. They are defined in physical and geographic terms.

- *Households* — These are the groups to which individual members belong. They are often defined as social subunits of the residential unit.

- *Individuals* — These are the people who are living in the residential units and households. They are the subject of main interest in any DSS.

Residential units

All DSSs identify residential units as a primary subject of interest, although they vary in the terms they use for these units (for example, *compounds* or *homesteads*) and may also differ slightly in their definition of them. Residency, or physical presence within a DSA at a fixed place of abode and for a sufficiently long period, is an essential prerequisite for the enumeration of individuals at risk for demographic events or disease exposure.

In most systems a distinction is made between places of residence and other structures, such as clinics, schools, churches, and stores. Identifying a unifying term for all these structural units may have conceptual merit, and some systems have attempted to do this, as these structural units share many characteristics and this approach simplifies the database hierarchy for handling this concept. In this system an inclusive term such as *bounded structure* may be used at a higher level and *compounds* (or *homesteads*) and *facilities* at the more specific level.

Households

Households may be variably defined in one or more of the following ways:

- A group of people who consume or make some contribution to food and other shared resources;

- A group of people who have a common allegiance to an acknowledged head of a household;

- A group of people, each of whom is recognized by other members of the household as belonging to a social group; or

- A group of people linked through ties of kinship.

The definition of *household* and its applicability both as a concept and as a separate DSS subject may vary greatly from one DSS to another. Households may simply be seen as fixed social subunits within residential units. In more complex systems, they may be seen as independent subjects able to change their place of residence while preserving their social identity, and they may have members who are resident elsewhere. In such a system, a clear distinction would be needed between **residency**, which defines the state of being physically present in a given residential unit for a defined threshold of time, and **membership**, which defines the state of belonging to a social group irrespective of physical presence. These concepts have a clear overlap with the related concepts of *de facto* population (persons who are physically present in a place) and *de jure* population (persons who usually reside in a given place), respectively. The concepts of residency and membership are discussed later in this chapter.

Individuals

The individuals are people of various ages, sex, and other personal characteristics who are residents or members of the DSS residential units or households, respectively. Their personal characteristics may be fixed (sex, date of birth) or change over time (age, marital status). Unless their changes are predictable (like the yearly increment of age), changing characteristics will need to be recorded repeatedly — or their changes will need to be recorded as events — to produce longitudinal trends.

Eligibility

Every DSS is required to define the population under surveillance. As most individuals within any population have places of residence and attachments to social groups, the task of defining the population begins with the identification of the residential units, households (where applicable), and individuals that will be visited and observed. Thereafter, a set of inclusion criteria must be applied to distinguish eligible from ineligible individuals or subjects within each subject category.

As residential units have fixed geographical positions in all DSSs, there are consistent and simple rules for their inclusion: they are included if they are situated in the DSA. In DSSs that deal with households as distinct (and potentially mobile) subjects, these households are eligible if (and while) they are situated in the DSA. This is what is referred to as household residency.

Rules for individuals, particularly in highly mobile populations, are more complex. The most typical approach is to simply base their eligibility on residence, that is, physical presence. Individuals are eligible if (and while) they are resident at eligible residential units. This is what is referred to as individual residency. Another approach, based on social linkages, rules that individuals are eligible if (and while) they are members of eligible households. This requires careful and consistent definitions of *household* and *membership* and can allow individuals who are not resident to remain as members of the household and therefore to qualify for observation.

Residency and membership

Clear geographical boundaries for the DSA and well-defined physical boundaries for residential units are minimal prerequisites for following up DSS subjects consistently and arriving at numerators and denominators for rate calculations. In systems where residential units and households are separate subjects and there is a separate relationship between individuals and each of those subjects — expressed as residency and membership, respectively — these concepts become substantially more complex.

Observing an individual's presence in, or absence from, a specific residential unit requires clear rules for residency status. The physical presence of an individual for a very short time may not be taken into account when the amount of time spent in the residential unit is computed. Conversely, the noncontinuous presence of an individual, with short periods of absence, may be considered continuous residency if he or she meets a threshold for inclusion.

Residency and membership statuses are assigned at the start of the DSS, based on prescribed eligibility rules. Thereafter, new residency episodes may commence as a result of births or in-migrations exceeding a prescribed threshold of duration, and current residency may end because of deaths or out-migrations, again exceeding a prescribed threshold of duration. New membership episodes may commence as a result of events that initiate a social relationship with a household, such as birth, marriage, adoption, or household formation, and may be terminated by events that end such a relationship, such as death, divorce, or household dissolution.

Core DSS events

To know the size of the registered resident population at any time, a DSS collects information about three core events that alter this size, namely, births, deaths, and migrations. These events are described by the following fundamental demographic equation:

$$P_{t_1} = P_{t_0} + B_{t_0,t_1} - D_{t_0,t_1} + I_{t_0,t_1} - O_{t_0,t_1} \qquad [1.1]$$

where P is the population; B is the number of births; D is the number of deaths; I is the number of in-migrants; O is the number of out-migrants; and t_0, t_1 is the time interval of their occurrence.

An underlying principle for recording events in a DSS is that of a **population at risk**. Mortality, fertility, and migration rates are calculated by counting the number of deaths, births, or migrations occurring within a registered population exposed to the risk. For example, an individual who is not resident within the DSA is not considered at risk of dying within the area. Consequently, most DSSs do not observe non-resident individuals or households and do not record their events.

Births and fertility

Pregnancies and their outcomes for all women registered in the DSS are recorded regardless of the place of occurrence of such events. The recording of births has two purposes: for estimating fertility and for identifying a criterion for registering an individual. To estimate fertility, a DSS should record all pregnancy outcomes, including miscarriages (<28 weeks), induced abortions, stillbirths (≥28 weeks), and live births. All live births are then registered as individual members of the DSS, independent of subsequent survival. In some DSSs, fieldworkers take note of live births to visitors to the DSA to alert the data collector in the next round to register the mother (if she becomes eligible) and her child. This procedure is very helpful, as it greatly improves the accuracy of dates of birth of newly born babies and increases reporting of births from eligible mothers with frequent in- and out-migration.

Although most DSSs will report their estimates of the fertility of a specific age group of women, usually 15–49 years, they should also record births to women outside this age group.

The underreporting of pregnancies and their outcomes is a major problem across all DSSs. Some DSSs have used the recording of pregnancies during routine update visits to improve birth coverage. Pregnancy observation has also been used to increase the reporting of other pregnancy outcomes, particularly miscarriages, induced abortions, and stillbirths. However, this requires an update-visit interval of <5 months so that a notification of pregnancy can be obtained in one round, followed by the recording of the pregnancy outcome in the next visit.

Deaths and mortality

Deaths of all registered and eligible individuals are recorded, regardless of the place of death. It may be impossible to record the deaths of previously eligible individuals who then out-migrated. In this case, observation of their survival is censored at the time of migration. Information about the death of visitors to the DSA is sometimes collected, but it is only used in mortality estimates if a *de facto* population estimate is available for each day.

Underreporting of deaths is typically less of a problem than that of births, because a death is widely known and remembered. Exceptions are the deaths of young (and yet unregistered) infants, particularly perinatal deaths, if cultural beliefs or grief hinders reporting.

Some DSSs collect more detailed information about deaths to establish the cause of death, generally through the so-called verbal autopsies (VAs).

Migrations and mobility

Two types of migration events occur:

- *External migration* — where residence changes between a residential unit in the DSA and one outside it; and

- *Internal migration* — where residence changes from one residential unit to another in the same DSA.

Where nonresident household members are ignored, only external migration affects the size of the population, resulting in either the registration of a new in-migrant or the termination of follow-up of an out-migrant. However, recording internal migration is very important to ensure the accuracy and validity of DSS data. The DSS needs to identify internal migrations and migrants and collect supporting information to avoid double counting of individuals and to ensure that their exposure to the social and physical environment is correctly apportioned. Migrations influence the registration of births and deaths; for example, a death would not be recorded for an individual who out-migrated before his or her death.

Defining the circumstances under which a migration is acknowledged to have occurred is notoriously difficult, not only for DSSs, but even for vital-registration systems and censuses. Different DSSs have different criteria. One approach, generally known as the "50% rule," considers individuals resident if they have spent most of the time between two data-collection visits within the DSA. Any former resident who has not spent at least 50% of the time in the DSA would be recorded as having out-migrated.

However, many rural communities have individuals who regularly and predictably change residence for seasonal work, employment, or educational opportunities. The terms *circular* and *pendular migration* are often used. In the Hlabisa DSS, a newly established system in an area of very high population mobility, individual residency has been replaced with household residency as a registration criterion. Consequently, although out-migrations are recorded, the fieldworkers do not automatically terminate follow-up observations.

Migration is a repeatable event — an individual may make several migrations over time, both internally and externally. To maintain longitudinal integrity of data concerning individuals, a DSS should establish whether an external in-migrant has previously been registered in the DSS. The individual's current and previous records should be matched so that he or she is not handled as a new individual in the system but as an individual under observation for several periods.

Episodes

Episodes are a logical complement to events. They are meaningful and identifiable segments of time started and ended by events. The life of an individual, for instance, can be understood as an episode that started with the individual's birth and ended with his or her death. In the same way, residential units or households can be said to be episodes that start when they are formed and end when they are dissolved.

The usefulness of the concept of episodes is not limited to primary subjects. It applies equally to associations between them and therefore provides a useful framework for handling residency, membership, marital status, and many other concepts. Episodes also make it much easier to formulate and implement validation rules regarding events.

Other events

In addition to births, deaths, and migrations, other events are of interest for our understanding of demographic, health, and social dynamics. One event on which data are commonly collected relates to nuptiality or marital status. Most DSSs collect information about events such as marriage, defined as an event that starts a marital relationship, and divorce, that is, an event that ends a marital union. Other events recorded by DSSs depend on their complexity and research interests but may include the change of a head of household, a household's formation or dissolution, or the construction or destruction of building structures.

Nuptiality and conjugal relationships

DSSs collect data on nuptiality primarily because of the important influence of marital patterns on fertility. Marriage as a start of an episode is easily identified, although a period of sexual union may have preceded marriage. The ending of a conjugal relationship can be less clearly marked, because it may not always be the death of one of the partners or a divorce, but a period of separation. In DSAs where the nonmarital fertility rate is high, other conjugal relationships become important, and the systems record informal relationships as well as formal marriages. However, in taking on this broader approach to sexual relationships, the DSSs must overcome two hurdles:

- The difficulty of establishing the starting and ending events of conjugal relationships that are not marked by official ceremonies; and

- The difficulty of establishing the link between two or more partners (in polygamous relationships, for example). For nonmarital conjugal relationships, where the partners often do not cohabit, greater efforts are needed to establish this link in a database than is the case for marital unions.

Construction and disintegration of residential units

At any given time, new residential units may be under construction and other residential units may be at various stages of disrepair following natural disasters or abandonment. The physical state may be distinct from the functionality of the residential unit; that is, it is possible that a residential unit is physically intact but long abandoned, and apparently broken-down units may still have households and individuals living in them. It is also possible that broken-down or destroyed units may subsequently be rebuilt, when the owner returns.

As the state of the residential unit is often — if not always — a good indication of its functionality, a DSS should make provision to track both its physical state and function.

Events occurring in households

Similarly, households can go through important changes affecting their composition and socioeconomic and health conditions. New households may form within an existing residential unit when, for example, a son takes a wife and establishes a family of his own or when a polygynous man takes another wife. Separate households may merge to form a new household, or a complete household may move to settle at another residential unit. Households may lose one or more members over time and decrease in size, or they may completely dissolve through a process of slow attrition or a major environmental or social disaster.

In environments with substantial social flux and instability, it is important to keep track of these events and their effects on the formation and dissolution of households. This is essential if DSSs have conceptualized households as subjects in their own right. Because they also influence patterns of individual presence at a residential unit, these household changes have important implications for the composition of the residential unit as a whole.

Chapter 2

DSS-GENERATED MORTALITY RATES AND MEASURES

Introduction

This chapter provides definitions and explanations of key DSS-generated mortality rates and measures, as well as describing the methodology employed in calculating them. It is intended for readers unfamiliar with these rates and measures. Their calculation is basic, and the various formulas can be found in standard textbooks (see for example, Shryock and Siegel 1976; Kpedekpo 1982; Newell 1994). These measures have been briefly discussed in this chapter for quick reference, as they form the basis for standardizing the results across DSS sites. Perhaps the most important reason for discussing them is the opportunity it affords to discuss the classic controversy over whether to define some of them as rates or ratios (for example, infant mortality, under-five mortality, and maternal mortality). Furthermore, this chapter provides an explanation of the need for a standard population and introduces the INDEPTH standard population for Africa south of the Sahara, discussed in greater detail in Part II.

Rates and ratios

Rates and ratios are frequently used in measuring demographic events. *Rate* refers to the frequency of events. A rate is estimated by taking the number of events in a given period and dividing it by the population at risk during that period. Pressat (1985, p. 194) stated that the term *rate*

> is also used more loosely to refer to the ratio between a sub-population and the total. ... In many other uses of rate, the measure in question would be better termed a ratio, proportion, or probability. The term can be justified only when a dynamic process is being measured, not a static description of a population at a given date, although its use in the latter sense is widespread. In general the word ratio is preferable to rate when the measure is not one relating events to a population at risk.

A **ratio** is the proportion between a numerator and a denominator that are related (for example, under-five child deaths per 1000 under-five person–years lived in a given year).

Crude death rate

The crude death rate (CDR) is defined as the number of deaths in a given period divided by the total population. Although the CDR can be computed for any segment of time, the period usually used is a year, and the denominator used in the rate calculation is the midyear population. The midyear population is the size of the population (or any specified group within the population) at the midpoint of a calendar year. This midpoint is often calculated as the arithmetic mean of the size of the population at the beginning and end of the year. Conventionally, the rate is expressed as a number per 1000 individuals.

In the case of a population under continuous surveillance, with possibly high in- and out-migration rates that may yield a strong variation in population size, the use of exact person–years lived is preferred. Person–years is the sum, expressed in years, of the time spent by all individuals in a given category of the population (Pressat 1985). Specifically, these years express the periods that eligible individuals spent in the DSA. Times or periods spent outside the DSA due to migration or death are excluded.

Age-specific death rate and ratio

Because of the differentials in exposure to the risk of dying, epidemiologists and demographers often use age-specific death rates (ASDRs) and sex-specific death rates, instead of the CDR. ASDRs are the most commonly used. The ASDR for an age group is defined as the number of deaths in the age group in a specific period divided by the total number of person–years lived in that age group during that period and multiplied by 1000. Demographers often use a slightly different notation. They express the ASDR of a particular age group as the deaths among individuals in that age group in the year, divided by the mid-year population of that age group and then multiplied by 1000. Five-year age groups are common, although age categories vary according to the purpose of study.

The following discussion of infant, under-five, and maternal mortality measures highlights the classic controversy over whether to define these measures as rates or ratios. The denominator used in calculating a measure determines whether it is a rate or a ratio. As stated earlier, the measure is a rate when the total number of individuals at risk is used as the denominator, and it is a ratio when some other event is used as the denominator.

Infant mortality

It is usually difficult to estimate the number of person–years lived for children <1 year old (infants). Consequently, the total number of live births is often used as the denominator to calculate the infant mortality rate. The total number of deaths among children <1 year old in a calendar year is divided by the live births in the same year, multiplied by 1000. Calculating the infant mortality rate in this way makes it more appropriately referred to as a ratio.

Infant deaths are unevenly distributed through the first year of life. A high proportion of infant deaths usually occurs in the first month of life. Of these deaths, a high proportion occurs during the first week of life; and of these, a high proportion occurs during the first day. The conventional infant mortality rate or ratio may use-fully be broken up into rates or ratios covering the early stages of life and a rate or ratio for the remainder of the year. The one for the first period is called the neonatal mortality rate or ratio, and that for the second period is called the postneonatal mortality rate or ratio. These concepts are briefly defined in the following paragraphs.

Neonatal mortality is defined as the number of deaths of infants <4 weeks old (or <1 month old) during a year. It is calculated by dividing the deaths of infants <28 days old during a year by the live births in the same year and multiplying by 1000. Early neonatal mortality is calculated by dividing the deaths of infants <7 days old during a year by live births in the same year and multiplying by 1000. Late neonatal mortality is calculated by dividing the deaths of infants 7–28 days old in a year by live births in the same year and multiplying by 1000. Postneonatal mortality is calculated by dividing the deaths of infants 4–51 weeks old during a year by live births in the same year and multiplying by 1000.

Infant mortality can also be expressed as a probability of dying before reaching the age of 1 year. Perinatal mortality is calculated by dividing the sum of stillbirths in the year and the deaths of infants <7 days old during the year by the sum of stillbirths in the year and live births in the same year.

Under-five mortality

Some consider the under-five mortality as a ratio expressing the number of deaths of children <5 years old divided by the number of live births in a year and then multi-plied by 1000. Others treat it as a rate, calculating it by dividing the number of deaths of children <5 years old by the total number of person–years of children <5 years old and multiplying by 1000. When under-five mortality is presented as a probability of dying before age 5, it is expressed as $_5q_0$.

Maternal mortality rate and ratio

Most DSSs record all pregnancies and their outcomes as well as deaths. As such, they have the potential to provide accurate, up-to-date estimates of maternal mortality rates and ratios. The maternal mortality ratio is conventionally defined as the number of deaths due to puerperal (pregnancy-related) factors per 100 000 live births. But strictly speaking, this is referred to as a ratio because the denominator is not the persons at risk of experiencing the event. In view of this, the following are the methods for esti-mating maternal mortality ratios and rates. The maternal mortality ratio is calculated by dividing the number of pregnancy-related deaths in a specified period by that of live births in the same period and multiplying by 100 000. The maternal mortality rate is calculated by dividing the number of pregancy-related deaths in a specified period by person–years lived by women of childbearing age and multiplying by 1000.

Maternal mortality can also be estimated by relating maternal deaths to women of reproductive age or to all pregnancies, including stillbirths and abortions.

Standardization

Age-standardized death rate

Crude mortality rates are inappropriate for comparing different populations within the DSS sites because of the different age structures within the sites. On the other hand, a single parameter is required for simple comparison. Therefore, standardized rates are used, in which the age-specific mortality rates are combined using a standard population. An INDEPTH standard population for sub-Saharan Africa (SSA) has been developed (see Table 6.2). More details on the INDEPTH standard population are provided in Chapter 6. The Segi (1960) and the new World Health Organization (WHO) standard age distributions are also shown in Table 6.2.

Age-specific rates are weighted averages of rates, where the weights are obtained as a proportion of the standard population in the respective age group. The summation goes over all age groups.

Confidence intervals for rates

Estimates of the mean and standard deviation of a population are usually needed if it is impossible to deal with the entire population. The standard deviation of a distribution of sample means is referred to as the standard error of the sample. It measures how precisely the sample mean estimates the population mean. For example, with a 95% confidence interval, about 95% of the sample means obtained by repeated sampling would lie within two standard errors below or above the population mean. Based on the sample mean and its standard error, a range of likely values can be constructed for a population mean that is not known. This range is referred to as a confidence interval. More precisely, there is a 95% probability that a particular sample mean lies within 1.96 standard errors above or below the population mean.

Confidence intervals can be calculated for the ASDRs. The variance of the CDRs or the ASDRs is used instead of the means. Estève et al. (1994) discussed the method in detail. For a small number of deaths or for small populations, however, confidence intervals for ASDRs are not reliable, because the formula used to calculate them is too imprecise. The question is then one of how large the numbers of deaths and populations must be to give reliable results. It is difficult to supply a rule of thumb, and as Estève et al. (1994, p. 58) noted,

> It is however difficult to tell what "sufficiently large" means in the present context because the numerator of a standardised rate is no longer a Poisson variable. Its variance depends not only on the total number of observed cases but also weighting scheme and the accuracy of the age-specific rates.

Chapter 3

DSS Methods of Data Collection

Introduction

Knowledge of the methods for collecting or compiling data at the DSS sites is essential because these methods influence the ways that data are processed, analyzed, and interpreted. The most common demographic methods used in data collection are censuses, sample surveys, and vital-events registration systems. The last method, however, is nonexistent or only partially applied in many developing countries. Given the paucity of vital-events registration and knowledge on population or health-status trends in such settings, demographic and health surveys have been introduced for health planning, practice, evaluation, and allocation of resources. Demographic estimates undertaken in developing countries have employed both indirect and direct methods, using retrospective single-round surveys and prospective multiround ones (Tablin 1984).

Indirect estimation methods rely on information obtained from subjects not directly at risk of a particular demographic phenomenon. The indirect methods can be used to estimate levels and trends of fertility, mortality, and migration where data sources are defective or incomplete. An example of an indirect method is the estimation of infant and child mortality from proportions of surviving children or the estimation of adult mortality from those orphaned. Indirect estimation methods are also used to assess data collected using conventional methods. Such data are compared with other information to infer a certain pattern, on the basis of certain assumptions. If this pattern is reproduced then data can be further inferred. Indirect estimation may, in addition, involve fitting of demographic models to fragmentary and incomplete data (Pressat 1985). The results obtained are used to estimate a particular parameter.

Direct methods use data on the people at risk to establish a demographic measure and pattern. These methods rely on data obtained from censuses, surveys, and recorded data on the components of change — that is, births, deaths, and migration. Data obtained from these methods are used directly to provide estimates of demographic phenomena, such as fertility, mortality, and migration. An example of a direct method is the use of the number of children born to women of a particular age group to estimate age-specific fertility rates.

In single-round surveys, a population is enumerated once during a survey, and retrospective data are gathered on past events (Kpedekpo 1982; Tablin 1984; Newell

1994), such as a birth or death that occurred in the last year (or a life and maternity history). This method may result in overestimation or underestimation of events, as a result of memory lapse. Respondents may exclude events from the reference period. It has been argued that an underestimation of 30–40% is likely using this method (Tablin 1984). Some examples of single-round surveys are the World Fertility Survey and the Demographic and Health Surveys.

Prospective surveys involve repeat visits (longitudinal data collection) to the same respondents or the same study area (Pressat 1985). All DSS sites employ this method of data collection. This does not mean, however, that the methodological approach is the same across all sites. Sites each have unique features, as shown in the various site chapters of this monograph. The purpose of this chapter is therefore to provide a general description of the data-collection methods used by the DSS sites. The data-collection methods are described to provide a quick reference for the reader, rather than describing experiences with data collection. Periodically, specific examples are provided from sites for clarification.

Establishing the monitored population

Selection and establishment of the DSA are prerequisites of any DSS site, but no specific sampling method has to be employed in the selection of an area. Depending on the nature of the study, sites employ probability or nonprobability sampling methods, or both, in drawing their sample population. Once an area has been selected the community has to be mobilized to prepare it to participate in the research and ensure its compliance. Mobilization activities involve conducting sensitization meetings with influential opinion leaders, such as councillors and village, hamlet, or religious leaders. During these meetings, the DSS staff presents and clarifies the project's objectives and expected output and outlines its anticipated activities. Other sensitization methods include drama and sports activities involving the project staff and the community.

As DSSs are longitudinal studies, staff also have to maintain the community's compliance with DSS activities longitudinally, and this means that mobilization of the community is not limited to the initial stages but has to be a continuous process. Compliance is maintained in a variety of ways across sites, including giving feedback to the community through presentation of results in simple tables or graphics, production and circulation of a newsletter, meetings with the key informants at regular intervals, and presentations of findings to health-management teams.

In terms of the minimum and maximum population size under DSS, there is no consensus. DSS sites can have a variety of population sizes under surveillance. For example, Butajira DSS (Ethiopia) began with a sample of 28 616 people (Berhane et al. 1999), whereas Navrongo DSS (Ghana) and Rufiji DSS (Tanzania) had, respectively, 124 857 and 85 102 people 1 year after they began operations (Binka et al. 1999; Mwageni and Irema 1999). The Adult Morbidity and Mortality Project (AMMP, Tanzania) has three sites and more than 300 000 people under surveillance (TMH 1997). The site chapters give more details on the sample sizes of the various DSS sites.

Planning for data collection

Any data-collection exercise requires advance planning and recruitment and training of field staff, such as enumerators and supervisors. It also involves the designing and printing of DSS forms and the preparation of field or training manuals. DSS enumerators are normally recruited from among those local individuals who meet minimum qualifications set for specific projects. Training focuses on proper ways to use DSS forms, conduct interviews, and handle various field forms. Field or interview manuals are used for training and are eventually provided to all field staff as reference materials during data collection. The training manuals clearly indicate the duties and responsibilities of the field staff. In addition, the staff may receive training on how to use or operate field equipment, such as motorcycles. The field staff are given periodic training on field operations to keep up to date on data-collection techniques.

Initial census

Data collection to establish the baseline population begins with a census, conducted by trained enumerators living in the study area. As stated earlier, they are trained on how to use DSS forms and conduct interviews. The initial census establishes the foundation for a longitudinal surveillance system and helps obtain background data on the subjects. Data are collected using standard questionnaires, with closed- or open-ended questions, or both. Separate questionnaires are used to collect household and individual data. The structured questionnaires comprise at least two sections: the header, for recording the unit of interest; and the main part, for recording basic information (see example 1 in Appendix 1).

The type of data collected during the initial censuses depends on the specific objectives of the site. In many sites, data are collected on variables such as household composition (household head, relation to household head, etc.), culture (religion and ethnicity), demographic data (age, sex, marital status), and socioeconomic data (education, occupation, etc.). In addition, the DSS can collect data on behavioural issues (alcohol consumption, smoking, etc.), housing, health-care use, and environmental conditions (source of drinking water, sanitation facility, etc.).

For identification purposes, each household and individual registered is assigned a unique number within its village and his or her household, respectively. A series of numbers for each individual may be used to identify the village, the household, and the individual within the household. The number allocated to the individual is permanent. In some systems, if an individual moves to a new area, the number is still used to identify that person. In this way, it is possible to monitor migrants, as will be shown.

Update rounds

The longitudinal system of data collection continues then with periodic visits to registered households. The purpose of the visits is to record vital changes or events since the previous visit. These may include births or other pregnancy outcomes, marital status (marriages, divorces, separations, reconciliations), deaths, and migrations. Regular data collection is undertaken to maintain accurate denominators for estimation of age-, sex-, and cause-specific death rates. The DSS approach has no specific interval for periodic visits to the registered households (Indome et al. 1995). Yet, it is important to ensure that the interval chosen between interview rounds is consistent for any given household or area. Provided they are consistent, periodic-visit cycles may range from 1 to 12 months.

During the periodic visits or updates, the status of each individual is verified using the household-registration or -record books (see example 2 in Appendix 1) or forms. The registration books are computer printouts of information on households and their members collected in the initial census. They are systematically arranged by household to facilitate further visits or household contacts. These books can be printed in rows and columns to maintain several rounds of data collection. The information on rows may correspond to individual members, as well as details of a household, whereas the columns have spaces for filling in vital events detected in each DSS round. However, all vital events have to be registered on specific event forms. These forms may include observation of pregnancies, births, deaths, and marital changes (see examples 3–5 in Appendix 1). These are forms used in the Butajira, Navrongo, and Rufiji DSSs.

All errors that the interviewers note during update rounds they correct accordingly in the respective book, along with filling out the changes form. The changes form requires the unique number of the household or individual, the change to be made, the original information, and the correction. Corrections that may require filling in the changes form include those for age, name, sex, missed members of a household, and relationship to the head of household. Eventually, these forms are taken to the data centre for correction of databases. This means that in DSS sites data are collected in conjunction with data-management operations (details on data management are provided later in this monograph). In most cases, the fieldwork and computer cycles coincide. Figure 3.1 summarizes the linkage between field and computer operations in Rufiji DSS. This linkage aims at maintaining the integrity of data, as well as ensuring timely reporting of findings. Upon completion of interviews in the household (during the initial census or updates), the forms are taken to the computer centre for data entry. Errors noted during quality control (for details, see Chapter 5) or data entry are verified, reported to the field staff for diagnosis, and later corrected in both the household-registration book and the computer databases.

Updating of vital events is not the only activity carried out during these periodic visits. During update rounds, enumerators register new people or households. These include the migrants, the newly married, and any individuals missed during the initial census. The longitudinal system allows individuals to enter or exit the DSS at any time. They enter through births or in-migration and exit through deaths or out-migration (Figure 3.2). As these individuals are under surveillance, it is possible to estimate the total time spent by each individual in the study population. This time contribution is called person–years of observation and is used as a denominator to estimate rates of events (such as fertility, mortality, and migration). Details on the uses of person–years of observation appear elsewhere in this monograph.

The periodic visits to registered households make DSS self-checking, allowing data collected in one round to be checked and corrected in successive rounds. This reduces the risk of omitting, forgetting, or misreporting variables or events. During the rounds it is also possible to select subsamples (nested studies) on which to collect data on specific items at marginal extra cost and without disturbing the original purpose of the surveillance. However, where the population is very mobile, a major problem of multiround surveillance is tracking subjects.

Figure 3.1. The linkage between field and computer operations at the Rufiji DSS site, Tanzania.
Source: After Binka et al. (1999). Note: HRB, household-registration book.

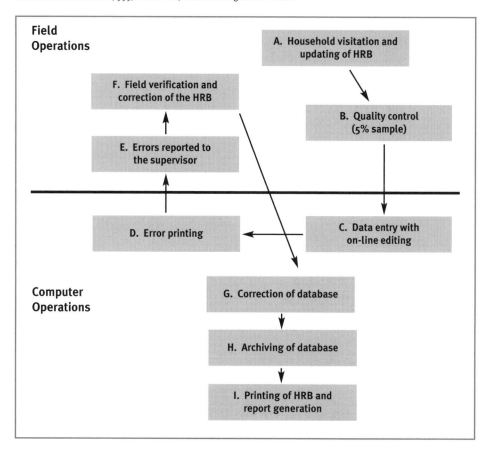

Figure 3.2. Prospective monitoring of demographic events.
Source: After Berhane et al. (1999).

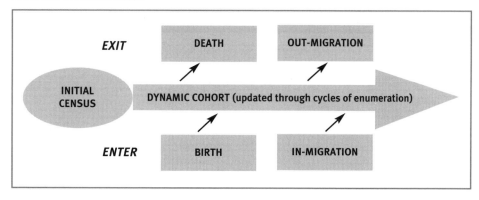

Recording demographic events

Monitoring of births and deaths in developing countries is very crucial, as these two events are easily omitted from routine statistical records and systems (Binka et al. 1999). This can lead researchers to underestimate their occurrence. A good recording system is needed to capture such events. Key informants can do this. Key informants are usually senior or respected members of the community (such as village or hamlet leaders) within the DSA. Key informants fill in their registers whenever an event has occurred, and they report this to the supervisors who visit them on regular basis. Ideally, being part of the community themselves, these people should not be individuals who have to find out about these pregnancies, births, and deaths but those who would hear about them in their course of normal life. As an incentive, a common practice is to pay key informants token fees for reporting such events, once they are confirmed by the system. An example of the system for recording events, as practiced in the Rufiji DSS, is summarized in Figure 3.3.

Figure 3.3. Vital-events reporting system at the Rufiji DSS site, Tanzania.
Source: After TEHIP (1996).

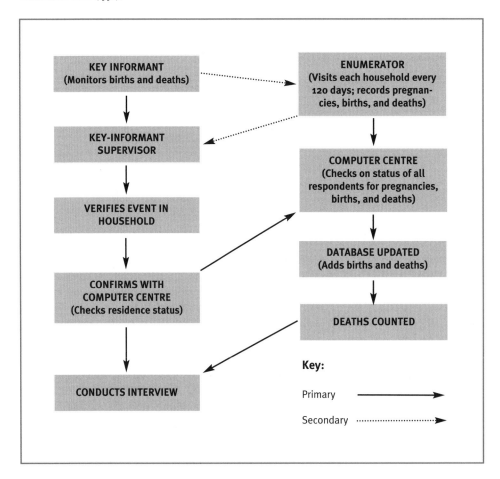

In the vital-events reporting system of the Rufiji DSS, key informants observe and record any birth or death occurring in the study area. This information is passed on to the DSS key-informant supervisor (or enumerator, who informs the key-informant supervisor). Within 2 weeks, the key-informant supervisor visits the households where a birth or death has been reported and contacts the data centre for verification of the event. If the information is correct, the key informant is paid a token fee. The key-informant supervisor then administers a verbal autopsy (VA) with one of the deceased's relatives (who is well informed of the trend of illness of the deceased) for all reported deaths. Enumerators also check births and deaths during fixed enumeration rounds.

Monitoring mortality

Documentation of causes of death has contributed to progress in knowledge of epidemiology and public health. Such documentation allows researchers and policymakers to assess the health status of a population, assign health priorities, study time trends in mortality from specific causes, and evaluate health interventions. Documenting deaths is a common practice in developed countries, where most deaths occur in a medical environment, postmortem autopsies are both feasible and culturally accepted, and vital-events registration is mandatory and complete. In developing countries, however, many deaths occur in the home, with limited or no medical attendance, and postmortem autopsies are rarely possible or complete and vital-events registration is impractical. To assess the cause of death, one must rely on an alternative source of information, that is, an attending relative's description of symptoms and events preceding death.

The VA is an indirect method employed in DSS sites to ascertain the causes of death from close associates whom the DSS interviewers question regarding their knowledge of the symptoms, signs, and circumstances leading to the death. Retrospective interviews of individuals who were there and can describe what happened during the hours, days, or months preceding a death are done, and then a most likely cause of death is inferred from the sequence and combination of symptoms and events. Specially designed forms (questionnaires) are used to suit the population of interest (TMH 1997). For example, if the study of interest is the mortality patterns of children <5 years old, then a form is designed and structured to cover all signs and symptoms of illnesses that affect mostly children of this age (see example 6 in Appendix 1). There are also special interview forms for deaths of children <31 days old and for deaths of those ≥5 years old. The DSSs use trained medical personnel or laypeople to conduct VAs.

VAs are used in health-care projects involved in research and evaluation of health services. As earlier described, key informants record deaths that occur in their area in a mortality register; this is reported to the interviewers who will conduct the VA. The interviewers make appointments to visit the houses of the bereaved families. On the appointment day, an interviewer visits the house and administers a VA with the caretaker or a close family member of the deceased. The VA questionnaires are designed to suit the settings of the area under surveillance (TMH 1997). Such information as name, age, sex, occupation, and other risk factors is usually collected, in addition to an open history of events leading to the death, previously diagnosed medical conditions, and signs and symptoms that appeared before death. The interviewer can use the questionnaires to record information on use of health facilities before the death, reasons for using or not using a particular health facility, the caretaker's perception of cause of death, and confirmatory evidence of a cause of death (if available). The cause of death is determined from a combination of these signs and symptoms.

Causes of death from the VA questionnaires can be reached by either asking physicians or using computer algorithms, depending on the design and structure of the questions. If physicians are asked to do this, then usually two physicians independently code the VA forms and determine the cause of death, using some kind of agreed classification (for example, the WHO International Classification of Diseases [ICD] for causes of diseases). In the case of discrepancies, a third physician is asked to code the forms. Computer algorithms are based strongly on the checklist of signs and symptoms recorded on the form. If discrepancies are noted at this level, then the cause of death is categorized as unknown. Discrepant VA forms produced by the algorithm are taken to physicians for diagnosis and coding. Usually, forms with discrepancies are fewer than others.

Tracking migrants

Migration is a complex subject, with a variety of definitions (Pressat 1985; Newell 1994). As such, the definition relies more on the way data are collected and the purpose for which they are collected. Generally, *migration* refers to movement of people (groups or individuals) that involves a permanent or temporal change of their usual place of residence (Pressat 1985). Migrants are therefore people who change their usual place of residence. According to Kpedekpo (1982), classification of migrants can be based on the following criteria:

- Those who are enumerated in a place different from where they were born;

- Those who resided in the place of enumeration for a period less than their own age; and

- Those who resided (for a fixed period) in a place different from their residence at the time of data collection.

Data on migration can be collected in several ways. Censuses, sample surveys, and continuous population registers are the most common (Shryock and Siegel 1976). Censuses and surveys can provide migration data directly (by asking questions about, for example, the number of moves, duration of residence, date of exit or entry, and previous residence) or indirectly (by estimating migration from total counts of population and natural increase of two censuses or counts). The problem with these methods is their failure to detect multiple moves or those that people cannot remember. In addition, past migrants are grouped together with most recent ones. Also, the indirect method requires very accurate data for the two censuses.

A migration history is another way to collect data on migrants. DSS sites collecting migration data employ this method. This is a continuous way of giving data on previous residence of individuals with dates of their moving out and in. In this way, migrants are linked to the database. Special in- or out-migration forms are used to track down migrants (see examples 7 and 8 in Appendix 1). The in-migration form requires more details than that for out-migration. In addition to personal particulars of an in-migrant (sex, date of birth, education, occupation, etc.), information on the date of and reasons for the migration and the place of origin are also gathered. If in-migration involves a household, a household questionnaire is also used to record household characteristics. On the out-migration form, information is recorded on the date of and reasons for the migration and the destination.

DSS sites do not record all the moves but only those within a certain period. For example, the Navrongo DSS considers an individual an in-migrant if this person is in the same place of residence for 3 months (Binka et al. 1994), whereas Rufiji DSS uses a 4-month criterion for the same purpose (TEHIP 1996). The opposite applies to an out-migrant. The purpose of setting these criteria is to find a proxy to determine the residency status of individuals. This status enables estimation of the individual's overall time contribution to supply denominators for calculation of other demographic measures, such as mortality and fertility.

Additional rounds of data collection

The previous sections have focused on collection of data for demographic variables — mainly, births, deaths, and migrations. All these can be considered extradynamic events, as they change frequently within a year. Other variables are constant or change slowly, such as socioeconomic aspects like education, occupation, housing conditions (floor, roofing material), health-care use (like vaccination), and environmental conditions (like source of drinking water and sanitation facilities). Such information can be collected once in a year, preferably at the beginning of each calendar year.

A DSS can have other nested studies to capitalize on its population database and organizational infrastructure. Such studies employ a variety of designs, such as cohort, cross-sectional, and case referent, depending on the specific primary purpose of each study, and these studies are usually linked to the longitudinal surveillance system. The Butajira DSS, for example, used its database as a sampling frame for a study population and used the routine surveillance to follow subjects in various studies of acute respiratory infections (Berhane et al. 1999). In Tanzania, a new study aimed at monitoring a program for antimalarial combination therapy uses the Ifakara, Morogoro (AMMP), and Rufiji DSAs.

Such nested studies in the DSS sites take advantage of the existing infrastructure and field organization for data collection. Sometimes these new studies may employ supplementary personnel trained to collect information specific to each study. As a result, many DSS sites become pools of trained field staff.

Geographic information systems

A GIS is a computer-assisted information-management system for geographically referenced data. It integrates the management (that is, acquisition, storage), analysis, and display (mapping) of geographic data (Loslier 1995). The GIS contains two integrated databases, namely, spatial (location information) and attribute (characteristics of the spatial features). The spatial database comprises digital coordinates obtained from maps, using GPS. These coordinates can take a variety of forms, such as points (dispensaries, hospitals, schools, households), lines (roads, railways, rivers), or polygons (wards, towns, villages, hamlets). The attribute database can include information such as population size or density and number of health facilities or personnel. The GIS can create a link between spatial data and their associated descriptive information. Its strength lies in its capacity for integration and analysis of data from many sources, such as population, topography, climate, vegetation, transportation network, social services, and epidemiological characteristics.

Many DSS sites use GPS to determine locations and boundaries of phenomena of interest, including boundaries of settlements, households, and villages, and to map health services in terms of access and coverage. Thus, Navrongo DSS used GPS coordinates to assess the child-mortality impact of insecticide-treated bednets in 96 clusters of contiguous compounds (Binka et al. 1996). The data collected using GPS are joined to spatial imagery with GIS. In this way, it is possible to combine and analyze the occurrence of features with various locations. Nouna DSS in Burkina Faso has a GIS with data on all households in 49 villages and information on such features as health facilities, sources of water, roads, schools, and religious places (Sauerborn and Kouyaté 2000[1]).

Conclusion

This chapter has presented a general picture of the major data-collection activities at the DSS sites. The data-collection process has been presented in terms of sequence of events carried out in DSS sites. It discussed the people involved in data collection and the tools used in obtaining information. (Part III will describe specific data-collection methods the DSS sites employ, including sampling procedures, type of information gathered, and key functions and responsibilities of the staff.) This chapter has also shown the potential of DSS sites to contribute reliable demographic and health-related data. Given developing countries' lack of complete vital-events registration systems and the costs of and long intervals between national censuses, the DSS approach is probably one of the best options for improving the quality of data. The DSS data-collection procedures are linked to data-management and quality-control procedures, which are the items discussed in detail in the next two chapters.

---

[1] Sauerborn, R.; Kouyaté, B., ed. 2000. Nouna Research Centre, a platform for interdisciplinary field research in Burkina Faso, West Africa. Internal report.

Chapter 4

PROCESSING DSS DATA

Introduction

Compiling longitudinal population information poses unique data-management challenges. Projects must maintain changing individual-level information on the composition and household structure of a large, geographically defined population. Events that arise — births, deaths, migrations, etc. — must be linked to individuals and other entities at risk of these events. These events affect not only demographic rates, for instance, but also relationships within and between households. As event histories grow, records of new events must be logically consistent with those of events in the past. Seemingly obvious checks on data to meet minimal standards of integrity can result in hundreds of lines of code.

Relating critically needed auxiliary data to dynamic population registers poses further challenges. Morbidity and cause-of-death data must be entered, linked, and stored. Most DSS projects also maintain socioeconomic data such as on marriage, family relationships, and economic conditions, owing to the strong correlation between health and socioeconomic status. These must be logically consistent with other longitudinal data on the population at risk and relationships among individuals under surveillance. Moreover, projects are often launched to assess the impacts of health technologies, service strategies, or policies, and this necessitates data entry, management, and checking procedures for the internal consistency of service information, as well as procedures to link this information to demographic histories. Variance in exposure to interventions must be monitored at the individual level, in conjunction with precise registration of demographic events and individual risk. Maintaining a detailed record of demographic events, relationships, and exposure to risks or interventions requires complex data-management operations, with a carefully controlled field-operation infrastructure to oversee and support data collection and entry, and a comprehensive computer system for the data-management operation.

Data-management systems required for this operation typically encompass thousands of lines of computer code. A key contribution of the INDEPTH network has been technology-sharing to offset the complexity of developing a data system and creating a reference data model for storage of DSS data. This generic model for data storage facilitates cross-site comparative analyses of the type described in this volume, as it standardizes data rules and concepts across sites. Future work of the network will address the need for generic analytical and data-management software compatible with the reference data model.

This chapter outlines features of this reference data model that pertain to the INDEPTH DSSs. In the not-too-distant past, developing DSS software was difficult, time-consuming, and prone to conceptual and programmatic errors. Software generators and object-oriented tools for software development greatly simply the task of developing a complex system, once common principles of software structure are instantiated in a common applications framework. The mechanisms of INDEPTH have marshalled these software innovations to meet the collective needs of member stations. The reference data model will facilitate exchange of information, swift formulation of site-specific data management software and common software for data analysis, and simplified technical assistance and capacity-building operations.

Background

The work of the INDEPTH Technical Working Group (TWG) has been informed by the achievements, limitations, and future needs of projects in Bangladesh, Burkina Faso, Ghana, Indonesia, Mali, Senegal, South Africa, Tanzania, and Uganda. One of the earlier systems, the Bangladesh DSS in Matlab District, was developed in the 1960s and has since been used for a wide range of studies of demographic dynamics, family planning, epidemiology, health-services research, and other issues (Rahman and D'Souza 1981; D'Souza 1984). Although the Bangladesh DSS has redeveloped its computer operations several times, its field operations have provided a model for a wide range of DSS applications in developing countries. The Bangladesh DSS precisely defined eligibility rules for members of a population under study; this, combined with a data system with rigorous logical-consistency checks, has provided high-quality data for many research papers. A number of software systems have been written, based on experiences with the Bangladesh DSS, including the Sample Registration System (Leon 1986a, b, 1987; Phillips et al. 1988; Mozumdar et al. 1990) and the Indramayu Child Survival Project of the University of Indonesia (Utomo et al. 1990). The DSS in Niakhar, Senegal, most recently described in Garenne (1997), has also influenced the technical design of a number of systems, including those of PRAPASS in Nouna, Burkina Faso (Sauerborn et al. 1996), and Agincourt, South Africa (Tollman et al. 1995). Garenne (1997) described the concept of entry–exit files (similar to the concept of "episodes" described here) as a means of modeling both intervals of residence at a location and intervals of relationships. Garenne also provided useful observations regarding the implementation of field and software systems for longitudinal population studies.

To develop its data model, TWG synthesized the experience of these disparate applications. The model specifies a demographic "core" common to field stations doing longitudinal research on populations (MacLeod et al. 1991; Phillips et al. 1991). Sites have developed software systems to manage this demographic core, maintain a consistent record of significant demographic events in the population of a fixed geographic region, generate registration books that the fieldworkers use, and compute basic demographic rates, such as birth, mortality, and total fertility. These core capabilities establish a computational framework to which projects add their site-specific data and consistency specifications. The concept of a core also entails some generic principles of data collection and management that apply to all INDEPTH sites.

The INDEPTH concept of a data core

All participating sites in INDEPTH collect and maintain a common core of data. Attempts to standardize data processing have led to the concept of a "core system" that provides many of the common software requirements of field research laboratories and can be extended and modified to tailor software to various specifications. This concept is based on the principle that certain characteristics of households, household members, relationships, and demographic events are common to all longitudinal studies of human populations, and software required to collect, enter, and manage data can therefore be generic to a family of applications. TWG has identified these features of a core system common to all DSS operations. In this framework, the core system maintains a consistent record of baseline and longitudinal data on all households, household members, and their relationships in a geographically defined population, including births, deaths, migrations, and marriages. The core system maintains information on events and observation dates to give each entity in the study corresponding "person-day" counts of risk for demographic events. Core computer operations structure data and maintain logical integrity on the following basic elements of a household unit:

- All households have defined members at any given point in time (rules unambiguously exclude nonmembers);

- All households have a single head at a given point in time, and members relate to one another and to the head in definable ways;

- Members have names, dates of birth, and other characteristics that do not change over time;

- Events can occur to members, such as death, birth, in- and out-migration, and marital-status change (attempts to enter event data on nonmembers are rejected at the point of data entry);

- Events change household membership and relationships according to fixed rules; and

- Episodes (such as pregnancies, conjugal relationships, or residencies) are associated with individuals at risk (that is, active members) and must follow simple logical rules.

Although these are seemingly trivial items, mundane relationships tend to become complex and unwieldy when arrayed as a logical system of longitudinal population data; and portraying even simple relationships requires rigorous standards to avoid error. For example, to be counted as a death in a resident population, a concerned household member must be resident in the study area at the time of death; a live birth to a woman 5 months after she gave birth to another child would be an inconsistent event. A central contribution of TWG has been to clarify such minimal system logic so that the system prevents errors resulting in violation of business rules and rendering data useless.

All INDEPTH computer systems maintain standard DSS-processing operations:

- *Data entry* — Software allows for entry, deletion, and editing of the baseline and longitudinal data. Baseline household information includes the household location, individuals within the household, relationships between individuals, and familial social groups. Longitudinal information includes basic information on pregnancies and their outcomes, deaths, migrations in and out of the study area, marriages, and any other measures the investigators specify.

- *Validation* — Software checks for the logical consistency of data.

Most INDEPTH sites have also developed software for reporting outcomes and managing data:

- *Reports and output* — Routine software calculates and displays demographic rates and life tables and can compute age-specific and overall rates.

- *Visitation register* — Software prints the household-registration book, which is used by the fieldworkers to update and record information during household interviews.

- *Utilities* — This option is primarily used by the system administrator. It includes capabilities for adding new user IDs, setting interview-round information, and generating reconciliation reports to help track down unreported pregnancy outcomes and unmatched internal migrants.

Tailoring the core system

Given the basic core model for data structure, each site has developed site-specific applications using building blocks of the core framework, which allow software developers to construct additional modules for project-specific data. At nine INDEPTH sites, standard tools of database-management packages have been used for an INDEPTH product known as the household-registration system (HRS) for the core specification.[1] Other INDEPTH sites have developed project-specific core capabilities to maintain the logical integrity of birth, death, migration, and marriage data over time and in a format consistent with the reference data model. Each site modifies the core to accommodate new cross-sectional data, special longitudinal modules, or variable classes or labels investigators want to add to field registers, along with logic to maintain the integrity of new variables.

The tools of commercially available database packages greatly facilitate the process of core modification. Standard features of commercially available database systems include those for easily adding data to the core system. For example, the HRS is built from the form menu (data-entry screen) and database builders of the Microsoft FoxPro system. These builders encourage and facilitate an object-oriented software-development approach through easily understandable mouse and menu procedures. To make changes to the core, a programmer locates the database table, menu, or form

---

[1] The HRS formed the basis for INDEPTH software systems in The Gambia, Ghana (Binka et al. 1995), Indonesia, Mali, Mozambique, Tanzania (three sites), and Uganda. Applications involve a wide range of INDEPTH studies, including family-planning research, malaria interventions, child and maternal health, and correlates of HIV transmission. The current INDEPTH data model improves on the original HRS and other INDEPTH systems by allowing investigators to track nonresident individuals; include more general relationships, rather than just marital relationships; and separate membership in social groups (such as the household or family) from the location.

object to be changed, then works with the small pieces of code, called code snippets, which are "attached" to the object. Some code snippets control the timing of the entry of data for a variable; others enforce rules of consistency. Some INDEPTH sites, such as Hlabisa, are developing similar capabilities, using systems in SQL Server and Access.

The reference data model

As explained in Chapter 3, a DSS tracks the presence of individuals in a defined study area. These individuals can enter and leave the study area in a small set of well-defined ways (for example, entering through birth or in-migration and leaving through death or out-migration). The INDEPTH reference model uses events to record the ways individuals enter (or return to) and leave the study area over time. Thus, events bracket the residency of any individual in the study area. In general, they occur in pairs, with one event (such as presence in the study area) initiating a state and another event (such as migrating out or death) terminating that state. Use of episodes in the reference model makes this pairing of initiating and terminating events explicit. The concept of episodes is diagramed in the centre section of Figure 4.1.

When a DSS tracks episodes, the concept of the "time resolution" of this tracking is very important. Below a certain time threshold, movements into or out of a particular place are not recorded. If a person leaves the physical location in the morning to go to the market and returns in the afternoon, this is not reflected in the DSS. If this period of absence increases beyond a certain threshold (6 weeks, 3 months, or some other period), it turns into an episode to be recorded in the DSS. This threshold varies from project to project, but the project always makes it explicit. The time resolution for "in" episodes should be consistent with the time resolution for "out" episodes, that is, the time before a visit becomes residency or the time after which an absence becomes an out-migration.

DSSs are concerned not only with the physical location or residence of individuals but also with their membership in social groups (such as households) and their relationships with other individuals (such as marital unions or parenthood). Many DSSs also need to reconstruct genealogies and to record isolated events, such as pregnancy outcomes or births and deaths external to the study area.

To support field operations and routine cleaning of data, a DSS must also keep track of where, when, and by whom a particular event was recorded. In this respect, the reference model provides a number of fields to facilitate construction of a good-quality data set. Another challenge for demographic field operations is to correctly identify migrating individuals. To resolve this problem, the reference data model includes fields to designate the place a migrant is moving to or coming from.

The INDEPTH reference model meets these requirements through its use of the following entities and the relationships between them (see Figure 4.1):

- *Physical location* — This entity records the physical locations where individuals can stay, either singly or in groups, such as a homestead, stand, or plot. At several INDEPTH sites, it is possible to pinpoint this location by using coordinates, such as latitudes and longitudes. This feature is easily linked to a GIS. External IDs, such as stand number or address, can be stored in addition to the unique location ID value. An individual is associated with a physical location at a given time through a "resident episode."

Figure 4.1. Reference Demographic Surveillance Data Model. Note: LMP, last menstrual period. Mandatory fields and entities are in bold.

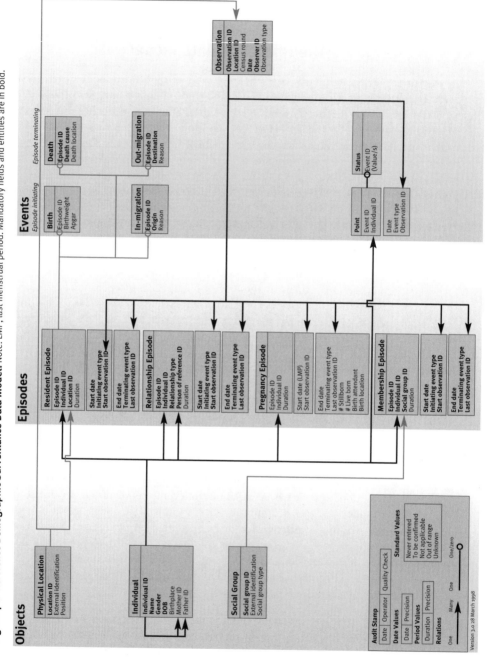

- *Individual* — This entity contains a record for every individual who has ever resided in the study area. Optionally, this entity may record individuals whose residence in the study area has not been recorded but is required to complete a genealogy or relationship record. Records are uniquely identified through an individual ID value. Genealogical linkages can be established by storing the IDs of the individual's father and mother. This information (mother's and father's ID) can also be useful for identification purposes, especially where name and date of birth are not clearly defined, as is often the case in SSA.

- *Social group* — This entity stores information on a defined social group, such as a household. An individual is associated with one or more social groups, through one or more membership episodes.

- *Observation* — The observation entity stores the information that a particular physical location has been observed at a given time. This entity can also store information on the person making the observation and optional information, such as the census round. The observation entity is linked to all the events recorded during the observation.

- *Events* — The events entity may indicate a change in the state of an individual (for example, from resident to nonresident, in the case of an out-migration). Events that initiate and terminate a particular state of interest (for example, residency) are combined and recorded as an episode (for example, resident episode). These types of events are known as "paired events." Events that do not record the start or end of a particular state are known as "point events." The information common to all events (such as date of occurrence, type of event, and ID of the observation during which the event was recorded) is stored as part of the episode that this event initiates or ends (in the case of paired events) or as part of the point-event table (in the case of point events). Additional data associated with an event are stored in a separate entity. The following event types are noted in Figure 4.1:
  - *Birth* — This event type records all live births to residents (stillbirths are recorded as a pregnancy-outcome event). The event is linked to the resident episode it initiates — it also initiates social-group membership and relationship episodes.
  - *Death* — This event type records all deaths of residents. A death event will terminate all open episodes belonging to the individual. The death-event record is linked to the resident episode that the event terminates and contains additional data, such as the location and cause of death.
  - *Relationship start* — This event type records the start of a relationship of one individual to another. By convention, relationship events are linked to the female in cases of heterosexual relationships and to the younger individual in cases of same-sex relationships. In the case of caretaking relationships, the relationship events are linked to the person receiving care.
  - *Relationship end* — This event type records the end of a relationship between two individuals.
  - *Membership start* — This event type records the start of an individual's membership in a social group.
  - *Membership end* — This event type records the end of an individual's membership in a social group.

- *In-migration* — An in-migration event initiates a new or changed physical location for an individual. It records the start of a new residence episode for an individual and can originate within or outside the study area. Additional data, such as origin, are usually stored in a separate entity linked to the episode via the episode ID.
- *Out-migration* — An out-migration event terminates a residence episode at a physical location for an individual. The destination of an out-migration can be within or outside the study area. Additional data, such as destination, are usually stored in a separate entity linked to the episode via the episode ID.
- *Status observation* — Any number of optional events can be defined to record status information observed for individuals, such as socioeconomic, nutritional, educational, or immunization status. Repeated status observations make no assumptions about the value of observed attributes during the observation interval, even if subsequent observations measure the same values.

- *Episodes* — As Figure 4.1 shows, episodes can occur to residents, relationships, pregnancies, and memberships in social groups:
  - *Resident episode* — A resident episode records the stay of an individual at a physical location. A resident episode can be initiated only by a DSS entry, a birth, or an in-migration event. It can be terminated only by a DSS exit, a death, or an out-migration event.
  - *Relationship episode* — A relationship episode records a time-dependent relationship, such as a marital union, between two individuals. The episode is started by a relationship-start event and concluded by a relationship-end event, a death, or a DSS exit. The relationship episode records the IDs of the two individuals involved in the relationship, but the events initiating and terminating the episode are linked to only one of the individuals, as described above.
  - *Pregnancy episode* — Pregnancy is recorded as an episode, with certain attributes recorded on the first observation of the pregnancy and others recorded when the outcome of the pregnancy is known. One lesson we have learned is that if you want to do a good job in child registration, you have to register pregnancies first. However, if a pregnancy is not observed, but only the outcome, the start of the pregnancy episode is still recorded as the date of the last menstrual period before the pregnancy. In this case the start and last observation IDs will point to the same observation instances. If a pregnancy is terminated by the woman's death or out-migration, the reason for termination is recorded as the terminating-event type, and the episode is concluded. In the normal course of events, the pregnancy outcome could be recorded in the terminating-event type as spontaneous abortion, induced abortion, normal delivery, assisted delivery, or caesarean section. The "birth location" field refers to the delivery environment (for example, the name of a hospital or clinic where the delivery took place).
  - *Membership episode* — A membership episode records the membership of an individual in a particular social group. A membership episode can be initiated only by a DSS entry, a birth, or a membership start event. It can be terminated only by a DSS exit, a death, or a membership end event.

In summary, Figure 4.1 illustrates the entities and relationships of the INDEPTH reference data model. Mandatory fields and entities are displayed in bold type, whereas optional fields and entities are displayed in normal (nonbold) type.

The role of the reference data model in maintaining data integrity

As explained in Chapter 3, any DSS must maintain a large volume of data over an extended period. Unless specific measures are taken, the integrity of the data will suffer, along with the accuracy and reliability of the information in the system. INDEPTH has taken steps to foster common standards for data integrity, based on a well-defined relational model. Although not all systems have the same measures to protect data quality, the following have been proposed or used at one or more INDEPTH site:

- *"Audit stamp"* — The audit stamp is part of every record in the database. The audit stamp records the operator and the date and time of the last update to the record. In addition, a quality-check indicator may record whether the record has been verified (for example, through a double-entry process).

- *Standard values* — Standard values should be used consistently throughout the database to indicate the status of a particular data value. The following standard values (and their meanings) are proposed:
  - *"Never entered"* — This is the default value for all data fields in a newly created record.
  - *"To be confirmed"* — This indicates a need to query the value as it appears on the input document and to take follow-up action.
  - *"Not applicable"* — Given the data in related fields or records, a value for this data field is not applicable.
  - *"Out of range"* — The value on the input document is out of range and could not be entered. Follow-up action yielded no better information or is not applicable.
  - *"Unknown"* — The value is not known. Follow-up action yielded no better information or is not applicable.

  (The actual values used to indicate the standard values depend on the data type of the field and the natural value range for the data item. Care should be taken to exclude these values from quantitative analysis of the data.)

- *Date values* — Date values are of particular importance in a DSS, and it is preferable to record the precision of date values in addition to the dates themselves. Each date or duration field should have an associated precision field for recording the precision of the date value (for example, minutes, hours, days, weeks, months, quarters, semesters, years, decades).

Extending the core

Although the INDEPTH reference data model covers aspects common to all INDEPTH DSSs, it makes no attempt to specify all site-specific needs. However, it is designed to accommodate new components to meet the needs of a wide spectrum of longitudinal studies, without losing its clear overall structure. Several ways are presented in this section:

- *Adding fields to existing entities* — The simplest core extension is to add a data field for a fixed-in-time attribute of objects, events, or episodes already implemented. Examples of this type of core modification are inauguration date of a physical location, membership in an ethnic group, an individual's Rh factor, the weaning age of a registered or member child, or the presence of a supervisor during an observation.

- *Defining new types of social groups and relationships* — Whenever the interaction of individuals can be formalized to permit specification of a start and an end point of this interaction, it can be expressed in terms of social-group membership (interaction with all other individuals being members of the same social group at the same time) or of a relationship to just one other individual. INDEPTH data systems have specified a wide variety of such relationships and episodes. For example, membership might be in a social group (such as a lineage), in a health-insurance scheme, or in any other type of group that suits the needs of a study. A relationship can also be of a patient to a health-care provider or of a tenant to a landowner. Membership is not always limited to social groups but sometimes involves a "membership" in a category of chronically ill individuals or "membership" in a nested cohort study (where fulfillment of some predefined criteria might be the start events; and of others, the end events).

- *Adding new types of episodes or events* — As illustrated in Figure 4.1, the system records four minimal, "predefined" types of episodes, and these can be adapted to various purposes. New event types are sometimes specified to facilitate storage of supplemental information (applicable only under specific conditions) while keeping the corresponding episode record as parsimonious as possible.

- *Defining events and episodes for physical locations and social groups* — Although events and episodes always refer to individuals, they sometimes relate individuals to other operations. An extended model can define additional events and episodes with reference to physical locations or social groups. Point events and status observations can be defined to record information collected or observations made about physical locations (such as housing type, water supply, number of rooms), social groups (such as ID of household chief, monthly household income, agricultural production), or other nonconstant attributes.

Social groups can be related to other social groups, or "first-level" social groups like households can be members of "second-level" social groups like clans or other types of networks. DSSs designed to track the interaction of households might define relationship and membership episodes for social groups, to store information about this topic.

Households are normally associated with only one homestead, even if the members of the household reside in more than one physical location. When social groups are used to record households, this association can be depicted by an episode that records the start and termination of occupation at a physical location. Households also normally have a head of household. This head may change with time, but the household will still retain its identity, and head of household can be recorded either as an updatable attribute ("Current head of household") or as a member of the social group. If the temporal dimension is important, the extension can be specified as an episode linking the household to an acting head of household.

In summary, the reference data model provides a structure to accommodate great flexibility in the design of longitudinal studies, and for this reason, INDEPTH includes sites engaged in various study designs, with a wide range of data-management needs. Despite this diversity, the model has a core of logic and structure lending integrity to operations and providing a crucial foundation for technical collaboration among sites.

Conclusion

This chapter has described the data model that INDEPTH has developed as the guiding framework for processing data at member sites. It makes attributes common to most health and family-planning studies explicit. As well, it serves as a structural framework for the addition of project-specific data. Much work still needs to be done to develop this model and a common data-processing system for INDEPTH core operations. However, the common framework for data management has already facilitated data sharing within the network, and nearly one-half of all INDEPTH sites use a common software system for core operations. If this use of generic software is more broadly accepted, the INDEPTH data model could serve as the basis for sharing system development, capacity-building, and collaborative research.

Chapter 5

ASSESSING THE QUALITY OF DSS DATA

Introduction

In a DSS, errors occur at all stages of the operation. These may take the form of coverage errors, resulting from omission or repeated counting of persons, or content errors, arising from incorrect reporting of the characteristics of respondents. To establish whether the data are of reasonable quality, INDEPTH sites use a variety of evaluation procedures at the field, data-processing, and analysis stages.

Assessing data quality in the field

It is important to note, at the outset, that however comprehensive the data-checking procedure is, it cannot substitute for careful, methodological, and conscientious interviewing (Shackleton 1998). During training, fieldworkers are made to understand that it is their primary responsibility to ensure accuracy and completeness of data. In addition, field monitoring of data quality is ensured through regular supervisory visits, form checking, and reinterviews.

Supervised visits

The field supervisor's role is to ensure that each fieldworker conducts interviews of optimum quality. An effective way for a field supervisor to do this is to join up with the fieldworker and observe one or more of the fieldworker's interviews. The frequency of the supervisory visits varies from site to site and may be daily, weekly, or fortnightly. Such visits are normally unannounced. They are intended to help monitor the performance of the fieldworker from several perspectives. The first is to check whether the fieldworker is actually making the field visits. The supervisor then observes interviews and discusses defects in interviewing techniques. Where necessary, a supervisor makes an effort to help resolve any problems the fieldworker may have. Supervisors pay particular attention to the sequence of the interview process, to prevent omission of questions and make sure fieldworkers follow a logical and systematic format for interviews.

Form checking

First and foremost, fieldworkers are expected to check their own work as part of their daily routine. Ideally, they should do this before leaving the site of an interview so that they can correct errors immediately. Key checks at this stage are to verify the number of event forms, ensure no omission of questions, and provide valid codes for questions. At some sites, each fieldworker gives completed forms to another team member to check before handing them over to the supervisor at the data centre. In addition to observing field interviews during visits, supervisors review samples of completed field questionnaires to identify inconsistencies and assess their completeness. They point out any obvious error for correction. In DSS activities, there is generally a high probability of obtaining missing information on a revisit. Therefore, to maximize the chance of identifying errors before the form leaves the field and minimize the effort required to do the revisit, the team supervisor carefully checks each form again. Here, the checking is more comprehensive and includes validity of dates, consistency of household relationships, and sensibleness of linked fields. Any error detected is returned to the fieldworker for correction, and if needed the fieldworker does a revisit to make corrections.

Duplicate visits

To further check on the reliability of the information, supervisors also carry out random field checks on compounds or households. On these visits, they re-administer portions of the questionnaires. The responses are compared with those obtained by the fieldworker, to provide an idea of the degree of accuracy of the data. At some sites, those responsible for the spot checks also ensure that all neighbouring households are registered. In addition to making random field visits, quality-control supervisors reinterview a 3–15% sample of all compounds or households at the site. They compare the data obtained from the re-enumeration with those of the fieldworker to determine whether the original interview was actually conducted. This also helps to reveal any systematic errors made by the interviewer and provides data for calculating error rates. It must be emphasized, however, that not all errors are completely attributable to the fieldworker, as they may arise if, for example, a different member of the compound or household serves as the respondent. At some DSS sites, efforts to improve on coverage include an independent annual listing of all households, which is then cross-checked against DSS households.

Assessing data quality at the data centre

General procedures

At the data centre, some sites have a second level of supervision: field headquarters' staff (senior supervisors) thoroughly examine completed questionnaires to identify errors missed by both interviewers and supervisors and ensure that data for individual respondents are consistent. The next stage involves computer editing, using computer programs with built-in checks to assess the validity of responses, either during or following data entry. These built-in consistency checks help to flush out illogical responses, invalid codes, double entries, and items with missing values. Verification of data is also carried out to detect systematic data-entry errors. This procedure helps to assess the performance of individual data-entry clerks and determine whether the general error rate of data entry is within acceptable limits. At the beginning of each data-collection and data-processing cycle, a verifier repeats the work of a data-entry clerk, until the clerk is qualified in terms of the maximum allowable error rate. Thereafter, only a sample of the work is verified to ensure that the clerk keeps up an acceptable level of accuracy.

Statistical techniques

Matching of records

The statistical procedure to determine the completeness of coverage and reliability of the data is to reinterview and to match individual records case-by-case from two data sources. To evaluate net coverage error, events from the DSS are matched one-on-one with corresponding records from the re-enumeration of 3–15% of the original population. The proportion of records in the re-enumerated sample that were missed in the registration process provides an estimate of the overall coverage error. To assess the accuracy of the data, records from the two data sources are matched, based on a central variable, such as age. By matching individual records from the reinterview with those from the DSS, it is possible to determine the number of individuals omitted from, or erroneously included in, each age group in the DSS. The assumption is that the probability of event omission from the quality-control sample is much lower than, and independent of, the probability of omission from the DSS, although surveys do have correlation biases. Another statistical approach for evaluating coverage and content errors is to compare both absolute and relative numbers from successive periods of the DSS to identify deviations from expected patterns. Occasionally, aggregate figures from the DSS are also compared with those from an independent source to test for consistency.

Population pyramid

The population pyramid is a graphic representation of a population's age–sex distribution. It is another method to assess the quality of age reporting and is used to give a detailed picture of the age–sex structure of the population. The basic form shows bars corresponding to age groups or single-year age distributions in ascending order, from youngest to oldest. These distributions may be in either absolute numbers or percentages calculated from the grand total for the population. In growing populations, the pyramid is expected to be triangular, with concave sides (that is, it narrows rapidly from the base up). Thus, the shape of the pyramid helps to reveal irregularities, such as age shifting and age heaping, in the age–sex structure of the population.

Alternative techniques

Undercounts and misplacements of events are very often encountered in DSS activities. Other errors resulting in the misclassification of population characteristics also occur. Even with the best quality assurance, it is impossible to overcome all these errors in the field and at the data centre. Several standard statistical and demographic methods are available to DSS sites for evaluating the accuracy of data.

Age preference

The degree of age preference can be used to test for deficiencies in the DSS data. Although age is the most important variable in demographic analysis, it is typically prone to errors of recall and other types of biases. Age misreporting takes two basic forms: "heaping," or digit preference, and "shifting." In less literate populations, the reporting of events, especially births, is usually clustered at certain preferred digits, as a result of ignorance, genuine reporting errors, or deliberate misreporting. Thus, it is common to find concentrations of people at ages with numbers ending in digits 0 and 5 and, to a lesser extent, 4, 6, or 9. Indexes such as Whipple's index and Myers' blended index have been developed to statistically assess the extent of age preference, based on the assumption that the population is rectangularly distributed over some age range (Shryock and Siegel 1976). Whereas Whipple's index is a measure of preference for ages ending in 0 and 5, Myers' index provides an overall measure of age heaping, as well as an index of preference for other terminal digits.

To measure the extent of heaping on digits 0 and 5, Whipple's index employs the assumption of rectangularity over a 10-year range and compares the population reporting ages ending in 0 and 5 in the range 23–62 years. The index varies between 100, indicating no preference for digits ending in 0 or 5, and 500, indicating that only digits ending in 0 or 5 were reported. A United Nations-developed scale can be used to evaluate the reliability of any data set based on the estimated Whipple's index, as follows: <105 = highly accurate; 105–109 = fairly accurate; 110–124 = approximate; 125–174 = rough; 175+ = very rough.

The Myers' blended index involves determining 10 times the proportion of the population reporting in each terminal digit for any 10-year age group. This yields an index of preference for each terminal digit representing the deviation from 10% of the total population reporting the particular digit. The overall index is derived as half the sum of the absolute deviations from 10% and is interpreted as the minimum proportion of individuals for whom an age with an incorrect final digit is reported. The index is 0 when no age heaping occurs and 90 when all age reports have the same terminal digit.

Sex ratios

Another way to appraise the accuracy of data is to examine the general and the age-specific sex composition of the population. The measure usually examined is the sex or masculinity ratio, which is expressed by the following equation:

$$\text{Sex ratio} = \frac{P_m}{P_f} \times 100 \qquad [5.1]$$

where P_m and P_f are the number of males and females, respectively. The point of balance for this measure is 100 and is interpreted as the number of males per 100 females. In real life, however, most vital events can be predictably proportioned between males and females. Generally, males outnumber females at birth, but higher rates of male mortality with advancing age offset this pattern. A sex ratio at birth, therefore, usually ranges between 95 and 102. Thus, failure to observe these typical sex distributions may signify either errors in the data or unusual population characteristics. To obtain a more accurate assessment, researchers normally compare the sex ratio estimated from the data with that obtained in previous years.

Age ratios

Another way to evaluate DSS data is to compare age ratios with expected or standard values. Age ratios are defined here as the ratio of the population in a given age group to one-third the sum of the populations in that age group and in the preceding and following groups, multiplied by 100. The age ratio is expressed for a 5-year age group as follows:

$$\text{Age ratio} = \frac{{}_5P_a}{{}^1\!/_3\left({}_5P_{a-5} + {}_5P_a + {}_5P_{a+5}\right)} \times 100 \qquad [5.2]$$

where ${}_5P_a$ is the population in the given age group; ${}_5P_{a-5}$ is the population in the preceding age group; and ${}_5P_{a+5}$ is the population in the following age group. In the absence of extreme fluctuations in the past vital events, the age ratios should be about equal to 100, based on the assumption that coverage errors are about the same for all age groups and that complementary errors in adjacent age groups offset age-reporting errors. The average absolute deviation from 100 of the age ratios, over all ages, gives the age-accuracy index, or overall measure of the accuracy of the age distribution: the lower the age-accuracy index, the more accurate the age data.

Comparison with population models

Yet another way to assess DSS data is to compare the actual percentage distribution of the population by age with an expected age distribution corresponding to a population model, such as that of the "stable population." With negligible migration and fairly constant fertility and mortality, the age distribution of a population will assume a definite, unchanging form. Thus, the percentage age distribution of a population with a fairly stable structure can be used to evaluate the accuracy of the reported age distributions. For each age group, an index may be calculated by dividing the percentage in the age group in a given country by the corresponding percentage in the stable population. Deviations from 100 signify under- or over-enumeration of the relative age groups. The stable-population model (with zero population growth) and the quasi-stable population model (similar to the stable-population model but with moderately declining mortality) may also be used to assess DSS population age–sex structures.

Conclusion

Right from the start of data collection, the DSS sites use various procedures to ensure sound data, including thorough, manual editing of the questionnaires in the field and at the data centre, partial or complete reinterviewing of a sample of respondents, and computer checks. At the analysis stage, depending on data requirements, specific techniques are applied to assess whether the data conform to an acceptable pattern. It is worth noting here that not all DSS sites have daily work routines. A few sites carry out only annual censuses. However, evaluations of DSS data at many sites suggest that the data are of reasonable quality and that they indicate an improvement over time.

PART II

MORTALITY AT INDEPTH SITES

Chapter 6

COMPARING MORTALITY PATTERNS AT INDEPTH SITES

Abstract

Empirical mortality life tables are chronically lacking for Africa. This chapter presents such tables for 19 INDEPTH sites for the 1995–99 period, with 17 of these in Africa. The data compiled for the calculations represent 4 194 627 person–years of exposure and 56 977 deaths. To compare the overall levels of mortality at the various sites, an INDEPTH population standard was developed and used to standardize observed crude death rates for Africa. Finally, the age- and sex-specific patterns and rates of infant, child, and adult mortality are provided for each DSS site, and mortality clusters are identified.

Introduction

Mortality data from Africa

Accurate data on mortality in Africa are still scarce. Until recently, the main tools for overcoming this shortcoming have been indirect demographic-estimation techniques and model age-specific mortality schedules produced by Brass et al. (1973) (the Brass relational system); Coale and Demeny (1966) (the CD model life-table system); and the United Nations (1982) (the UN model life-table system). The Brass relational system is based on empirical data collected in West Africa during the middle of the 20th century. In contrast, neither the CD nor the UN model life-table system is built using significant amounts of data collected from Africa. Moreover, all three of the systems are based on data that are 30–50 years old. Given the dramatic demographic changes that have affected Africa in the past 20–30 years and the fact that two of the systems are based largely on data collected from other regions and the third is based on data from only one region of Africa, it may be problematic to use them in the current African context. No doubt, the World Fertility Survey (WFS) and the Demographic and Health Surveys (DHS) have remedied in part the above situation by increasing our knowledge of the level trends and differentials in infant and child mortality in the developing world (Cleland and Scott 1987). However, complete mortality life tables

51

cannot be constructed from WFS and DHS data without relying on indirect methods. Finally, several African countries have since independence undertaken national censuses, but mortality data from these sources are often plagued with underreporting and need to be adjusted using hypotheses that are not always realistic.

Mortality data from INDEPTH sites

Data collected at DSS sites are often dismissed because they are collected from small areas, a fact presumed to make the resulting mortality measures neither accurate nor representative. The modest population size of a DSS site does not really constitute a major flaw, however, as even sites monitoring small populations can produce robust measures of age-specific mortality when data are aggregated over several years. Moreover, data collected over long periods from the same population living in the same area can reveal important age-specific trends in the risk of death. Furthermore, when data from a number of widely dispersed sites are brought together, they provide a measure both geographically and temporally representative of mortality conditions. Currently, only DSS sites provide data of use in depicting the temporal and geographic contours of mortality patterns in Africa.

Each DSS site monitors a well-defined, prospectively linked population over a period of years. The longitudinal nature of the DSS ensures that demographic events (such as births, deaths, and migrations) and person–years of exposure are accurately recorded. Keeping the data-collection rounds short, usually 3–4 months, minimizes the likelihood of "losing" a respondent or failing to observe an event. Consequently, the data presented here are of unusually high quality with respect to coverage, completeness, and accuracy of age.

This chapter presents data for age-specific counts of deaths and person–years of exposure at 19 INDEPTH sites in the period 1995–99. The data are used to construct life tables describing the mortality conditions at each of the sites in this period. The levels of child, adult, and overall mortality are compared across the sites, and standardized CDRs are presented for wider comparison. The next chapter presents a detailed examination of the age patterns of mortality revealed in these data.

Age-specific mortality rates and life tables

Data

The data used in this chapter come from sites for which information on mortality was available for at least a full year during the 1995–99 period (Table 6.1). The overall average length of the observation period for the contributing sites is 3.7 years. In total, the data yield 4 194 627 person–years of exposure, during which 56 977 deaths occurred. An average of 16% of the person–years exposed were lived at ages younger than 5 years old, and an average of 37% of the deaths also occurred between birth and 5 years of age. The CDR for both sexes combined ranges from a low of 7 per 1000 in Agincourt, South Africa, to 39 per 1000 in Bandim, Guinea-Bissau.

Table 6.1. Summary of mortality data from 19 INDEPTH sites, 1995–99.

DSS site	Reporting period	Period (years)	Observed deaths	Observed PYs	CDR	% deaths < age 5	% PYs < age 5
Agincourt, South Africa	1995–99	5	1 738	304 530	7.11	15.54	13.79
Bandafassi, Senegal	1995–99	5	901	41 286	33.57	53.16	19.86
Bandim, Guinea-Bissau	1995–97	3	1 830	64 434	38.65	56.01	27.69
Butajira, Ethiopia	1995–96	2	834	72 873	19.20	41.49	16.94
Dar es Salaam, Tanzania	1994/95–1998/99[a]	5	4 515	354 041	21.75	27.44	13.87
Farafenni, The Gambia	1995–99	5	1 201	81 872	21.23	45.05	17.12
Gwembe, Zambia	1991–95	5	576	37 089	26.89	59.72	19.37
Hai, Tanzania	1994/95–1998/99[a]	5	8 106	746 864	16.09	23.14	14.30
Ifakara, Tanzania	1997–99	3	1 812	159 639	20.28	41.17	16.23
Manhiça, Mozambique	1998–99	2	973	67 344	20.97	35.66	17.06
Matlab comp.,[b] Bangladesh	1998	1	857	105 900	16.16	31.39	12.27
Matlab treat.,[c] Bangladesh	1998	1	764	109 573	12.45	24.74	11.37
Mlomp, Senegal	1995–99	5	374	37 051	13.75	20.59	10.80
Morogoro, Tanzania	1994/95–1998/99[a]	5	9 548	538 286	30.01	29.03	13.01
Navrongo, Ghana	1995–99	5	11 278	691 679	27.72	34.46	14.10
Niakhar, Senegal	1995–98	4	1 993	116 133	24.30	51.03	18.05
Nouna, Burkina Faso	1995–98	4	1 650	117 156	17.00	40.48	18.24
Oubritenga, Burkina Faso	1995–98	4	6 967	478 315	24.83	49.63	17.40
Rufiji, Tanzania	1999	1	1 060	70 563	33.96	35.47	16.32
Average		3.68			13.58	37.64	16.20

Note: CDR, crude death rate (actual number of deaths per 1000 population); PY, person–years.
[a] Reporting in midyear to midyear annual periods resulted in a 5-year reporting period running from 15 July 1994 to 15 July 1998.
[b] Comparison area.
[c] Treatment area.

Method of analysis

Although many sites reported data for longer periods, the following analysis is restricted to the 1995–99 period. The aim here is to present the mortality profile of the INDEPTH sites for a recent period for which there was a maximum number of contributing sites.

Life tables were constructed in the standard fashion (Preston et al. 2001). For each site, $_nM_x$, the age-specific mortality rates for the age group $x,x+n$ were calculated as the ratio of deaths, $_nD_x$, to person–years exposed, $_nPY_x$, in the same age group. When calculating $_nq_x$, the probability of dying in age group $x,x+n$, one assumes that the average age at death, $_na_x$, equals half of the age interval, except for ages <5 years. In the age intervals 0–<1 and 1–4 years, the values of $_na_x$ are calculated using the relationships developed by Coale and Demeny, based on the their West model life-table system (Preston et al. 2001). The open age interval encompassing ages ≥85 years is closed in the usual way, by letting $_nL_{85}$ equal the ratio of l_{85} to $_\infty M_{85}$. Standard errors are calculated using formulae developed by Chiang (1984).

Crude death rate

To examine the overall level of mortality reported at each site and to compare those across sites, we calculated the age-standardized crude death rate (ASCDR) and life expectancy at birth. The CDR is the overall death rate obtained by taking the ratio of the total deaths in the population to the total person–years of exposure over a given period. Life expectancy at birth is the number of years a newborn is expected to live if

Table 6.2. **Standard age distributions.**

Age group (years)	INDEPTH[a]	Segi[b]	WHO[c]
0–4	0.149 418	0.120 0	0.088 6
5–9	0.142 497	0.100 0	0.086 9
10–14	0.131 040	0.090 0	0.086 0
15–19	0.104 564	0.090 0	0.084 7
20–24	0.078 289	0.080 0	0.082 2
25–29	0.063 646	0.080 0	0.079 3
30–34	0.057 554	0.060 0	0.076 1
35–39	0.054 802	0.060 0	0.071 5
40–44	0.043 456	0.060 0	0.065 9
45–49	0.036 307	0.060 0	0.060 4
50–54	0.033 110	0.050 0	0.053 7
55–59	0.030 741	0.040 0	0.045 5
60–64	0.025 024	0.040 0	0.037 2
65–69	0.019 660	0.030 0	0.029 6
70–74	0.013 432	0.020 0	0.022 1
75–79	0.008 473	0.010 0	0.015 2
80–84	0.004 740	0.005 0	0.009 1
≥85	0.003 246	0.005 0	0.006 4

[a] Standard age distribution proposed by INDEPTH for sub-Saharan
Africa.
[b] Standard age distribution proposed by Segi (1960).
[c] Standard global age distribution proposed by WHO (see Estève et
al. 1994).

at each age he or she is subjected to the age-specific mortality rates under consideration. Both measures reflect the total risk of death faced by the population as a whole.

The CDR can also be expressed as the age-weighted average of age-specific
mortality rates. As a result, the CDR is a function of both the age structure of the population and its age-specific mortality rates, and variations in either schedule, from one
site to another, may yield spurious differences in CDRs. Because diverse populations
may have significantly different age distributions, the CDR cannot be directly compared across different populations. To remove the influence of the age structure and
make such a comparison possible, it is necessary to substitute a standard age distribution in place of the population's true age distribution when calculating the CDR. The
result is an ASCDR. There are several widely used standard age distributions, including the Segi and WHO standard age distributions (see Segi 1960; Estève et al. 1994).
Both of these standards reflect populations with fairly low fertility and mortality.
Consequently, they give significant weight to the middle years of life. All of the
INDEPTH sites record information from fairly young populations with high fertility
and mortality. Under those conditions, the population has proportionally more young
people, giving it a "younger" age distribution. When the Segi or WHO standard age
distributions are applied to the INDEPTH data, they give too much weight to the high
mortality rates prevailing at middle and older ages and too little to mortality at
younger ages. Consequently, the absolute level of the ASCDRs produced using those
standards significantly overestimates the true level of mortality at the INDEPTH sites.

To address this problem and create ASCDRs that more accurately reflect the
true level of mortality at the INDEPTH sites, we calculated the INDEPTH standard
age distribution. We constructed an average age distribution for each site over the
period 1995–99 by taking the weighted average of the person–years of exposure in

each age group across all of the years for which data had been reported. The weight for each year is the total number of person–years reported for all ages during that year. We calculated the INDEPTH standard age distribution by taking the weighted average of the individual site average age distributions in each age group. In this case, the weights are the total number of person–years in each of the individual site average age distributions. The result is displayed in Table 6.2, along with Segi and WHO standards.

In Figure 6.1, the younger age distribution of the INDEPTH standard, which is typical of developing countries, is contrasted with the much older population structures of the Segi and WHO standards.

Figure 6.1. CDR and life expectancy at birth.
Source: Segi and WHO standards (see Segi 1960; Estève et al. 1994). Note: WHO, World Health Organization.

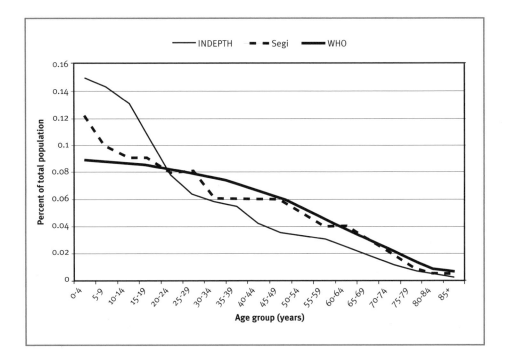

Table 6.3 displays the CDR for each site and the ASCDRs calculated using both the INDEPTH and Segi standard age distributions along with the values for life expectancy at birth taken from Tables 6A.1–6A.19 (see Annex). Differences in the ASCDRs are the result of differences in the underlying age-specific mortality schedules measured at each site. Because they control for the age distribution of the population, both of the ASCDRs may be directly compared across the sites.

The INDEPTH standardized CDRs range from about 7 to about 33 per 1000 for males and from about 5 to about 27 per 1000 for females, revealing a very wide range of mortality at the INDEPTH sites. The figures for life expectancy at birth vary in a relationship that is loosely inverse to the values of the CDR (Figure 6.2), and they cover a similarly wide range: from 66 to 39 years for males and from 74 to 40 years for females. The data from Bandim are anomalous and reflect some unresolved questions about the way in which they were collected and reported.

Some geographic clustering occurs. Agincourt, in South Africa, is grouped with the two sites in Bangladesh: the Matlab comparison and treatment areas. Also together at the low end of the spectrum are three rural sites in Tanzania: Hai, Rufiji, and Ifakara; and one site in Senegal: Mlomp. In the middle of the pack are three sites in West Africa: Nouna, Oubritenga, and Farafenni. At the high end is a mixture of sites from West, East, and southern Africa. The absolute level of mortality varies considerably over space, with sites located close to each other having similar levels of mortality, but with a wide range of mortality levels measured in all major regions of Africa.

Table 6.3. Crude death rates and life expectancies at birth for 19 INDEPTH sites, 1995–99.

DSS site	Male				Female			
	CDR	ASCDR[a]	ASCDR[b]	e_0 (years)	CDR	ASCDR[a]	ASCDR[b]	e_0 (years)
Agincourt, South Africa	5.93	7.42	9.43	66.12	4.65	4.90	5.90	74.38
Matlab treat.,[c] Bangladesh	7.30	7.60	9.20	66.93	6.66	7.70	8.93	67.02
Matlab comp.,[d] Bangladesh	8.70	9.58	11.24	63.40	7.50	9.14	10.37	64.87
Mlomp, Senegal	10.35	10.80	12.51	60.46	9.83	8.59	9.68	64.78
Hai, Tanzania	12.33	11.56	13.49	56.26	9.49	8.65	9.74	62.80
Rufiji, Tanzania	14.67	12.19	13.57	53.40	15.35	12.61	13.28	52.18
Ifakara, Tanzania	11.70	12.45	13.98	55.73	11.01	11.37	12.28	58.22
Butajira, Ethiopia	11.65	12.50	13.79	55.81	11.25	12.44	13.50	56.68
Nouna, Burkina Faso	13.74	13.62	14.46	54.20	14.42	14.41	15.71	53.06
Oubritenga, Burkina Faso	15.68	14.93	15.95	51.63	13.58	13.05	13.53	55.08
Farafenni, The Gambia	16.24	15.84	17.47	50.83	13.17	13.56	14.08	55.05
Dar es Salaam, Tanzania	12.84	17.15	20.52	50.32	12.66	16.45	19.42	49.76
Niakhar, Senegal	18.45	17.45	18.26	48.80	15.89	14.40	14.81	53.59
Manhiça, Mozambique	17.00	17.50	20.11	47.47	12.41	11.36	12.60	58.12
Navrongo, Ghana	17.66	18.07	20.42	47.22	15.10	15.82	17.66	51.39
Gwembe, Zambia	18.69	19.27	21.89	47.32	16.82	17.95	19.67	53.66
Morogoro, Tanzania	18.70	19.27	21.90	44.44	16.82	17.95	19.67	46.11
Bandafassi, Senegal	23.49	20.62	21.62	44.74	20.36	18.30	18.71	47.54
Bandim, Guinea-Bissau	31.35	32.86	38.63	35.86	25.65	27.48	31.42	38.91

Note: ASCDR, age-standardized crude death rate; CDR, crude death rate (actual number of deaths per 1000 population); e_0, life expectancy at birth.
[a] Standardized with INDEPTH standard age structure.
[b] Standardized with Segi standard age structure (see Segi 1960).
[c] Treatment area.
[d] Comparison area.

For the most part the sex differentials are small, but they generally favour females, as expected. Two of the sites in southern Africa with significant male migration — Agincourt, South Africa, and Manhiça, Mozambique — register substantial sex differentials, standing out in contrast to the rest of the sites. Bandim, in West Africa, also records a very substantial sex differential, but as noted above there may be a methodological explanation for this.

Figure 6.2. ASCDR and life expectancy at birth.
Note: ASCDR, age-standardized crude death rate; comp., comparison area; e_0, life expectancy at birth; treat., treatment area.

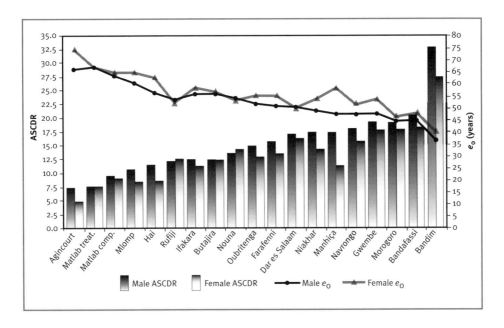

Child mortality

The measures of child mortality displayed in Table 6.4 are the life-table probabilities of dying in a specified age group: $_1q_0$ for ages 0–<1 year, $_4q_1$ for ages 1–4 years, and $_5q_0$ for ages 0–<5 years — all taken from the life tables in Tables 6A.1–6A.19 (see Annex). The conventional infant mortality rate is also included. The life-table measures represent the probability that a child who survives to the beginning of the specified age interval will die before reaching the end of that interval. A value of 0.1 for $_1q_0$ indicates that 10% of newborns will die before their first birthday, and correspondingly a value of 0.25 for $_4q_1$ indicates that 25% of the children reaching their first birthday will die before reaching their fifth birthday. We chose to present these measures because they are intuitive and powerful and represent the fundamental probability of death, rather than a potentially ambiguously defined and difficult-to-interpret rate or ratio to live births, which would be affected by differentials in fertility between sites.

As shown in Figure 6.3, a wide range occurs in the level of child mortality. The probability that a newborn dies before reaching its fifth birthday ranges from 32 to 255 per 1000 for males and from 34 to 217 per 1000 for females. The Agincourt site in South Africa has recorded a comparatively very low level of child mortality. In another cluster, composed of the Matlab sites in Bangladesh, Mlomp in Senegal, and Hai in Tanzania, all have reported low levels of child mortality, but not nearly as low as the level reported from the South Africa site. The next higher cluster is composed of sites

Table 6.4. Infant and child mortality at 19 INDEPTH sites, 1995–99.

DSS Site	IMR per 1000	Male (per 1000)				Female (per 1000)			
		$_1q_0$	$_4q_1$	$_5q_0$	$_1q_0/_4q_1$	$_1q_0$	$_4q_1$	$_5q_0$	$_1q_0/_4q_1$
Agincourt, South Africa	16.93	15.06	17.52	32.32	0.86	16.63	17.35	33.69	0.96
Matlab treat.,[a] Bangladesh	50.58	47.38	15.92	62.54	2.98	59.88	20.88	79.51	2.87
Matlab comp.,[b] Bangladesh	70.05	65.96	23.67	88.08	2.79	80.24	21.64	100.15	3.71
Mlomp, Senegal	45.18	48.24	42.61	88.80	1.13	49.42	51.74	98.60	0.96
Hai, Tanzania	67.13	66.78	26.73	91.73	2.50	56.54	26.68	81.71	2.12
Dar es Salaam, Tanzania	71.13	66.38	50.86	113.86	1.30	67.20	52.49	116.16	1.28
Butajira, Ethiopia	67.82	65.62	57.73	119.56	1.14	71.09	62.20	128.87	1.14
Ifakara, Tanzania	93.22	76.12	52.23	124.37	1.46	86.09	50.27	132.03	1.71
Nouna, Burkina Faso	40.85	34.31	107.53	138.15	0.32	42.71	106.82	144.97	0.40
Manhiça, Mozambique	72.65	85.75	68.91	148.75	1.24	59.37	60.41	116.19	0.98
Farafenni, The Gambia	74.65	68.04	110.47	171.00	0.62	66.46	109.12	168.32	0.61
Rufiji, Tanzania	143.00	147.54	37.54	179.55	3.93	175.60	33.10	202.88	5.31
Navrongo, Ghana	109.59	106.58	83.54	181.21	1.28	102.96	73.23	168.65	1.41
Gwembe, Zambia	NA	105.24	87.26	183.32	1.21	111.94	78.78	181.90	1.42
Morogoro, Tanzania	116.73	105.24	87.26	183.32	1.21	111.94	78.78	181.90	1.42
Oubritenga, Burkina Faso	96.49	102.25	95.97	188.41	1.07	91.88	104.84	187.09	0.88
Niakhar, Senegal	NA	89.80	146.84	223.45	0.61	72.16	129.14	191.98	0.56
Bandim, Guinea-Bissau	NA	112.37	129.78	227.57	0.87	101.52	128.31	216.80	0.79
Bandafassi, Senegal	124.88	138.60	134.59	254.54	1.03	116.43	114.29	217.42	1.02

Note: IMR, infant mortality rate (number of deaths of infants <1 year old per 1000 live births in a given year); NA, not available; $_1q_0$, probability that a newborn will die before reaching its 1st birthday; $_4q_1$, probability that a child that has reached its 1st birthday will die before its reaching its 5th birthday; $_5q_0$, probability that a newborn will die before reaching its 5th birthday; $_1q_0/_4q_1$, ratio of probability of death faced by children before and after their 1st birthday.

[a] Treatment area.

[b] Comparison area.

from various regions of Africa, including Dar es Salaam, Tanzania; Butajira, Ethiopia; Ifakara, Tanzania; Nouna, Burkina Faso; and Manhiça, Mozambique. Following after, with $_5q_0$ very close to 175 per 1000 for males and females, are Farafenni, The Gambia; Rufiji, Tanzania; Navrongo, Ghana; Gwembe, Zambia; Morogoro, Tanzania; and Oubritenga, Burkina Faso. The three remaining sites — Niakhar, Senegal; Bandim, Guinea-Bissau; and Bandafassi, Senegal — all have substantially higher values of $_5q_0$, closer to 225 per 1000. A wide range occurs in the level of child mortality, but except at the very lowest and very highest levels, no geographical clustering is apparent. The lowest levels are definitely found in South Africa and Asia, and the highest levels are reported from West Africa.

It is also worth noting the very high levels of $_1q_0$ reported from Rufiji,[1] Tanzania, and Bandafassi, Senegal. Both of those values are extraordinarily high and indicate that the conditions for infants in those areas are among the most unfavourable anywhere on the globe. Table 6.4 also displays the ratio of $_1q_0$ to $_4q_1$, to elucidate the changing risk of death children face before and after their first birthday. This ratio reveals that children in Rufiji who survive to age 1 year face a probability of death improved by nearly a factor of four, whereas children in Bandafassi face a nearly constant probability of dying throughout the first 5 years of life.

Sex differentials in child mortality are fairly small and do not appear to consistently favour one sex over the other. Interestingly, this pattern is broken by four sites: Manhiça, Mozambique; Rufiji, Tanzania; Niakhar, Senegal; and Bandafassi, Senegal. In the last two cases, there is a clear differential favouring females, as there is in Manhiça. In contrast, Rufiji records a substantial differential favouring males.

Figure 6.3. Child mortality.
Note: Cont., control area; $_5q_0$, probablity of dying between birth and <5 years of age; treat., treatment area.

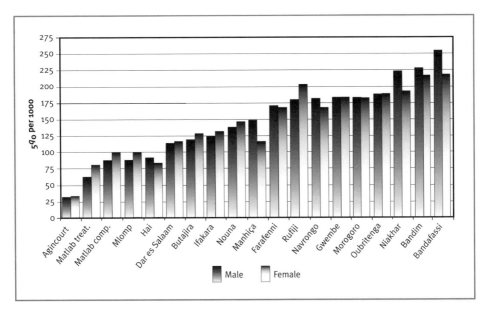

Adult mortality

In keeping with the life-table treatment of child mortality, the index chosen for adult mortality, $_{30}q_{20}$, is the probability that a person who has survived to age 20 will die before his or her 50th birthday. Values for $_{30}q_{20}$ taken from Tables 6A.1–6A.19 (see Annex) are displayed in Table 6.5 along with values of $_5q_0$ and the ratio of $_5q_0$ to $_{30}q_{20}$. The information on child mortality is included to allow the calculation and display of the relationship between child and adult mortality for each site, embodied in the ratio of $_5q_0$ to $_{30}q_{20}$.

Very substantial ranges occur in the level of adult mortality: 63–501 per 1000 for males and 59–421 per 1000 for females. A value of 500 per 1000 for $_{30}q_{20}$ indicates that fully half of the people who survive to age 20 do not live to reach their 50th birthday. Additionally, a number of sites record substantial sex differentials in adult mortality — Mlomp, Senegal; Agincourt, South Africa; Navrongo, Ghana; Hai, Tanzania; and Manhiça, Mozambique, in particular. Also apparent is the opposite differential, in which female rates exceed those of males in two sites: Rufiji, Tanzania, and Dar es Salaam, Tanzania. HIV–AIDS and maternal mortality may play roles. Without more information from the sites, we are unable to explain these differentials.

For the first time, Agincourt, South Africa, does not define the low end of the range. Where adult mortality is concerned, the Matlab sites in Bangladesh clearly stand out, with substantially lower risks of death than anywhere else, and in both these sites a very small sex differential favours females. In both cases, nearly 95% of adults

---

1 Rufiji is the newest INDEPTH site and is reporting data for its first year of operation (see Table 7.2). The apparent high risk of death for infants revealed by the data from Rufiji may be in part an artifact, resulting from an age-reporting bias for an infant's date of birth in first-year DSSs. This is due to the fact that in the first year of any DSS, unlike subsequent years, a large portion of the infants would be born before the DSS started and their birth dates would be subject to maternal recall error. These errors decrease for infants born during the DSS, as such infants become registered soon after birth. This start-up bias would have less of an effect on under-five mortality rates.

Table 6.5. Adult mortality and child–adult mortality ratio at 19 INDEPTH sites, 1995–99.

DSS site	Male (per 1000)			Female (per 1000)		
	$_5q_0$	$_{30}q_{20}$	$_5q_0/_{30}q_{20}$	$_5q_0$	$_{30}q_{20}$	$_5q_0/_{30}q_{20}$
Matlab treat,[a] Bangladesh	62.54	63.45	0.9856	79.51	59.43	1.3378
Matlab comp.,[b] Bangladesh	88.08	72.35	1.2173	100.15	60.28	1.6614
Mlomp, Senegal	88.80	159.03	0.5584	98.60	111.51	0.8842
Niakhar, Senegal	223.45	165.25	1.3522	191.98	141.86	1.3533
Agincourt, South Africa	32.32	196.35	0.1646	33.69	100.77	0.3344
Nouna, Burkina Faso	138.15	199.93	0.6910	144.97	184.51	0.7857
Farafenni, The Gambia	171.00	205.13	0.8336	168.32	149.85	1.1231
Oubritenga, Burkina Faso	188.41	210.62	0.8945	187.09	157.60	1.1871
Bandafassi, Senegal	254.54	226.27	1.1249	217.42	200.42	1.0848
Butajira, Ethiopia	119.56	227.19	0.5263	128.87	193.86	0.6648
Rufiji, Tanzania	179.55	236.29	0.7599	202.88	259.63	0.7814
Ifakara, Tanzania	124.37	240.09	0.5180	132.03	185.07	0.7135
Navrongo, Ghana	181.21	298.01	0.6081	168.65	188.86	0.8930
Hai, Tanzania	91.73	304.77	0.3010	81.71	229.38	0.3562
Dar es Salaam, Tanzania	113.86	331.46	0.3435	116.16	369.74	0.3142
Manhiça, Mozambique	148.75	382.13	0.3893	116.19	197.39	0.5887
Gwembe, Zambia	183.32	408.82	0.4484	181.90	372.81	0.4879
Morogoro, Tanzania	183.32	409.03	0.4482	181.90	372.81	0.4879
Bandim, Guinea-Bissau	227.57	500.75	0.4545	216.80	421.42	0.5145

Note: $_5q_0$, probability that a newborn will die before reaching its 5th birthday; $_{30}q_{20}$, probability that an adult who has survived to age 20 will die before reaching his or her 50th birthday; $_5q_0/_{30}q_{20}$, ratio of the probability that a newborn will die before reaching its 5th birthday to the probability that an adult who has survived to age 20 will die before reaching his or her 50th birthday.

[a] Treatment area.

[b] Comparison area.

reaching age 20 years survive to their 50th birthday. The next cluster appears at between 150 and 200 per 1000 and includes sites ranging from Mlomp in Senegal to Rufiji in Tanzania (Figure 6.4). In all of these cases, the sex differential is small, except for Agincourt, South Africa, and favours females in all cases except for Rufiji, Tanzania. The last cluster covers a wide range: about 250–475 per 1000. This group includes the remainder of the sites and is marked by the very high risk of adult mortality in Bandim and the substantial sex differentials in Navrongo, Ghana; Hai, Tanzania; and Manhiça, Mozambique.

As was the case with child mortality, the geographic clustering clearly separates the Asian sites from the African sites, but beyond that, there does not appear to be any substantial geographical clustering of similar risk of adult mortality within Africa. The cluster with moderate risk includes sites from all major regions of Africa, as does the high-risk cluster.

The relationship between child and adult mortality reveals three distinct groups: sites in Asia, sites in West Africa, and sites in the rest of Africa. The Asian and some of the West African sites clearly record levels of child mortality that are higher than the corresponding levels of adult mortality. Mortality at all ages is relatively low in Asia, so this finding is primarily the result of exceptionally low adult mortality. In four West African sites — Niakhar and Bandafassi, Senegal; Farafenni, The Gambia; and Oubritenga, Burkina Faso — this is the result of unusually high child mortality, coupled with substantial adult mortality. It is our guess that in these cases malaria is the primary reason why child mortality is so high, but this must be confirmed with more information from those sites.

Figure 6.4. Adult mortality.
Note: Cont., control area; $_{30}q_{20}$, probability of dying between ages 20 and 50 years; treat., treatment area.

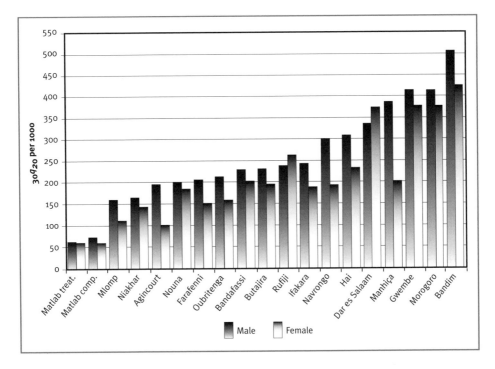

Discussion

The data presented here are the first large compilation of high-quality data collected over a large area of Africa at intensively operated longitudinal field sites. In light of the general lack of high-quality information describing contemporary mortality in Africa, this is a unique and useful collection of data. The level of mortality varies considerably across the sites that have produced these data, and all but one or two appear to have produced very reasonable age-specific mortality schedules. A great deal of additional analysis will be applied to these data in the near future. The first extension of the basic description of the levels and age patterns of mortality presented here is the identification and thorough examination of the common underlying age patterns of mortality embodied in these data, presented in the following chapter.

ANNEX: LIFE TABLES

Table 6A.1. Life table for the Agincourt DSS site, South Africa, 1995–99.

Age (years)	$_nD_x$	$_nPY_x$	$_nM_x$	SE_{nM_x}	$_nq_x$	SE_{nq_x}	l_x	SE_{l_x}	$_nd_x$	$_nL_x$	T_x	e_x (years)	SE_{e_x} (years)
Male													
<1	59	3 877	0.015 218	0.001 966	0.015 064	0.001 946	100 000	0.0000	1 506	98 991	6 611 576	66.12	0.639 9
1–4	76	17 147	0.004 432	0.000 504	0.017 522	0.001 992	98 494	0.3788	1 726	389 370	6 512 585	66.12	0.626 6
5–9	14	23 175	0.000 604	0.000 161	0.003 016	0.000 805	96 768	0.7507	292	483 110	6 123 215	63.28	0.613 1
10–14	14	20 119	0.000 696	0.000 186	0.003 473	0.000 927	96 476	0.8068	335	481 542	5 640 105	58.46	0.611 2
15–19	16	17 741	0.000 902	0.000 225	0.004 499	0.001 122	96 141	0.8811	433	479 623	5 158 563	53.66	0.609 2
20–24	32	14 014	0.002 283	0.000 401	0.011 352	0.001 995	95 708	0.9896	1 086	475 826	4 678 940	48.89	0.606 6
25–29	46	11 122	0.004 136	0.000 604	0.020 469	0.002 987	94 622	1.3320	1 937	468 267	4 203 115	44.42	0.600 0
30–34	53	9 027	0.005 871	0.000 795	0.028 933	0.003 916	92 685	2.0768	2 682	456 721	3 734 847	40.30	0.587 7
35–39	61	7 198	0.008 474	0.001 062	0.041 493	0.005 201	90 003	3.2759	3 735	440 681	3 278 126	36.42	0.570 4
40–44	44	5 634	0.007 810	0.001 155	0.038 303	0.005 663	86 269	5.2012	3 304	423 084	2 837 445	32.89	0.545 9
45–49	69	4 559	0.015 133	0.001 754	0.072 909	0.008 451	82 965	7.1969	6 049	399 701	2 414 361	29.10	0.523 6
50–54	48	3 322	0.014 448	0.002 011	0.069 724	0.009 707	76 916	11.1018	5 363	371 171	2 014 661	26.19	0.483 4
55–59	56	2 697	0.020 765	0.002 634	0.098 700	0.012 522	71 553	15.1816	7 062	340 109	1 643 489	22.97	0.444 4
60–64	41	1 980	0.020 706	0.003 070	0.098 435	0.014 597	64 491	20.3599	6 348	306 583	1 303 381	20.21	0.395 1
65–69	56	1 733	0.032 311	0.003 982	0.149 481	0.018 422	58 142	25.4104	8 691	268 984	996 798	17.14	0.349 1
70–74	58	1 352	0.042 889	0.005 057	0.193 680	0.022 836	49 451	29.8539	9 578	223 312	727 814	14.72	0.296 5
75–79	70	1 021	0.068 566	0.006 892	0.292 662	0.029 419	39 874	32.1623	11 669	170 194	504 502	12.65	0.242 1
80–84	29	415	0.069 925	0.010 882	0.297 600	0.046 315	28 204	29.8521	8 394	120 037	334 308	11.85	0.173 9
≥85	27	292	0.092 455	NA	1.000 000	NA	19 811	31.7918	19 811	214 271	214 271	10.82	NA
Female													
<1	65	3 866	0.016 813	0.002 068	0.016 631	0.002 046	100 000	0.0000	1 663	98 919	7 438 159	74.38	0.645 5
1–4	75	17 093	0.004 388	0.000 502	0.017 350	0.001 986	98 337	0.4185	1 706	388 845	7 339 240	74.63	0.626 9
5–9	19	23 002	0.000 826	0.000 189	0.004 122	0.000 944	96 631	0.7855	398	482 158	6 950 395	71.93	0.609 7
10–14	12	19 943	0.000 602	0.000 173	0.003 004	0.000 866	96 232	0.8621	289	480 440	6 468 237	67.21	0.606 4
15–19	18	17 494	0.001 029	0.000 242	0.005 131	0.001 206	95 943	0.9264	492	478 486	5 987 798	62.41	0.604 0
20–24	30	15 098	0.001 987	0.000 361	0.009 886	0.001 796	95 451	1.0509	944	474 896	5 509 312	57.72	0.600 0
25–29	30	12 356	0.002 428	0.000 441	0.012 067	0.002 190	94 507	1.3241	1 140	469 686	5 034 416	53.27	0.592 3
30–34	36	10 365	0.003 473	0.000 574	0.017 217	0.002 845	93 367	1.7206	1 608	462 816	4 564 729	48.89	0.582 7
35–39	37	8 572	0.004 316	0.000 702	0.021 351	0.003 472	91 759	2.3673	1 959	453 900	4 101 913	44.70	0.569 0
40–44	36	7 025	0.005 124	0.000 843	0.025 297	0.004 163	89 800	3.2825	2 272	443 322	3 648 013	40.62	0.552 2
45–49	20	5 111	0.003 913	0.000 866	0.019 375	0.004 290	87 529	4.5158	1 696	433 404	3 204 691	36.61	0.532 5
50–54	22	3 572	0.006 159	0.001 293	0.030 326	0.006 367	85 833	5.7526	2 603	422 057	2 771 288	32.29	0.516 2
55–59	19	3 285	0.005 784	0.001 308	0.028 507	0.006 446	83 230	8.3953	2 373	410 218	2 348 631	28.22	0.488 2
60–64	48	3 132	0.015 326	0.002 129	0.073 803	0.010 252	80 857	10.8017	5 968	389 367	1 938 413	23.97	0.467 0
65–69	63	3 351	0.018 800	0.002 260	0.089 779	0.010 791	74 890	16.1376	6 724	357 640	1 549 046	20.68	0.425 7
70–74	66	2 086	0.031 641	0.003 598	0.146 609	0.016 671	68 166	19.9014	9 994	315 847	1 191 406	17.48	0.393 9
75–79	65	1 583	0.041 055	0.004 594	0.186 167	0.020 831	58 172	27.4077	10 830	263 788	875 559	15.05	0.339 6
80–84	33	507	0.065 149	0.009 622	0.280 119	0.041 373	47 343	32.8374	13 262	203 559	611 772	12.92	0.283 6
≥85	40	479	0.083 489	NA	1.000 000	NA	34 081	55.3825	34 081	408 212	408 212	11.98	NA

Note: $_nD_x$, observed deaths between ages x and $x+n$; $_nd_x$, number dying between ages x and $x+n$; e_x, expectation of life at age x for the life-table population; l_x, number of survivors at age x in the life-table population; $_nL_x$, person-years lived by the life-table population between ages x and $x+n$; $_nM_x$, observed mortality rate for ages x to $x+n$; NA, not applicable; $_nPY_x$, observed person-years between ages x and $x+n$; $_nq_x$, probability of dying between ages x and $x+n$; SE_{l_x}, standard error in l_x; $SE_{_nM_x}$, standard error in $_nM_x$; $SE_{_nq_x}$, standard error in $_nq_x$; SE_{e_x}, standard error in e_x; T_x, person-years lived by the life-table population at ages older than x.

Table 6A.2. Life table for the Bandafassi DSS site, Senegal, 1995–99.

Age (years)	$_nD_x$	$_nPY_x$	$_nM_x$	SE$_{_nM_x}$	$_nq_x$	SE$_{_nq_x}$	l_x	SE$_{l_x}$	$_nd_x$	$_nL_x$	T_x	e_x (years)	SE$_{e_x}$ (years)
Male													
<1	145	949	0.152 785	0.011 776	0.138 597	0.010 683	100 000	0.000 0	13 860	90 714	4 473 789	44.74	1.254 6
1–4	118	3 192	0.036 967	0.003 166	0.134 593	0.011 526	86 140	11.411 6	11 594	313 631	4 388 075	50.88	1.127 3
5–9	12	3 304	0.003 633	0.001 039	0.017 999	0.005 149	74 546	18.404 6	1 342	369 378	4 069 444	54.59	0.973 4
10–14	6	1 632	0.003 677	0.001 487	0.018 217	0.007 369	73 205	19.221 3	1 334	362 689	3 700 067	50.54	0.951 9
15–19	10	1 936	0.005 164	0.001 612	0.025 493	0.007 958	71 871	21.437 5	1 832	354 775	3 337 377	46.44	0.914 6
20–24	10	1 633	0.006 125	0.001 908	0.030 165	0.009 394	70 039	23.629 9	2 113	344 912	2 982 603	42.58	0.877 4
25–29	4	947	0.004 222	0.002 089	0.020 891	0.010 336	67 926	26.554 8	1 419	336 083	2 637 690	38.83	0.834 2
30–34	7	863	0.008 114	0.003 005	0.039 761	0.014 727	66 507	30.385 7	2 644	325 924	2 301 607	34.61	0.792 5
35–39	11	831	0.013 236	0.003 861	0.064 062	0.018 687	63 863	37.610 1	4 091	309 085	1 975 683	30.94	0.721 7
40–44	6	628	0.009 548	0.003 806	0.046 626	0.018 586	59 771	47.187 1	2 787	291 890	1 666 597	27.88	0.624 0
45–49	8	796	0.010 051	0.003 465	0.049 024	0.016 902	56 985	55.230 7	2 794	277 939	1 374 707	24.12	0.549 5
50–54	12	803	0.014 953	0.004 158	0.072 069	0.020 041	54 191	59.225 2	3 905	261 191	1 096 768	20.24	0.503 9
55–59	15	546	0.027 487	0.006 625	0.128 598	0.030 996	50 285	62.790 9	6 467	235 261	835 577	16.62	0.459 2
60–64	12	407	0.029 450	0.007 897	0.137 150	0.036 777	43 819	71.972 8	6 010	204 070	600 316	13.70	0.383 5
65–69	28	398	0.070 370	0.011 133	0.299 211	0.047 336	37 809	79.554 2	11 313	160 763	396 246	10.48	0.321 4
70–74	26	265	0.097 973	0.014 964	0.393 486	0.060 098	26 496	71.101 0	10 426	106 416	235 483	8.89	0.248 6
75–79	10	125	0.079 992	0.020 654	0.333 304	0.086 061	16 070	51.511 9	5 356	66 961	129 067	8.03	0.183 5
80–84	11	49	0.223 159	0.035 843	0.716 218	0.115 038	10 714	42.023 6	7 674	34 386	62 106	5.80	0.143 2
≥85	3	27	0.109 685	NA	1.000 000	NA	3 040	18.575 2	3 040	27 720	27 720	9.12	NA
Female													
<1	120	953	0.125 969	0.010 809	0.116 435	0.009 991	100 000	0.000 0	11 643	92 432	4 754 185	47.54	1.280 8
1–4	96	3 106	0.030 903	0.002 968	0.114 292	0.010 978	88 357	9.982 1	10 098	326 776	4 661 753	52.76	1.164 4
5–9	25	3 423	0.007 303	0.001 434	0.035 859	0.007 042	78 258	17.239 5	2 806	384 275	4 334 977	55.39	1.019 3
10–14	12	2 368	0.005 067	0.001 444	0.025 018	0.007 131	75 452	19.062 3	1 888	372 540	3 950 702	52.36	0.973 4
15–19	10	2 213	0.004 519	0.001 413	0.022 343	0.006 986	73 564	21.015 6	1 644	363 711	3 578 163	48.64	0.933 7
20–24	7	1 095	0.006 390	0.002 126	0.031 447	0.011 697	71 920	22.728 3	2 262	353 948	3 214 451	44.69	0.901 7
25–29	12	1 599	0.007 503	0.002 126	0.036 824	0.010 433	69 659	28.398 7	2 565	341 881	2 860 503	41.06	0.823 8
30–34	8	829	0.009 645	0.003 329	0.047 090	0.016 252	67 094	31.627 1	3 159	327 570	2 518 622	37.54	0.770 7
35–39	10	1 129	0.008 861	0.002 741	0.043 344	0.013 406	63 934	40.608 5	2 771	312 743	2 191 053	34.27	0.658 2
40–44	4	888	0.004 504	0.002 227	0.022 268	0.011 009	61 163	44.511 1	1 362	302 410	1 878 309	30.71	0.593 5
45–49	8	1 022	0.007 825	0.002 713	0.038 373	0.013 304	59 801	47.084 9	2 295	293 268	1 575 899	26.35	0.560 8
50–54	11	715	0.015 387	0.004 464	0.074 084	0.021 494	57 506	49.870 5	4 260	276 881	1 282 631	22.30	0.524 9
55–59	15	723	0.020 740	0.005 084	0.098 589	0.024 168	53 246	58.032 7	5 249	253 106	1 005 750	18.89	0.453 5
60–64	15	595	0.025 231	0.006 116	0.118 670	0.028 765	47 997	63.714 1	5 696	225 743	752 643	15.68	0.388 4
65–69	25	549	0.045 502	0.008 118	0.204 271	0.036 443	42 301	68.550 7	8 641	189 902	526 900	12.46	0.329 0
70–74	20	362	0.055 206	0.010 744	0.242 553	0.047 203	33 660	67.170 1	8 164	147 889	336 998	10.01	0.266 5
75–79	22	212	0.103 602	0.016 945	0.411 445	0.067 297	25 496	63.781 5	10 490	101 253	189 109	7.42	0.215 0
80–84	14	68	0.204 614	0.031 087	0.676 841	0.102 833	15 006	51.532 4	10 156	49 637	87 856	5.85	0.160 2
≥85	13	102	0.126 877	NA	1.000 000	NA	4 849	29.192 0	4 849	38 220	38 220	7.88	NA

Note: $_nD_x$, observed deaths between ages x and $x+n$; $_nd_x$, number of deaths between ages x and $x+n$; $_nd_x$, number dying between ages x and $x+n$; l_x, number of survivors at age x in the life-table population; $_nL_x$, person-years lived by the life-table population between ages x and $x+n$; $_nM_x$, observed mortality rate for ages x to $x+n$; NA, not applicable; $_nPY_x$, observed person-years between ages x and $x+n$; $_nq_x$, probability of dying between ages x and $x+n$; SE$_{l_x}$, standard error in l_x; SE$_{_nM_x}$, standard error in $_nM_x$; SE$_{_nq_x}$, standard error in $_nq_x$; SE$_{e_x}$, standard error in e_x; T_x, person-years lived by the life-table population at ages older than x.

Table 6A.3. Life table for the Bandim DSS site, Guinea-Bissau, 1995–97.

Age (years)	nD_x	nPY_x	nM_x	SE_{nM_x}	nq_x	SE_{nq_x}	l_x	SE_{l_x}	nd_x	nL_x	T_x	e_x(years)	SE_{e_x} (years)
					Male								
0	306	2 518	0.121 521	0.006 545	0.112 372	0.006 052	100 000	0.000 0	11 237	92 471	3 585 686	35.86	0.733 7
1–4	236	6 644	0.035 521	0.002 157	0.129 784	0.007 881	88 763	3.662 9	11 520	324 318	3 493 215	39.35	0.692 5
5–9	47	3 702	0.012 697	0.001 794	0.061 530	0.008 695	77 243	7.667 3	4 753	374 332	3 168 897	41.03	0.621 4
10–14	21	3 153	0.006 660	0.001 429	0.032 756	0.007 030	72 490	11.263 2	2 374	356 514	2 794 565	38.55	0.556 9
15–19	15	2 831	0.005 298	0.001 350	0.026 145	0.006 662	70 116	13.134 3	1 833	345 995	2 438 051	34.77	0.523 5
20–24	17	2 441	0.006 964	0.001 660	0.034 226	0.008 158	68 282	14.638 2	2 337	335 569	2 092 056	30.64	0.500 1
25–29	29	2 278	0.012 731	0.002 090	0.061 693	0.011 097	65 945	16.756 2	4 068	319 556	1 756 487	26.64	0.473 0
30–34	30	2 094	0.014 327	0.002 524	0.069 159	0.012 182	61 877	20.107 8	4 279	298 687	1 436 931	23.22	0.434 0
35–39	27	1 676	0.016 108	0.002 977	0.077 420	0.014 311	57 598	23.104 8	4 459	276 840	1 138 244	19.76	0.400 2
40–44	41	1 163	0.035 251	0.005 040	0.161 979	0.023 158	53 138	26.460 3	8 607	244 174	861 404	16.21	0.369 3
45–49	41	772	0.053 121	0.007 259	0.234 469	0.032 039	44 531	33.725 3	10 441	196 553	617 230	13.86	0.309 6
50–54	25	581	0.043 006	0.007 721	0.194 156	0.034 858	34 090	40.119 6	6 619	153 903	420 677	12.34	0.225 9
55–59	34	501	0.067 799	0.009 798	0.289 863	0.041 891	27 471	40.174 0	7 963	117 449	266 774	9.71	0.173 1
60–64	29	276	0.105 107	0.014 913	0.416 177	0.059 050	19 508	33.503 1	8 119	77 244	149 325	7.65	0.127 7
65–69	29	195	0.148 699	0.018 687	0.542 006	0.068 114	11 389	24.689 8	6 173	41 154	72 081	6.33	0.077 3
70–74	17	104	0.163 781	0.025 712	0.581 009	0.091 214	5 216	11.197 2	3 031	18 505	30 567	5.86	0.042 0
75–79	19	106	0.178 709	0.025 353	0.617 614	0.087 618	2 186	4.229 5	1 350	7 553	12 062	5.52	0.017 6
80–84	7	40	0.176 584	0.041 546	0.612 519	0.144 111	836	0.985 1	512	2 899	4 509	5.40	0.009 0
≥85	5	25	0.201 146	NA	1.000 000	NA	324	0.293 0	324	1 610	1 610	4.97	NA
					Female								
<1	264	2 429	0.108 687	0.006 341	0.101 515	0.005 922	100 000	0.000 0	10 152	93 402	3 890 969	38.91	0.806 9
1–4	219	6 249	0.035 045	0.002 211	0.128 314	0.008 095	89 848	3.507 3	11 529	328 969	3 797 567	42.27	0.795 9
5–9	40	3 919	0.010 206	0.001 573	0.049 762	0.007 670	78 320	7.955 3	3 897	381 855	3 468 598	44.29	0.685 6
10–14	17	3 561	0.004 773	0.001 144	0.023 585	0.005 652	74 422	10.791 7	1 755	367 723	3 086 743	41.48	0.632 7
15–19	10	3 456	0.002 893	0.000 908	0.014 363	0.004 509	72 667	12.058 2	1 044	360 726	2 719 020	37.42	0.610 0
20–24	27	3 613	0.007 472	0.001 411	0.036 677	0.006 928	71 623	12.788 0	2 627	351 549	2 358 294	32.93	0.598 8
25–29	31	2 723	0.011 384	0.001 987	0.055 343	0.009 661	68 996	14.329 2	3 818	335 436	2 006 745	29.08	0.578 0
30–34	29	2 065	0.014 043	0.002 518	0.067 832	0.012 161	65 178	17.230 2	4 421	314 837	1 671 309	25.64	0.546 7
35–39	24	1 643	0.014 609	0.002 875	0.070 469	0.013 868	60 757	21.255 0	4 281	293 080	1 356 472	22.33	0.510 0
40–44	29	1 046	0.027 716	0.004 802	0.129 599	0.022 452	56 475	25.464 6	7 319	264 079	1 063 392	18.83	0.477 3
45–49	28	822	0.034 070	0.005 912	0.156 978	0.027 238	49 156	35.370 2	7 716	226 490	799 313	16.26	0.413 8
50–54	23	538	0.042 718	0.008 002	0.192 979	0.036 148	41 440	43.064 4	7 997	187 206	572 823	13.82	0.351 4
55–59	32	455	0.070 318	0.010 407	0.299 024	0.044 257	33 443	50.486 6	10 000	142 213	385 617	11.53	0.281 6
60–64	24	282	0.085 044	0.013 989	0.350 667	0.057 680	23 443	46.713 7	8 221	96 661	243 403	10.38	0.207 2
65–69	13	240	0.054 234	0.013 123	0.238 791	0.057 783	15 222	37.979 4	3 635	67 023	146 742	9.64	0.126 5
70–74	17	140	0.121 464	0.021 530	0.465 858	0.082 577	11 587	29.743 2	5 398	44 441	79 719	6.88	0.095 9
75–79	11	72	0.152 210	0.030 742	0.551 276	0.111 343	6 189	17.641 2	3 412	22 416	35 278	5.70	0.055 2
80–84	9	42	0.214 272	0.039 274	0.697 645	0.127 871	2 777	8.301 0	1 938	9 042	12 862	4.63	0.025 0
≥85	8	36	0.219 830	NA	1.000 000	NA	840	2.020 0	840	3 820	3 820	4.55	NA

Note: nD_x, observed deaths between ages x and $x+n$; nd_x, number dying between ages x and $x+n$ in the life-table population; l_x, number of survivors at age x in the life-table population; L_x, person-years lived by the life-table population between ages x and $x+n$; M_x, observed mortality rate for ages x to $x+n$; NA, not applicable; PY_x, observed person-years between ages x and $x+n$; nq_x, probability of dying between ages x and $x+n$; SE_{l_x}, standard error in l_x; SE_{nM_x}, standard error in nM_x; SE, standard error in e_x; T_x, person-years lived by the life-table population at ages older than x; e_x, expectation of life at age x for the life-table population; SE_{e_x}, standard error in e_x; SE_{nq_x}, standard error in nq_x.

Table 6A.4. Life table for the Butajira DSS site, Ethiopia, 1995–96.

Age (years)	$_nD_x$	$_nPY_x$	$_nM_x$	$SE_{_nM_x}$	$_nq_x$	$SE_{_nq_x}$	l_x	SE_{l_x}	$_nd_x$	$_nL_x$	T_x	e_x (years)	SE_{e_x} (years)
Male													
<1	92	1 340	0.068 633	0.006 917	0.065 616	0.006 613	100 000	0.000 0	6 562	95 604	5 581 033	55.81	1.204 2
1–4	73	4 863	0.015 011	0.001 705	0.057 732	0.006 559	93 438	4.372 8	5 394	359 362	5 485 429	58.71	1.138 4
5–9	38	5 608	0.006 776	0.001 081	0.033 317	0.005 314	88 044	7.638 5	2 933	432 887	5 126 067	58.22	1.075 5
10–14	16	4 944	0.003 236	0.000 802	0.016 050	0.003 980	85 111	9.327 0	1 366	422 138	4 693 180	55.14	1.041 2
15–19	18	4 292	0.004 194	0.000 978	0.020 753	0.004 841	83 745	10.177 6	1 738	414 378	4 271 042	51.00	1.025 3
20–24	20	3 464	0.005 774	0.001 273	0.028 459	0.006 272	82 007	11.402 7	2 334	404 199	3 856 664	47.03	1.005 4
25–29	14	2 082	0.006 726	0.001 768	0.033 073	0.008 692	79 673	13.408 8	2 635	391 776	3 452 465	43.33	0.977 4
30–34	7	1 448	0.004 835	0.001 806	0.023 887	0.008 920	77 038	17.332 2	1 840	380 588	3 060 689	39.73	0.932 6
35–39	11	1 541	0.007 137	0.002 114	0.035 057	0.010 383	75 198	21.236 2	2 636	369 397	2 680 101	35.64	0.895 0
40–44	17	1 436	0.011 840	0.002 788	0.057 496	0.013 538	72 561	25.869 6	4 172	352 377	2 310 704	31.84	0.853 9
45–49	20	1 314	0.015 221	0.003 276	0.073 313	0.015 781	68 389	32.630 1	5 014	329 412	1 958 327	28.63	0.797 2
50–54	12	960	0.012 494	0.003 496	0.060 578	0.016 949	63 376	39.668 9	3 839	307 280	1 628 915	25.70	0.736 8
55–59	11	747	0.014 719	0.004 278	0.070 982	0.020 628	59 536	46.546 9	4 226	287 117	1 321 635	22.20	0.687 4
60–64	16	514	0.031 111	0.007 195	0.144 329	0.033 377	55 310	55.256 7	7 983	256 594	1 034 518	18.70	0.636 2
65–69	14	459	0.030 480	0.007 547	0.141 609	0.035 065	47 327	74.537 9	6 702	219 882	777 924	16.44	0.531 5
70–74	17	298	0.057 047	0.011 985	0.249 633	0.052 446	40 625	82.462 2	10 141	177 774	558 042	13.74	0.458 2
75–79	7	159	0.044 025	0.014 899	0.198 300	0.067 109	30 484	91.827 2	6 045	137 308	380 268	12.47	0.328 8
80–84	5	98	0.050 782	0.019 989	0.225 306	0.088 686	24 439	100.870 3	5 506	108 429	242 960	9.94	0.208 2
≥85	7	50	0.140 732	NA	1.000 000	NA	18 933	107.513 2	18 933	134 531	134 531	7.11	NA
Female													
<1	104	1 395	0.074 539	0.007 045	0.071 094	0.006 719	100 000	0.000 0	7 109	95 379	5 667 969	56.68	1.216 3
1–4	77	4 748	0.016 216	0.001 790	0.062 203	0.006 865	92 891	4.514 5	5 778	356 314	5 572 590	59.99	1.146 0
5–9	34	5 613	0.006 057	0.001 023	0.029 836	0.005 040	87 113	8.036 4	2 599	429 065	5 216 276	59.88	1.074 4
10–14	14	5 130	0.002 729	0.000 724	0.013 552	0.003 597	84 513	9.491 5	1 145	419 704	4 787 211	56.64	1.042 6
15–19	16	4 380	0.003 653	0.000 905	0.018 098	0.004 483	83 368	10.160 3	1 509	413 069	4 367 507	52.39	1.029 1
20–24	11	3 320	0.003 313	0.000 991	0.016 431	0.004 913	81 859	11.192 9	1 345	405 934	3 954 438	48.31	1.011 4
25–29	11	2 345	0.004 691	0.001 398	0.023 183	0.006 908	80 514	12.445 8	1 867	397 905	3 548 504	44.07	0.993 9
30–34	14	2 022	0.006 925	0.001 819	0.034 036	0.008 940	78 648	14.969 3	2 677	386 547	3 150 599	40.06	0.965 3
35–39	12	2 171	0.005 529	0.001 574	0.027 266	0.007 763	75 971	18.917 7	2 071	374 676	2 764 052	36.38	0.925 8
40–44	11	1 604	0.006 859	0.002 033	0.033 718	0.009 993	73 899	21.372 7	2 492	363 268	2 389 376	32.33	0.902 7
45–49	23	1 458	0.015 773	0.003 162	0.075 873	0.015 209	71 408	25.409 7	5 418	343 494	2 026 108	28.37	0.873 5
50–54	7	853	0.008 211	0.003 040	0.040 228	0.014 896	65 990	33.494 2	2 655	323 313	1 682 614	25.50	0.818 8
55–59	17	728	0.023 354	0.005 342	0.110 327	0.025 239	63 335	40.516 1	6 988	299 207	1 359 302	21.46	0.784 2
60–64	12	457	0.026 258	0.007 098	0.123 201	0.033 302	56 348	57.621 7	6 942	264 383	1 060 095	18.81	0.706 4
65–69	14	389	0.036 035	0.008 799	0.165 285	0.040 359	49 406	79.510 7	8 166	226 613	795 712	16.11	0.614 0
70–74	14	278	0.050 445	0.011 877	0.223 978	0.052 733	41 240	95.157 5	9 237	183 106	569 099	13.80	0.521 0
75–79	12	194	0.061 814	0.015 270	0.267 702	0.066 131	32 003	104.596 5	8 567	138 596	385 993	12.06	0.413 7
80–84	8	89	0.089 878	0.025 283	0.366 939	0.103 222	23 436	100.881 4	8 599	95 679	247 397	10.56	0.307 9
≥85	8	82	0.097 788	NA	1.000 000	NA	14 836	98.948 5	14 836	151 718	151 718	10.23	NA

Note: $_nD_x$, observed deaths between ages x and $x+n$; $_nd_x$, number dying between ages x and $x+n$; e_x, expectation of life at age x for the life-table population; l_x, number of survivors at age x in the life-table population; $_nL_x$, person-years lived by the life-table population between ages x to $x+n$; NA, not applicable; $_nPY_x$, observed person-years between ages x and $x+n$; $_nM_x$, observed mortality rate for ages x to $x+n$; $_nq_x$, probability of dying between ages x and $x+n$; $SE_{_nM_x}$, standard error in $_nM_x$; $SE_{_nq_x}$, standard error in $_nq_x$; SE_{l_x}, standard error in e_x; T_x, person-years lived by the life-table population at ages older than x.

Table 6A.5. Life table for the Dar es Salaam DSS site, Tanzania, 1994/95–1998/99[a]

Age (years)	$_nD_x$	$_nPY_x$	$_nM_x$	$SE_{_nM_x}$	$_nq_x$	$SE_{_nq_x}$	l_x	SE_{l_x}	$_nd_x$	$_nL_x$	T_x	e_x (years)	SE_{e_x} (years)
Male													
0	358	5 154	0.069 465	0.003 547	0.066 375	0.003 390	100 000	0.000 0	6 638	95 553	5 031 982	50.32	0.424 7
1–4	258	19 602	0.013 162	0.000 798	0.050 862	0.003 085	93 362	1.149 0	4 749	360 781	4 936 429	52.87	0.384 0
5–9	80	20 289	0.003 943	0.000 437	0.019 522	0.002 161	88 614	1.864 6	1 730	438 744	4 575 648	51.64	0.350 7
10–14	42	16 686	0.002 517	0.000 386	0.012 507	0.001 918	86 884	2.159 3	1 087	431 703	4 136 903	47.61	0.337 3
15–19	36	17 950	0.002 006	0.000 333	0.009 978	0.001 655	85 797	2.383 3	856	426 846	3 705 201	43.19	0.328 6
20–24	97	20 672	0.004 692	0.000 471	0.023 190	0.002 327	84 941	2.537 5	1 970	419 781	3 278 355	38.60	0.323 4
25–29	184	20 495	0.008 978	0.000 647	0.043 903	0.003 165	82 971	2.811 9	3 643	405 750	2 858 574	34.45	0.315 0
30–34	170	15 402	0.011 038	0.000 823	0.053 706	0.004 007	79 329	3.259 9	4 260	385 992	2 452 824	30.92	0.302 5
35–39	201	12 357	0.016 267	0.001 102	0.078 155	0.005 293	75 068	3.929 5	5 867	360 674	2 066 831	27.53	0.287 1
40–44	165	9 416	0.017 523	0.001 306	0.083 940	0.006 254	69 201	4.918 0	5 809	331 485	1 706 157	24.65	0.266 0
45–49	150	6 822	0.021 987	0.001 699	0.104 206	0.008 053	63 393	6.000 3	6 606	300 448	1 374 673	21.69	0.244 6
50–54	107	4 804	0.022 274	0.002 037	0.105 496	0.009 646	56 787	7.420 9	5 991	268 957	1 074 224	18.92	0.218 8
55–59	65	3 262	0.019 927	0.002 351	0.094 905	0.011 199	50 796	8.938 0	4 821	241 928	805 268	15.85	0.194 3
60–64	103	2 009	0.051 263	0.004 440	0.227 199	0.019 680	45 975	10.558 1	10 445	203 762	563 340	12.25	0.175 3
65–69	62	1 197	0.051 796	0.005 775	0.229 288	0.025 564	35 530	14.491 8	8 147	157 282	359 578	10.12	0.133 0
70–74	74	765	0.096 727	0.008 786	0.389 457	0.035 375	27 383	16.857 9	10 665	110 254	202 296	7.39	0.098 0
75–79	57	384	0.148 387	0.013 313	0.541 177	0.048 554	16 719	15.667 6	9 048	60 974	92 042	5.51	0.060 0
80–84	36	157	0.229 387	0.019 905	0.728 922	0.063 252	7 671	9.887 7	5 591	24 376	31 068	4.05	0.027 7
≥85	35	113	0.310 697	NA	1.000 000	NA	2 079	3.080 8	2 079	6 693	6 693	3.22	NA
Female													
<1	362	5 151	0.070 272	0.003 567	0.067 202	0.003 411	100 000	0.000 0	6 720	95 632	4 976 327	49.76	0.473 4
1–4	261	19 203	0.013 592	0.000 819	0.052 485	0.003 162	93 280	1.163 7	4 896	360 199	4 880 695	52.32	0.437 5
5–9	54	21 130	0.002 556	0.000 346	0.012 697	0.001 717	88 384	1.914 9	1 122	439 114	4 520 496	51.15	0.407 8
10–14	31	18 767	0.001 652	0.000 295	0.008 225	0.001 471	87 262	2.096 8	718	434 514	4 081 382	46.77	0.400 8
15–19	65	22 735	0.002 859	0.000 352	0.014 194	0.001 748	86 544	2.227 3	1 228	429 649	3 646 867	42.14	0.396 7
20–24	144	25 522	0.005 642	0.000 464	0.027 819	0.002 286	85 316	2.393 4	2 373	420 645	3 217 218	37.71	0.392 0
25–29	268	20 169	0.013 288	0.000 785	0.064 303	0.003 800	82 942	2.642 4	5 333	401 378	2 796 573	33.72	0.385 6
30–34	249	14 022	0.017 758	0.001 076	0.085 018	0.005 154	77 609	3.306 6	6 598	371 549	2 395 195	30.86	0.371 0
35–39	176	9 564	0.018 403	0.001 325	0.087 966	0.006 332	71 011	4.368 0	6 247	339 437	2 023 646	28.50	0.349 7
40–44	125	6 710	0.018 628	0.001 590	0.088 995	0.007 598	64 764	5.655 3	5 764	309 412	1 684 209	26.01	0.325 3
45–49	85	4 582	0.018 549	0.001 921	0.088 634	0.009 178	59 001	7.114 6	5 229	281 929	1 374 797	23.30	0.299 5
50–54	73	2 870	0.025 435	0.002 793	0.119 571	0.013 131	53 771	8.841 5	6 429	252 782	1 092 868	20.32	0.272 9
55–59	38	2 009	0.018 914	0.002 926	0.090 299	0.013 971	47 342	11.839 2	4 275	226 021	840 087	17.75	0.232 4
60–64	50	1 344	0.037 203	0.004 793	0.170 186	0.021 924	43 067	14.172 4	7 329	197 010	614 066	14.26	0.204 3
65–69	32	970	0.033 006	0.005 372	0.152 452	0.024 811	35 737	18.674 4	5 448	165 066	417 056	11.67	0.154 4
70–74	74	755	0.098 077	0.008 877	0.393 822	0.035 644	30 289	21.276 4	11 929	121 624	251 990	8.32	0.120 9
75–79	44	589	0.074 721	0.009 324	0.314 798	0.039 284	18 361	19.473 8	5 780	77 353	130 366	7.10	0.062 3
80–84	53	240	0.220 879	0.016 296	0.711 505	0.052 494	12 581	14.345 4	8 951	40 525	53 013	4.21	0.039 2
≥85	51	175	0.290 648	NA	1.000 000	NA	3 629	5.555 4	3 629	12 488	12 488	3.44	NA

Note: $_nD_x$, observed deaths between ages x and $x+n$; $_nd_x$, number dying between ages x and $x+n$ in the life-table population; l_x, number of survivors at age x in the life-table population; $_nL_x$, person-years lived by the life-table population between ages x and $x+n$; e_x, expectation of life at age x for the life-table population; $_nM_x$, observed mortality rate for ages x to $x+n$; NA, not applicable; $_nPY_x$, observed person–years between ages x and $x+n$; $_nq_x$, probability of dying between ages x and $x+n$ in the life-table population; $SE_{_nM_x}$, standard error in $_nM_x$; $SE_{_nq_x}$, standard error in $_nq_x$; SE_{l_x}, standard error in l_x; T_x, person–years lived by the life-table population at ages older than x.
[a] Data were reported from midyear to midyear.

Table 6A.6. Life table for the Farafenni DSS site, The Gambia, 1995–99.

Age (years)	nD_x	nPY_x	SE_{nM_x}	nM_x	nq_x	SE_{nq_x}	l_x	SE_{l_x}	nd_x	nL_x	T_x	e_x (years)	SE_{e_x} (years)
Male													
<1	113	1 585	0.006 475	0.071 293	0.068 043	0.006 179	100 000	0.000 0	6 804	95 441	5 083 047	50.83	0.956 5
1–4	185	6 205	0.002 067	0.029 815	0.110 474	0.007 660	93 196	3.818 4	10 296	345 315	4 987 606	53.52	0.895 9
5–9	40	7 284	0.000 856	0.005 491	0.027 085	0.004 224	82 900	8.118 2	2 245	408 886	4 642 290	56.00	0.792 0
10–14	25	5 645	0.000 876	0.004 429	0.021 901	0.004 332	80 655	8.910 7	1 766	398 857	4 233 404	52.49	0.768 2
15–19	10	4 348	0.000 723	0.002 300	0.011 434	0.003 595	78 888	9.745 4	902	392 186	3 834 547	48.61	0.747 2
20–24	11	2 838	0.001 157	0.003 876	0.019 195	0.005 732	77 986	10.328 2	1 497	386 188	3 442 361	44.14	0.735 4
25–29	3	1 848	0.000 934	0.001 624	0.008 086	0.004 650	76 489	11.933 5	619	380 900	3 056 173	39.96	0.710 5
30–34	9	1 517	0.001 948	0.005 932	0.029 228	0.009 599	75 871	13.006 1	2 218	373 810	2 675 273	35.26	0.697 7
35–39	15	1 585	0.002 387	0.009 465	0.046 232	0.011 658	73 653	17.561 0	3 405	359 753	2 301 464	31.25	0.653 0
40–44	19	1 420	0.002 969	0.013 381	0.064 740	0.014 364	70 248	23.347 5	4 548	339 870	1 941 711	27.64	0.599 5
45–49	14	1 204	0.003 018	0.011 626	0.056 490	0.014 665	65 700	30.603 3	3 711	319 222	1 601 840	24.38	0.534 6
50–54	26	1 071	0.004 478	0.024 266	0.114 389	0.021 112	61 989	36.526 5	7 091	292 217	1 282 618	20.69	0.485 7
55–59	19	954	0.004 347	0.019 918	0.094 864	0.020 705	54 898	45.774 4	5 208	261 470	990 401	18.04	0.404 5
60–64	35	913	0.005 886	0.038 335	0.174 913	0.026 856	49 690	50.422 1	8 691	226 722	728 931	14.67	0.354 3
65–69	36	635	0.008 197	0.056 729	0.248 413	0.035 893	40 999	52.133 7	10 185	179 532	502 210	12.25	0.294 6
70–74	28	424	0.010 569	0.066 069	0.283 516	0.045 353	30 814	51.104 7	8 736	132 230	322 678	10.47	0.224 4
75–79	27	296	0.013 911	0.091 155	0.371 185	0.056 646	22 078	45.764 5	8 195	89 902	190 448	8.63	0.161 8
80–84	20	147	0.021 339	0.135 962	0.507 357	0.079 628	13 883	33.736 2	7 044	51 805	100 547	7.24	0.106 4
≥85	15	107	NA	0.140 318	1.000 000	NA	6 839	20.408 1	6 839	48 741	48 741	7.13	NA
Female													
<1	104	1 497	0.006 581	0.069 458	0.066 458	0.006 296	100 000	0.000 0	6 646	95 680	5 505 050	55.05	1.057 3
1–4	139	4 729	0.002 353	0.029 395	0.109 117	0.008 736	93 354	3.964 6	10 186	346 535	5 409 370	57.94	0.990 8
5–9	40	5 852	0.001 062	0.006 835	0.033 601	0.005 223	83 168	9.797 1	2 795	408 852	5 062 835	60.88	0.844 7
10–14	14	5 730	0.000 649	0.002 443	0.012 141	0.003 225	80 373	11.036 5	976	399 426	4 653 983	57.90	0.802 9
15–19	15	4 525	0.000 849	0.003 315	0.016 439	0.004 210	79 397	11.442 1	1 305	393 724	4 254 557	53.59	0.789 6
20–24	13	2 949	0.001 209	0.004 408	0.021 800	0.005 980	78 092	12.186 1	1 702	386 204	3 860 813	49.44	0.770 3
25–29	10	2 378	0.001 316	0.004 206	0.020 810	0.006 512	76 390	13.841 3	1 590	377 974	3 474 629	45.49	0.737 0
30–34	14	2 205	0.001 670	0.006 349	0.031 249	0.008 220	74 800	15.745 7	2 337	368 156	3 096 655	41.40	0.703 9
35–39	12	2 239	0.001 526	0.005 358	0.026 438	0.007 530	72 463	18.557 6	1 916	357 523	2 728 498	37.65	0.659 2
40–44	11	2 327	0.001 408	0.004 726	0.023 356	0.006 959	70 547	20.567 0	1 648	348 615	2 370 975	33.61	0.629 0
45–49	12	1 616	0.002 104	0.007 425	0.036 449	0.010 328	68 899	22.027 8	2 511	338 217	2 022 360	29.35	0.609 3
50–54	13	1 425	0.002 473	0.009 122	0.044 593	0.012 089	66 388	25.515 3	2 960	324 538	1 684 142	25.37	0.576 1
55–59	20	1 269	0.003 389	0.015 766	0.075 840	0.016 303	63 427	29.731 4	4 810	305 111	1 359 604	21.44	0.543 1
60–64	35	1 372	0.004 045	0.025 510	0.119 904	0.019 014	58 617	36.084 9	7 028	275 514	1 054 493	17.99	0.500 1
65–69	27	750	0.006 330	0.036 000	0.165 138	0.029 038	51 589	40.371 9	8 519	236 645	778 979	15.10	0.460 0
70–74	24	444	0.009 633	0.054 066	0.238 142	0.042 430	43 069	50.580 5	10 257	189 706	542 333	12.59	0.400 6
75–79	23	298	0.013 248	0.077 259	0.323 761	0.055 515	32 813	62.752 8	10 624	137 505	352 628	10.75	0.319 2
80–84	14	135	0.021 269	0.103 781	0.412 007	0.084 436	22 189	61.879 2	9 142	88 091	215 123	9.69	0.229 3
≥85	11	107	NA	0.102 708	1.000 000	NA	13 047	56.496 4	13 047	127 032	127 032	9.74	NA

Note: D_x, observed deaths between ages x and $x+n$; d_x, number dying between ages x and $x+n$; d_x, number dying between ages x and $x+n$ in the life-table population; L_x, person-years lived by the life-table population between ages x and $x+n$; M_x, observed mortality rate for ages x to $x+n$; NA, not applicable; PY_x, observed person-years between ages x and $x+n$; q_x, probability of dying between ages x and $x+n$; SE_{l_x}, standard error in l_x; SE_{nM_x}, standard error in nM_x; SE_{nq_x}, standard error in nq_x; SE_{e_x}, standard error in e_x; T_x, person-years lived by the life-table population at ages older than x.

Table 6A.7. Life table for the Gwembe DSS site, Zambia, 1991–95.

Age (years)	nD_x	nPY_x	nM_x	SE_{nM_x}	nq_x	SE_{nq_x}	l_x	SE_{l_x}	nd_x	nL_x	T_x	e_x (years)	SE_{e_x} (years)
Male
<1	97	853	0.113 716	0.010 919	0.105 666	0.010 146	100 000	0.000 0	10 567	92 920	4 731 883	47.32	1.619 7
1–4	90	2 795	0.032 200	0.003 187	0.118 607	0.011 737	89 433	10.294 3	10 607	329 420	4 638 962	51.87	1.529 4
5–9	12	2 665	0.004 503	0.001 285	0.022 263	0.006 355	78 826	19.016 3	1 755	389 743	4 309 542	54.67	1.406 0
10–14	11	2 153	0.005 109	0.001 521	0.025 224	0.007 509	77 071	20.688 4	1 944	386 495	3 919 799	50.86	1.380 3
15–19	5	1 848	0.002 706	0.001 202	0.013 437	0.005 969	75 127	23.006 8	1 010	373 111	3 539 304	47.11	1.350 2
20–24	3	1 814	0.001 654	0.000 951	0.008 235	0.004 735	74 118	24.403 5	610	369 062	3 166 193	42.72	1.334 8
25–29	11	1 349	0.008 154	0.002 409	0.039 956	0.011 804	73 507	25.234 7	2 937	360 193	2 797 131	38.05	1.327 2
30–34	19	1 096	0.017 336	0.003 808	0.083 078	0.018 251	70 570	30.787 3	5 863	338 193	2 436 938	34.53	1.287 8
35–39	15	751	0.019 973	0.004 906	0.095 117	0.023 362	64 707	42.472 4	6 155	308 149	2 098 744	32.43	1.206 6
40–44	10	586	0.017 065	0.005 171	0.081 833	0.024 796	58 552	57.629 0	4 792	280 784	1 790 595	30.58	1.098 1
45–49	5	461	0.010 846	0.004 721	0.052 798	0.022 980	53 761	69.663 0	2 838	261 709	1 509 811	28.08	1.004 3
50–54	8	386	0.020 725	0.006 957	0.098 522	0.033 072	50 922	77.764 2	5 017	242 070	1 248 103	24.51	0.947 2
55–59	7	264	0.026 515	0.009 378	0.124 334	0.043 975	45 905	91.559 0	5 708	215 258	1 006 033	21.92	0.853 3
60–64	9	253	0.035 573	0.010 846	0.163 339	0.049 802	40 198	110.958 6	6 566	184 575	790 774	19.67	0.726 5
65–69	1	141	0.007 092	0.006 968	0.034 843	0.034 231	33 632	117.248 1	1 172	165 230	606 200	18.02	0.599 2
70–74	3	88	0.034 091	0.018 071	0.157 068	0.083 258	32 460	122.939 4	5 098	149 555	440 970	13.58	0.569 9
75–79	3	44	0.068 182	0.033 140	0.291 262	0.141 568	27 362	160.390 4	7 969	116 885	291 415	10.65	0.445 5
80–84	0	14	0.000 000	0.000 000	0.000 000	0.000 000	19 392	230.609 3	0	96 961	174 530	9.00	0.000 0
≥85	4	16	0.250 000	NA	1.000 000	NA	19 392	230.609 3	19 392	77 569	77 569	4.00	NA
Female
<1	82	794	0.103 275	0.010 839	0.096 705	0.010 150	100 000	0.000 0	9 670	93 638	5 365 525	53.66	1.777 9
1–4	75	2 741	0.027 362	0.002 994	0.102 089	0.011 170	90 330	10.301 8	9 222	337 021	5 271 887	58.36	1.673 9
5–9	9	2 782	0.003 235	0.001 070	0.016 046	0.005 305	81 108	18.486 7	1 301	402 286	4 934 866	60.84	1.546 5
10–14	5	2 353	0.002 125	0.000 945	0.010 569	0.004 701	79 806	19.749 9	843	396 924	4 532 580	56.79	1.525 3
15–19	5	2 347	0.002 130	0.000 948	0.010 595	0.004 713	78 963	20.742 4	837	392 723	4 135 656	52.37	1.511 3
20–24	11	1 981	0.005 553	0.001 651	0.027 384	0.008 143	78 126	21.690 3	2 139	385 283	3 742 933	47.91	1.499 7
25–29	11	1 585	0.006 940	0.002 057	0.034 109	0.010 107	75 987	24.565 6	2 592	373 455	3 357 650	44.19	1.470 0
30–34	12	1 210	0.009 917	0.002 793	0.048 387	0.013 626	73 395	28.816 9	3 551	358 097	2 984 194	40.66	1.432 1
35–39	8	899	0.008 899	0.003 077	0.043 526	0.015 050	69 844	36.097 3	3 040	341 619	2 626 097	37.60	1.374 8
40–44	6	680	0.008 824	0.003 524	0.043 165	0.017 238	66 804	44.072 5	2 884	326 810	2 284 478	34.20	1.319 6
45–49	4	496	0.008 065	0.003 952	0.039 526	0.019 368	63 920	53.610 3	2 526	313 285	1 957 668	30.63	1.263 2
50–54	11	495	0.022 222	0.006 338	0.105 263	0.030 021	61 394	64.783 2	6 462	290 812	1 644 383	26.78	1.210 1
55–59	3	392	0.007 653	0.004 335	0.037 547	0.021 267	54 931	85.833 0	2 062	269 500	1 353 571	24.64	1.101 9
60–64	4	330	0.012 121	0.005 880	0.058 824	0.028 534	52 869	93.155 8	3 110	256 569	1 084 072	20.50	1.068 6
65–69	6	242	0.024 793	0.009 513	0.116 732	0.044 788	49 759	105.275 4	5 808	234 273	827 503	16.63	1.028 9
70–74	7	121	0.057 851	0.018 902	0.252 708	0.082 569	43 950	131.797 7	11 107	191 985	593 230	13.50	0.965 1
75–79	1	37	0.027 027	0.025 259	0.126 582	0.118 300	32 844	205.292 2	4 157	153 825	401 245	12.22	0.803 9
80–84	2	19	0.105 263	0.056 849	0.416 667	0.225 026	28 686	307.573 0	11 953	113 550	247 420	8.63	0.677 8
≥85	1	8	0.125 000	NA	1.000 000	NA	16 734	521.351 4	16 734	133 870	133 870	8.00	NA

Note: nD_x, observed deaths between ages x and $x+n$; nd_x, number dying between ages x and $x+n$ in the life-table population; nL_x, person-years lived by the life-table population between ages x and $x+n$; l_x, number of survivors at age x in the life-table population; e_x, expectation of life at age x for the life-table population; nM_x, observed mortality rate for ages x to $x+n$; NA, not applicable; nPY_x, observed person-years between ages x and $x+n$; nq_x, probability of dying between ages x and $x+n$; SE_{nM_x}, standard error in nM_x; SE_{nq_x}, standard error in nq_x; SE_{l_x}, standard error in l_x; SE_{e_x}, standard error in e_x; T_x, person-years lived by the life-table population at ages older than x.

Table 6A.8. Life table for the Hai DSS site, Tanzania, 1994/95–1998/99.[a]

Age (years)	nD_x	nPY_x	nM_x	SE_{nM_x}	nq_x	SE_{nq_x}	l_x	SE_{l_x}	nd_x	nL_x	T_x	e_x (years)	SE_{e_x} (years)
Male													
<1	699	9 999	0.069 906	0.002 554	0.066 778	0.002 440	100 000	0.000 0	6 678	95 526	5 626 254	56.26	0.349 4
1–4	297	43 648	0.006 804	0.000 390	0.026 733	0.001 530	93 322	0.595 4	2 495	366 633	5 530 728	59.26	0.317 3
5–9	161	54 209	0.002 970	0.000 232	0.014 741	0.001 153	90 827	0.767 9	1 339	450 790	5 164 095	56.86	0.305 7
10–14	79	48 642	0.001 624	0.000 182	0.008 088	0.000 906	89 489	0.855 1	724	445 634	4 713 305	52.67	0.300 2
15–19	94	36 738	0.002 559	0.000 262	0.012 712	0.001 303	88 765	0.907 1	1 128	441 003	4 267 671	48.08	0.297 4
20–24	110	25 682	0.004 283	0.000 404	0.021 189	0.001 999	87 636	1.017 9	1 857	433 540	3 826 668	43.67	0.292 6
25–29	164	22 076	0.007 429	0.000 569	0.036 467	0.002 795	85 780	1.282 1	3 128	421 077	3 393 128	39.56	0.281 1
30–34	252	20 518	0.012 282	0.000 750	0.059 579	0.003 640	82 651	1.765 2	4 924	400 946	2 972 050	35.96	0.267 7
35–39	272	18 068	0.015 054	0.000 879	0.072 541	0.004 236	77 727	2.466 0	5 638	374 540	2 571 104	33.08	0.245 4
40–44	236	14 725	0.016 027	0.001 002	0.077 047	0.004 818	72 089	3.205 3	5 554	346 558	2 196 564	30.47	0.220 1
45–49	215	12 219	0.017 595	0.001 148	0.084 270	0.005 500	66 534	3.936 8	5 607	318 655	1 850 006	27.81	0.193 3
50–54	197	10 877	0.018 111	0.001 233	0.086 632	0.005 899	60 928	4.640 2	5 278	291 442	1 531 351	25.13	0.164 7
55–59	154	10 084	0.015 271	0.001 184	0.073 547	0.005 705	55 649	5.162 8	4 093	268 015	1 239 909	22.28	0.138 5
60–64	221	10 048	0.021 995	0.001 400	0.104 244	0.006 637	51 556	5.439 1	5 374	244 346	971 894	18.85	0.120 8
65–69	211	7 186	0.029 361	0.001 878	0.136 768	0.008 748	46 182	5.534 9	6 316	215 120	727 548	15.75	0.103 4
70–74	247	5 917	0.041 743	0.002 392	0.188 993	0.010 830	39 866	5.756 6	7 534	180 493	512 428	12.85	0.082 8
75–79	225	3 867	0.058 188	0.003 351	0.253 992	0.014 625	32 331	5.650 2	8 212	141 127	331 935	10.27	0.061 7
80–84	182	2 407	0.075 623	0.004 629	0.317 997	0.019 466	24 120	5.380 4	7 670	101 423	190 808	7.91	0.037 3
≥85	412	2 239	0.184 030	NA	1.000 000	NA	16 450	4.707 0	16 450	89 385	89 385	5.43	NA
Female													
<1	587	10 000	0.058 700	0.002 353	0.056 543	0.002 267	100 000	0.000 0	5 654	96 325	6 280 020	62.80	0.359 9
1–4	293	43 160	0.006 789	0.000 391	0.026 677	0.001 538	94 346	0.513 9	2 517	370 741	6 183 695	65.54	0.327 1
5–9	118	53 555	0.002 203	0.000 202	0.010 956	0.001 001	91 829	0.697 2	1 006	456 629	5 812 954	63.30	0.312 8
10–14	61	47 642	0.001 280	0.000 163	0.006 382	0.000 814	90 823	0.766 9	580	452 665	5 356 325	58.98	0.307 6
15–19	56	38 453	0.001 456	0.000 194	0.007 255	0.000 966	90 243	0.811 8	655	449 579	4 903 660	54.34	0.304 8
20–24	150	31 591	0.004 748	0.000 383	0.023 463	0.001 893	89 588	0.876 1	2 102	442 687	4 454 081	49.72	0.301 3
25–29	236	27 682	0.008 525	0.000 543	0.041 738	0.002 660	87 486	1.123 1	3 651	428 304	4 011 394	45.85	0.290 0
30–34	268	25 263	0.010 608	0.000 631	0.051 672	0.003 074	83 835	1.572 7	4 332	408 345	3 583 090	42.74	0.270 2
35–39	211	21 215	0.009 946	0.000 668	0.048 523	0.003 258	79 503	2.078 4	3 858	387 871	3 174 745	39.93	0.247 1
40–44	171	18 479	0.009 254	0.000 691	0.045 222	0.003 379	75 645	2.552 7	3 421	369 675	2 786 874	36.84	0.225 1
45–49	126	13 965	0.009 022	0.000 786	0.044 117	0.003 843	72 225	2.980 4	3 186	353 157	2 417 200	33.47	0.205 4
50–54	105	12 920	0.008 127	0.000 777	0.039 824	0.003 808	69 038	3.493 4	2 749	338 318	2 064 043	29.90	0.184 7
55–59	115	11 229	0.010 242	0.000 931	0.049 930	0.004 538	66 289	3.912 0	3 310	323 170	1 725 725	26.03	0.168 8
60–64	122	10 030	0.012 163	0.001 068	0.059 021	0.005 183	62 979	4.436 1	3 710	305 602	1 402 556	22.27	0.151 4
65–69	133	7 266	0.018 305	0.001 516	0.087 519	0.007 249	59 262	4.993 6	5 187	283 343	1 096 953	18.51	0.135 0
70–74	146	5 879	0.024 836	0.001 932	0.116 919	0.009 093	54 075	6.003 3	6 322	254 571	813 610	15.05	0.112 0
75–79	145	3 859	0.037 575	0.002 880	0.171 742	0.012 980	47 753	7.099 4	8 201	218 262	559 039	11.71	0.087 6
80–84	161	2 867	0.056 156	0.003 842	0.246 216	0.016 847	39 552	8.712 2	9 738	173 443	340 777	8.62	0.054 1
≥85	474	2 661	0.178 136	NA	1.000 000	NA	29 813	9.390 2	29 813	167 364	167 364	5.61	NA

Note: nD_x, observed deaths between ages x and $x+n$; nd_x, number dying between ages x and $x+n$ in the life-table population; nPY_x, person-years lived by the life-table population between ages x and $x+n$; M_x, observed mortality rate for ages x to $x+n$; NA, not applicable; PY_x, observed person-years between ages x and $x+n$; nq_x, probability of dying between ages x and $x+n$ by the life-table population at age x for the life-table population; l_x, number of survivors at age x in the life-table population; l_x, person-years lived by the life-table population between ages x to $x+n$; e_x, expectation of life at age x; T_x, person-years lived by the life-table population at ages older than x.
error in e_x; T_x, person-years lived by the life-table population at ages older than x.
SE_{nM_x}, standard error in nM_x; SE_{nq_x}, standard error in nq_x; SE_{l_x}, standard error in l_x; SE_{e_x}, standard

[a] Data were reported from midyear to midyear.

Table 6A.9. Life table for the Ifakara DSS site, Tanzania, 1997–99.

Age (years)	$_nD_x$	$_nPY_x$	$_nM_x$	$SE_{_nM_x}$	$_nq_x$	$SE_{_nq_x}$	l_x	SE_{l_x}	$_nd_x$	$_nL_x$	T_x	e_x (years)	SE_{e_x} (years)
Male													
<1	218	2 718	0.080 206	0.005 221	0.076 116	0.004 955	100 000	0.000 0	7 612	94 900	5 573 486	55.73	0.748 4
1–4	133	9 830	0.013 530	0.001 142	0.052 235	0.004 409	92 388	2.455 3	4 826	356 679	5 478 586	59.30	0.686 9
5–9	29	11 525	0.002 516	0.000 464	0.012 503	0.002 307	87 563	3.865 1	1 095	435 076	5 121 907	58.49	0.640 1
10–14	12	10 368	0.001 157	0.000 333	0.005 770	0.001 661	86 468	4.177 2	499	431 092	4 686 831	54.20	0.629 8
15–19	19	9 180	0.002 070	0.000 472	0.010 295	0.002 350	85 969	4.335 4	885	427 632	4 255 739	49.50	0.625 4
20–24	25	6 385	0.003 915	0.000 775	0.019 387	0.003 840	85 084	4.654 6	1 650	421 295	3 828 108	44.99	0.618 0
25–29	32	5 237	0.006 110	0.001 064	0.030 092	0.005 239	83 434	5.543 2	2 511	410 894	3 406 813	40.83	0.601 5
30–34	47	4 492	0.010 463	0.001 487	0.059 982	0.007 244	80 923	7.125 2	4 126	394 303	2 995 918	37.02	0.576 2
35–39	46	3 896	0.011 807	0.001 690	0.057 342	0.008 209	76 798	9.854 0	4 404	372 980	2 601 615	33.88	0.535 3
40–44	36	3 182	0.011 314	0.001 833	0.055 012	0.008 913	72 394	12.730 5	3 983	352 014	2 228 635	30.78	0.492 4
45–49	29	2 569	0.011 288	0.002 038	0.054 893	0.009 910	68 412	15.537	3 755	332 669	1 876 621	27.43	0.453 0
50–54	36	2 225	0.016 180	0.002 590	0.077 754	0.012 445	64 656	18.469 3	5 027	310 713	1 543 951	23.88	0.416 2
55–59	51	1 854	0.027 508	0.003 596	0.128 690	0.016 821	59 629	22.183 4	7 674	278 961	1 233 238	20.68	0.372 0
60–64	37	1 754	0.021 095	0.003 290	0.100 190	0.015 624	51 955	26.901 5	5 205	246 763	954 278	18.37	0.307 6
65–69	36	1 315	0.027 376	0.004 260	0.128 114	0.019 938	46 750	28.370 5	5 989	218 776	707 515	15.13	0.272 2
70–74	44	813	0.054 121	0.007 121	0.238 353	0.031 360	40 761	30.254 7	9 715	179 514	488 738	11.99	0.236 4
75–79	47	677	0.069 424	0.008 498	0.295 784	0.036 206	31 045	33.889 9	9 183	132 269	309 224	9.96	0.174 6
80–84	19	214	0.088 785	0.016 253	0.363 289	0.066 504	21 863	29.440 8	7 942	89 457	176 955	8.09	0.127 7
≥85	21	132	0.159 091	NA	1.000 000	NA	13 920	33.074 8	13 920	87 498	87 498	6.29	NA
Female													
<1	258	2 829	0.091 198	0.005 428	0.086 095	0.005 124	100 000	0.000 0	8 609	94 404	5 822 136	58.22	0.769 8
1–4	137	10 540	0.012 998	0.001 082	0.050 268	0.004 485	91 391	2.625 6	4 594	353 438	5 727 733	62.67	0.698 0
5–9	39	11 657	0.003 346	0.000 531	0.016 589	0.002 634	86 797	3.831 4	1 440	430 383	5 374 294	61.92	0.652 9
10–14	16	9 995	0.001 601	0.000 399	0.007 972	0.001 985	85 357	4.228 1	680	425 082	4 943 911	57.92	0.638 1
15–19	22	8 119	0.002 710	0.000 574	0.013 457	0.002 850	84 676	4.448 1	1 140	420 532	4 518 830	53.37	0.631 1
20–24	29	7 014	0.004 135	0.000 760	0.020 461	0.003 761	83 537	4.911 4	1 709	413 410	4 098 298	49.06	0.618 7
25–29	37	5 940	0.006 229	0.001 008	0.030 667	0.004 964	81 827	5.699 3	2 509	402 863	3 684 888	45.03	0.600 4
30–34	39	4 768	0.008 180	0.001 283	0.040 078	0.006 288	79 318	7.004 9	3 179	388 642	3 282 025	41.38	0.573 3
35–39	26	4 249	0.006 119	0.001 182	0.030 134	0.005 820	76 139	8.941 9	2 294	374 959	2 893 382	38.00	0.536 6
40–44	29	3 495	0.008 298	0.001 509	0.040 645	0.007 393	73 845	10.374 9	3 001	361 720	2 518 423	34.10	0.511 5
45–49	22	2 762	0.007 965	0.001 665	0.039 049	0.008 161	70 843	12.528 7	2 766	347 300	2 156 704	30.44	0.478 8
50–54	26	2 542	0.010 228	0.001 955	0.049 866	0.009 533	68 077	14.912 0	3 395	331 898	1 809 404	26.58	0.448 3
55–59	28	2 226	0.012 579	0.002 304	0.060 976	0.011 166	64 682	17.673 2	3 944	313 551	1 477 506	22.84	0.417 1
60–64	38	1 970	0.019 289	0.002 982	0.092 010	0.014 223	60 738	20.800 4	5 588	289 719	1 163 955	19.16	0.386 6
65–69	37	1 517	0.024 390	0.003 772	0.114 943	0.017 777	55 150	24.611 3	6 339	259 901	874 236	15.85	0.352 6
70–74	42	797	0.052 698	0.007 122	0.232 816	0.031 466	48 811	28.890 8	11 364	215 643	614 335	12.59	0.320 1
75–79	35	507	0.069 034	0.009 802	0.294 365	0.041 797	37 447	40.593 0	11 023	159 676	398 692	10.65	0.248 4
80–84	18	220	0.081 818	0.015 671	0.339 623	0.065 051	26 424	44.709 0	8 974	109 683	239 016	9.05	0.170 4
≥85	17	126	0.134 921	NA	1.000 000	NA	17 450	49.043 7	17 450	129 332	129 332	7.41	NA

Note: $_nD_x$, observed deaths between ages x and $x+n$; $_nd_x$, number dying between ages x and $x+n$; $_nd_x$, number of survivors at age x in the life-table population; $_nPY_x$, person–years lived by the life-table population between ages x and $x+n$; NA, not applicable; $_nPY_x$, observed person–years between ages x and $x+n$; $_nq_x$, probability of dying between ages x and $x+n$; SE_{l_x}, standard error in l_x; $SE_{_nM_x}$, standard error in $_nM_x$; $SE_{_nq_x}$, standard error in e_x; T_x, person–years lived by the life-table population at ages older than x.

Table 6A.10. Life table for the Manhiça DSS site, Mozambique, 1998–99.

Age (years)	$_nD_x$	$_nPY_x$	$_nM_x$	$SE_{_nM_x}$	$_nq_x$	$SE_{_nq_x}$	l_x	SE_{l_x}	$_nd_x$	$_nL_x$	T_x	e_x (years)	SE_{e_x} (years)
Male													
<1	119	1 308	0.090 979	0.007 974	0.085 752	0.007 516	100 000	0.000 0	8 575	94 255	4 746 753	47.47	1.090 4
1–4	81	4 486	0.018 056	0.001 936	0.068 905	0.007 388	91 425	5.649 4	6 300	348 893	4 652 499	50.89	1.019 2
5–9	11	4 561	0.002 412	0.000 723	0.011 986	0.003 592	85 125	9.459 5	1 020	423 075	4 303 606	50.56	0.953 7
10–14	12	4 429	0.002 709	0.000 777	0.013 456	0.003 858	84 105	10.169 3	1 132	417 695	3 880 531	46.14	0.942 1
15–19	12	3 828	0.003 135	0.000 898	0.015 552	0.004 454	82 973	10.950 4	1 290	411 640	3 462 836	41.73	0.931 1
20–24	6	1 991	0.003 014	0.001 221	0.014 955	0.006 060	81 683	11.978 5	1 222	405 360	3 051 196	37.35	0.919 3
25–29	13	1 357	0.009 580	0.002 594	0.046 779	0.012 667	80 461	14.072 7	3 764	392 896	2 645 837	32.88	0.902 5
30–34	25	1 128	0.022 163	0.004 193	0.104 998	0.019 867	76 697	23.174 9	8 053	363 353	2 252 941	29.37	0.842 0
35–39	22	1 257	0.017 502	0.003 572	0.083 841	0.017 109	68 644	41.780 7	5 755	328 833	1 889 588	27.53	0.706 9
40–44	30	1 204	0.024 917	0.004 274	0.117 279	0.020 117	62 889	48.861 9	7 376	296 006	1 560 755	24.82	0.629 9
45–49	17	893	0.019 037	0.004 402	0.090 861	0.021 012	55 513	54.079 4	5 044	264 957	1 264 749	22.78	0.542 6
50–54	20	730	0.027 397	0.005 720	0.128 205	0.026 767	50 469	58.304 4	6 470	236 171	999 792	19.81	0.476 1
55–59	32	777	0.041 184	0.006 566	0.186 698	0.029 764	43 999	62.562 4	8 215	199 459	763 621	17.36	0.393 4
60–64	26	664	0.039 157	0.006 961	0.178 326	0.031 701	35 784	58.532 6	6 381	162 969	564 163	15.77	0.312 3
65–69	27	627	0.043 062	0.007 438	0.194 384	0.033 577	29 403	52.387 2	5 716	132 727	401 194	13.64	0.252 9
70–74	14	262	0.053 435	0.012 485	0.235 690	0.055 070	23 688	43.747 2	5 583	104 481	268 467	11.33	0.212 9
75–79	15	199	0.075 377	0.016 083	0.317 125	0.067 664	18 105	42.572 2	5 741	76 170	163 986	9.06	0.150 3
80–84	9	94	0.095 745	0.025 003	0.386 266	0.100 868	12 363	34.859 1	4 776	49 877	87 816	7.10	0.093 5
≥85	17	85	0.200 000	NA	1.000 000	NA	7 588	28.682 0	7 588	37 939	37 939	5.00	NA
Female													
<1	77	1 247	0.061 748	0.006 825	0.059 365	0.006 561	100 000	0.000 0	5 937	96 141	5 811 687	58.12	1.094 0
1–4	70	4 450	0.015 730	0.001 822	0.060 413	0.006 999	94 063	4.305 2	5 683	361 257	5 715 546	60.76	1.017 1
5–9	15	4 547	0.003 299	0.000 845	0.016 359	0.004 189	88 381	8.135 4	1 446	438 289	5 354 289	60.58	0.928 1
10–14	6	4 201	0.001 428	0.000 581	0.007 116	0.002 895	86 935	9.242 2	619	433 128	4 916 000	56.55	0.901 9
15–19	11	4 068	0.002 704	0.000 810	0.013 429	0.004 022	86 316	9.744 4	1 159	428 683	4 482 872	51.94	0.891 5
20–24	23	3 460	0.006 647	0.001 363	0.032 694	0.006 705	85 157	10.689 6	2 784	418 825	4 054 188	47.61	0.874 3
25–29	17	2 321	0.007 324	0.001 744	0.035 964	0.008 564	82 373	13.262 0	2 962	404 459	3 635 363	44.13	0.832 8
30–34	15	2 050	0.007 317	0.001 855	0.035 928	0.009 108	79 411	17.301 9	2 853	389 920	3 239 904	40.69	0.775 1
35–39	9	1 908	0.004 717	0.001 554	0.023 310	0.007 679	76 558	21.312 7	1 785	378 326	2 840 984	37.11	0.720 2
40–44	11	1 765	0.006 232	0.001 850	0.030 683	0.009 108	74 773	23.786 7	2 294	368 129	2 462 657	32.94	0.689 4
45–49	17	1 449	0.011 732	0.002 763	0.056 990	0.013 422	72 479	26.987 8	4 131	352 067	2 094 528	28.90	0.655 4
50–54	16	1 298	0.012 327	0.002 988	0.059 791	0.014 494	68 348	33.463 5	4 087	331 524	1 742 461	25.49	0.596 2
55–59	34	1 279	0.026 583	0.004 265	0.124 633	0.019 998	64 262	39.395 0	8 009	301 285	1 410 937	21.96	0.544 7
60–64	25	1 041	0.024 015	0.004 523	0.113 276	0.021 333	56 252	46.702 3	6 372	265 332	1 109 652	19.73	0.463 8
65–69	20	885	0.022 599	0.004 775	0.106 952	0.022 600	49 880	51.122 5	5 335	236 065	844 320	16.93	0.401 0
70–74	28	554	0.050 542	0.008 412	0.224 359	0.037 342	44 546	53.480 1	9 994	197 742	608 256	13.65	0.357 2
75–79	32	532	0.060 150	0.009 138	0.261 438	0.039 718	34 551	59.844 0	9 033	150 174	410 513	11.88	0.265 3
80–84	17	207	0.082 126	0.016 173	0.340 681	0.067 092	25 518	51.475 7	8 694	105 858	260 339	10.20	0.200 0
≥85	22	202	0.108 911	NA	1.000 000	NA	16 825	51.688 7	16 825	154 481	154 481	9.18	NA

Note: $_nD_x$, observed deaths between ages x and $x+n$; $_nd_x$, number dying between ages x and $x+n$; l_x, number of survivors at age x for the life-table population; l_x, number of survivors at age x in the life-table population; $_nL_x$, person-years lived by the life-table population between ages x and $x+n$; $_nM_x$, observed mortality rate for ages x to $x+n$; NA, not applicable; $_nPY_x$, observed person-years between ages x and $x+n$; $_nq_x$, probability of dying between ages x and $x+n$; SE_{l_x}, standard error in l_x; $SE_{_nM_x}$, standard error in $_nM_x$; $SE_{_nM_x}$, standard error in $_nM_x$; $SE_{_nq_x}$, standard error in $_nq_x$; SE_{e_x}, standard error in e_x; T_x, person-years lived by the life-table population at ages older than x.

Table 6A.11. Life table for the comparison area of the Matlab DSS site, Bangladesh, 1998.

Age (years)	$_nD_x$	$_nPY_x$	$_nM_x$	$SE_{_nM_x}$	$_nq_x$	$SE_{_nq_x}$	l_x	SE_{l_x}	$_nd_x$	$_nL_x$	T_x	e_x (years)	SE_{e_x} (years)
Male												
<1	98	1 420	0.069 014	0.006 738	0.065 964	0.006 440	100 000	0.000 0	6 596	95 580	6 339 807	63.40	0.810 7
1-4	31	5 155	0.006 014	0.001 067	0.023 674	0.004 201	93 404	4.147 2	2 211	367 715	6 244 227	66.85	0.684 2
5-9	9	7 274	0.001 237	0.000 411	0.006 167	0.002 049	91 192	5.493 1	562	454 556	5 876 512	64.44	0.631 5
10-14	9	7 295	0.001 234	0.000 410	0.006 150	0.002 044	90 630	5.774 9	557	451 756	5 421 956	59.83	0.620 6
15-19	7	6 146	0.001 139	0.000 429	0.005 679	0.002 140	90 073	6.047 1	511	449 084	4 970 200	55.18	0.611 4
20-24	3	4 095	0.000 733	0.000 422	0.003 656	0.002 107	89 561	6.350 2	327	446 987	4 521 116	50.48	0.602 8
25-29	5	3 243	0.001 542	0.000 687	0.007 679	0.003 421	89 234	6.660 0	685	444 455	4 074 129	45.66	0.595 9
30-34	4	2 949	0.001 356	0.000 676	0.006 759	0.003 368	88 548	7.490 0	599	441 246	3 629 674	40.99	0.580 9
35-39	12	3 279	0.003 660	0.001 047	0.018 132	0.005 187	87 950	8.278 6	1 595	435 762	3 188 429	36.25	0.569 3
40-44	11	2 506	0.004 389	0.001 309	0.021 709	0.006 474	86 355	10.062 0	1 875	427 089	2 752 666	31.88	0.547 3
45-49	6	1 796	0.003 341	0.001 353	0.016 565	0.006 707	84 480	12.755 5	1 399	418 904	2 325 577	27.53	0.520 9
50-54	14	1 613	0.008 679	0.002 270	0.042 476	0.011 108	83 081	15.546 4	3 529	406 583	1 906 674	22.95	0.500 5
55-59	28	1 476	0.018 970	0.003 419	0.090 556	0.016 320	79 552	22.771 2	7 204	379 750	1 500 091	18.86	0.460 1
60-64	43	1 442	0.029 820	0.004 220	0.138 754	0.019 637	72 348	35.689 9	10 039	336 644	1 120 341	15.49	0.396 4
65-69	44	1 016	0.043 307	0.005 856	0.195 382	0.026 421	62 309	46.656 7	12 174	281 112	783 597	12.58	0.333 6
70-74	36	647	0.055 641	0.008 062	0.244 233	0.035 387	50 135	57.308 8	12 245	220 065	502 585	10.02	0.262 2
75-79	44	406	0.108 374	0.012 374	0.426 357	0.048 682	37 891	64.210 1	16 155	149 066	282 520	7.46	0.193 8
80-84	25	190	0.131 579	0.018 700	0.495 050	0.070 356	21 736	55.154 5	10 760	81 778	133 454	6.14	0.110 2
≥85	24	113	0.212 389	NA	1.000 000	NA	10 975	37.448 9	10 975	51 676	51 676	4.71	NA
Female												
<1	112	1 323	0.084 656	0.007 672	0.080 241	0.007 271	100 000	0.000 0	8 024	94 784	6 486 850	64.87	0.820 4
1-4	28	5 101	0.005 489	0.001 026	0.021 643	0.004 046	91 976	5.287 4	1 991	362 650	6 392 066	69.50	0.642 5
5-9	5	7 268	0.000 688	0.000 307	0.003 434	0.001 533	89 985	6.445 6	309	449 154	6 029 415	67.00	0.588 0
10-14	7	6 915	0.001 012	0.000 382	0.005 049	0.001 903	89 676	6.591 7	453	447 250	5 580 261	62.23	0.581 1
15-19	4	5 438	0.000 736	0.000 367	0.003 671	0.001 832	89 224	6.816 7	328	445 299	5 133 012	57.53	0.572 0
20-24	10	4 470	0.002 237	0.000 703	0.011 123	0.003 498	88 896	7.034 0	989	442 008	4 687 713	52.73	0.564 9
25-29	4	4 037	0.000 991	0.000 494	0.004 942	0.002 465	87 907	7.845 3	434	438 450	4 245 705	48.30	0.542 3
30-34	9	3 885	0.002 317	0.000 768	0.011 516	0.003 817	87 473	8.237 4	1 007	434 845	3 807 255	43.53	0.533 1
35-39	6	3 360	0.001 786	0.000 726	0.008 889	0.003 613	86 465	9.163 3	769	430 405	3 372 410	39.00	0.514 8
40-44	9	2 551	0.003 528	0.001 166	0.017 486	0.005 777	85 697	9.976 9	1 498	424 738	2 942 004	34.33	0.501 7
45-49	3	1 904	0.001 576	0.000 906	0.007 847	0.004 513	84 198	12.082 4	661	419 340	2 517 266	29.90	0.475 4
50-54	15	1 982	0.007 568	0.001 917	0.037 138	0.009 409	83 538	13.337 3	3 102	409 932	2 097 927	25.11	0.463 7
55-59	13	1 842	0.007 058	0.001 923	0.034 676	0.009 449	80 435	18.543 4	2 789	395 203	1 687 995	20.99	0.425 3
60-64	26	1 512	0.017 196	0.003 230	0.082 435	0.015 486	77 646	23.056 3	6 401	372 228	1 292 792	16.65	0.399 7
65-69	28	1 038	0.026 975	0.004 765	0.126 354	0.022 319	71 245	33.870 3	9 002	333 721	920 564	12.92	0.354 0
70-74	36	595	0.060 504	0.008 658	0.262 774	0.037 604	62 243	51.136 9	16 356	270 326	586 843	9.43	0.299 0
75-79	36	388	0.092 784	0.012 210	0.376 569	0.049 555	45 887	82.576 0	17 280	186 237	316 516	6.90	0.202 5
80-84	28	144	0.194 444	0.021 609	0.654 206	0.072 702	28 608	83.802 8	18 715	96 250	130 279	4.55	0.123 5
≥85	25	86	0.290 698	NA	1.000 000	NA	9 892	53.277 0	9 892	34 030	34 030	3.44	NA

Note: $_nD_x$, observed deaths between ages x and $x+n$; $_nd_x$, number dying between ages x and $x+n$; e_x, expectation of life at age x for the life-table population; l_x, number of survivors at age x in the life-table population; $_nL_x$, person-years lived by the life-table population between ages x and $x+n$; $_nM_x$, observed mortality rate for ages x to $x+n$; NA, not applicable; $_nPY_x$, observed person-years between ages x and $x+n$; $_nq_x$, probability of dying between ages x and $x+n$; SE_{l_x}, standard error in l_x; $SE_{_nM_x}$, standard error in $_nM_x$; $SE_{_nq_x}$, standard error in $_nq_x$; SE_{e_x}, standard error in e_x; T_x, person-years lived by the life-table population at ages older than x.

Table 6A.12. Life table for the treatment area of the Matlab DSS site, Bangladesh, 1998.

Age (years)	$_nD_x$	$_nPY_x$	$SE_{_nM_x}$	$_nM_x$	$SE_{_nq_x}$	$_nq_x$	l_x	SE_{l_x}	$_nd_x$	$_nL_x$	T_x	e_x (years)	SE_{e_x} (years)
Male													
<1	64	1 308	0.005 970	0.048 930	0.005 780	0.047 377	100 000	0.000 0	4 738	96 826	6 692 804	66.93	0.818 9
1–4	20	4 973	0.000 892	0.004 022	0.003 531	0.015 916	95 262	3.340 9	1 516	377 004	6 595 978	69.24	0.712 3
5–9	9	6 397	0.000 467	0.001 407	0.002 328	0.007 010	93 746	4.366 9	657	467 088	6 218 974	66.34	0.673 4
10–14	4	6 870	0.000 291	0.000 582	0.001 451	0.002 907	93 089	4.782 0	271	464 768	5 751 886	61.79	0.658 6
15–19	5	6 166	0.000 362	0.000 811	0.001 806	0.004 046	92 818	4.936 8	376	463 153	5 287 118	56.96	0.653 7
20–24	3	4 908	0.000 352	0.000 611	0.001 759	0.003 052	92 443	5.177 9	282	461 509	4 823 965	52.18	0.647 3
25–29	2	3 614	0.000 391	0.000 553	0.001 951	0.002 763	92 161	5.410 8	255	460 167	4 362 456	47.34	0.642 2
30–34	4	3 172	0.000 629	0.001 261	0.003 133	0.006 285	91 906	5.704 3	578	458 086	3 902 289	42.46	0.637 1
35–39	4	3 675	0.000 543	0.001 088	0.002 706	0.005 427	91 328	6.461 8	496	455 403	3 444 203	37.71	0.626 4
40–44	12	2 779	0.001 233	0.004 318	0.006 100	0.021 360	90 833	7.002 8	1 940	449 313	2 988 800	32.90	0.620 3
45–49	11	2 084	0.001 571	0.005 278	0.007 751	0.026 048	88 893	9.776 7	2 315	438 674	2 539 487	28.57	0.595 9
50–54	20	1 789	0.002 431	0.011 179	0.011 824	0.054 377	86 577	14.021 0	4 708	421 116	2 100 813	24.27	0.566 7
55–59	34	1 678	0.003 303	0.020 262	0.015 720	0.096 427	81 869	23.016 9	7 894	389 610	1 679 697	20.52	0.515 4
60–64	39	1 557	0.003 767	0.025 048	0.017 726	0.117 860	73 975	35.354 3	8 719	348 078	1 290 086	17.44	0.447 0
65–69	41	1 166	0.005 028	0.035 163	0.023 110	0.161 608	65 256	44.705 6	10 546	299 916	942 009	14.44	0.387 9
70–74	39	761	0.007 214	0.051 248	0.031 975	0.227 140	54 710	54.165 9	12 427	242 484	642 093	11.74	0.323 1
75–79	33	454	0.010 529	0.072 687	0.044 550	0.307 549	42 283	62.956 8	13 004	178 906	399 609	9.45	0.246 3
80–84	26	247	0.015 767	0.105 263	0.062 411	0.416 667	29 279	65.671 8	12 200	115 897	220 703	7.54	0.157 8
≥85	22	135	NA	0.162 963	NA	1.000 000	17 079	55.738 3	17 079	104 806	104 806	6.14	NA
Female													
<1	79	1 268	0.006 797	0.062 303	0.006 532	0.059 878	100 000	0.000 0	5 988	96 108	6 701 577	67.02	0.827 6
1–4	26	4 912	0.001 027	0.005 293	0.004 052	0.020 881	94 012	4.266 7	1 963	370 868	6 605 470	70.26	0.685 8
5–9	3	6 211	0.000 279	0.000 483	0.001 391	0.002 412	92 049	5.541 6	222	459 691	6 234 601	67.73	0.631 3
10–14	6	6 784	0.000 360	0.000 884	0.001 797	0.004 412	91 827	5.678 8	405	458 123	5 774 911	62.89	0.625 7
15–19	4	5 415	0.000 369	0.000 739	0.001 840	0.003 687	91 422	5.901 2	337	456 267	5 316 788	58.16	0.617 6
20–24	7	5 123	0.000 515	0.001 366	0.002 565	0.006 809	91 085	6.140 7	620	453 874	4 860 521	53.36	0.610 4
25–29	4	4 497	0.000 444	0.000 889	0.002 214	0.004 438	90 465	6.603 1	401	451 320	4 406 647	48.71	0.598 6
30–34	12	4 462	0.000 771	0.002 689	0.003 830	0.013 357	90 063	6.945 7	1 203	447 309	3 955 327	43.92	0.591 3
35–39	8	3 850	0.000 731	0.002 078	0.003 635	0.010 336	88 860	7.951 3	918	442 005	3 508 018	39.48	0.573 3
40–44	7	2 827	0.000 930	0.002 476	0.004 622	0.012 304	87 942	8.831 3	1 082	437 004	3 066 013	34.86	0.560 5
45–49	6	2 178	0.001 117	0.002 755	0.005 546	0.013 680	86 860	10.267 4	1 188	431 328	2 629 009	30.27	0.544 4
50–54	12	2 213	0.001 544	0.005 423	0.007 618	0.026 750	85 672	12.309 4	2 292	422 628	2 197 681	25.65	0.527 3
55–59	23	2 041	0.002 284	0.011 269	0.011 109	0.054 801	83 380	15.919 2	4 569	405 476	1 775 052	21.29	0.503 9
60–64	25	1 608	0.002 991	0.015 547	0.014 395	0.074 828	78 811	22.802 4	5 897	379 310	1 369 576	17.38	0.469 1
65–69	42	1 079	0.005 448	0.038 925	0.024 823	0.177 365	72 913	32.387 5	12 932	332 236	990 267	13.58	0.432 1
70–74	37	735	0.007 292	0.050 340	0.032 386	0.223 565	59 981	54.674 7	13 410	266 381	658 031	10.97	0.356 8
75–79	38	374	0.012 713	0.101 604	0.050 688	0.405 117	46 571	70.695 3	18 867	185 690	391 650	8.41	0.287 0
80–84	16	170	0.018 513	0.094 118	0.074 933	0.380 952	27 705	80.742 7	10 554	112 137	205 960	7.43	0.165 5
≥85	17	93	NA	0.182 796	NA	1.000 000	17 150	74.039 2	17 150	93 823	93 823	5.47	NA

Note: $_nD_x$, observed deaths between ages x and $x+n$; $_nd_x$, number dying between ages x and $x+n$; e_x, expectation of life at age x for the life-table population; l_x, number of survivors at age x in the life-table population; $_nL_x$, person–years lived by the life-table population for ages x to $x+n$; $_nM_x$, observed mortality rate for ages x in the life-table population; NA, not applicable; $_nPY_x$, observed person–years between ages x and $x+n$; $_nq_x$, probability of dying between ages x and $x+n$; SE_{l_x}, standard error in l_x; $SE_{_nM_x}$, standard error in $_nM_x$; $SE_{_nq_x}$, standard error in $_nq_x$; SE_{e_x}, standard error in e_x; T_x, person–years lived by the life-table population at ages older than x.

Table 6A.13. Life table for the Mlomp DSS site, Senegal, 1995–99.

Age (years)	$_nD_x$	$_nPY_x$	$SE_{_nM_x}$	$_nM_x$	$_nq_x$	$SE_{_nq_x}$	l_x	SE_{l_x}	$_nd_x$	$_nL_x$	T_x	e_x (years)	SE_{e_x} (years)
Male													
<1	18	361	0.011 464	0.049 856	0.048 245	0.011 094	100 000	0.000 0	4 824	96 768	6 045 562	60.46	1.479 1
1–4	17	1 551	0.002 602	0.010 963	0.042 606	0.010 111	95 176	12.307 0	4 055	369 884	5 948 794	62.50	1.302 5
5–9	7	2 097	0.001 251	0.003 339	0.016 556	0.006 206	91 120	20.541 2	1 509	451 831	5 578 910	61.23	1.148 3
10–14	4	2 298	0.000 867	0.001 741	0.008 666	0.004 314	89 612	23.064 2	777	446 118	5 127 080	57.21	1.097 5
15–19	5	2 417	0.000 920	0.002 069	0.010 291	0.004 579	88 835	24.160 9	914	441 891	4 680 962	52.69	1.076 5
20–24	4	2 097	0.000 949	0.001 907	0.009 490	0.004 722	87 921	25.320 6	834	437 519	4 239 071	48.21	1.056 6
25–29	5	1 884	0.001 179	0.002 653	0.013 180	0.005 855	87 087	26.566 2	1 148	432 564	3 801 552	43.65	1.039 1
30–34	3	1 187	0.001 449	0.002 526	0.012 553	0.007 202	85 939	28.470 6	1 079	426 997	3 368 989	39.20	1.017 1
35–39	8	824	0.003 350	0.009 709	0.047 393	0.016 354	84 860	31.590 9	4 022	414 246	2 941 991	34.67	0.990 7
40–44	2	558	0.002 511	0.003 583	0.017 756	0.012 444	80 838	47.927 9	1 435	400 603	2 527 746	31.27	0.872 9
45–49	7	491	0.005 198	0.014 253	0.068 811	0.025 097	79 403	56.359 9	5 464	383 355	2 127 143	26.79	0.821 6
50–54	5	484	0.004 593	0.010 334	0.050 367	0.021 950	73 939	88.582 8	3 724	360 385	1 743 788	23.58	0.636 3
55–59	9	719	0.004 043	0.012 514	0.060 674	0.019 602	70 215	106.225 0	4 260	340 424	1 383 403	19.70	0.524 4
60–64	10	664	0.004 588	0.015 067	0.072 600	0.022 109	65 955	112.668 4	4 788	317 803	1 042 979	15.81	0.459 9
65–69	20	509	0.007 962	0.039 293	0.178 892	0.036 247	61 166	118.166 2	10 942	278 477	725 176	11.86	0.409 5
70–74	25	408	0.010 500	0.061 267	0.265 645	0.045 529	50 224	128.826 0	13 342	217 767	446 699	8.89	0.322 3
75–79	30	221	0.017 425	0.135 983	0.507 415	0.065 019	36 882	121.760 3	18 715	137 625	228 933	6.21	0.253 4
80–84	7	38	0.042 154	0.182 547	0.626 720	0.144 724	18 168	87.051 5	11 386	62 373	91 307	5.03	0.177 9
≥85	9	38	NA	0.234 385	1.000 000	NA	6 782	81.262 4	6 782	28 934	28 934	4.27	NA
Female													
<1	19	372	0.011 420	0.051 058	0.049 418	0.011 054	100 000	0.000 0	4 942	96 788	6 478 388	64.78	1.523 5
1–4	23	1 717	0.002 719	0.013 393	0.051 742	0.010 506	95 058	12.218 1	4 919	367 253	6 381 601	67.13	1.326 6
5–9	7	2 076	0.001 264	0.003 373	0.016 722	0.006 267	90 140	20.960 4	1 507	446 930	6 014 348	66.72	1.131 3
10–14	1	2 209	0.000 452	0.000 453	0.002 261	0.002 258	88 632	23.456 8	200	442 661	5 567 418	62.81	1.069 5
15–19	0	2 488	0.000 000	0.000 000	0.000 000	0.000 000	88 432	23.751 5	0	442 160	5 124 757	57.95	1.062 6
20–24	4	1 943	0.001 024	0.002 059	0.010 241	0.005 094	88 432	23.751 5	906	439 896	4 682 597	52.95	1.062 6
25–29	3	1 438	0.001 199	0.002 087	0.010 380	0.005 962	87 526	25.297 1	908	435 360	4 242 701	48.47	1.037 5
30–34	1	982	0.001 015	0.001 018	0.005 077	0.005 064	86 618	27.497 3	440	431 990	3 807 341	43.96	1.008 8
35–39	2	630	0.002 227	0.003 175	0.015 749	0.011 048	86 178	29.143 0	1 357	427 497	3 375 352	39.17	0.992 1
40–44	2	491	0.002 853	0.004 075	0.020 172	0.014 119	84 821	37.297 6	1 711	419 826	2 947 855	34.75	0.926 5
45–49	6	534	0.004 458	0.011 230	0.054 615	0.021 679	83 110	50.150 3	4 539	404 201	2 528 028	30.42	0.838 5
50–54	1	524	0.001 899	0.001 908	0.009 496	0.009 451	78 571	77.285 0	746	390 988	2 123 827	27.03	0.648 0
55–59	7	665	0.003 877	0.010 530	0.051 299	0.018 885	77 825	81.338 5	3 992	379 142	1 732 839	22.27	0.621 4
60–64	13	620	0.005 516	0.020 958	0.099 575	0.026 206	73 832	94.809 1	7 352	350 782	1 353 696	18.33	0.540 7
65–69	5	569	0.003 846	0.008 791	0.043 010	0.018 817	66 480	114.304 3	2 859	325 254	1 002 915	15.09	0.420 2
70–74	20	433	0.009 204	0.046 227	0.207 192	0.041 252	63 621	120.331 7	13 182	285 151	677 661	10.65	0.386 6
75–79	22	293	0.013 235	0.075 057	0.315 993	0.055 718	50 439	144.512 8	15 938	212 350	392 510	7.78	0.276 9
80–84	23	143	0.021 897	0.160 789	0.573 439	0.078 093	34 501	146.595 0	19 784	123 044	180 160	5.22	0.171 9
≥85	20	78	NA	0.257 663	1.000 000	NA	14 717	99.265 2	14 717	57 116	57 116	3.88	NA

Note: $_nD_x$, observed deaths between ages x and $x+n$; $_nd_x$, number dying between ages x and $x+n$; e_x, expectation of life at age x for the life-table population; l_x, number of survivors at age x in the life-table population; $_nL_x$, person-years lived by the life-table population between ages x to $x+n$; $_nM_x$, observed mortality rate for ages x to $x+n$; NA, not applicable; $_nPY_x$, observed person–years between ages x and $x+n$; $_nq_x$, probability of dying between ages x and $x+n$; SE_{l_x}, standard error in l_x; $SE_{_nM_x}$, standard error in $_nM_x$; $SE_{_nq_x}$, standard error in $_nq_x$; SE_{e_x}, standard error in e_x; T_x, person–years lived by the life-table population at ages older than x.

Table 6A.14. Life table for the Morogoro DSS site, Tanzania, 1994/95–1998/99.[a]

Age (years)	nDx	nPYx	nMx	SE_nMx	nqx	SE_nqx	lx	SE_lx	ndx	nLx	Tx	ex (years)	SE_ex (years)
					Male								
<1	725	6 403	0.113 226	0.003 978	0.105 242	0.003 697	100 000	0.000 0	10 524	92 949	4 444 446	44.44	0.361 9
1–4	648	27 974	0.023 164	0.000 869	0.087 265	0.003 275	89 476	1.366 9	7 808	337 072	4 351 497	48.63	0.312 7
5–9	227	37 856	0.005 996	0.000 392	0.029 539	0.001 931	81 668	1.997 5	2 412	402 307	4 014 425	49.16	0.273 3
10–14	91	34 925	0.002 606	0.000 271	0.012 944	0.001 348	79 255	2.130 0	1 026	393 712	3 612 118	45.58	0.262 6
15–19	104	29 781	0.003 492	0.000 339	0.017 309	0.001 683	78 229	2.189 4	1 354	387 762	3 218 406	41.14	0.258 4
20–24	127	20 814	0.006 102	0.000 533	0.030 050	0.002 626	76 875	2.287 5	2 310	378 601	2 830 644	36.82	0.253 2
25–29	239	17 289	0.013 824	0.000 864	0.066 812	0.004 175	74 565	2.559 7	4 982	360 371	2 452 043	32.88	0.242 9
30–34	246	16 442	0.014 962	0.000 919	0.072 111	0.004 429	69 583	3.198 1	5 018	335 372	2 091 671	30.06	0.220 7
35–39	249	13 795	0.018 051	0.001 093	0.086 356	0.005 231	64 566	3.703 2	5 576	308 889	1 756 299	27.20	0.200 8
40–44	262	10 864	0.024 117	0.001 403	0.113 729	0.006 615	58 990	4.231 9	6 709	278 178	1 447 410	24.54	0.178 9
45–49	273	9 735	0.028 044	0.001 582	0.131 031	0.007 393	52 281	4.846 6	6 850	244 279	1 169 232	22.36	0.150 3
50–54	232	8 666	0.026 770	0.001 644	0.125 455	0.007 703	45 431	5.153 5	5 700	212 904	924 953	20.36	0.121 6
55–59	206	8 002	0.025 744	0.001 682	0.120 935	0.007 900	39 731	5.166 0	4 805	186 643	712 048	17.92	0.098 4
60–64	244	7 066	0.034 530	0.002 027	0.158 929	0.009 331	34 926	4.977 3	5 551	160 754	525 405	15.04	0.081 5
65–69	268	5 304	0.050 527	0.002 718	0.224 301	0.012 067	29 375	4.583 0	6 589	130 405	364 651	12.41	0.065 4
70–74	272	4 329	0.062 829	0.003 252	0.271 501	0.014 051	22 787	4.014 2	6 187	98 466	234 246	10.28	0.047 2
75–79	210	2 616	0.080 284	0.004 520	0.334 319	0.018 823	16 600	3.155 5	5 550	69 126	135 780	8.18	0.032 6
80–84	131	1 238	0.105 797	0.007 050	0.418 338	0.027 876	11 050	2.374 6	4 623	43 694	66 654	6.03	0.018 7
≥85	177	632	0.279 948	NA	1.000 000	NA	6 428	1.752 2	6 428	22 960	22 960	3.57	NA
					Female								
<1	795	6 585	0.120 723	0.004 035	0.111 939	0.003 741	100 000	0.000 0	11 194	92 724	4 610 918	46.11	0.375 0
1–4	604	29 075	0.020 774	0.000 811	0.078 775	0.003 076	88 806	1.399 7	6 996	336 763	4 518 194	50.88	0.321 6
5–9	210	37 882	0.005 543	0.000 377	0.027 339	0.001 861	81 810	1.934 3	2 237	403 460	4 181 432	51.11	0.286 1
10–14	84	34 064	0.002 466	0.000 267	0.012 254	0.001 329	79 574	2.061 7	975	395 431	3 777 971	47.48	0.275 8
15–19	117	28 958	0.004 040	0.000 370	0.020 000	0.001 830	78 599	2.123 3	1 572	389 063	3 382 540	43.04	0.271 6
20–24	220	24 299	0.009 054	0.000 597	0.044 267	0.002 918	77 027	2.246 2	3 410	376 609	2 993 477	38.86	0.265 0
25–29	334	19 878	0.016 802	0.000 882	0.080 625	0.004 230	73 617	2.556 8	5 935	353 246	2 616 867	35.55	0.250 8
30–34	313	16 906	0.018 514	0.000 999	0.088 474	0.004 775	67 682	3.130 8	5 988	323 438	2 263 621	33.45	0.224 5
35–39	270	14 413	0.018 733	0.001 088	0.089 473	0.005 196	61 694	3.645 6	5 520	294 668	1 940 183	31.45	0.195 8
40–44	183	12 606	0.014 517	0.001 035	0.070 042	0.004 993	56 174	4.049 9	3 934	271 032	1 645 516	29.29	0.167 2
45–49	178	11 389	0.015 629	0.001 127	0.075 207	0.005 421	52 239	4.289 1	3 929	251 374	1 374 484	26.31	0.146 4
50–54	149	10 869	0.013 709	0.001 085	0.066 272	0.005 246	48 310	4.470 2	3 202	233 548	1 123 110	23.25	0.127 0
55–59	145	8 392	0.017 279	0.001 374	0.082 817	0.006 587	45 109	4.539 7	3 736	216 204	889 563	19.72	0.113 8
60–64	178	7 345	0.024 233	0.001 709	0.114 242	0.008 059	41 373	4.701 7	4 727	195 048	673 359	16.28	0.099 2
65–69	194	5 125	0.037 853	0.002 472	0.172 903	0.011 290	36 646	4.800 4	6 336	167 391	478 310	13.05	0.084 6
70–74	179	3 221	0.055 579	0.003 612	0.243 993	0.015 857	30 310	4.995 6	7 395	133 062	310 919	10.26	0.066 1
75–79	135	2 049	0.065 888	0.004 802	0.282 849	0.020 615	22 915	5.165 2	6 481	98 370	177 857	7.76	0.043 9
80–84	160	984	0.162 539	0.008 349	0.577 876	0.029 682	16 433	4.888 1	9 496	58 425	79 487	4.84	0.027 0
≥85	169	513	0.329 358	NA	1.000 000	NA	6 937	3.250 2	6 937	21 062	21 062	3.04	NA

Note: $_nD_x$, observed deaths between ages x and $x+n$; $_nD_x$, number dying between ages x and $x+n$; e_x, expectation of life at age x for the life-table population; l_x, number of survivors at age x in the life-table population; $_nL_x$, person-years lived by the life-table population between ages x to $x+n$; NA, not applicable; $_nPY_x$, observed person-years between ages x and $x+n$; $_nq_x$, probability of dying between ages x and $x+n$; SE, standard error in $_nM_x$; SE, standard error in $_nq_x$; SE, standard error in $_nq_x$; T_x, person-years lived by the life-table population at ages older than x.

[a] Data were reported from midyear to midyear.

Table 6A.15. Life table for the Navrongo DSS site, Ghana, 1995–99.

Age (years)	nD_x	nPY_x	nM_x	SE_nM_x	nq_x	SE_nq_x	l_x	SE_{l_x}	nd_x	nL_x	T_x	e_x (years)	SE_{e_x} (years)
Male													
<1	1 160	10 107	0.114 772	0.003 185	0.106 577	0.002 958	100 000	0.000 0	10 658	92 859	4 721 624	47.22	0.324 8
1–4	858	38 795	0.022 116	0.000 723	0.083 536	0.002 730	89 342	0.874 8	7 463	337 458	4 628 765	51.81	0.285 3
5–9	243	51 644	0.004 705	0.000 298	0.023 253	0.001 474	81 879	1.329 7	1 904	404 635	4 291 307	52.41	0.251 7
10–14	164	50 035	0.003 278	0.000 254	0.016 255	0.001 259	79 975	1.414 3	1 300	396 625	3 886 671	48.60	0.244 0
15–19	117	37 926	0.003 085	0.000 283	0.015 307	0.001 404	78 675	1.470 1	1 204	390 365	3 490 046	44.36	0.239 4
20–24	87	22 522	0.003 863	0.000 410	0.019 130	0.002 031	77 471	1.547 5	1 482	383 649	3 099 681	40.01	0.234 8
25–29	99	15 415	0.006 422	0.000 635	0.031 604	0.003 126	75 989	1.736 5	2 402	373 940	2 716 032	35.74	0.226 9
30–34	145	14 669	0.009 885	0.000 801	0.048 232	0.003 908	73 587	2.192 6	3 549	359 063	2 342 092	31.83	0.221 8
35–39	172	15 006	0.011 462	0.000 849	0.055 714	0.004 128	70 038	2.813 1	3 902	340 435	1 983 028	28.31	0.192 3
40–44	227	12 138	0.018 702	0.001 185	0.089 331	0.005 658	66 136	3.344 3	5 908	315 910	1 642 594	24.84	0.175 3
45–49	255	12 502	0.020 397	0.001 214	0.097 036	0.005 774	60 228	4.173 8	5 844	286 529	1 326 684	22.03	0.149 4
50–54	286	11 099	0.025 768	0.001 429	0.121 043	0.006 710	54 384	4.612 5	6 583	255 461	1 040 155	19.13	0.129 1
55–59	385	11 409	0.033 745	0.001 580	0.155 600	0.007 287	47 801	4.895 2	7 438	220 410	784 694	16.42	0.109 1
60–64	348	7 522	0.046 264	0.002 208	0.207 340	0.009 895	40 363	4.703 7	8 369	180 893	564 284	13.98	0.092 7
65–69	404	6 812	0.059 307	0.002 541	0.258 246	0.011 066	31 994	4.550 7	8 262	139 315	383 391	11.98	0.072 5
70–74	253	3 869	0.065 392	0.003 486	0.281 017	0.014 981	23 732	3.757 2	6 669	101 986	244 076	10.28	0.056 6
75–79	293	2 728	0.107 405	0.004 765	0.423 349	0.018 781	17 063	3.206 2	7 224	67 255	142 089	8.33	0.041 5
80–84	115	1 076	0.106 877	0.007 579	0.421 709	0.029 905	9 839	2.093 1	4 149	38 823	74 834	7.61	0.026 0
≥85	149	943	0.158 006	NA	1.000 000	NA	5 690	1.565 7	5 690	36 011	36 011	6.33	NA
Female													
<1	1 130	10 241	0.110 341	0.003 109	0.102 957	0.002 901	100 000	0.000 0	10 296	93 308	5 138 770	51.39	0.312 5
1–4	738	38 364	0.019 237	0.000 682	0.073 230	0.002 595	89 704	0.841 5	6 569	341 482	5 045 462	56.25	0.265 4
5–9	197	49 662	0.003 967	0.000 280	0.019 639	0.001 385	83 135	1.264 6	1 633	411 595	4 703 981	56.58	0.226 8
10–14	122	45 385	0.002 688	0.000 242	0.013 351	0.001 201	81 503	1.348 1	1 088	404 793	4 292 386	52.67	0.217 7
15–19	76	32 598	0.002 331	0.000 266	0.011 590	0.001 322	80 414	1.408 1	932	399 742	3 887 593	48.34	0.211 9
20–24	97	23 960	0.004 048	0.000 407	0.020 039	0.002 014	79 483	1.488 6	1 593	393 431	3 487 851	43.88	0.206 1
25–29	132	22 666	0.005 824	0.000 500	0.028 701	0.002 462	77 890	1.685 9	2 235	383 860	3 094 420	39.73	0.194 7
30–34	167	21 913	0.007 621	0.000 579	0.037 393	0.002 839	75 654	1.958 2	2 829	371 199	2 710 560	35.83	0.180 3
35–39	137	23 658	0.005 791	0.000 488	0.028 541	0.002 403	72 825	2.275 8	2 079	358 930	2 339 361	32.12	0.164 2
40–44	150	18 833	0.007 965	0.000 637	0.039 046	0.003 125	70 747	2.454 1	2 762	346 828	1 980 431	27.99	0.155 3
45–49	195	18 382	0.010 608	0.000 740	0.051 671	0.003 603	67 984	2.755 0	3 513	331 140	1 633 603	24.03	0.143 8
50–54	313	18 091	0.017 301	0.000 937	0.082 920	0.004 488	64 472	3.077 8	5 346	308 993	1 302 462	20.20	0.132 6
55–59	443	16 672	0.026 571	0.001 181	0.124 582	0.005 538	59 126	3.425 9	7 366	277 213	993 469	16.80	0.120 3
60–64	339	9 513	0.035 635	0.001 770	0.163 602	0.008 126	51 760	3.697 7	8 468	237 628	716 256	13.84	0.107 8
65–69	479	8 024	0.059 696	0.002 347	0.259 719	0.010 210	43 292	4.355 9	11 244	188 349	478 628	11.06	0.091 4
70–74	320	3 522	0.090 857	0.004 031	0.370 199	0.016 423	32 048	4.340 9	11 864	130 580	290 279	9.06	0.075 8
75–79	279	2 558	0.109 070	0.004 936	0.428 506	0.019 394	20 184	4.492 1	8 649	79 297	159 699	7.91	0.052 4
80–84	101	743	0.135 935	0.009 494	0.507 283	0.035 431	11 535	2.999 4	5 851	43 046	80 402	6.97	0.037 1
≥85	103	677	0.152 142	NA	1.000 000	NA	5 683	2.398 5	5 683	37 356	37 356	6.57	NA

Note: nD_x, observed deaths between ages x and $x+n$; d_x, number dying between ages x and $x+n$; e_x, expectation of life at age x for the life-table population; l_x, number of survivors at age x in the life-table population; nL_x, person–years lived by the life-table population between ages x and $x+n$; M_x, observed mortality rate for ages x to $x+n$; NA, not applicable; nPY_x, observed person–years between ages x and $x+n$; nq_x, probability of dying between ages x and $x+n$; SE_nM_x, standard error in nM_x; SE_{l_x}, standard error in l_x; SE_{nq_x}, standard error in nq_x; SE_{e_x}, standard error in e_x; T_x, person–years lived by the life-table population at ages older than x.

Table 6A.16. Life table for the Niakhar DSS site, Senegal, 1995–98.

Age (years)	$_nD_x$	$_nPY_x$	$_nM_x$	$SE_{_nM_x}$	$_nq_x$	$SE_{_nq_x}$	l_x	SE_{l_x}	$_nd_x$	$_nL_x$	T_x	e_x (years)	SE_{e_x} (years)
Male													
<1	223	2 334	0.095 544	0.006 104	0.089 796	0.005 737	100 000	0.000 0	8 980	93 984	4 879 773	48.80	0.803 1
1–4	334	8 207	0.040 697	0.002 057	0.146 844	0.007 422	91 020	3.291 1	13 366	328 424	4 785 790	52.58	0.742 7
5–9	72	9 281	0.007 758	0.000 897	0.038 051	0.004 398	77 655	6.958 8	2 955	380 886	4 457 366	57.40	0.622 0
10–14	32	8 313	0.003 849	0.000 674	0.019 064	0.003 338	74 700	7.605 8	1 424	369 939	4 076 480	54.57	0.590 7
15–19	21	6 787	0.003 094	0.000 670	0.015 352	0.003 324	73 276	7.940 2	1 125	363 566	3 706 542	50.58	0.575 7
20–24	15	4 344	0.003 453	0.000 884	0.017 117	0.004 382	72 151	8.291 6	1 235	357 666	3 342 976	46.33	0.563 3
25–29	15	2 692	0.005 572	0.001 419	0.027 478	0.006 997	70 916	9.009 7	1 949	349 707	2 985 309	42.10	0.545 3
30–34	8	2 517	0.003 178	0.001 115	0.015 767	0.005 530	68 967	10.983 1	1 087	342 117	2 635 602	38.22	0.506 5
35–39	22	2 623	0.008 387	0.001 751	0.041 075	0.008 576	67 880	12.094 2	2 788	332 428	2 293 485	33.79	0.487 3
40–44	16	2 312	0.006 920	0.001 700	0.034 014	0.008 358	65 092	14.509 6	2 214	319 923	1 961 057	30.13	0.448 7
45–49	14	1 626	0.008 610	0.002 252	0.042 143	0.011 023	62 878	16.498 7	2 650	307 763	1 641 134	26.10	0.420 9
50–54	23	1 342	0.017 139	0.003 424	0.082 172	0.016 415	60 228	19.941 6	4 949	288 766	1 333 371	22.14	0.384 7
55–59	23	1 412	0.016 289	0.003 261	0.078 258	0.015 666	55 279	26.573 0	4 326	265 578	1 044 605	18.90	0.321 3
60–64	39	1 192	0.032 718	0.004 827	0.151 221	0.022 309	50 953	30.076 5	7 705	235 501	779 026	15.29	0.282 0
65–69	47	1 011	0.046 489	0.006 034	0.208 241	0.027 028	43 248	34.588 7	9 006	193 723	543 526	12.57	0.224 0
70–74	42	688	0.061 047	0.008 077	0.264 817	0.035 036	34 242	35.346 2	9 068	148 539	349 803	10.22	0.167 5
75–79	41	484	0.084 711	0.010 670	0.349 531	0.044 026	25 174	33.497 3	8 799	103 872	201 264	7.99	0.110 5
80–84	36	302	0.119 205	0.014 611	0.459 184	0.056 281	16 375	26.456 3	7 519	63 076	97 393	5.95	0.058 8
≥85	40	155	0.258 065	NA	1.000 000	NA	8 856	16.231 2	8 856	34 316	34 316	3.88	NA
Female													
<1	173	2 285	0.075 711	0.005 545	0.072 160	0.005 285	100 000	0.000 0	7 216	95 310	5 359 093	53.59	0.816 2
1–4	287	8 132	0.035 293	0.001 944	0.129 143	0.007 114	92 784	2.792 7	11 982	339 515	5 263 783	56.73	0.757 8
5–9	69	9 386	0.007 351	0.000 869	0.036 094	0.004 266	80 802	6.474 6	2 916	396 717	4 924 269	60.94	0.631 0
10–14	23	7 155	0.003 215	0.000 665	0.015 945	0.003 298	77 885	7.203 8	1 242	386 321	4 527 552	58.13	0.595 4
15–19	15	5 111	0.002 935	0.000 752	0.014 567	0.003 734	76 643	7.635 7	1 116	380 426	4 141 230	54.03	0.577 4
20–24	16	4 298	0.003 723	0.000 922	0.018 442	0.004 568	75 527	8.233 8	1 393	374 152	3 760 805	49.79	0.557 6
25–29	14	3 219	0.004 349	0.001 150	0.021 512	0.005 687	74 134	9.123 1	1 595	366 683	3 386 652	45.68	0.532 3
30–34	9	2 949	0.003 052	0.001 010	0.015 144	0.005 010	72 539	10.512 4	1 099	359 950	3 019 969	41.63	0.498 7
35–39	11	3 208	0.003 429	0.001 025	0.016 999	0.005 082	71 441	11.516 9	1 214	354 168	2 660 019	37.23	0.477 4
40–44	15	2 474	0.006 063	0.001 542	0.029 863	0.007 594	70 226	12.446 6	2 097	345 889	2 305 852	32.83	0.459 8
45–49	19	1 904	0.009 979	0.002 233	0.048 681	0.010 893	68 129	14.558 8	3 317	332 354	1 959 963	28.77	0.428 5
50–54	17	1 793	0.009 481	0.002 246	0.046 309	0.010 968	64 813	18.683 3	3 001	316 560	1 627 608	25.11	0.376 3
55–59	26	1 829	0.014 215	0.002 690	0.068 638	0.012 991	61 811	22.046 6	4 243	298 450	1 311 049	21.21	0.336 5
60–64	28	1 525	0.018 361	0.003 314	0.087 774	0.015 843	57 569	25.571 7	5 053	275 211	1 012 599	17.59	0.295 3
65–69	36	1 222	0.029 460	0.004 561	0.137 195	0.021 239	52 516	29.598 3	7 205	244 566	737 389	14.04	0.253 8
70–74	51	994	0.051 308	0.006 315	0.227 374	0.027 986	45 311	34.475 2	10 302	200 797	492 823	10.88	0.205 3
75–79	37	492	0.075 203	0.010 221	0.316 510	0.043 018	35 008	36.659 8	11 080	147 340	292 026	8.34	0.152 5
80–84	48	379	0.126 649	0.013 170	0.480 962	0.050 014	23 928	39.806 1	11 508	90 868	144 686	6.05	0.081 8
≥85	36	156	0.230 769	NA	1.000 000	NA	12 419	25.045 1	12 419	53 818	53 818	4.33	NA

Note: $_nD_x$, observed deaths between ages x and $x+n$; $_nd_x$, number dying between ages x and $x+n$; e_x, expectation of life at age x for the life-table population; l_x, number of survivors at age x in the life-table population; $_nL_x$, person-years lived by the life-table population between ages x and $x+n$; $_nM_x$, observed mortality rate for ages x to $x+n$; NA, not applicable; $_nPY_x$, observed person-years between ages x and $x+n$; $_nq_x$, probability of dying between ages x and $x+n$; SE_{l_x}, standard error in l_x; $SE_{_nM_x}$, standard error in $_nM_x$; $SE_{_nq_x}$, standard error in $_nq_x$; SE_{e_x}, standard error in e_x; T_x, person-years lived by the life-table population at ages older than x.

Table 6A.17. Life table for the Nouna DSS site, Burkina Faso, 1995–98.

Age (years)	$_nD_x$	$_nPY_x$	$_nM_x$	$SE_{_nM_x}$	$_nq_x$	$SE_{_nq_x}$	l_x	SE_{l_x}	$_nd_x$	$_nL_x$	T_x	e_x (years)	SE_{e_x} (years)
Male													
<1	78	2 221	0.035 116	0.003 907	0.034 309	0.003 817	100 000	0.000 0	3 431	97 701	5 419 511	54.20	0.8737
1–4	238	8 218	0.028 960	0.001 773	0.107 531	0.006 585	96 569	1.457 3	10 384	358 573	5 321 809	55.11	0.8474
5–9	85	9 408	0.009 035	0.000 958	0.044 117	0.004 685	86 185	5.204 3	3 807	421 406	4 963 236	57.59	0.755 8
10–14	30	7 484	0.004 009	0.000 725	0.019 844	0.003 587	82 378	6.384 7	1 635	407 801	4 541 830	55.13	0.719 1
15–19	21	5 791	0.003 626	0.000 784	0.017 968	0.003 886	80 743	7.006 9	1 451	400 087	4 134 029	51.20	0.701 4
20–24	27	4 304	0.006 273	0.001 189	0.030 883	0.005 851	79 292	7.741 6	2 449	390 338	3 733 942	47.09	0.683 9
25–29	20	3 632	0.005 507	0.001 215	0.027 162	0.005 991	76 843	9.423 2	2 087	378 998	3 343 603	43.51	0.649 7
30–34	21	3 135	0.006 698	0.001 437	0.032 939	0.007 069	74 756	11.037 3	2 462	367 624	2 964 605	39.66	0.620 1
35–39	18	2 688	0.006 695	0.001 552	0.032 926	0.007 632	72 294	13.114 4	2 380	355 518	2 596 980	35.92	0.585 9
40–44	19	2 154	0.008 820	0.001 979	0.043 148	0.009 683	69 913	15.309 1	3 017	342 025	2 241 463	32.06	0.554 0
45–49	21	1 979	0.010 612	0.002 255	0.051 689	0.010 984	66 897	18.599 3	3 458	325 839	1 899 437	28.39	0.513 0
50–54	14	1 659	0.008 439	0.002 208	0.041 325	0.010 814	63 439	22.125 6	2 622	310 640	1 573 598	24.80	0.472 2
55–59	24	1 359	0.017 663	0.003 450	0.084 581	0.016 519	60 817	25.041 0	5 144	291 226	1 262 958	20.77	0.444 4
60–64	35	1 170	0.029 906	0.004 690	0.139 130	0.021 820	55 673	31.076 8	7 746	259 002	971 731	17.45	0.396 6
65–69	29	977	0.029 685	0.005 117	0.138 172	0.023 819	47 928	37.788 1	6 622	223 082	712 729	14.87	0.335 8
70–74	38	651	0.058 336	0.008 171	0.254 555	0.035 653	41 305	41.099 6	10 514	180 240	489 647	11.85	0.293 1
75–79	31	411	0.075 387	0.011 189	0.317 162	0.047 072	30 791	44.526 0	9 766	129 540	309 407	10.05	0.227 4
80–84	30	229	0.131 216	0.017 041	0.494 022	0.064 158	21 025	41.767 8	10 387	79 159	179 867	8.55	0.161 4
≥85	12	114	0.105 634	NA	1.000 000	NA	10 638	28.889 4	10 638	100 709	100 709	9.47	NA
Female													
<1	110	2 504	0.043 926	0.004 098	0.042 707	0.003 984	100 000	0.000 0	4 271	97 224	5 306 169	53.06	0.805 2
1–4	242	8 423	0.028 731	0.001 745	0.106 823	0.006 490	95 729	1.587 3	10 226	355 930	5 208 945	54.41	0.774 8
5–9	67	9 593	0.006 984	0.000 838	0.034 321	0.004 120	85 503	5.125 9	2 935	420 180	4 853 015	56.76	0.681 3
10–14	31	7 829	0.003 960	0.000 704	0.019 604	0.003 486	82 569	6.021 2	1 619	408 797	4 432 835	53.69	0.651 9
15–19	30	5 904	0.005 081	0.000 916	0.025 088	0.004 523	80 950	6.616 1	2 031	399 673	4 024 038	49.71	0.634 3
20–24	20	4 544	0.004 401	0.000 973	0.021 768	0.004 814	78 919	7.628 6	1 718	390 301	3 624 366	45.93	0.699 0
25–29	25	3 736	0.006 691	0.001 316	0.032 907	0.006 472	77 201	8.743 6	2 540	379 655	3 234 065	41.89	0.585 2
30–34	16	3 230	0.004 953	0.001 223	0.024 461	0.006 040	74 661	10.674 2	1 826	368 738	2 854 410	38.23	0.548 7
35–39	15	2 832	0.005 296	0.001 349	0.026 135	0.006 659	72 834	12.192 0	1 904	359 414	2 485 671	34.13	0.523 2
40–44	22	2 219	0.009 915	0.002 062	0.048 375	0.010 061	70 931	13.915 5	3 431	346 077	2 126 258	29.98	0.498 9
45–49	19	1 993	0.009 532	0.002 135	0.046 548	0.010 427	67 500	17.694 5	3 142	329 643	1 780 181	26.37	0.454 4
50–54	24	1 727	0.013 897	0.002 740	0.067 154	0.013 239	64 358	21.039 6	4 322	310 984	1 450 538	22.54	0.418 8
55–59	30	1 422	0.021 090	0.003 653	0.100 168	0.017 348	60 036	25.568 8	6 014	285 145	1 139 554	18.98	0.376 7
60–64	35	1 144	0.030 596	0.004 790	0.142 109	0.022 249	54 022	31.550 3	7 677	250 918	854 409	15.82	0.324 9
65–69	47	1 016	0.046 257	0.006 007	0.207 310	0.026 923	46 345	37.666 3	9 608	207 706	603 491	13.02	0.266 0
70–74	36	656	0.054 903	0.007 970	0.241 384	0.035 040	36 737	39.236 7	8 868	161 517	395 785	10.77	0.208 1
75–79	44	439	0.100 289	0.011 702	0.400 926	0.046 782	27 870	39.1517	11 174	111 414	234 268	8.41	0.153 6
80–84	21	227	0.092 450	0.015 943	0.375 469	0.064 750	16 696	31.049 8	6 269	67 808	122 854	7.36	0.084 1
≥85	25	132	0.189 423	NA	1.000 000	NA	10 427	23.797 6	10 427	55 047	55 047	5.28	NA

Note: $_nD_x$, observed deaths between ages x and x+n; $_nd_x$, number dying between ages x and x+n; e_x, expectation of life at age x for the life-table population; l_x, number of survivors at age x in the life-table population; $_nL_x$, person-years lived by the life-table population between ages x and x+n; $_nM_x$, observed mortality rate for ages x to x+n; NA, not applicable; PY_x, observed person-years between ages x and x+n; $_nq_x$, probability of dying between ages x and x+n; SE_{l_x}, standard error in l_x; $SE_{_nM_x}$, standard error in $_nM_x$; $SE_{_nq_x}$, standard error in $_nq_x$; SE_{e_x}, standard error in e_x; T_x, person-years lived by the life-table population at ages older than x.

Table 6A.18. Life table for the Oubritenga DSS site, Burkina Faso, 1995–98.

Age (years)	$_nD_x$	$_nPY_x$	$_nM_x$	$SE_{_nM_x}$	$_nq_x$	$SE_{_nq_x}$	l_x	SE_{l_x}	$_nd_x$	$_nL_x$	T_x	e_x (years)	SE_{e_x} (years)
Male													
<1	882	8 035	0.109 774	0.003 502	0.102 253	0.003 262	100 000	0.000 0	10 225	93 149	5 163 358	51.63	0.434 4
1–4	876	34 175	0.025 633	0.000 823	0.095 968	0.003 083	89 775	1.064 2	8 615	336 114	5 070 209	56.48	0.392 3
5–9	189	38 961	0.004 851	0.000 349	0.023 965	0.001 722	81 159	1.635 8	1 945	400 934	4 734 095	58.33	0.354 2
10–14	82	35 857	0.002 287	0.000 251	0.011 369	0.001 248	79 214	1.753 7	901	393 820	4 333 161	54.70	0.345 0
15–19	62	25 399	0.002 441	0.000 308	0.012 131	0.001 531	78 314	1.811 8	950	389 193	3 939 341	50.30	0.341 0
20–24	39	14 117	0.002 763	0.000 439	0.013 719	0.002 182	77 364	1.911 9	1 061	384 164	3 550 148	45.89	0.336 1
25–29	72	10 603	0.006 790	0.000 787	0.033 385	0.003 868	76 302	2.144 7	2 547	375 143	3 165 984	41.49	0.327 8
30–34	88	10 302	0.008 542	0.000 891	0.041 816	0.004 363	73 755	2.875 0	3 084	361 064	2 790 841	37.84	0.305 4
35–39	77	8 098	0.009 508	0.001 058	0.046 438	0.005 168	70 671	3.675 3	3 282	345 149	2 429 777	34.38	0.281 4
40–44	57	6 692	0.008 518	0.001 104	0.041 702	0.005 407	67 389	4.675 7	2 810	329 919	2 084 627	30.93	0.253 5
45–49	70	6 265	0.011 174	0.001 299	0.054 350	0.006 317	64 579	5.621 6	3 510	314 119	1 754 708	27.17	0.229 3
50–54	67	5 330	0.012 571	0.001 488	0.060 940	0.007 215	61 069	6.691 3	3 722	296 041	1 440 589	23.59	0.203 1
55–59	87	4 671	0.018 627	0.001 906	0.088 992	0.009 106	57 347	7.841 8	5 103	273 978	1 144 548	19.96	0.177 3
60–64	94	4 531	0.020 746	0.002 032	0.098 615	0.009 657	52 244	9.235 5	5 152	248 339	870 570	16.66	0.146 4
65–69	185	4 483	0.041 265	0.002 735	0.187 031	0.012 398	47 092	10.049 1	8 868	213 440	622 231	13.21	0.123 1
70–74	169	3 096	0.054 588	0.003 660	0.240 166	0.016 104	38 284	10.050 6	9 195	168 435	408 791	10.68	0.096 0
75–79	173	2 032	0.085 142	0.005 215	0.350 998	0.021 498	29 090	9.603 7	10 210	119 922	240 356	8.26	0.069 4
80–84	147	1 127	0.130 470	0.007 671	0.491 902	0.028 920	18 879	7.956 1	9 287	71 179	120 434	6.38	0.041 7
≥85	101	519	0.194 755	NA	1.000 000	NA	9 593	5.034 9	9 593	49 254	49 254	5.13	NA
Female													
<1	765	7 829	0.097 714	0.003 367	0.091 878	0.003 166	100 000	0.000 0	9 188	94 028	5 507 751	55.08	0.420 2
1–4	935	33 206	0.028 158	0.000 871	0.104 841	0.003 244	90 812	1.002 1	9 521	338 123	5 413 723	59.61	0.374 4
5–9	145	38 667	0.003 750	0.000 309	0.018 576	0.001 528	81 291	1.670 8	1 510	402 681	5 075 600	62.44	0.321 6
10–14	61	33 928	0.001 798	0.000 229	0.008 949	0.001 141	79 781	1.763 7	714	397 121	4 672 918	58.57	0.312 5
15–19	94	26 582	0.003 536	0.000 362	0.017 526	0.001 792	79 067	1.815 1	1 386	391 872	4 275 797	54.08	0.308 2
20–24	83	20 811	0.003 988	0.000 433	0.019 744	0.002 146	77 682	1.952 7	1 534	384 573	3 883 925	50.00	0.299 1
25–29	78	15 542	0.005 019	0.000 561	0.024 782	0.002 771	76 148	2.154 2	1 887	376 021	3 499 351	45.95	0.288 0
30–34	78	13 805	0.005 650	0.000 631	0.027 858	0.003 110	74 261	2.494 0	2 069	366 132	3 123 330	42.06	0.272 2
35–39	64	11 483	0.005 573	0.000 687	0.027 484	0.003 388	72 192	2.890 4	1 984	356 000	2 757 198	38.19	0.255 5
40–44	68	9 590	0.007 090	0.000 845	0.034 835	0.004 150	70 208	3.331 9	2 446	344 925	2 401 199	34.20	0.239 2
45–49	59	8 458	0.006 976	0.000 892	0.034 281	0.004 386	67 762	3.952 7	2 323	333 004	2 056 274	30.35	0.219 2
50–54	81	8 364	0.009 684	0.001 050	0.047 276	0.005 127	65 439	4.569 6	3 094	319 462	1 723 270	26.33	0.201 8
55–59	64	6 000	0.010 666	0.001 298	0.051 945	0.006 322	62 346	5.273 5	3 239	303 631	1 403 808	22.52	0.183 5
60–64	87	5 571	0.015 617	0.001 610	0.075 153	0.007 749	59 107	6.293 5	4 442	284 430	1 100 177	18.61	0.163 5
65–69	153	5 550	0.027 567	0.002 080	0.128 949	0.009 730	54 665	7.480 7	7 049	255 702	815 747	14.92	0.142 8
70–74	226	4 426	0.051 061	0.002 987	0.226 403	0.013 246	47 616	8.504 6	10 780	211 129	560 044	11.76	0.120 9
75–79	169	2 283	0.074 012	0.004 721	0.312 281	0.019 921	36 836	9.067 7	11 503	155 420	348 915	9.47	0.094 5
80–84	104	1 169	0.088 957	0.006 957	0.363 865	0.028 458	25 333	9.673 2	9 218	103 619	193 495	7.64	0.058 2
≥85	136	759	0.179 301	NA	1.000 000	NA	16 115	9.111 5	16 115	89 876	89 876	5.58	NA

Note: $_nD_x$, observed deaths between ages x and $x+n$; $_nd_x$, number dying between ages x and $x+n$; e_x, expectation of life at age x for the life-table population; l_x, number of survivors at age x in the life-table population; $_nL_x$, person–years lived by the life-table population between ages x and $x+n$; $_nM_x$, observed mortality rate for ages x to $x+n$; NA, not applicable; PY_x, observed person–years between ages x and $x+n$; $_nq_x$, probability of dying between ages x and $x+n$; SE_{l_x}, standard error in l_x; $SE_{_nM_x}$, standard error in $_nM_x$; $SE_{_nq_x}$, standard error in $_nq_x$; SE_{e_x}, standard error in e_x; T_x, person–years lived by the life-table population at ages older than x.

Table 6A.19. Life table for the Rufiji DSS site, Tanzania, 1999.

Age (years)	$_nD_x$	$_nPY_x$	$_nM_x$	$SE_{_nM_x}$	$_nq_x$	$SE_{_nq_x}$	l_x	SE_{l_x}	$_nd_x$	$_nL_x$	T_x	e_x (years)	SE_{e_x} (years)
Male													
<1	130	794	0.163 728	0.013 258	0.147 543	0.011 948	100 000	0.000 0	14 754	90 115	5 339 664	53.40	1.242 4
1–4	49	5 090	0.009 627	0.001 349	0.037 543	0.005 262	85 246	14.274 7	3 200	332 445	5 249 550	61.58	0.995 2
5–9	16	5 376	0.002 976	0.000 739	0.014 771	0.003 665	82 045	15.234 7	1 212	407 197	4 917 105	59.93	0.954 8
10–14	6	4 861	0.001 334	0.000 502	0.006 153	0.002 504	80 833	15.692 4	497	402 924	4 509 908	55.79	0.938 5
15–19	7	3 615	0.001 936	0.000 728	0.009 635	0.003 624	80 336	15.909 6	774	399 746	4 106 984	51.12	0.932 2
20–24	2	2 339	0.000 855	0.000 603	0.004 266	0.003 010	79 562	16.452 2	339	396 962	3 707 238	46.60	0.921 2
25–29	6	2 000	0.003 000	0.001 216	0.014 888	0.006 033	79 223	16.885 7	1 179	393 164	3 310 276	41.78	0.915 1
30–34	15	1 553	0.009 659	0.002 434	0.047 155	0.011 885	78 043	18.670 8	3 680	381 105	2 917 112	37.38	0.895 0
35–39	17	1 415	0.012 014	0.002 828	0.058 319	0.013 726	74 363	25.554 6	4 337	360 973	2 536 096	34.10	0.828 1
40–44	10	912	0.010 965	0.003 374	0.053 362	0.016 418	70 026	33.079 0	3 737	340 789	2 175 123	31.06	0.754 0
45–49	15	862	0.017 401	0.004 302	0.083 380	0.020 611	66 290	42.860 9	5 527	317 630	1 834 334	27.67	0.669 4
50–54	13	826	0.015 738	0.004 197	0.075 713	0.020 189	60 762	54.679 9	4 601	292 310	1 516 704	24.96	0.554 4
55–59	18	836	0.021 531	0.004 809	0.102 157	0.022 816	56 162	61.761 3	5 737	266 466	1 224 394	21.80	0.467 4
60–64	25	884	0.028 281	0.005 269	0.132 066	0.024 607	50 424	66.206 0	6 659	235 474	957 928	19.00	0.377 6
65–69	17	729	0.023 320	0.005 335	0.110 175	0.025 206	43 765	65.269 7	4 822	206 771	722 454	16.51	0.294 9
70–74	25	706	0.035 411	0.006 481	0.162 655	0.029 768	38 943	63.849 5	6 334	178 881	515 683	13.24	0.238 4
75–79	35	522	0.067 050	0.009 569	0.287 121	0.040 977	32 609	58.206 8	9 363	139 638	336 802	10.33	0.186 3
80–84	28	328	0.085 366	0.012 989	0.351 759	0.053 522	23 246	47.435 2	8 177	95 789	197 163	8.48	0.114 8
≥85	66	444	0.148 649	NA	1.000 000	NA	15 069	35.413 3	15 069	101 375	101 375	6.73	NA
Female													
<1	156	787	0.198 221	0.014 410	0.175 597	0.012 765	100 000	0.000 0	17 560	88 586	5 217 766	52.18	1.250 2
1–4	41	4 847	0.008 459	0.001 299	0.033 097	0.005 083	82 440	16.294 7	2 728	322 561	5 129 179	62.22	0.958 6
5–9	11	5 164	0.002 130	0.000 639	0.010 594	0.003 177	79 712	16.989 7	844	396 448	4 806 619	60.30	0.921 6
10–14	12	4 348	0.002 760	0.000 791	0.013 705	0.003 929	78 867	17.273 0	1 081	391 635	4 410 171	55.92	0.909 7
15–19	7	3 448	0.002 030	0.000 763	0.010 100	0.003 798	77 786	17.763 1	786	386 968	4 018 536	51.66	0.894 1
20–24	18	2 804	0.006 419	0.001 489	0.031 590	0.007 327	77 001	18.278 9	2 432	378 923	3 631 567	47.16	0.881 9
25–29	26	2 676	0.009 716	0.001 860	0.047 428	0.009 078	74 568	20.325 5	3 537	364 001	3 252 644	43.62	0.842 7
30–34	21	1 862	0.011 278	0.002 393	0.054 845	0.011 635	71 032	23.025 8	3 896	345 420	2 888 644	40.67	0.790 4
35–39	22	1 595	0.013 793	0.002 841	0.066 667	0.013 731	67 136	27.399 9	4 476	324 491	2 543 224	37.88	0.716 5
40–44	12	1 117	0.010 743	0.003 019	0.052 310	0.014 700	62 660	32.366 9	3 278	305 107	2 218 733	35.41	0.625 4
45–49	10	1 226	0.008 157	0.002 527	0.039 968	0.012 384	59 383	37.554 1	2 373	290 979	1 913 625	32.23	0.537 5
50–54	13	1 235	0.010 526	0.002 844	0.051 282	0.013 854	57 009	40.020 1	2 924	277 737	1 622 646	28.46	0.486 9
55–59	14	933	0.015 005	0.003 863	0.072 314	0.018 615	54 086	42.258 3	3 911	260 650	1 344 909	24.87	0.436 2
60–64	13	1 078	0.012 059	0.003 245	0.058 532	0.015 752	50 174	46.503 9	2 937	243 530	1 084 259	21.61	0.362 5
65–69	28	1 030	0.027 184	0.004 799	0.127 273	0.022 470	47 238	47.465 5	6 012	221 158	840 729	17.80	0.325 0
70–74	24	772	0.031 088	0.005 870	0.144 231	0.027 235	41 226	47.418 1	5 946	191 263	619 571	15.03	0.266 5
75–79	24	527	0.045 541	0.008 292	0.204 429	0.037 220	35 280	47.332 8	7 212	158 367	428 308	12.14	0.209 8
80–84	31	414	0.074 879	0.011 128	0.315 361	0.046 866	28 067	47.201 0	8 851	118 209	269 940	9.62	0.136 8
≥85	77	608	0.126 645	NA	1.000 000	NA	19 216	39.427 5	19 216	151 732	151 732	7.90	NA

Note: D_x, observed deaths between ages x and x+n; $_nd_x$, number dying between ages x and x+n; d_x, number dying between ages x and x+n by the life-table population; l_x, number of survivors at age x in the life-table population; $_nL_x$, person-years lived by the life-table population between ages x and x+n; $_nM_x$, observed mortality rate for ages x to x+n; NA, not applicable; PY_x, observed person-years between ages x and x+n; $_nM_x$, observed mortality rate in $_nM_x$; $_nq_x$, probability of dying between ages x and x+n; l_x; SE$_{_nM_x}$, standard error in $_nM_x$; SE$_{l_x}$, standard error in l_x; SE$_{_nq_x}$, standard error in $_nq_x$; SE$_{e_x}$, standard error in e_x; T_x, person-years lived by the life-table population at ages older than x.

Chapter 7

INDEPTH MORTALITY PATTERNS FOR AFRICA

Abstract

Mortality data from Africa compiled by the INDEPTH Network and including over 6.4 million person–years of exposure are used to identify new mortality patterns. Seven age patterns of mortality emerge from these data, two of which clearly show excess mortality due to HIV–AIDS. The emergent patterns are compared with the existing model mortality patterns produced by Coale and Demeny (CD) and the United Nations (UN) and are demonstrated to be substantially different. The principal-components technique is used to calculate 15 principal components that account for all of the variation in the data. It is demonstrated that the components are sufficiently general to accurately reproduce the existing CD and UN model mortality patterns. The resulting component model of mortality is demonstrated through the construction of a hypothetical set of life tables combining the HIV–AIDS pattern of mortality with an underlying pattern of mortality that is not affected by HIV–AIDS. This general technique yields mortality patterns that might prevail if the population described by the underlying mortality pattern were infected with HIV–AIDS.

Mortality models and Africa

An individual's probability of dying depends primarily on sex, age, health, genetic endowment, and the environment, all of which determine the risk of falling victim to illness or accident. The primary determinants of mortality interact in complex ways and depend in turn on a large and variable set of complex social determinants. As a result, it has not been possible to formulate a general, theory-driven model of individual risk of death. In lieu of a good general model, two widely used sets of model life tables are the CD model, created by Coale and Demeny (1966), and the later UN model (United Nations 1982). In both cases, a large set of empirical mortality rates are summarized to yield a small number of characteristic age patterns of mortality. Coale and Demeny identified four patterns, which they called North, South, East, and West to reflect the fact that each pattern is representative of the mortality pattern in a particular region of Europe. For a similar reason, the UN's patterns also bear regional names: Latin America, Chile, Far East, South Asia, and General. The UN General pattern is, as its name suggests, a general pattern that is not specific to a single location.

Each of the eight existing model mortality patterns (excluding the UN General pattern) results from the characteristic epidemiological profile of the region it represents. For example, the UN South Asia pattern describes an age pattern of mortality with "very high rates under age fifteen and very high rates again at the oldest ages, with correspondingly lower mortality for the prime age groups." This pattern is ascribed to "high incidences of infectious, parasitic and diarrheal diseases at the youngest ages and high mortality from diarrheal and respiratory diseases at the oldest ages" (United Nations 1982, p. 13).

For large areas of the developing world, accurate information describing the mortality of the population is not available because vital registration systems are incomplete and inaccurate. Where that is true, model mortality patterns are used to substitute for real information. Two important examples are population projections and estimates of child mortality. All population projections must include both existing mortality conditions and educated estimates of future mortality regimes. The Brass estimators of child mortality (United Nations 1983), widely used in areas where accurate data on child mortality are unavailable, rely on estimates of the age pattern of child mortality, and in most cases a model mortality pattern is used for that purpose. Moreover, model mortality patterns are used to evaluate data, to produce smoothed or corrected versions of faulty data, and to extend or fill in the age range of incomplete data. Demographers working in regions where mortality data are inaccurate or incomplete depend heavily on model mortality patterns to allow them to evaluate the data they have and to make reasonable estimates and predictions.

None of the data used to create either of the widely used collections of model mortality patterns came from sub-Saharan Africa. Consequently, it is not evident that the existing model mortality patterns adequately describe the age patterns of mortality in Africa, and it is only because there is nothing else that they are applied to African populations at all. Furthermore, the emergence of the HIV–AIDS pandemic in Africa has radically altered the age pattern of mortality in large areas of the continent. Because the existing model mortality patterns do not contain an AIDS pattern of mortality, they are no longer appropriate under any circumstance where AIDS is a significant cause of death or where AIDS is anticipated as a significant cause of death in the near future. This is an even more serious problem than it might first appear because of the crucial role that model mortality patterns play in routine demographic work in Africa — precisely because of the substantial lack of comprehensive, accurate mortality data.

This chapter presents seven age patterns of mortality derived almost exclusively from data collected in Africa, including two patterns resulting from excess mortality caused by AIDS. A 15-factor model is constructed to summarize the data, and that model is used to isolate the AIDS-related component of mortality in the AIDS pattern. Last, the AIDS component is superimposed in various amounts on one of the patterns to generate a coarse set of model life tables that illustrates the effects of AIDS mortality.

Mortality data

To allow maximum flexibility in analysis, individual sites provided counts of deaths and person–years observed in standard 0 to 85+ age groups by sex for single years of observation for as many years of observation as possible. The majority of sites were able to provide data in this format, although one or two provided time-aggregated data. Table 7.1 summarizes the data for this work.

The overall aim of this work is to identify age patterns of mortality for Africa and Asia using longitudinal data from INDEPTH field sites. To adequately capture the variation in mortality over time, the data from each site are grouped into 3-year intervals, or as close to 3-year intervals as possible and practical, to yield 70 site–periods. The annual data in each of those periods is aggregated to yield 70 site–period data sets for each sex: 140 site–period data sets in all. Table 7.2 shows the periods chosen for each site.

Table 7.1. Temporal aspects of INDEPTH mortality data.

DSS site	Period of data collection	Total years of data	Aggregated years	Total person–years observed
Agincourt, South Africa	1992–99	8	—	405 311.46
Bandafassi, Senegal	1980–99	14	—	144 475.61
Bandim, Guinea-Bissau	1990–97	8	—	193 832.91
Butajira, Ethiopia	1987–96	10	—	336 075.71
Dar es Salaam, Tanzania	1992–99	8	—	485 446.30
Farafenni, The Gambia	1990–99	10	—	98 073.70
Gwembe, Zambia	1956–95	39	—	187 034.00
Hai, Tanzania	1992–99	8	—	1 045 152.69
Ifakara, Tanzania	1997–99	3	—	159 639.00
Manhiça, Mozambique	1998–99	2	—	67 344.00
Matlab comp.,[a] Bangladesh	NA	2	1988, 1998	203 744.00
Matlab treat.,[b] Bangladesh	NA	2	1988, 1998	211 770.00
Mlomp, Senegal	1985–99	14	—	106 593.48
Morogoro, Tanzania	1992–99	8	—	741 412.41
Navrongo, Ghana	1993–99	7	—	930 187.50
Niakhar, Senegal	1985–98	14	1985–89, 1990–94, 1995–98	372880.00
Nouna, Burkina Faso	1993–98	6	—	174 689.62
Oubritenga, Burkina Faso	1994–98	5	—	482 100.40
Rufiji, Tanzania	1999–99	1	—	67 842.50

Note: NA, not applicable.
[a] Comparison area.
[b] Treatment area.

Table 7.2. Periods chosen for analysis from each site: site–periods.

DSS site	1950–79	1980	1981	1982	1983	1984	1985	1986	1987	1988	1989	1990	1991	1992	1993	1994	1995	1996	1997	1998	1999
Agincourt, South Africa														1		2		3			4
Bandafassi, Senegal				1							3			4			5			6	
Bandim, Guinea-Bissau												1		2		3		4			
Butajira, Ethiopia										1		2		3		4					
Dar es Salaam, Tanzania														1	2	3	4	5	6	7	
Farafenni, The Gambia																1		2		3	
Gwembe, Zambia	1			2			3			4			5			6					
Hai, Tanzania														1	2	3	4	5	6	7	
Ifakara, Tanzania																				1	
Manhiça, Mozambique																					
Matlab comp.,[a] Bangladesh										1									2		
Matlab treat.,[b] Bangladesh										1									2		
Mlomp, Senegal								1			2			3			4			5	
Morogoro, Tanzania														1	2	3	4	5	6	7	
Navrongo, Ghana																1		2		3	
Niakhar, Senegal									1					2					3		
Nouna, Burkina Faso																1			2		
Oubritenga, Burkina Faso																	1		2		
Rufiji, Tanzania																					1

Note: Numerals label the periods chosen at each site. Observations at the AMMP sites in Tanzania — Dar es Salaam, Hai, and Morogoro — go from midyear to midyear and are reported in midyear to midyear intervals instead of calendar-year intervals. In each of these cases, seven 1-year periods are reported.
[a] Comparison area.
[b] Treatment area.

Principal-components analysis

Data summary

The goal is to identify a compact representation of the information contained in a large set of observations of similar items. Principal-components analysis transforms the observations to produce an equal number of components. These can reproduce all of the original observations when combined in the appropriate proportions. The components differ from the original observations in that they capture as much variation as possible in as few components as possible. The first component accounts for the maximum variation that one component can account for. After the analyst removes the variation associated with the first component, the second component accounts for as much of the remaining variation as can be accounted for with one component. The analyst continues this process until all the variation in the original data set has been accounted for and the number of components equals the number of original observations. The important consequence is that the majority of the variation in the data set is accounted for in the first few components.

In this way a large set of observations may be summarized using a small number of components. After deciding how much of the original variation must be retained, the analyst may choose to discard the higher order components accounting for the residual variation.

Component model of mortality

The component model of mortality constructed here makes no substantive assumptions regarding the underlying form of the age-specific mortality schedule. The model makes the general assumption that an arbitrary age-specific mortality schedule can be decomposed into a small number of individual components and a negligible residual term. Additionally, it is assumed that a small number of components together form a universal set of age-specific mortality components and that, when combined in the appropriate proportions, they can reproduce any age-specific mortality schedule. For the purposes of this work, these assumptions encompass only the complete set of mortality data examined here; however, it has been demonstrated that the "universal" mortality components generated from the INDEPTH data are capable of reproducing all of the CD and UN model life-table mortality schedules to within a very small tolerance.

Assume there are n separate components of the age-specific mortality schedule and g age groups. Let m represent the $g \times 1$ vector of age-specific logit ($_nq_x$) values, and let C represent the $g \times n$ matrix whose ith column is the $g \times 1$ vector containing the ith component of mortality. Let a be an $n \times 1$ vector of coefficients that determines how much of each component is used to generate the mortality schedule, and let r be a $g \times 1$ vector of residuals, one for each age. Then equation [7.1] is a compact representation of the full-component model of mortality:

$$m = Ca + r \qquad [7.1]$$

where m, C, a, and r are as defined above. Expanding this around the row for the 20–24 age group reveals

$$\begin{bmatrix} \vdots \\ \text{logit}\left(_5 q_{20}\right) \\ \vdots \end{bmatrix} = \begin{bmatrix} \vdots \\ _5 C_{20}^i \\ \vdots \end{bmatrix} \cdot a_i + \ldots + \begin{bmatrix} \vdots \\ _5 C_{20}^n \\ \vdots \end{bmatrix} \cdot a_n + \begin{bmatrix} \vdots \\ r_{20} \\ \vdots \end{bmatrix}$$

where $_5 C_{20}^i$ is the value of the ith component for the 20–24 age group; a_i is the value of the coefficient on the ith component; and r_{20} is the value of the residual for the 20–24 age group. Each of the column vectors contains g elements, one for each age group.

Once the matrix C has been identified through principal-components analysis (described below), the model may be used in many ways. First, it is informative to examine the shape of the components themselves. The primary component (accounting for the bulk of the variation in the data) represents the common underlying shape of the schedule as a function of age. The second and higher order components define age-specific variations on the basic shape. Moreover, it may be possible to associate certain substantive interpretations with the components; for example, one may appear to affect the balance between child and adult mortality, and one may appear to contribute to or remove from a particular age group affected by a specific condition, such as maternal or AIDS-related mortality.

Estimates of the coefficients a that transform the components into a given mortality schedule may be obtained through an ordinary linear least-squares regression of the mortality schedule against the components C. The residual identified in the regression is equivalent to r, and the regression coefficients are the elements of the vector a with the addition of an extra element to store the constant estimated in the regression. Let a' be the $(n + 1) \times 1$ coefficient vector with the additional element to store the constant generated in the regression model, and let C' be the $g \times (n + 1)$ matrix of components with one additional column containing all ones to accommodate the constant in a'. The constant is interpreted as a measure of the overall **level** of the mortality schedule, whereas the coefficients indicate how much of each age pattern (component) is necessary to reproduce the overall age pattern in the original data. Interpreted in this way, the regression controls for level and provides an estimate of how much of each component is contained within the data, or how important each individual age pattern is in generating the age pattern observed in the data. Equation [7.2] represents the regression component model of mortality:

$$m = C' a' \tag{7.2}$$

where m, C', and a' are defined as above. Expanding this around the row for the 20–24-year age group reveals

$$\begin{bmatrix} \vdots \\ \text{logit}\left(_5 q_{20}\right) \\ \vdots \end{bmatrix} = \begin{bmatrix} \vdots \\ _5 C_{20}^i \\ \vdots \end{bmatrix} \cdot a_i + \ldots + \begin{bmatrix} \vdots \\ _5 C_{20}^n \\ \vdots \end{bmatrix} \cdot a_n + \begin{bmatrix} \vdots \\ 1 \\ \vdots \end{bmatrix} \cdot a_c$$

where $_5C_{20}^i$ is the value of the ith component for the 20–24 age group; a_i is the value of the coefficient estimated on the ith component; and a_c is the constant term estimated in the regression, taking the same value for all age groups. Each of the column vectors contains g elements, one for each age group.

Ignoring the residual and postmultiplying C' by a' (equation [7.2]) yields the original mortality schedule purged of the residual r. Together with C', the $(n + 1) \times 1$ vector a' contains all the information needed to reproduce the original mortality schedule to within r. In most cases the number of components $(n + 1)$ necessary to adequately encode the mortality schedule is much less than g, the number of age groups. As a result, a' is a compact representation of the mortality schedule that encodes the fundamental shape of the schedule without the "noise" associated with the high-order components and the residual term. Additionally, by adjusting the constant term contained in the last element of a', it is possible to arbitrarily set the level of the mortality schedule without affecting its age pattern.

The individual coefficient vectors associated with each mortality schedule represent the most important dimensions of the mortality schedules and can be compared and grouped without worrying about the high-order noise associated with the individual schedules. Moreover, by comparing only the coefficients corresponding to the components and ignoring the constant, it is possible to compare individual mortality schedules based only on their individual age patterns and **not on differences in their level.** Correspondingly, by comparing only the constants associated with two mortality schedules, the influence of the age pattern is effectively removed (controlled for), and it is possible to compare the mortality schedules based only on their level.

Principal components of INDEPTH mortality data

For each sex, logit $(_nq_x)$ values are calculated for the standard 0–85 age groups (18 in all)[1] in each of the site–periods according to equations [7.3] and [7.4]. This yields a 70×18 data set consisting of one column for each site–period and one row for each age group, with each cell containing a value of logit $(_nq_x)$ corresponding to the specified site–period and age group.

Equation [7.3] gives $_nq_x$ as a function of $_nM_x$:

$$_nq_x = \frac{_nM_x}{1 + n(1 - _na_x)\,_nM_x} \qquad [5.1]$$

where $_nq_x$ is the life-table probability of death between ages x and $x + n$ for those who survive to age x; $_nM_x$ is the observed mortality rate (the ratio of deaths to person–years lived) for those between ages x and $x + n$; and $_na_x$ is the average proportion of years between ages x and $x + n$ lived by those who die in that age interval.[2]

---

[1] 0, 1–4, 5–9, 10–14, 15–19, 20–24, 25–29, 30–34, 35–39, 40–44, 45–49, 50–54, 55–59, 60–64, 65–69, 70–74, 75–79, 80–84.

[2] Without substantially more data tabulated by single year of age it is impossible to directly calculate or estimate the values of $_na_x$. Moreover, except for the youngest ages, the value of $_na_x$ is always near 0.5. At the youngest ages, the values are much closer to 0.25. Additionally, the life table is not highly sensitive to the exact values chosen as long as they are close to 0.25 for ages <5 years and close to 0.5 for ages >5 years. In this work, the value of $_na_x$ used for ages >5 years is 0.5. For ages <5 years, the values for $_na_x$ are for males 0.33 for ages 0–1 years and 0.25 for ages 1–4 years; and for females, 0.35 for ages 0–1 years and 0.25 for ages 1–4 years. These are loosely adapted from the CD West model life-table system (Coale and Demeny 1966).

Table 7.3. First 15 principal components of INDEPTH male mortality.

Age (years)	PC1	PC2	PC3	PC4	PC5	PC6	PC7	PC8	PC9	PC10	PC11	PC12	PC13	PC14	PC15
0	3.5206	-0.9092	-0.5861	0.7908	-0.9517	-0.1341	-0.0818	0.0137	-0.0715	-0.0257	-0.0624	0.0275	-0.0939	-0.0773	-0.0056
1-4	2.1060	-1.3263	-0.4162	0.2302	-0.0323	0.1009	-0.0104	-0.0263	0.0459	-0.0008	0.0371	-0.0160	0.0626	0.0489	0.0025
5-9	-0.6237	-1.3939	-0.2097	-0.2409	0.3600	0.1113	0.0420	0.0000	-0.0094	-0.0129	-0.0139	0.0089	-0.0443	-0.0346	0.0001
10-14	-3.8913	-0.6672	0.2893	-0.2781	-0.2373	-0.2707	-0.0414	0.0790	-0.1137	0.0415	-0.0198	0.0100	0.0234	0.0162	0.0013
15-19	-4.2300	0.2142	0.5140	0.2019	-0.1094	0.0091	0.1223	-0.1077	0.2174	-0.0260	0.0616	-0.0360	-0.0171	-0.0103	-0.0055
20-24	-2.9701	1.0178	0.2872	0.5311	0.2605	0.2447	-0.0343	0.0151	-0.0975	-0.0369	-0.1389	0.0622	0.0185	0.0144	0.0003
25-29	-1.3633	1.5292	-0.2994	0.2827	0.2560	-0.0229	-0.2078	0.1704	-0.1585	0.0290	0.1827	-0.0389	-0.0237	-0.0082	0.0135
30-34	-0.0101	1.6798	-0.8204	-0.1323	0.1790	-0.3111	-0.1093	-0.1431	0.1191	0.1215	-0.1161	-0.0862	0.0321	-0.0231	-0.0333
35-39	1.1271	1.5442	-0.5701	-0.3670	-0.0745	-0.2137	0.0288	-0.0588	0.1346	-0.1331	0.0150	0.1368	-0.0566	0.0521	0.0674
40-44	2.0278	1.4749	-0.2600	-0.3663	-0.2405	0.1735	0.3823	0.1487	-0.0608	-0.1717	0.0395	0.0461	0.0853	-0.0358	-0.0863
45-49	2.9895	1.1639	0.0904	-0.3435	-0.3401	0.4071	0.3410	0.1576	-0.0829	0.0946	-0.0489	-0.1475	-0.0459	0.0031	0.0489
50-54	3.9242	0.7764	0.4165	-0.2790	-0.2578	0.4380	-0.0074	-0.2064	-0.0613	0.2585	-0.0078	0.0370	-0.0202	0.0447	0.0390
55-59	5.0339	0.4222	0.6651	-0.3319	-0.1043	0.1733	-0.3776	-0.3370	-0.0928	0.0997	0.1143	0.1160	-0.0040	-0.0381	-0.0896
60-64	6.4716	0.1705	0.9022	-0.2772	-0.0053	-0.0324	-0.4303	-0.1194	-0.0338	-0.3066	-0.0430	-0.1138	0.1070	-0.0853	0.1084
65-69	8.2046	-0.0280	0.8817	-0.1134	0.1607	-0.1749	-0.3034	0.1980	0.0741	-0.2004	-0.0884	-0.1207	-0.1348	0.1284	-0.1121
70-74	9.9266	-0.0834	0.9652	0.1994	0.3252	-0.2939	-0.0499	0.5487	0.3829	0.1610	-0.0376	0.0641	-0.0381	0.0069	-0.0222
75-79	11.7097	-0.0984	1.0259	0.5481	0.5681	-0.6360	0.4503	0.3546	0.2699	0.3511	0.0297	0.1869	0.1476	-0.1304	0.0800
80-84	13.7690	-0.1067	1.0401	1.0822	1.0750	-1.5415	1.4284	-0.8888	-0.9189	-0.1067	0.0850	-0.1085	-0.0877	0.0748	0.0021
Var.[a]	0.8712	0.0889	0.0153	0.0077	0.0062	0.0037	0.0024	0.0014	0.0012	0.0007	0.0004	0.0003	0.0002	0.0001	0.0001
Cum. var.[b]	0.8712	0.9601	0.9755	0.9832	0.9894	0.9931	0.9955	0.9969	0.9981	0.9988	0.9992	0.9995	0.9997	0.9998	0.9999

Note: Units of logit ($_nq_x$).
[a] Percent of variance explained by the component.
[b] Cumulative percent of variance explained by the component(s).

Equation [7.4] shows the calculation for logit $(_nq_x)$:

$$\text{logit } (_nq_n) = \tfrac{1}{2} \ln \left(\frac{_nq_x}{1 - {}_nq_x} \right)$$ [7.4]

The **factor**[3] and **score** routines provided with the STATA statistical software package release 5.0 (StataCorp 1997)[4] are used to calculate the principal components of the 70 × 18 covariance matrix[5] associated with the data set described above. Each age group (row) in the data set is given a weight equal to the total number of person–years of observation for the age group summed across all site–periods. Fifteen of the resulting 70 principal components are retained, and for both males and females those 15 components account for greater than 99.99% of the variation in the data.

Male

The first 15 principal components of INDEPTH male mortality are contained in Table 7.3, and the first 5 components are shown in Figure 7.1. The primary (first) component, PC1, obviously represents the underlying age pattern of mortality, and together PC2–PC4 modify the age pattern in a way that is consistent with mortality caused by AIDS. PC2 in particular has the shape necessary to account for increased mortality between the ages of 20 and 64 years. PC3 and PC4 allow modifications between the ages of 20 and 49 years and during childhood.

Figure 7.1. First five principal components of INDEPTH male mortality. The first five principal components explain 98.94% of total variance.

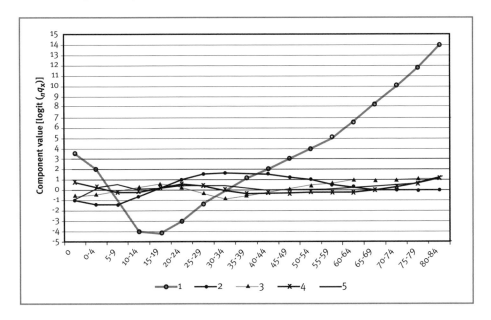

<hr>

[3] The factor routine is used with the options [pc] to request principal-components analysis; [covariance], to specify that the covariance matrix is analyzed; and [weight], to specify the weighting.

[4] Mention of a proprietary name does not constitute endorsement of the product and is given only for information.

[5] The covariance matrix is used so that the observations are not standardized before the calculation. The resulting principal components refer to the unstandardized observations and can be directly recombined to produce age-specific mortality schedules that need no further transformation, except for the inverse logit, to produce values of $_nq_x$.

Table 7.4. First 15 principal components of INDEPTH female mortality.

Age (years)	PC1	PC2	PC3	PC4	PC5	PC6	PC7	PC8	PC9	PC10	PC11	PC12	PC13	PC14	PC15
0	3.5313	-0.4696	-0.2823	0.9837	0.6458	-0.4557	-0.5026	-0.2507	0.0375	-0.0815	-0.0516	-0.0245	0.0183	-0.0096	-0.1023
1–4	2.3801	-1.1570	-0.3886	0.3453	-0.0051	-0.1870	-0.0543	0.0899	-0.0276	0.0054	0.0376	0.0227	-0.0123	0.0075	0.0693
5–9	-0.3553	-1.5460	-0.4143	-0.1775	-0.3376	0.0598	0.0976	0.0563	-0.0250	0.0135	-0.0422	-0.0158	0.0003	-0.0028	-0.0467
10–14	-3.9597	-1.0972	0.1003	-0.2918	0.2469	0.2186	-0.0422	-0.2020	0.0855	-0.0112	0.0366	0.0076	0.0187	0.0038	0.0187
15–19	-3.8199	0.0125	0.6053	0.2285	0.3222	-0.0854	0.1449	0.1722	-0.1569	-0.0147	-0.0341	0.0008	-0.0486	-0.0082	-0.0065
20–24	-2.2312	1.0535	0.2788	0.5568	-0.3124	-0.1589	0.1621	0.0696	0.2258	-0.0418	0.0319	-0.0306	0.0716	-0.0062	-0.0014
25–29	-0.8902	1.6924	-0.1814	0.5557	-0.2909	0.3444	-0.0841	-0.1418	-0.0648	0.1300	0.0070	0.0948	-0.0527	0.0294	-0.0112
30–34	-0.1141	1.8996	-0.6129	-0.0698	0.0584	0.3515	-0.1415	0.0030	-0.0994	-0.0446	-0.0620	-0.1350	0.0061	-0.0375	0.0314
35–39	0.3159	1.7325	-0.6989	-0.7004	0.3716	-0.0558	-0.0309	0.2363	-0.0152	-0.0941	0.0901	0.0743	0.0619	0.0360	-0.0306
40–44	0.7540	1.2876	-0.2148	-0.7254	0.0605	-0.5754	0.1212	-0.0973	0.2371	0.1248	-0.0473	0.0139	-0.1273	-0.0655	0.0098
45–49	1.4083	0.8007	0.4921	-0.5216	-0.2276	-0.5815	0.1042	-0.2427	-0.2023	0.0497	-0.0439	-0.0532	0.0521	0.1314	0.0018
50–54	2.4523	0.2582	0.7844	-0.3784	-0.4306	-0.1563	-0.2427	-0.1569	-0.2432	-0.0833	0.0309	0.0400	0.0773	-0.1118	0.0475
55–59	3.8123	-0.0959	1.0571	-0.4104	-0.4334	0.2157	-0.4918	0.1446	0.0872	-0.2270	0.1135	-0.0077	-0.1201	0.0071	-0.0628
60–64	5.4730	-0.2709	0.9026	-0.2793	0.2074	0.4606	-0.3685	0.2549	0.2940	0.1110	-0.2140	-0.0096	0.0205	0.0886	0.0637
65–69	7.4297	-0.1483	0.6562	-0.1330	0.3840	0.3041	0.2144	0.0973	-0.0260	0.3456	-0.0498	0.0983	0.1588	-0.0981	-0.0650
70–74	9.2290	-0.1971	0.4828	0.1217	0.4232	0.3758	0.5258	-0.0544	-0.0405	0.2968	0.2371	-0.1387	-0.0093	-0.0193	-0.0319
75–79	11.2081	0.0265	0.2309	0.2767	0.3649	0.4929	0.8747	-0.2562	0.0128	-0.1368	0.2313	-0.1680	-0.1436	0.0685	-0.0035
80–84	13.4986	0.8028	-0.0993	0.3120	0.2427	0.6651	1.5584	-0.5054	0.0902	-0.9873	-0.3832	0.2796	-0.0019	-0.0200	0.0403
Var.[a]	0.8249	0.1176	0.0191	0.015	0.0074	0.0063	0.004	0.0019	0.0014	0.001	0.0004	0.0003	0.0003	0.0002	0.0001
Cum var.[b]	0.8249	0.9425	0.9616	0.9766	0.9840	0.9903	0.9944	0.9963	0.9977	0.9987	0.9991	0.9994	0.9996	0.9998	0.9999

Note: Units of logit ($_nq_x$).

[a] Percent of variance explained by the component.

[b] Cumulative percent of variance explained by the component(s).

Figure 7.2. First five principal components of INDEPTH female mortality. The first five principal components explain 98.40% of total variance.

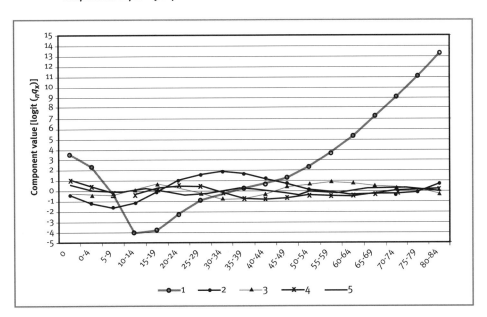

The primary component crosses the *x*-axis between ages 5 and 9 years and again between ages 30 and 34 years, with the result that as the coefficient of the primary component increases, child and adult mortality increases while the mortality of teenagers and young adults decreases. Consequently, the first coefficient determines the ratio of child and adult mortality to teenage and young-adult mortality. This is likely due to the fact that mortality of the very young and elderly is more sensitive to adverse (or advantageous) conditions than the mortality of the generally healthy and robust teenagers and young adults.[6] Naturally then, this balance accounts for a great deal of the variation in the data and is therefore encoded in the first component. Remember that the overall level of mortality is governed by the value of the constant term in equation [7.2], so the coefficient of the first component is really only responsible for the age balance, not for the absolute level of mortality at any age.

Female

The first 15 principal components of INDEPTH female mortality are contained in Table 7.4, and the first 5 components are shown in Figure 7.2. In broad terms they are very similar to the male components. However, the primary component contains a significant positive bulge between ages 20 and 44 years, which is absent on the male primary component (see Figure 7.3). The most likely explanation for this is that it accounts for the maternal mortality experienced in the female population. Additionally, the second component describes a somewhat narrower, younger pattern of deviation that at its peak is of slightly greater magnitude than that for the males (see Figure 7.4). This likely results from the general fact that the effect of AIDS on female mortality occurs at a younger and more focused age than its effect on male mortality.

---

[6] It is also worth noting that the impact of the first component is not constant with age: when the value of the first component is close to zero, the absolute impact is much smaller than when the value of the first component is more distant from zero. An examination of the curve reveals that the absolute effect of the first component increases significantly with age past 39 years.

The third and fourth components are virtually identical for males and females, except at older ages. The data for older ages will not be interpreted, because they are more likely to be inaccurate and the differences are large only for the oldest ages.

Male and female principal components contrasted

Figures 7.3–7.6 plot the first four principal components of INDEPTH mortality for the males and females together, to clearly demonstrate the differences between the male and female components. These differences are discussed briefly above.

To examine the generality of the INDEPTH components of mortality, the existing CD and UN model mortality patterns (at levels corresponding to a life expectancy at birth of 55 years) were regressed against the INDEPTH components of mortality in a simple linear ordinary least-squares regression. The regressions were run against all 15 of the INDEPTH components, the first 10, and finally the first 5. In each case, the fit statistics were examined and the predicted mortality patterns were calculated and visually compared with the fit patterns. Table 7.5 displays the R^2 fit statistic for those regressions. Using all 15 components produces near-perfect fits that are able to faithfully reproduce the existing patterns in all respects. Reducing the number of components used has the expected effect of reducing the quality of the overall fit and failing to correctly model the high-frequency variation in the model patterns. Using 10 components still produces a very reasonable fit, and using 5 or 6 components is acceptable in most circumstances; however, with a small number of components, a substantial "smoothing" occurs, as a result of the lack of high-frequency components. This is actually useful if the aim is to capture the fundamental shape of the mortality curve or if the data are "dirty" and the analyst needs the data to fit the basic shape but can ignore the smaller bumps and dips, which may be meaningless.

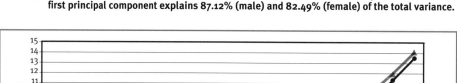

Figure 7.3. First principal component of INDEPTH male mortality and female mortality contrasted. The first principal component explains 87.12% (male) and 82.49% (female) of the total variance.

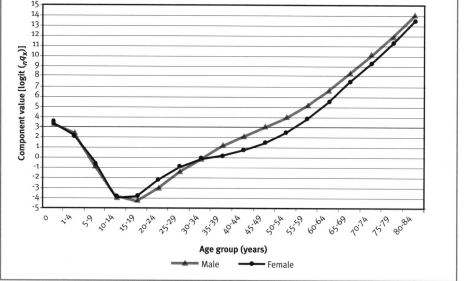

Figure 7.4. Second principal component of INDEPTH male mortality and female mortality contrasted. The second principal component explains 8.89% (male) and 11.76% (female) of the total variance.

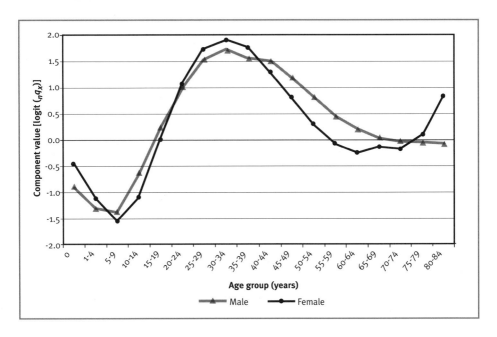

Figure 7.5. Third principal component of INDEPTH male mortality and female mortality contrasted. The third principal component explains 1.53% (male) and 1.91% (female) of the total variance.

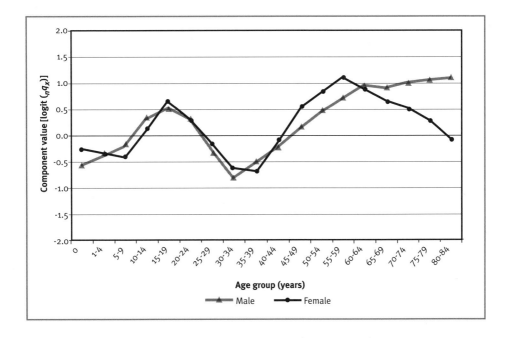

Figure 7.6. Fourth principal component of INDEPTH male mortality and female mortality contrasted. The fourth principal component explains 0.77% (male) and 1.50% (female) of the total variance.

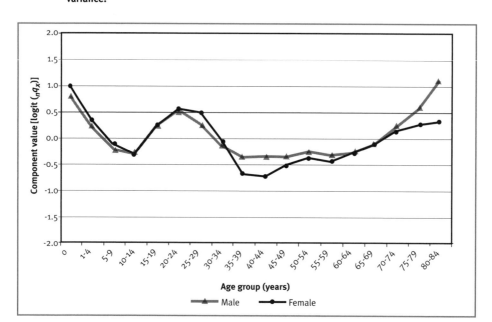

INDEPTH mortality patterns

The overall aim of this work is to identify common age patterns of mortality in the INDEPTH data. The resulting patterns provide a distilled representation of the important mortality conditions experienced by the populations from which the data were collected. Moreover, some understanding of the age patterns of mortality in Africa, based on empirical data from Africa, is invaluable to demographers and planners of all kinds, who must account for present and future mortality in much of their work.

Component-clustering method

The most critical task in identifying the common underlying mortality patterns is to identify clusters of similar patterns — in this case, clusters of site–periods with similar age patterns of mortality. This is a particularly difficult exercise that necessarily involves some subjective input from the analyst.

A given **age** pattern of mortality can be observed at various **levels** resulting from the fact that there may be causes of mortality that affect all ages in roughly the same way and consequently do not produce an age pattern. Given that, mortality schedules may cluster along two dimensions: age pattern and level. The age pattern of a mortality schedule contains a lot of information regarding the epidemiological profile of the population and is consequently of primary interest here.

One of the substantial advantages of the component model of mortality is the distilled, parsimonious representation of a mortality pattern that results from regressing it on the components. The vector of regression coefficients contains independent information on the age pattern and level of the mortality schedule. That fact allows the creation of clusters of age patterns without respect to level.

Table 7.5. The R^2 values from linear regressions of existing model mortality patterns on the INDEPTH components.

Model	Male	Female
Fit with first 15 components		
North	0.999 999 77	0.999 956 79
South	0.999 429 47	0.999 041 30
East	0.999 991 92	0.999 997 87
West	0.999 935 68	0.999 872 75
Latin America	0.999 711 66	0.999 081 25
Chile	0.999 993 61	0.999 869 67
South Asia	0.999 841 72	0.999 336 33
Far East	0.999 977 82	0.999 998 68
General	0.999 950 98	0.999 775 79
Fit with first 10 components		
North	0.999 855 85	0.998 970 05
South	0.996 437 55	0.993 827 83
East	0.999 569 20	0.999 577 40
West	0.999 556 50	0.997 920 47
Latin America	0.998 883 54	0.995 959 77
Chile	0.999 496 56	0.999 092 39
South Asia	0.998 156 76	0.996 751 65
Far East	0.999 651 67	0.999 109 22
General	0.999 659 60	0.998 246 04
Fit with first 5 components		
North	0.998 866 69	0.996 337 04
South	0.993 827 70	0.988 258 46
East	0.996 563 74	0.994 030 00
West	0.996 784 75	0.994 526 55
Latin America	0.994 807 25	0.988 185 31
Chile	0.994 486 95	0.980 204 60
South Asia	0.992 722 03	0.983 421 85
Far East	0.996 987 49	0.995 609 08
General	0.996 377 00	0.994 121 56

Source: CD model (North, South, East, West) is from Coale and Demeny (1966); UN model (Latin America, Chile, South Asia, Far East, General) is from United Nations (1982).

To create the age-pattern clusters, all 70 of the INDEPTH mortality schedules for both males and females are regressed against the appropriate sex-specific components of INDEPTH mortality. The coefficients corresponding to the first 4 principal components are retained, and the other 11 plus the constant are discarded. The first four principal components account for 98.32% of the variation in the male data and 97.66% of the variation in the female data, making them sufficient to capture all but the finest nuances in the age pattern of mortality. These form a collection of 70 4 × 1 coefficient vectors for each sex.

The agglomerative hierarchical clustering algorithm provided with the S-PLUS 2000 Professional statistical software package (release 3) is used to identify clusters of similar coefficient vectors for each sex.[7] The Ward method used here is described by the provider of the software as follows (MathSoft Inc. 1999, p. 102):

> The basic hierarchical agglomerative algorithm starts with each object in a separate group. At each iteration it merges two groups to form a new group; the merger chosen is the one that leads to the smallest increase in the sum of within-group sums of squares. The number of iterations is equal to the number of objects minus one, and at the end all the objects are together in a single group.

[7] S-Plus's "agnes" routine was used with options: metric = euclidean, standardize = true, and linkage type = word.

Table 7.6. INDEPTH mortality age-pattern clusters

	Male			Female	
ID	Site–period	Pattern	ID	Site–period	Pattern
26	Bandafassi, Senegal: 1980–84	1	26	Bandafassi, Senegal: 1980–84	1
27	Bandafassi, Senegal: 1985–87	1	27	Bandafassi, Senegal: 1985–87	1
28	Bandafassi, Senegal: 1988–90	1	28	Bandafassi, Senegal: 1988–90	1
29	Bandafassi, Senegal: 1991–93	1	29	Bandafassi, Senegal: 1991–93	1
30	Bandafassi, Senegal: 1994–96	1	30	Bandafassi, Senegal: 1994–96	1
31	Bandafassi, Senegal: 1997–99	1	31	Bandafassi, Senegal: 1997–99	1
36	Butajira, Ethiopia: 1987–89	1	32	Bandim, Guinea-Bissau: 1990–91	1
37	Butajira, Ethiopia: 1990–91	1	40	Oubritenga, Burkina Faso: 1994–95	1
38	Butajira, Ethiopia: 1992–93	1	41	Oubritenga, Burkina Faso: 1996–98	1
39	Butajira, Ethiopia: 1994–96	1	43	Farafenni, The Gambia: 1996–97	1
40	Oubritenga, Burkina Faso: 1994–95	1	44	Farafenni, The Gambia: 1998–99	1
47	Gwembe, Zambia: 1984–86	1	45	Gwembe, Zambia: 1950–80	1
65	Niakhar, Senegal: 1985–89	1	49	Gwembe, Zambia: 1990–92	1
66	Niakhar, Senegal: 1990–94	1	50	Gwembe, Zambia: 1993–95	1
67	Niakhar, Senegal: 1995–98	1	51	Ifakara, Tanzania: 1997–99	1
69	Nouna, Burkina Faso: 1996–98	1	52	Manhiça, Mozambique: 1998–99	1
54	Matlab comp.,[a] Bangladesh: 1998	2	65	Niakhar, Senegal: 1985–89	1
55	Matlab treat.,[b] Bangladesh: 1988	2	66	Niakhar, Senegal: 1990–94	1
56	Matlab treat.,[b] Bangladesh: 1998	2	67	Niakhar, Senegal: 1995–98	1
59	Mlomp, Senegal: 1991–93	2	70	Rufiji, Tanzania: 1999	1
60	Mlomp, Senegal: 1994–96	2	53	Matlab comp.,[a] Bangladesh: 1988	2
1	Agincourt, South Africa: 1992–93	3	54	Matlab comp.,[a] Bangladesh: 1998	2
2	Agincourt, South Africa: 1994–95	3	55	Matlab treat.,[b] Bangladesh: 1988	2
3	Agincourt, South Africa: 1996–97	3	56	Matlab treat.,[b] Bangladesh: 1998	2
11	Dar es Salaam, Tanzania: 1998–99	3	57	Mlomp, Senegal: 1985–87	2
35	Bandim, Guinea-Bissau: 1996–97	3	61	Mlomp, Senegal: 1997–99	2
5	Dar es Salaam, Tanzania: 1992–93	4	2	Agincourt, South Africa: 1994–95	3
32	Bandim, Guinea-Bissau: 1990–91	4	3	Agincourt, South Africa: 1996–97	3
33	Bandim, Guinea-Bissau: 1992–93	4	4	Agincourt, South Africa: 1998–99	3
34	Bandim, Guinea-Bissau: 1994–95	4	7	Dar es Salaam, Tanzania: 1994–95	3
42	Farafenni, The Gambia: 1994–95	4	8	Dar es Salaam, Tanzania: 1995–96	3
43	Farafenni, The Gambia: 1996–97	4	9	Dar es Salaam, Tanzania: 1996–97	3
44	Farafenni, The Gambia: 1998–99	4	10	Dar es Salaam, Tanzania: 1997–98	3
45	Gwembe, Zambia: 1950–80	4	11	Dar es Salaam, Tanzania: 1998–99	3
46	Gwembe, Zambia: 1981–83	4	35	Bandim, Guinea-Bissau: 1996–97	3
49	Gwembe, Zambia: 1990–92	4	1	Agincourt, South Africa: 1992–93	4
53	Matlab comp.,[a] Bangladesh: 1988	4	33	Bandim, Guinea-Bissau: 1992–93	4
57	Mlomp, Senegal: 1985–87	4	34	Bandim, Guinea-Bissau: 1994–95	4
58	Mlomp, Senegal: 1988–90	4	42	Farafenni, The Gambia: 1994–95	4
61	Mlomp, Senegal: 1997–99	4	62	Navrongo, Ghana: 1993–95	4
62	Navrongo, Ghana: 1993–95	4	63	Navrongo, Ghana: 1996–97	4
63	Navrongo, Ghana: 1996–97	4	64	Navrongo, Ghana: 1998–99	4
64	Navrongo, Ghana: 1998–99	4	68	Nouna, Burkina Faso: 1993–95	4
68	Nouna, Burkina Faso: 1993–95	4	5	Dar es Salaam, Tanzania: 1992–93	5
70	Rufiji, Tanzania: 1999	4	6	Dar es Salaam, Tanzania: 1993–94	5
4	Agincourt, South Africa: 1998–99	5	12	Hai, Tanzania: 1992–93	5
6	Dar es Salaam, Tanzania: 1993–94	5	13	Hai, Tanzania: 1993–94	5
7	Dar es Salaam, Tanzania: 1994–95	5	14	Hai, Tanzania: 1994–95	5
8	Dar es Salaam, Tanzania: 1995–96	5	15	Hai, Tanzania: 1995–96	5
9	Dar es Salaam, Tanzania: 1996–97	5	16	Hai, Tanzania: 1996–97	5
10	Dar es Salaam, Tanzania: 1997–98	5	17	Hai, Tanzania: 1997–98	5
12	Hai, Tanzania: 1992–93	5	18	Hai, Tanzania: 1998–99	5
13	Hai, Tanzania: 1993–94	5	19	Morogoro, Tanzania: 1992–93	5
14	Hai, Tanzania: 1994–95	5	20	Morogoro, Tanzania: 1993–94	5
15	Hai, Tanzania: 1995–96	5	21	Morogoro, Tanzania: 1994–95	5
16	Hai, Tanzania: 1996–97	5	22	Morogoro, Tanzania: 1995–96	5
17	Hai, Tanzania: 1997–98	5	23	Morogoro, Tanzania: 1996–97	5
18	Hai, Tanzania: 1998–99	5	24	Morogoro, Tanzania: 1997–98	5
19	Morogoro, Tanzania: 1992–93	5	25	Morogoro, Tanzania: 1998–99	5

(continued)

Table 7.6. *(concluded)*

Male			Female		
ID	Site–period	Pattern	ID	Site–period	Pattern
20	Morogoro, Tanzania: 1993–945	5	36	Butajira, Ethiopia: 1987–89	6
21	Morogoro, Tanzania: 1994–95	5	37	Butajira, Ethiopia: 1990–91	6
22	Morogoro, Tanzania: 1995–96	5	38	Butajira, Ethiopia: 1992–93	6
23	Morogoro, Tanzania: 1996–97	5	39	Butajira, Ethiopia: 1994–96	6
24	Morogoro, Tanzania: 1997–98	5	58	Mlomp, Senegal: 1988–90	6
25	Morogoro, Tanzania: 1998–99	5	69	Nouna, Burkina Faso: 1996–98	6
41	Oubritenga, Burkina Faso: 1996–98	5	46	Gwembe, Zambia: 1981–83	7
48	Gwembe, Zambia: 1987–89	5	47	Gwembe, Zambia: 1984–86	7
50	Gwembe, Zambia: 1993–95	5	48	Gwembe, Zambia: 1987–89	7
51	Ifakara, Tanzania: 1997–995	5	59	Mlomp, Senegal: 1991–93	7
52	Manhiça, Mozambique: 1998–99	5	60	Mlomp, Senegal: 1994–96	7

[a] Comparison area.
[b] Treatment area.

Detailed discussions of clustering techniques and this particular algorithm are found in Kaufman and Rousseeuw (1990), Struyf and Hubert (1997), and MathSoft Inc. (1999).[8] This routine was applied separately to the male and female data sets, each consisting of four columns (one for each coefficient described above) and 70 rows (one for each site–period).

Clusters

The method described above identified five robust clusters in the male data and seven robust clusters in the female data, presented in Table 7.6. Because females are subject to the additional risk of maternal mortality, their age patterns are always more complex, and so it is not surprising that two more clusters were identified in the female data. Categorizing the male data into the seven female clusters produces seven male clusters that can be directly compared with the female clusters.

In many cases, periods from the same site are grouped in the same cluster, reassuring us that the clustering algorithm is identifying and grouping fundamentally similar mortality schedules. Where periods from the same site are assigned to various clusters, mortality has been changing significantly over time, and the mortality schedules from two periods are substantially different.

Mortality patterns

After the clusters are identified, a characteristic age pattern of mortality is identified for each cluster. In keeping with the use of the component model of mortality, we then calculate, for each of the 15 coefficients derived from the regression of the individual site–period mortality schedules on the 15 components of INDEPTH mortality, the weighted average across the site–periods in each cluster. The weights used are the person–years of observation in each site–period. This yields the average amount of

---

[8] A number of clustering techniques were applied to both the raw and the transformed data and to the coefficient vectors, including agglomerative hierarchical clustering, partitioning around K-means, partitioning around K-medoids, fuzzy partitioning, and divisive hierarchical clustering. Three different statistical software packages — STATA (StataCorp 1997), S-PLUS (MathSoft Inc. 1999), and MVSP (Multi-Variate Statistical Package [KCS 1998]) — were used, and in each case all of their clustering routines were tried. All of the methods produced essentially the same clusters but differed in the clarity of their output and in how they managed ambiguous cases. The agglomerative hierarchical algorithm provided with S-PLUS was eventually chosen, based on its clear and robust theoretical underpinnings and the fact that its output is easily understood and interpreted. Moreover, it appeared to provide the most robust clusters and the most efficient means of categorizing ambiguous cases.

each of the 15 components and the constant needed for each of the mortality schedules in a given cluster. When these average values are combined with the components through equation [7.2], the result is the weighted average mortality schedule for each cluster. By varying the constant, the analyst can adjust mortality schedules to an arbitrary level, and for convenience's sake, the seven INDEPTH mortality patterns presented in Table 7.7 are adjusted to a level that yields a life expectancy at birth of 55 years. Table 7.7 organizes the male and female patterns into the seven female-derived clusters. This arrangement facilitates comparison of the male and female patterns. The five male-derived patterns are retained when the male data are organized into the female-derived patterns; this simply creates two sets of two slightly redundant male patterns. The author verified this by producing the male patterns based on both the male- and female-derived clusters.

Table 7.7. INDEPTH mortality patterns.

Age (years)	Pattern						
	1	2	3	4	5	6	7
				Male			
0	−1.1821	−1.0939	−1.6252	−1.3192	−1.3260	−1.3778	−1.2170
1–4	−1.3230	−1.4728	−1.7509	−1.4661	−1.5931	−1.3428	−1.3911
5–9	−1.6722	−1.9849	−2.0255	−1.7771	−1.9413	−1.5184	−1.7003
10–14	−2.1807	−2.3702	−2.3544	−2.1811	−2.2056	−1.8187	−2.0821
15–19	−2.2586	−2.5108	−2.2378	−2.2402	−2.1341	−1.8875	−2.1865
20–24	−2.1049	−2.4333	−1.9393	−2.1120	−1.8661	−1.8463	−2.1345
25–29	−1.9047	−2.2779	−1.6891	−1.9157	−1.6286	−1.8062	−2.0705
30–34	−1.7481	−2.1099	−1.5053	−1.7563	−1.4667	−1.7737	−2.0261
35–39	−1.6588	−1.9003	−1.3908	−1.5743	−1.3647	−1.7097	−1.8115
40–44	−1.5905	−1.7467	−1.2490	−1.4380	−1.2778	−1.5853	−1.6832
45–49	−1.4908	−1.5228	−1.1515	−1.3033	−1.2277	−1.4725	−1.4792
50–54	−1.3599	−1.2380	−1.0762	−1.1844	−1.2131	−1.3443	−1.3307
55–59	−1.2138	−0.9758	−0.9546	−1.0316	−1.1841	−1.2052	−1.1678
60–64	−1.0475	−0.7508	−0.7807	−0.8254	−1.0605	−1.0625	−0.8985
65–69	−0.8344	−0.5340	−0.5862	−0.6689	−0.8813	−0.8767	−0.6242
70–74	−0.6132	−0.3143	−0.3531	−0.5276	−0.6934	−0.6775	−0.3279
75–79	−0.3790	−0.0674	−0.1027	−0.3782	−0.4948	−0.4865	−0.1158
80–84	−0.1107	0.2082	0.1747	−0.2005	−0.2477	−0.3257	−0.0226
				Female			
0	−1.1678	−1.0304	−1.4926	−1.2429	−1.2667	−1.4005	−1.1935
1–4	−1.2698	−1.3893	−1.6489	−1.4084	−1.5306	−1.3479	−1.2674
5–9	−1.6070	−1.9119	−1.9691	−1.7526	−1.8930	−1.5252	−1.5658
10–14	−2.1126	−2.3759	−2.3076	−2.1760	−2.1958	−1.8319	−2.1678
15–19	−2.0958	−2.3195	−2.1232	−2.2106	−2.0281	−1.8767	−2.5014
20–24	−1.9525	−2.1988	−1.8469	−2.0725	−1.6854	−1.8322	−2.3502
25–29	−1.8484	−2.1152	−1.6241	−1.9094	−1.4610	−1.7935	−2.1065
30–34	−1.8019	−2.1711	−1.4641	−1.8040	−1.3720	−1.7781	−1.7919
35–39	−1.7623	−2.1811	−1.3715	−1.7224	−1.3793	−1.7215	−1.5495
40–44	−1.7020	−1.9609	−1.3386	−1.6330	−1.4161	−1.6174	−1.5311
45–49	−1.6005	−1.6935	−1.2734	−1.4865	−1.4478	−1.4856	−1.6743
50–54	−1.4831	−1.4249	−1.2305	−1.3010	−1.4333	−1.2875	−1.5927
55–59	−1.3321	−1.1522	−1.0773	−1.0693	−1.3500	−1.1067	−1.4082
60–64	−1.1252	−0.8883	−0.9092	−0.7946	−1.1827	−0.9697	−1.0982
65–69	−0.8707	−0.6080	−0.6508	−0.6352	−0.9797	−0.8405	−0.7822
70–74	−0.6243	−0.3002	−0.4577	−0.4904	−0.7919	−0.7177	−0.5037
75–79	−0.3983	−0.0193	−0.2001	−0.3331	−0.5537	−0.6067	−0.1865
80–84	−0.2084	0.2012	0.1935	−0.1574	−0.2269	−0.4946	0.1573

Note: Units of logit $(_nq_x)$.

Figures 7.7 and 7.8 plot the seven INDEPTH age patterns of mortality for males and females, respectively. Figures 7.9–7.15 compare each of the seven INDEPTH age patterns of mortality for males and females. The patterns are arbitrarily named 1–7,[9] and a discussion of the patterns accompanies the plots.

Figure 7.7. Seven INDEPTH age patterns of mortality for males, adjusted to yield a life expectancy at birth of 55 years.

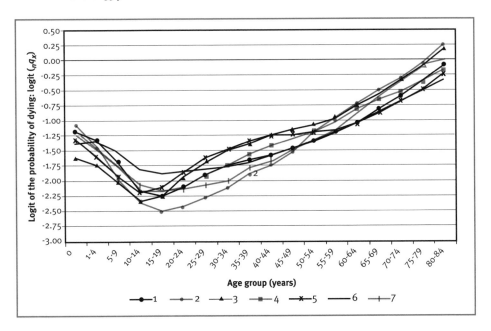

Figure 7.8. Seven INDEPTH age patterns of mortality for females, adjusted to yield a life expectancy at birth of 55 years.

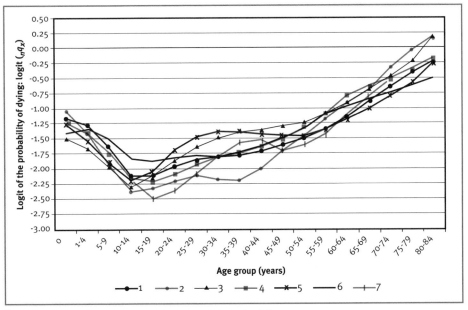

9 This is done to avoid the potential stigmatization from use of more descriptive names.

Figure 7.9. INDEPTH mortality pattern 1, adjusted to yield a life expectancy at birth of 55 years.

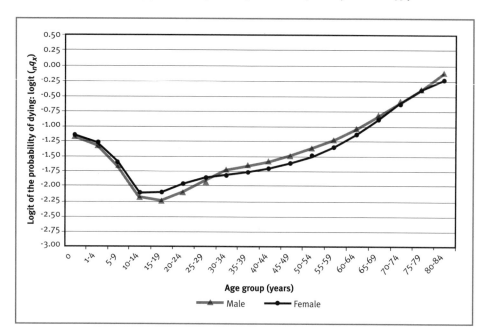

Pattern 1

The first pattern (Figure 7.9) is similar to the CD North and UN Latin American model life-table age patterns of mortality (see "Comparisons with the Coale and Demeny and United Nations model life tables," below). There is no indication that HIV–AIDS affects pattern 1, and the male and female age patterns are similar, with the exception of a bulge in the female pattern during the reproductive years, presumably caused by maternal mortality. Pattern 1 is primarily derived from sites in West Africa over the entire period covered by the INDEPTH data set. HIV–AIDS has not yet become as significant a problem in West Africa as it is in Central and southern Africa, so a large impact of AIDS is not expected to be seen in the data from West Africa. It is worth noting that child mortality between the ages of 1 and 9 is significant and substantially elevated above that shown by the most similar existing models, below. This is in keeping with the fact that malaria is a significant cause of death in West Africa, and it has a large impact on those age groups.

Figure 7.10. INDEPTH mortality pattern 2, adjusted to yield a life expectancy at birth of 55 years.

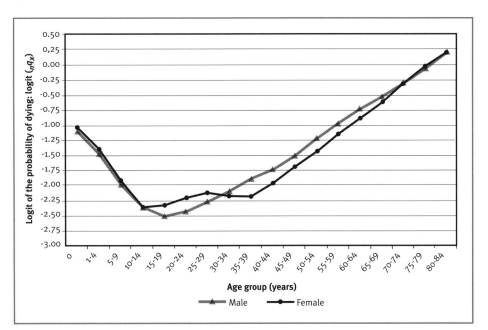

Pattern 2

Pattern 2 (Figure 7.10) is the only pattern to contain significant contributions from Asia, and it is in fact dominated by data from the Matlab project, in Bangladesh. The only other site to contribute data to this pattern is the Mlomp site, in Senegal. Again, the male and female patterns are similar, with the exception of maternal mortality. However, pattern 2 is strikingly different from all of the others in that the mortality of children, teenagers, and young adults is comparatively very low, and correspondingly the mortality of older adults is comparatively high. In keeping with the fact that the data contributing to this pattern come from Bangladesh and Senegal, it is not surprising that there is no evidence at all of an HIV–AIDS impact. Pattern 2 is very similar to the UN South Asia pattern, as it should be, coming largely from South Asia (see below).

Figure 7.11. INDEPTH mortality pattern 3, adjusted to yield a life expectancy at birth of 55 years.

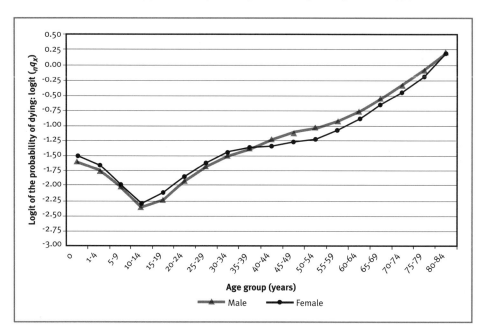

Pattern 3

The sites contributing to pattern 3 (Figure 7.11) are almost exclusively located in southern and East Africa: South Africa and Tanzania in particular. This pattern obviously contains some influence of HIV–AIDS, but not nearly to the degree observed in pattern 5. The South African data come from the Agincourt site, where mortality is extraordinarily low compared with the other INDEPTH sites in Africa and where HIV–AIDS is recognized but not yet impacting the population in the catastrophic way that it is in other parts of southern and East Africa. The remainder of the data come from the Dar es Salaam site, where there appears to be a greater impact of HIV–AIDS. This pattern is most similar to the UN Far East pattern of mortality, corresponding to the fact that infant and child mortality are very low compared with mortality at older ages. A noteworthy feature of this pattern is the fact that infant and child mortality does not appear to be substantially elevated, as might be expected when HIV–AIDS is an important contributor to mortality.

Figure 7.12. INDEPTH mortality pattern 4, adjusted to yield a life expectancy at birth of 55 years.

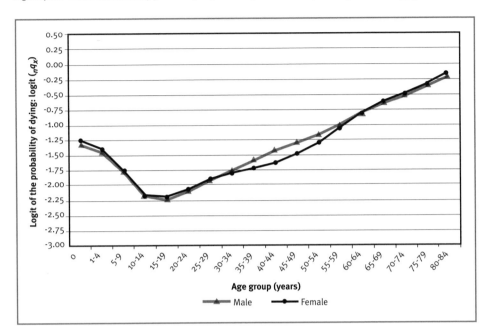

Pattern 4

Pattern 4 (Figure 7.12) is a variation on pattern 1, with the important difference manifested in the 35-69 years age range. At all other ages, patterns 1 and 4 are negligibly different, except that infant and child mortality in pattern 4 is consistently slightly lower than in pattern 1. But between ages 35 and roughly 69 years, pattern 4 reveals significantly higher mortality than pattern 1. This pattern is most similar to the UN General pattern for females and UN Latin America for males. As was the case with pattern 1, most of the data contributing to pattern 4 come from West Africa.

Figure 7.13. INDEPTH mortality pattern 5, adjusted to yield a life expectancy at birth of 55 years.

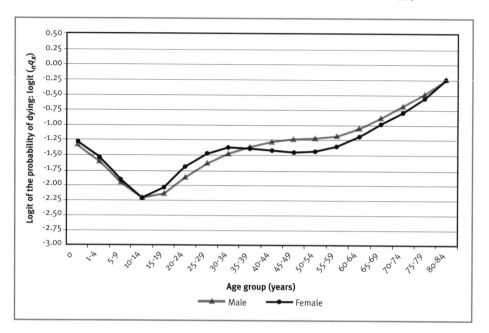

Pattern 5

The HIV–AIDS pattern of mortality is most clearly visible in pattern 5 (Figure 7.13). The data contributing to pattern 5 are derived from the three Tanzanian sites run by the Adult Morbidity and Mortality Project in Dar es Salaam, Hai, and Morogoro. A very striking bulge appears in the mortality of males between the ages of 20 and 54 years and for females between the ages of 15 and 49 years. Additionally, the female bulge is significantly narrower and more pronounced, corresponding to the fact that the female population is infected earlier and within a tighter age range. This pattern is not particularly similar to any of the existing model patterns, but it is most closely matched with the UN General (female) and UN Latin American (male) model patterns. Pattern 5 differs from pattern 3 mainly in the shape of the HIV–AIDS impact. The effect is more diffuse with age in pattern 3, meaning that mortality is elevated through a broader age range, the magnitude of the elevation is more consistent, and the differences between the sexes are less apparent. Pattern 3 is derived largely from the Dar es Salaam data, and this may reflect the fact that the epidemic is more mature in Dar es Salaam and has consequently had enough time to infect a wider age range of people of both sexes. As with pattern 3, it is worth noting that infant and child mortality do not appear to be substantially affected in a manner comparable to adult mortality, and this is in contradiction to what is known about HIV prevalence and vertical transmission. Further investigation is needed to determine why this effect is not prominently measured in these data.

Figure 7.14. INDEPTH mortality pattern 6, adjusted to yield a life expectancy at birth of 55 years.

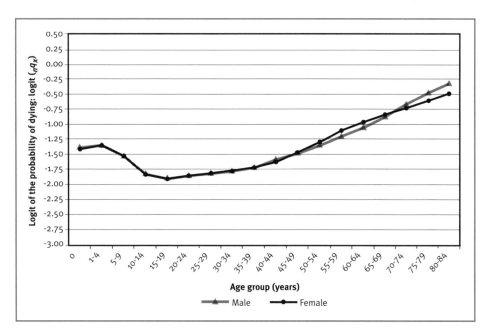

Pattern 6

Pattern 6 (Figure 7.14) is one of the two additional patterns identified in the female data. It is an interesting pattern that reveals very high mortality of children and teenagers, together with comparatively low mortality of infants and adults of all ages. This pattern is exhibited at sites in northeast and West Africa, with most of the data coming from Ethiopia. Without additional information, it is impossible to speculate on what may be producing this unique pattern. The male pattern is most similar to the CD North model pattern, and the female pattern is closest to the CD West model, both of which embody high mortality in the same age ranges. They deviate from those patterns in that infant mortality is substantially lower than would be found in either model pattern, and child and adolescent mortality is significantly higher: this might be called the "Super North" pattern.

Figure 7.15. INDEPTH mortality pattern 7, adjusted to yield a life expectancy at birth of 55 years.

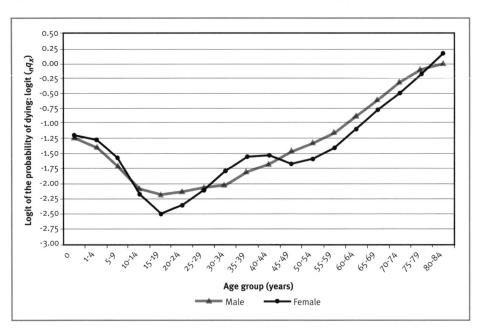

Pattern 7

Pattern 7 (Figure 7.15), the other additional pattern identified in the female data, is also of interest. It is derived from two sites in Central and West Africa. The reason why it was identified in the female data is obvious: a very substantial bulge appears in the female age pattern between ages 25 and 44 years. This most likely results from very serious maternal mortality, the risk of which increases with age. The site in Zambia is a rural site without easy access to modern medical facilities, and this may contribute to an unusual risk of maternal mortality. The corresponding male pattern is similar to pattern 6, and both are similar to the CD North model pattern. The CD North model pattern contains higher child and teenage mortality, coupled with comparatively low mortality at older ages. This is consistent with the fact that malaria is an important contributor to mortality at both sites.

Comparisons with the Coale and Demeny and United Nations model life tables

The INDEPTH mortality patterns are explicitly compared with the existing CD and UN models to ensure that they are indeed new patterns and to demonstrate exactly how they differ from the existing model mortality patterns. The method used is a simple minimum sum of squared differences. Each INDEPTH mortality pattern is compared with all of the existing CD and UN model mortality patterns: CD patterns North, South, East, and West; and UN patterns Latin America, Chile, South Asia, Far East, and General. For each pair of patterns, the difference between the two is calculated for each age group, and those differences are squared and summed to yield the sum (over all ages) of the squared differences (SSD) between the two patterns. For each INDEPTH pattern, the SDDs derived from the seven comparisons are ranked, and the members of the pair with the smallest SDD are considered to be most similar. All of the mortality patterns used in the comparisons are adjusted to a level corresponding to an life expectancy at birth of 55 years.[10] The SDDs are presented in Table 7.8, where both the minimum and the next greater SDDs for each comparison are identified.

For each INDEPTH pattern, the age-specific deviations from the closest fit existing model pattern are calculated and presented in Figures 7.16 and 7.17. Those figures clearly reveal that all of the INDEPTH patterns are systematically different from the existing model mortality patterns. Both figures reveal clear peaks in the deviations for children (1-14 years) and young to middle-aged adults (25-49 years). Interestingly, infant and child mortality between the ages of 1 and 4 years is generally lower than the corresponding pattern. The peak in the deviations during childhood may be due to malaria and other diseases that have a large impact on children in Africa but not elsewhere in the world, and it is clear that continued investigation is needed to identify all of the factors contributing to childhood deviations. The peak during the adult years is most pronounced for patterns 3 and 5, which are the two patterns affected by HIV–AIDS, and it is reasonable to assume that this peak is primarily due to the impact of HIV–AIDS. It is curious to note that infant and child mortality in patterns 3 and 5 does not appear to be elevated in a manner corresponding to the increase in adult mortality. This suggests that the HIV–AIDS epidemic does not have an enormous impact on infant and child mortality or that all of the data used to generate patterns 3 and 5 are defective with regard to infants and children. It seems unlikely that all the data would be defective, along with being defective to the same degree, and this points to the need for considerable investigation of the impact of HIV–AIDS on infant and child mortality.

Table 7.8. Sum of squared differences comparing INDEPTH and existing mortality patterns.

Pattern	North	South	East	West	LA	CH	SA	FE	GL
					Model				
					Male				
1	**0.2670**	0.5550	0.7599	0.6035	*0.3111*	1.1682	0.8744	1.6724	0.6458
2	1.3819	0.6787	*0.6538*	0.9190	0.8760	1.0439	**0.2265**	1.1394	0.6918
3	1.1060	1.6448	1.2875	0.8313	1.0938	0.9075	2.3094	**0.5066**	*0.7774*
4	*0.4041*	0.7742	0.7219	0.4561	**0.3640**	0.8273	1.0159	0.9664	0.4344
5	**0.6760**	1.4443	1.3789	0.8996	*0.7961*	1.1767	2.3346	1.6279	1.0265
6	**0.5118**	1.4451	1.6459	1.2315	*0.9998*	2.2118	2.1365	2.5333	1.4486
7	**0.4017**	0.4548	0.5344	0.4985	*0.4233*	1.1231	0.5451	1.1824	0.4866
					Female				
1	*0.1763*	0.4823	0.4573	0.3666	**0.1727**	0.6523	0.6724	1.0096	0.3428
2	1.4695	1.0966	*0.8080*	1.2731	1.0356	1.0373	**0.4703**	1.4209	0.9744
3	1.4447	2.2012	1.5312	1.0859	1.3253	1.1886	2.4018	**0.4426**	*0.9283*
4	0.4823	1.0188	0.7003	0.4749	*0.3982*	0.6471	1.0570	0.6098	**0.3752**
5	0.7861	1.5676	1.2496	**0.7118**	0.8045	0.9274	2.1636	0.7916	*0.7728*
6	**0.3860**	1.1897	1.2256	*0.7723*	0.7730	1.4854	1.7386	1.6242	0.9320
7	**0.3837**	0.5397	0.4040	0.4859	*0.3905*	0.7709	0.4704	1.0079	0.4050

Source: CD model (North, South, East, West) is from Coale and Demeny (1966); UN model (Latin America, Chile, South Asia, Far East, General) is from United Nations (1982).
Note: CH, Chile; FE, Far East; GL, General; LA, Latin America; SA, South Asia. Bold, minimum; italic, next best.

---

[10] The level of the INDEPTH patterns is set by adjusting the constant term in the component model of morality, and the CD- and UN-model mortality patterns used in the comparisons are generated by the United Nation's computer program for the analysis of mortality data, MortPak-Lite (United Nations 1988), at a level corresponding to a life expectancy at birth of 55 years.

Figure 7.16. Age-specific deviations of INDEPTH male mortality patterns from those of best-fit existing models [logit ($_nq_x$)], adjusted to yield a life expectancy at birth of 55 years.

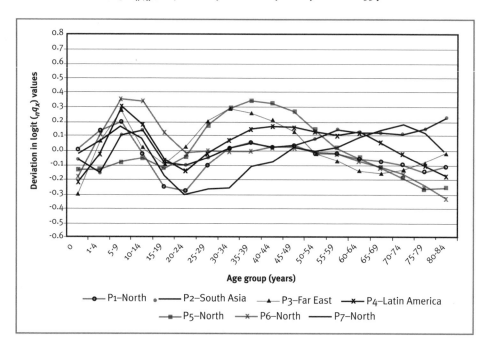

Figure 7.17. Age-specific deviations of INDEPTH female mortality patterns from those of best-fit existing models [logit ($_nq_x$)], adjusted to yield a life expectancy at birth of 55 years.

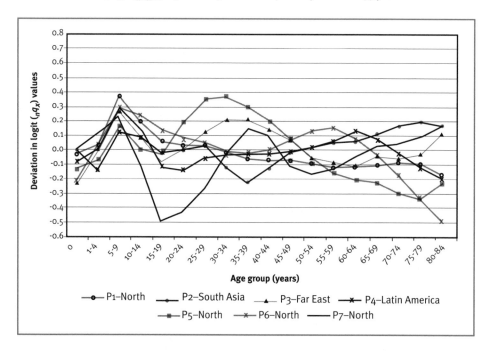

Demonstration of the HIV–AIDS model life-table system

Model life-table construction

The component model of mortality is capable of generating (and fitting) a very wide range of arbitrary mortality patterns. This makes it particularly well-suited for the creation of model life tables. To demonstrate how the component model can be used to create a set of model life tables, we use the INDEPTH mortality components to isolate (in a set of coefficient deviations) the general age pattern of the impact of HIV–AIDS, and then add that impact in increasing quantities to the INDEPTH pattern-1 mortality schedule, thus creating a set of life tables with decreasing life expectancies at birth corresponding to an increasing impact of HIV. The result is a set of life tables with the underlying age pattern defined by INDEPTH pattern 1 but with various levels of HIV–AIDS mortality added to that.

Figures 7.18 and 7.19 display the male and female INDEPTH pattern-5 mortality schedules with and without what is presumed to be the increase in mortality due to HIV–AIDS. Figure 7.20 presents the male INDEPTH pattern-1 mortality with and without an increase in mortality over the infant and childhood ages.[11] In each case, the difference between the two curves is fitted against the first 15 components of mortality (for the appropriate sex) to yield the coefficients presented in Table 7.9.

Figure 7.18. INDEPTH male mortality pattern 5, without and with the presumed increase in mortality due to HIV–AIDS (the HIV–AIDS bulge).

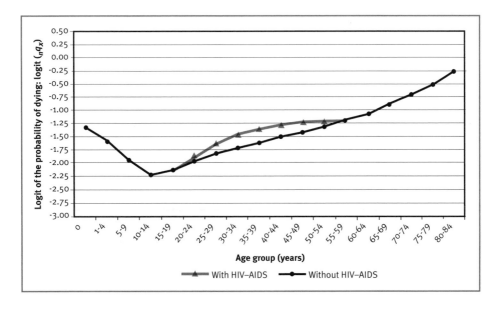

---

[11] There is no empirical pattern used to create the increase in infant and child mortality. It is simply created so that it could be included in the model life tables.

Figure 7.19. INDEPTH female mortality pattern 5, without and with the presumed increase in mortality due to HIV–AIDS (the HIV–AIDS bulge).

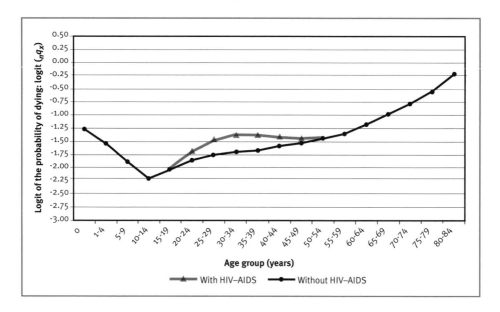

Figure 7.20. INDEPTH male mortality pattern 1, with and without HIV–AIDS mortality for infants and children.

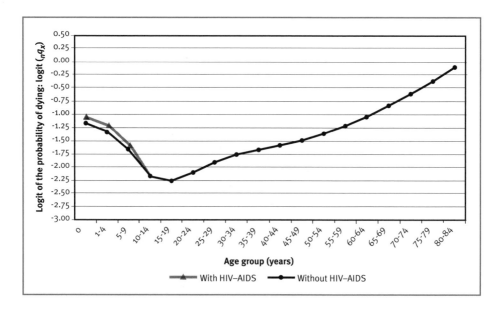

Table 7.9. Coefficient values estimated in fit of HIV-derived deviations in logit ($_n q_x$) on the mortality components.

Component	Fit of adult deviations		Fit of child deviations	
	Male	Female	Male	Female
1	0.001 794	−0.004 217	−0.002 822	−0.003 926
2	0.069 515	0.086 812	0.030 939	0.024 063
3	−0.087 825	−0.093 468	0.048 722	0.046 546
4	−0.046 538	0.007 340	−0.030 034	−0.033 062
5	0.014 998	−0.053 602	−0.002 600	0.017 291
6	0.007 024	0.071 480	−0.042 015	0.044 176
7	0.057 843	−0.026 918	−0.001 601	0.029 769
8	0.067 342	0.011 817	0.015 266	−0.036 031
9	−0.035 387	0.055 790	−0.012 263	0.029 199
10	−0.030 752	0.070 519	0.028 062	0.006 903
11	−0.048 241	0.037 762	−0.013 452	0.043 736
12	0.040 329	−0.028 917	−0.001 339	−0.004 031
13	0.003 209	0.082 885	0.032 003	0.025 621
14	0.091 293	0.089 362	0.050 373	−0.013 287
15	0.126 678	−0.048 030	−0.008 452	0.030 330
Constant	0.062 364	0.079 854	−0.030 420	−0.028 344

The model life tables are constructed to produce a family of life tables with the underlying mortality of INDEPTH pattern-1 mortality. The HIV–AIDS pattern of mortality is added to each of the members of the family in amounts sufficient to reduce the life expectancy at birth in 5-year increments. Equation [7.5] is a simple extension of the component model of mortality that describes the relationship used to accomplish this. In this case, the $(n + 1) \times 1$ vector d' of HIV–AIDS coefficient deviations is multiplied by α and added to the $(n + 1) \times 1$ vector of coefficients, a'.[12] The scaling factor α determines how much of the HIV–AIDS pattern to add to the basic pattern of mortality represented by the vector of coefficients, a'. Once that addition has been accomplished, the resulting vector is premultiplied by the matrix of components C' to yield the logit-transformed probabilities of dying, logit ($_n q_x$). The relationship governing the HIV-augmented model life table is given by the following equation:

$$m = C'(a' + \alpha d')$$ [7.5]

where m, C', a', α, and d' are as defined above. Expanding this around the row for the 20–24 age group reveals

$$\begin{bmatrix} \vdots \\ \text{logit}(_5 q_{20}) \\ \vdots \end{bmatrix} = \begin{bmatrix} \vdots \\ _5 C_{20}^i \cdot (a_i + \alpha \cdot d_i) \\ \vdots \end{bmatrix} + \ldots + \begin{bmatrix} \vdots \\ _5 C_{20}^n \cdot (a_n + \alpha \cdot d_n) \\ \vdots \end{bmatrix} + \begin{bmatrix} \vdots \\ 1 \cdot (a_c + \alpha \cdot d_c) \\ \vdots \end{bmatrix}$$

---

[12] Remember that the prime (′) indicates that the matrices and vectors include the column and row needed to store the constant and its coefficient. Also, n is the number of components used, and g is the number of age groups.

where $_5C_{20}^i$ is the value of the ith component for the 20–24 age group; a_i is the value of the coefficient on the ith component; α is a single scalar applied to the vector of coefficient deviations; d_i is the coefficient deviation for the ith component; a_c is the constant term, which takes the same value for all age groups; and d_c is the deviation for the constant term. Each of the column vectors contains g elements, one for each age group.

Once the logit $(_nq_x)$ values have been calculated, the inverse logit produces values for $_nq_x$ to be substituted into a life table and used to calculate its other columns, including life expectancy. The model life tables are calculated through an iterative, target-seeking process that varies α until the desired value for the life expectancy is attained (see Figures 7A.1–7A6 and Tables 7A.1–7A.4 in the Annex).

Conclusion

Data describing mortality at 19 sites in Africa and Asia are used to identify seven new age patterns of mortality, six of which originate solely from Africa. A component model of mortality is constructed from the raw data and used to identify clusters of similar age patterns of mortality, and these patterns are compared with the existing CD and UN model life-table age patterns of mortality and demonstrated to be systematically and individually different from the existing models. This finding supports the notion that unique age patterns of mortality occur in Africa and that routine demographic and epidemiological estimations calculated from African data must take this into account. To make these data useful to practicing demographers and epidemiologists, a set of model life tables based on these patterns must be constructed. INDEPTH is pursuing the construction of a set of INDEPTH model life tables for Africa, using the component model of mortality and based on the age patterns of mortality presented here.

ANNEX: AIDS-DECREMENTED MODEL LIFE TABLES

Figure 7A.1. Male life-table probability of dying ($_nq_x$), decreased by AIDS mortality in 5-year increments (initial life expectancy at birth, 45 years).

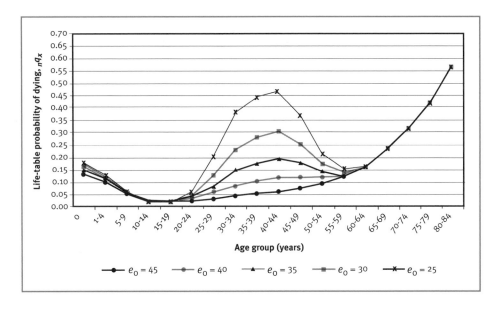

Figure 7A.2. Female life-table probability of dying ($_nq_x$), decreased by AIDS mortality in 5-year increments (initial life expectancy at birth, 45 years).

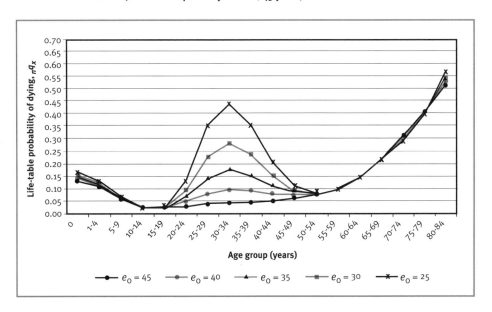

Figure 7A.3. Male life-table probability of surviving (P_x), decreased by AIDS mortality in 5-year increments (initial life expectancy at birth, 45 years).

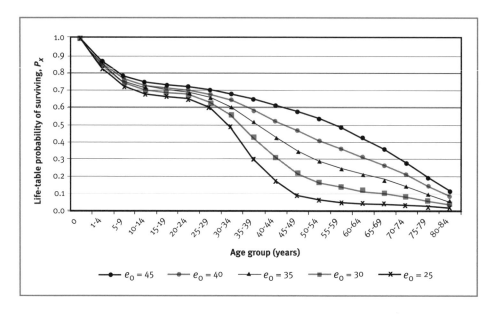

Figure 7A.4. Female life-table probability of surviving (P_x), decreased by AIDS mortality in 5-year increments (initial life expectancy at birth, 45 years).

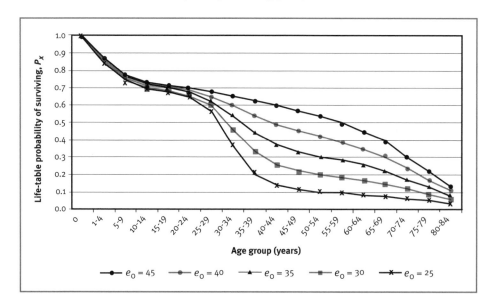

Figure 7A.5. Male life expectancy (e_x, or average remaining lifetime for a person who survives to the beginning of the indicated age interval), decreased by AIDS mortality in 5-year increments (initial life expectancy at birth, 45 years).

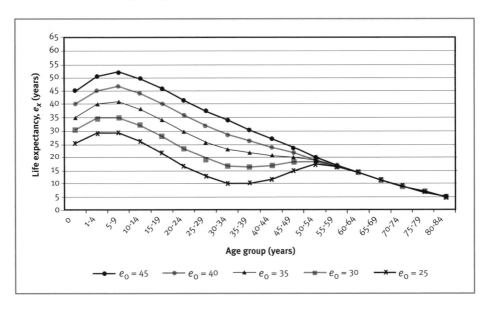

Figure 7A.6. Female life expectancy (e_x, or average remaining lifetime for a person who survives to the beginning of the indicated age interval), decreased by AIDS mortality in 5-year increments (initial life expectancy at birth, 45 years).

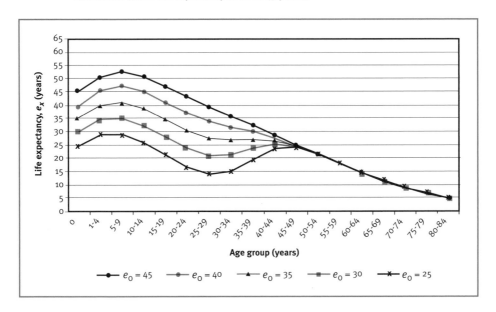

Table 7A.1. Model life tables for INDEPTH pattern 1: life expectancy of 60.0 years decremented by HIV–AIDS mortality.

$_nq_x$

Age (years)	Male					Female				
	0.0	5.0	10.0	15.0	20.0	0.0	5.0	10.0	15.0	20.0
0	0.068 354	0.076 013	0.081 963	0.087 230	0.092 413	0.070 648	0.076 841	0.081 025	0.084 427	0.087 546
1–4	0.051 414	0.055 626	0.058 835	0.061 634	0.064 355	0.057 153	0.061 250	0.063 991	0.066 204	0.068 222
5–9	0.026 085	0.027 408	0.028 394	0.029 240	0.030 051	0.030 118	0.031 523	0.032 448	0.033 187	0.033 854
10–14	0.010 159	0.010 162	0.010 164	0.010 165	0.010 167	0.011 862	0.011 849	0.011 840	0.011 834	0.011 828
15–19	0.008 511	0.009 057	0.009 469	0.009 825	0.010 169	0.011 452	0.012 871	0.013 861	0.014 683	0.015 450
20–24	0.011 362	0.015 591	0.019 531	0.023 537	0.027 986	0.015 359	0.027 156	0.038 818	0.051 094	0.064 944
25–29	0.016 697	0.030 949	0.047 772	0.068 061	0.093 905	0.018 947	0.048 985	0.087 589	0.134 870	0.193 185
30–34	0.022 747	0.049 920	0.085 953	0.132 372	0.193 248	0.021 038	0.059 561	0.111 710	0.176 657	0.256 096
35–39	0.027 520	0.061 020	0.105 336	0.161 762	0.234 230	0.022 694	0.054 981	0.094 380	0.140 965	0.196 943
40–44	0.031 406	0.068 631	0.117 010	0.177 538	0.253 830	0.025 472	0.045 196	0.064 552	0.084 710	0.107 149
45–49	0.038 409	0.069 160	0.103 772	0.143 428	0.191 043	0.030 371	0.038 020	0.043 802	0.048 876	0.053 829
50–54	0.048 610	0.064 737	0.079 184	0.093 381	0.108 628	0.038 946	0.041 139	0.042 592	0.043 757	0.044 813
55–59	0.063 546	0.068 230	0.071 772	0.074 846	0.077 819	0.051 958	0.051 479	0.051 178	0.050 944	0.050 738
60–64	0.087 337	0.087 156	0.087 026	0.086 919	0.086 818	0.076 859	0.076 105	0.075 630	0.075 262	0.074 937
65–69	0.129 704	0.130 249	0.130 641	0.130 967	0.131 271	0.121 951	0.120 671	0.119 865	0.119 240	0.118 690
70–74	0.186 536	0.185 707	0.185 117	0.184 626	0.184 170	0.180 792	0.175 174	0.171 681	0.168 998	0.166 653
75–79	0.265 402	0.262 574	0.260 564	0.258 900	0.257 356	0.254 473	0.251 341	0.249 368	0.247 837	0.246 489
80–84	0.384 085	0.385 585	0.386 658	0.387 551	0.388 385	0.343 509	0.361 047	0.372 376	0.381 299	0.389 263

P_x

Age (years)	Male					Female				
	0.0	5.0	10.0	15.0	20.0	0.0	5.0	10.0	15.0	20.0
0	1.000 000	1.000 000	1.000 000	1.000 000	1.000 000	1.000 000	1.000 000	1.000 000	1.000 000	1.000 000
1–4	0.931 646	0.923 987	0.918 037	0.912 770	0.907 587	0.929 352	0.923 159	0.918 975	0.915 573	0.912 454
5–9	0.883 747	0.872 589	0.864 024	0.856 513	0.849 180	0.876 236	0.866 616	0.860 169	0.854 958	0.850 205
10–14	0.860 695	0.848 673	0.839 491	0.831 468	0.823 661	0.849 846	0.839 297	0.832 258	0.826 585	0.821 422
15–19	0.851 951	0.840 049	0.830 959	0.823 016	0.815 287	0.839 765	0.829 352	0.822 403	0.816 803	0.811 707
20–24	0.844 700	0.832 441	0.823 091	0.814 930	0.806 996	0.830 148	0.818 677	0.811 004	0.804 810	0.799 166
25–29	0.835 103	0.819 462	0.807 015	0.795 749	0.784 412	0.817 397	0.796 445	0.779 523	0.763 690	0.747 265
30–34	0.821 160	0.794 100	0.768 462	0.741 590	0.710 751	0.801 910	0.757 431	0.711 246	0.660 691	0.602 905
35–39	0.802 481	0.754 459	0.702 410	0.643 424	0.573 400	0.785 039	0.712 318	0.631 793	0.543 975	0.448 503
40–44	0.780 396	0.708 421	0.628 421	0.539 342	0.439 092	0.767 223	0.673 154	0.572 164	0.467 294	0.360 173
45–49	0.755 887	0.659 802	0.554 890	0.443 589	0.327 637	0.747 681	0.642 730	0.535 230	0.427 709	0.321 581
50–54	0.726 854	0.614 170	0.497 308	0.379 966	0.265 045	0.724 973	0.618 293	0.511 786	0.406 804	0.304 271
55–59	0.691 522	0.574 411	0.457 929	0.344 484	0.236 253	0.696 739	0.592 857	0.489 988	0.389 004	0.290 636

Age	60.00	55.00	50.00	45.00	40.00	60.00	55.00	50.00	45.00	40.00
60–64	0.647 578	0.535 218	0.425 062	0.318 701	0.217 868	0.660 537	0.562 337	0.464 912	0.369 186	0.275 889
65–69	0.591 020	0.488 571	0.388 071	0.291 000	0.198 953	0.609 769	0.519 541	0.429 751	0.341 401	0.255 215
70–74	0.514 363	0.424 935	0.337 373	0.252 889	0.172 837	0.535 408	0.456 847	0.378 239	0.300 692	0.224 924
75–79	0.418 415	0.346 021	0.274 920	0.206 199	0.141 005	0.438 610	0.376 819	0.313 302	0.249 876	0.187 440
80–84	0.307 367	0.255 165	0.203 285	0.152 814	0.104 717	0.326 996	0.282 109	0.235 175	0.187 947	0.141 238

e_x (years)

Age	60.00	55.00	50.00	45.00	40.00	60.00	55.00	50.00	45.00	40.00
0	60.00	55.00	50.00	45.00	40.00	60.00	55.00	50.00	45.00	40.00
1–4	58.48	53.42	48.25	43.02		63.52	58.54	53.36	48.10	42.79
5–9	57.81	52.63	47.29	41.84		63.25	58.23	52.88	47.37	41.78
10–14	54.37	49.10	43.64	38.06		60.14	55.04	49.57	43.91	38.15
15–19	49.90	44.58	39.06	33.43		55.83	50.67	45.13	39.41	33.58
20–24	45.33	39.98	34.43	28.75		51.45	46.30	40.73	34.96	29.07
25–29	41.01	35.73	30.19	24.50		47.21	42.52	37.27	31.71	25.91
30–34	37.24	32.39	27.22	21.78		43.08	39.58	35.61	31.26	26.52
35–39	34.07	30.20	25.99	21.40		38.95	36.93	34.77	32.43	29.79
40–44	31.12	28.47	25.52	22.18		34.79	33.93	33.14	32.34	31.48
45–49	28.23	26.91	25.49	23.88		30.64	30.42	30.25	30.10	29.96
50–54	25.14	24.73	24.34	23.92		26.52	26.52	26.52	26.52	26.52
55–59	21.71	21.64	21.59	21.54		22.49	22.55	22.59	22.62	22.64
60–64	18.11	18.13	18.13	18.14		18.59	18.64	18.68	18.70	18.72
65–69	14.61	14.61	14.62	14.63		14.93	14.97	15.00	15.02	15.04
70–74	11.42	11.44	11.45	11.46		11.65	11.68	11.70	11.71	11.72
75–79	8.45	8.46	8.47	8.48		8.67	8.64	8.61	8.59	8.57
80–84	5.57	5.57	5.56	5.56		5.78	5.69	5.64	5.59	5.55

Note: e_0, life expectancy at birth (number of years a child is expected to live as calculated at the time of birth); P_x, probability of surviving at age x; e_x, life expectancy at age x; $_nq_x$, probability of dying between ages x and $x+n$.

Table 7A.2. Model life tables for INDEPTH pattern 1: life expectancy of 55.0 years decremented by HIV–AIDS mortality.

$_nq_x$

Age (years)	Male					Female				
	Reduction in e_0 (years)									
	0.0	5.0	10.0	15.0	20.0	0.0	5.0	10.0	15.0	20.0
0	0.086 457	0.095 211	0.102 372	0.109 000	0.115 902	0.088 792	0.095 816	0.100 835	0.105 077	0.109 142
1–4	0.065 345	0.070 215	0.074 132	0.077 708	0.081 390	0.072 101	0.076 786	0.080 106	0.082 896	0.085 555
5–9	0.033 394	0.034 950	0.036 176	0.037 278	0.038 398	0.038 281	0.039 916	0.041 057	0.042 006	0.042 903
10–14	0.013 065	0.013 069	0.013 071	0.013 074	0.013 076	0.015 155	0.015 139	0.015 129	0.015 120	0.015 112
15–19	0.010 951	0.011 599	0.012 116	0.012 585	0.013 065	0.014 633	0.016 296	0.017 522	0.018 584	0.019 622
20–24	0.014 608	0.019 565	0.024 393	0.029 535	0.035 628	0.019 603	0.033 111	0.046 933	0.062 021	0.079 914
25–29	0.021 433	0.037 844	0.057 782	0.082 836	0.116 851	0.024 158	0.057 774	0.101 617	0.156 753	0.227 435
30–34	0.029 149	0.060 017	0.101 670	0.157 114	0.233 660	0.026 809	0.069 618	0.128 095	0.202 532	0.296 503
35–39	0.035 218	0.073 105	0.123 957	0.190 613	0.280 180	0.028 906	0.065 058	0.109 890	0.164 281	0.232 142
40–44	0.040 146	0.082 148	0.137 483	0.208 616	0.302 143	0.032 418	0.054 837	0.077 539	0.101 974	0.130 432
45–49	0.048 998	0.083 893	0.124 091	0.171 658	0.231 688	0.038 600	0.047 420	0.054 425	0.060 814	0.067 345
50–54	0.061 832	0.080 307	0.097 550	0.115 199	0.135 262	0.049 381	0.051 917	0.053 699	0.055 186	0.056 597
55–59	0.080 487	0.085 865	0.090 160	0.094 061	0.098 056	0.065 641	0.065 090	0.064 720	0.064 421	0.064 146
60–64	0.109 876	0.109 669	0.109 513	0.109 377	0.109 242	0.096 432	0.095 576	0.095 001	0.094 538	0.094 110
65–69	0.161 244	0.161 849	0.162 310	0.162 712	0.163 110	0.151 128	0.149 709	0.148 758	0.147 989	0.147 281
70–74	0.228 271	0.227 379	0.226 704	0.226 116	0.225 538	0.220 511	0.214 469	0.210 459	0.207 246	0.204 304
75–79	0.317 886	0.314 969	0.312 765	0.310 851	0.308 969	0.304 365	0.301 131	0.298 958	0.297 202	0.295 583
80–84	0.445 796	0.447 247	0.448 348	0.449 309	0.450 256	0.401 458	0.418 649	0.430 372	0.439 940	0.448 835

P_x

Age (years)	Male					Female				
	0.0	5.0	10.0	15.0	20.0	0.0	5.0	10.0	15.0	20.0
0	1.000 000	1.000 000	1.000 000	1.000 000	1.000 000	1.000 000	1.000 000	1.000 000	1.000 000	1.000 000
1–4	0.913 543	0.904 789	0.897 628	0.891 000	0.884 098	0.911 208	0.904 184	0.899 165	0.894 923	0.890 858
5–9	0.853 847	0.841 259	0.831 085	0.821 762	0.812 141	0.845 509	0.834 755	0.827 136	0.820 738	0.814 640
10–14	0.825 334	0.811 858	0.801 020	0.791 128	0.780 957	0.813 142	0.801 435	0.793 176	0.786 262	0.779 690
15–19	0.814 550	0.801 248	0.790 549	0.780 785	0.770 745	0.800 819	0.789 302	0.781 177	0.774 374	0.767 907
20–24	0.805 630	0.791 954	0.780 971	0.770 959	0.760 675	0.789 101	0.776 440	0.767 489	0.759 983	0.752 839
25–29	0.793 862	0.776 459	0.761 920	0.748 188	0.733 573	0.773 632	0.750 731	0.731 468	0.712 848	0.692 677
30–34	0.776 846	0.747 075	0.717 895	0.686 211	0.647 854	0.754 942	0.707 358	0.657 138	0.601 107	0.535 138
35–39	0.754 202	0.702 238	0.644 907	0.578 398	0.496 476	0.734 703	0.658 114	0.572 962	0.479 363	0.376 468
40–44	0.727 641	0.650 901	0.564 966	0.468 148	0.357 374	0.713 466	0.615 298	0.510 000	0.400 613	0.289 074
45–49	0.698 429	0.597 430	0.487 293	0.370 485	0.249 396	0.690 337	0.581 556	0.470 455	0.359 761	0.251 370
50–54	0.664 207	0.547 310	0.426 824	0.306 888	0.191 614	0.663 690	0.553 979	0.444 850	0.337 882	0.234 441
55–59	0.623 138	0.503 357	0.385 187	0.271 535	0.165 696	0.630 916	0.525 218	0.420 962	0.319 236	0.221 172

Age										
60–64	0.572 984	0.460 137	0.350 459	0.245 994	0.149 448	0.589 502	0.491 032	0.393 718	0.298 670	0.206 985
65–69	0.510 027	0.409 674	0.312 079	0.219 088	0.133 122	0.532 655	0.444 101	0.356 314	0.270 435	0.187 506
70–74	0.427 788	0.343 368	0.261 426	0.183 440	0.111 409	0.452 156	0.377 615	0.303 310	0.230 413	0.159 890
75–79	0.330 137	0.265 294	0.202 159	0.141 961	0.086 282	0.352 451	0.296 628	0.239 475	0.182 661	0.127 223
80–84	0.225 191	0.181 734	0.138 931	0.097 832	0.059 623	0.245 177	0.207 304	0.167 882	0.128 374	0.089 618

e_x (years)

Age										
0	55.00	50.00	45.00	40.00	35.00	55.00	50.00	45.00	40.00	35.00
1–4	59.16	54.21	49.08	43.83	38.52	59.31	54.25	48.99	43.64	38.23
5–9	59.15	54.15	48.84	43.36	37.76	59.76	54.59	49.08	43.40	37.62
10–14	56.11	51.02	45.58	39.94	34.17	57.04	51.76	46.08	40.19	34.19
15–19	51.82	46.66	41.15	35.43	29.59	52.88	47.51	41.75	35.77	29.68
20–24	47.37	42.18	36.63	30.85	24.94	48.63	43.26	37.45	31.40	25.22
25–29	43.03	37.97	32.48	26.72	20.77	44.55	39.66	34.17	28.31	22.19
30–34	38.92	34.37	29.32	23.90	18.19	40.59	36.93	32.75	28.11	22.99
35–39	35.01	31.41	27.36	22.89	17.98	36.64	34.51	32.19	29.62	26.63
40–44	31.20	28.68	25.87	22.70	19.00	32.66	31.74	30.86	29.95	28.92
45–49	27.40	26.03	24.60	23.02	21.14	28.67	28.43	28.24	28.07	27.89
50–54	23.68	23.18	22.73	22.27	21.77	24.72	24.72	24.72	24.72	24.72
55–59	20.08	19.99	19.92	19.85	19.78	20.88	20.94	20.99	21.02	21.05
60–64	16.62	16.63	16.64	16.65	16.66	17.17	17.23	17.26	17.30	17.32
65–69	13.36	13.37	13.38	13.39	13.40	13.73	13.78	13.81	13.84	13.86
70–74	10.45	10.47	10.49	10.50	10.52	10.73	10.77	10.79	10.81	10.83
75–79	7.80	7.82	7.83	7.84	7.85	8.06	8.03	8.00	7.98	7.96
80–84	5.27	5.26	5.26	5.25	5.25	5.49	5.41	5.35	5.30	5.26

Note: e_0, life expectancy at birth (number of years a child is expected to live as calculated at the time of birth); e_x, life expectancy at age x; P_x, probability of surviving at age x; ${}_nq_x$, probability of dying between ages x and $x+n$.

Table 7A.3. Model life tables for INDEPTH pattern 1: life expectancy of 50.0 years decremented by HIV–AIDS mortality.

$_nq_x$

Age (years)	Male					Female				
	0.0	5.0	10.0	15.0	20.0	0.0	5.0	10.0	15.0	20.0
0	0.107 006	0.117 042	0.125 659	0.134 058	0.143 537	0.109 195	0.117 155	0.123 135	0.128 417	0.133 799
1–4	0.081 323	0.086 976	0.091 759	0.096 363	0.101 503	0.089 043	0.094 403	0.098 400	0.101 912	0.105 474
5–9	0.041 910	0.043 748	0.045 276	0.046 726	0.048 322	0.047 685	0.049 590	0.050 992	0.052 212	0.053 439
10–14	0.016 485	0.016 490	0.016 493	0.016 496	0.016 499	0.018 990	0.018 971	0.018 958	0.018 947	0.018 936
15–19	0.013 826	0.014 601	0.015 253	0.015 877	0.016 571	0.018 338	0.020 296	0.021 816	0.023 193	0.024 630
20–24	0.018 424	0.024 301	0.030 294	0.037 051	0.045 852	0.024 536	0.040 164	0.056 745	0.075 678	0.099 802
25–29	0.026 984	0.046 177	0.070 323	0.102 350	0.150 137	0.030 202	0.068 421	0.119 279	0.185 467	0.275 133
30–34	0.036 623	0.072 313	0.121 688	0.190 360	0.292 481	0.033 492	0.081 882	0.148 955	0.236 782	0.352 657
35–39	0.044 177	0.087 770	0.147 553	0.229 008	0.345 758	0.036 092	0.077 161	0.129 137	0.194 322	0.280 152
40–44	0.050 293	0.098 477	0.163 232	0.249 528	0.370 014	0.040 442	0.066 165	0.093 074	0.123 237	0.160 738
45–49	0.061 241	0.101 344	0.148 810	0.207 374	0.286 862	0.048 078	0.058 291	0.066 783	0.074 881	0.083 717
50–54	0.077 021	0.098 342	0.119 063	0.141 348	0.168 860	0.061 337	0.064 274	0.066 449	0.068 348	0.070 266
55–59	0.099 771	0.105 966	0.111 170	0.116 151	0.121 678	0.081 198	0.080 563	0.080 113	0.079 733	0.079 361
60–64	0.135 167	0.134 932	0.134 744	0.134 572	0.134 388	0.118 362	0.117 392	0.116 703	0.116 122	0.115 552
65–69	0.195 759	0.196 429	0.196 968	0.197 464	0.197 994	0.182 977	0.181 413	0.180 303	0.179 365	0.178 447
70–74	0.272 473	0.271 517	0.270 753	0.270 052	0.269 305	0.262 462	0.256 013	0.251 477	0.247 668	0.243 960
75–79	0.371 096	0.368 105	0.365 717	0.363 526	0.361 195	0.355 004	0.351 692	0.349 338	0.347 346	0.345 392
80–84	0.504 579	0.505 975	0.507 094	0.508 122	0.509 220	0.457 623	0.474 353	0.486 322	0.496 497	0.506 508

P_x

Age (years)	Male					Female				
	0.0	5.0	10.0	15.0	20.0	0.0	5.0	10.0	15.0	20.0
0	1.000 000	1.000 000	1.000 000	1.000 000	1.000 000	1.000 000	1.000 000	1.000 000	1.000 000	1.000 000
1–4	0.892 994	0.882 958	0.874 341	0.865 942	0.856 463	0.890 805	0.882 845	0.876 865	0.871 583	0.866 201
5–9	0.820 373	0.806 162	0.794 112	0.782 497	0.769 529	0.811 486	0.799 502	0.790 581	0.782 758	0.774 839
10–14	0.785 991	0.770 893	0.758 158	0.745 934	0.732 344	0.772 790	0.759 855	0.750 268	0.741 889	0.733 432
15–19	0.773 034	0.758 182	0.745 654	0.733 629	0.720 261	0.758 115	0.745 440	0.736 044	0.727 832	0.719 544
20–24	0.762 346	0.747 112	0.734 280	0.721 981	0.708 326	0.744 212	0.730 310	0.719 987	0.710 952	0.701 822
25–29	0.748 301	0.728 956	0.712 036	0.695 231	0.675 847	0.725 952	0.700 978	0.679 131	0.657 148	0.631 778
30–34	0.728 108	0.695 295	0.661 963	0.624 074	0.574 378	0.704 027	0.653 016	0.598 125	0.535 269	0.457 955
35–39	0.701 443	0.645 016	0.581 411	0.505 275	0.406 383	0.680 448	0.599 546	0.509 031	0.408 527	0.296 454
40–44	0.670 455	0.588 403	0.495 622	0.389 564	0.265 873	0.655 889	0.553 284	0.443 297	0.329 142	0.213 402
45–49	0.636 736	0.530 459	0.414 720	0.292 356	0.167 496	0.629 364	0.516 676	0.402 038	0.288 579	0.179 100
50–54	0.597 741	0.476 700	0.353 006	0.231 729	0.119 448	0.599 105	0.486 559	0.375 188	0.266 970	0.164 106
55–59	0.551 703	0.429 820	0.310 976	0.198 975	0.099 278	0.562 358	0.455 286	0.350 257	0.248 723	0.152 575

Probability of dying

Age										
60–64	0.496 659	0.384 274	0.276 405	0.175 864	0.087 198	0.516 695	0.418 607	0.322 197	0.228 892	0.140 467
65–69	0.429 527	0.332 423	0.239 161	0.152 197	0.075 480	0.455 538	0.369 466	0.284 596	0.202 312	0.124 235
70–74	0.345 443	0.267 125	0.192 054	0.122 144	0.060 535	0.372 185	0.302 440	0.233 282	0.166 025	0.102 066
75–79	0.251 319	0.194 596	0.140 055	0.089 159	0.044 233	0.274 500	0.225 011	0.174 617	0.124 906	0.077 166
80–84	0.158 056	0.122 964	0.088 834	0.056 747	0.028 256	0.177 052	0.145 877	0.113 617	0.081 520	0.050 513

e_x (years)

Age	50.00	45.00	40.00	35.00	30.00	50.00	45.00	40.00	35.00	30.00
0	50.00	45.00	40.00	35.00	30.00	50.00	45.00	40.00	35.00	30.00
1–4	54.93	49.90	44.68	39.34	33.94	55.07	49.91	44.55	39.08	33.56
5–9	55.62	50.46	44.99	39.32	33.55	56.25	50.90	45.19	39.29	33.28
10–14	52.94	47.66	42.00	36.13	30.13	53.95	48.42	42.48	36.32	30.02
15–19	48.79	43.41	37.67	31.69	25.59	49.94	44.31	38.26	31.97	25.55
20–24	44.43	39.02	33.21	27.16	20.98	45.83	40.18	34.05	27.67	21.13
25–29	40.22	34.93	29.17	23.11	16.87	41.92	36.76	30.95	24.73	18.19
30–34	36.27	31.50	26.19	20.46	14.41	38.15	34.27	29.81	24.79	19.15
35–39	32.55	28.76	24.47	19.69	14.33	34.38	32.10	29.59	26.71	23.22
40–44	28.94	26.29	23.27	19.79	15.59	30.58	29.58	28.60	27.55	26.29
45–49	25.34	23.88	22.32	20.54	18.27	26.76	26.50	26.28	26.07	25.84
50–54	21.83	21.30	20.79	20.26	19.61	22.98	22.98	22.98	22.98	22.97
55–59	18.44	18.35	18.26	18.18	18.09	19.32	19.39	19.44	19.48	19.52
60–64	15.21	15.22	15.23	15.24	15.25	15.81	15.87	15.92	15.95	15.99
65–69	12.20	12.21	12.22	12.22	12.23	12.60	12.65	12.69	12.72	12.75
70–74	9.56	9.58	9.60	9.62	9.63	9.86	9.90	9.93	9.95	9.98
75–79	7.20	7.22	7.23	7.25	7.26	7.47	7.45	7.42	7.41	7.39
80–84	4.98	4.97	4.96	4.96	4.95	5.21	5.13	5.07	5.02	4.97

Note: e_0, life expectancy at birth (number of years a child is expected to live as calculated at the time of birth); e_x, life expectancy at age x; P_x, probability of surviving at age x; $_nq_x$, probability of dying between ages x and x+n.

Table 7A.4. Model life tables for INDEPTH pattern 1: life expectancy of 45.0 years decremented by HIV–AIDS mortality.

| | Male | | | | | Female | | | | |
| | Reduction in e_0 (years) | | | | | | | | | |
Age (years)	0.0	5.0	10.0	15.0	20.0	0.0	5.0	10.0	15.0	20.0
$_nq_x$										
0	0.130 408	0.142 000	0.152 464	0.163 365	0.177 364	0.132 228	0.141 286	0.148 429	0.155 094	0.162 575
1–4	0.099 735	0.106 357	0.112 256	0.118 335	0.126 060	0.108 342	0.114 505	0.119 334	0.123 819	0.128 833
5–9	0.051 903	0.054 101	0.056 029	0.057 987	0.060 440	0.058 597	0.060 833	0.062 566	0.064 160	0.065 927
10–14	0.020 546	0.020 551	0.020 555	0.020 560	0.020 565	0.023 498	0.023 475	0.023 459	0.023 444	0.023 427
15–19	0.017 243	0.018 183	0.019 017	0.019 874	0.020 961	0.022 695	0.025 023	0.026 924	0.028 750	0.030 861
20–24	0.022 951	0.030 035	0.037 641	0.046 910	0.061 008	0.030 319	0.048 669	0.068 924	0.093 586	0.128 831
25–29	0.033 543	0.056 429	0.086 545	0.129 663	0.204 725	0.037 270	0.081 539	0.142 109	0.224 795	0.346 988
30–34	0.045 415	0.087 531	0.147 904	0.237 255	0.386 298	0.041 297	0.097 061	0.176 087	0.283 708	0.435 645
35–39	0.054 680	0.105 837	0.178 214	0.282 343	0.446 914	0.044 476	0.091 937	0.153 658	0.234 709	0.350 954
40–44	0.062 155	0.118 483	0.196 399	0.305 597	0.472 510	0.049 783	0.079 693	0.112 158	0.150 603	0.203 719
45–49	0.075 480	0.122 298	0.179 636	0.254 615	0.368 924	0.059 074	0.071 008	0.081 403	0.091 897	0.104 601
50–54	0.094 559	0.119 443	0.144 724	0.173 778	0.214 795	0.075 127	0.078 551	0.081 218	0.083 682	0.086 423
55–59	0.121 807	0.128 996	0.135 355	0.141 867	0.150 082	0.098 982	0.098 248	0.097 699	0.097 209	0.096 682
60–64	0.163 599	0.163 330	0.163 104	0.162 881	0.162 612	0.143 019	0.141 916	0.141 091	0.140 355	0.139 561
65–69	0.233 495	0.234 239	0.234 870	0.235 492	0.236 244	0.217 770	0.216 044	0.214 754	0.213 601	0.212 358
70–74	0.319 129	0.318 106	0.317 242	0.316 393	0.315 369	0.306 695	0.299 831	0.294 730	0.290 194	0.285 335
75–79	0.424 780	0.421 720	0.419 136	0.416 599	0.413 540	0.406 242	0.402 864	0.400 332	0.398 063	0.395 614
80–84	0.560 367	0.561 711	0.562 846	0.563 963	0.565 311	0.511 918	0.528 150	0.540 312	0.551 190	0.562 900
P_x										
0	1.000 000	1.000 000	1.000 000	1.000 000	1.000 000	1.000 000	1.000 000	1.000 000	1.000 000	1.000 000
1–4	0.869 592	0.858 000	0.847 536	0.836 635	0.822 636	0.867 772	0.858 714	0.851 571	0.844 906	0.837 425
5–9	0.782 863	0.766 745	0.752 396	0.737 631	0.718 934	0.773 756	0.760 388	0.749 949	0.740 291	0.729 537
10–14	0.742 231	0.725 264	0.710 240	0.694 858	0.675 482	0.728 416	0.714 131	0.703 028	0.692 793	0.681 441
15–19	0.726 981	0.710 359	0.695 641	0.680 572	0.661 591	0.711 300	0.697 367	0.686 536	0.676 552	0.665 477
20–24	0.714 445	0.697 442	0.682 412	0.667 046	0.647 724	0.695 157	0.679 916	0.668 051	0.657 101	0.644 940
25–29	0.698 048	0.676 495	0.656 725	0.635 755	0.608 207	0.674 080	0.646 825	0.621 983	0.595 605	0.561 851
30–34	0.674 634	0.638 321	0.599 888	0.553 322	0.483 692	0.648 958	0.594 084	0.533 594	0.461 716	0.366 896
35–39	0.643 995	0.582 448	0.511 163	0.422 043	0.296 843	0.622 157	0.536 422	0.439 635	0.330 724	0.207 060
40–44	0.608 781	0.520 803	0.420 067	0.302 882	0.164 180	0.594 486	0.487 104	0.372 081	0.253 100	0.134 391
45–49	0.570 942	0.459 097	0.337 566	0.210 322	0.086 603	0.564 891	0.448 285	0.330 350	0.214 982	0.107 013
50–54	0.527 848	0.402 951	0.276 927	0.156 771	0.054 653	0.531 520	0.416 454	0.303 458	0.195 226	0.095 819
55–59	0.477 935	0.354 821	0.236 849	0.129 528	0.042 914	0.491 589	0.383 741	0.278 812	0.178 889	0.087 538

Age										
60–64	0.419 719	0.309 050	0.204 790	0.111 152	0.036 473	0.442 931	0.346 039	0.251 572	0.161 500	0.079 075
65–69	0.351 053	0.258 573	0.171 388	0.093 047	0.030 542	0.379 583	0.296 931	0.216 078	0.138 832	0.068 039
70–74	0.269 084	0.198 005	0.131 134	0.071 136	0.023 327	0.296 921	0.232 780	0.169 674	0.109 178	0.053 591
75–79	0.183 212	0.135 019	0.089 533	0.048 629	0.015 970	0.205 857	0.162 986	0.119 666	0.077 495	0.038 299
80–84	0.105 387	0.078 079	0.052 006	0.028 370	0.009 366	0.122 229	0.097 325	0.071 760	0.046 647	0.023 148

e_x (years)

Age										
0	45.00	40.00	35.00	30.00	25.00	45.00	40.00	35.00	30.00	25.00
1–4	50.67	45.54	40.21	34.76	29.28	50.78	45.50	40.01	34.42	28.76
5–9	52.07	46.72	41.04	35.16	29.22	52.71	47.12	41.16	35.00	28.71
10–14	49.78	44.25	38.32	32.17	25.94	50.83	45.01	38.74	32.22	25.56
15–19	45.77	40.12	34.08	27.79	21.43	47.00	41.04	34.62	27.94	21.12
20–24	41.53	35.82	29.69	23.30	16.83	43.03	37.03	30.50	23.69	16.71
25–29	37.45	31.85	25.75	19.33	12.76	39.30	33.79	27.58	20.88	13.81
30–34	33.66	28.61	22.96	16.83	10.41	35.72	31.57	26.73	21.21	14.82
35–39	30.14	26.11	21.51	16.29	10.38	32.15	29.69	26.91	23.62	19.33
40–44	26.74	23.91	20.63	16.72	11.76	28.53	27.45	26.34	25.09	23.43
45–49	23.35	21.78	20.06	17.98	15.05	24.90	24.61	24.36	24.10	23.79
50–54	20.05	19.47	18.90	18.26	17.38	21.30	21.29	21.29	21.29	21.28
55–59	16.88	16.77	16.68	16.58	16.45	17.83	17.90	17.95	18.00	18.05
60–64	13.88	13.89	13.90	13.91	13.92	14.51	14.58	14.63	14.67	14.72
65–69	11.10	11.11	11.12	11.12	11.13	11.52	11.58	11.62	11.66	11.70
70–74	8.72	8.75	8.76	8.78	8.80	9.03	9.08	9.11	9.14	9.18
75–79	6.64	6.66	6.67	6.69	6.71	6.92	6.89	6.88	6.86	6.84
80–84	4.70	4.69	4.69	4.68	4.67	4.94	4.86	4.80	4.74	4.69

Note: e_0, life expectancy at birth (number of years a child is expected to live as calculated at the time of birth); e_x, life expectancy at age x; P_x, probability of surviving at age x; $_nq_x$, probability of dying between ages x and $x+n$.

PART III

INDEPTH DSS SITE PROFILES

INTRODUCTION

Part III of this monograph contains detailed profiles of all INDEPTH DSS sites contributing mortality data to the comparative analyses presented in Part II. Part III is intended as a reference for those who wish to know more about any particular site and the context of the population it monitors, the specific methods it uses, and some of its additional demographic outputs.

Information for each site is provided in separate profiles, presented in a standardized format to allow easy comparisons of selected features between sites. A map panel is also provided to help the reader appreciate the exact location of each DSS site.

The first section of each profile provides full details of the physical and human geography of the DSS area. These details include the following:

- Geographic location, including longitude, latitude, and altitude;
- Administrative location (regions, districts, etc);
- DSS dimensions and area;
- Main geoecological and climatic zone;
- Seasonality (temperature ranges, annual rainfall, seasons); and
- Unique features.

The first section of each profile also provides population characteristics of the DSS site, including

- Monitored population and population density;
- Status, whether rural, peri-urban, or urban;
- Main ethnic groups;
- Major religions;
- Major languages;
- Main occupations;
- Schools;
- Literacy among those ≥15 years old, male and female;
- Housing;
- Water and sanitation;
- Access (paved or unpaved roads, public-transportion services, telecommunications);
- Electrification;
- Health services (for example, number of hospitals, health centres, dispensaries, health posts; user fees or free health services; coverage of major health interventions, such as immunization; use of major health interventions);
- Main health problems;

- Other socioeconomic indicators, such as household income, if available;
- History pertinent to site demographics (for example, epidemics, war, droughts, floods, famines, refugee situations); and
- Any other unique features.

The second section of each site profile is dedicated to the site itself. This section contains introductory information on the site, including

- Original and current objectives of the DSS site;
- Start-up year and evolution of the DSS site (original population and current population under surveillance, etc.);
- Main DSS features (for example, update-round intervals, definitions of residency, types of verbal autopsy ([VA], software systems);
- Main demographic, health, and socioeconomic variables that the DSS site measures routinely;
- Additional parameters measured in special nested surveys at the DSS site;
- DSS organization (staff, infrastructure, institutional base, etc.);
- Unique features (for example, other models of data linkage); and
- Usual consumers of site DSS data (dissemination).

In the second section of each site profile, you will also find details on the site's procedures for DSS data collection and processing, including field procedures such as the following:

- Mapping;
- Initial census;
- Regular update rounds;
- Continuous surveillance (vital and other events, VA); and
- Supervision and quality control.

You will also find data-management procedures, such as

- Data handling and data processing;
- Data-quality assurance and links back to field operations; and
- Data analysis and packaging.

The third section of each site profile provides the basic outputs of the DSS site, including demographic indicators generated by the site, such as

- Population size;
- Main age-group structure (percentage <1, 0–4, 5–14, 15–64, and ≥65 years old);
- Age-dependency ratio [(population <15 years old + population ≥65 years old) ÷ (population 15–64 years old)];
- Sex ratio;
- Total fertility rate;
- Infant mortality rate;
- Under-five mortality rate;
- Maternal mortality ratio;
- Average household size;

- Household headship; and
- Percentage literate by sex at ≥15 years old.

A graphic of the current population pyramid for the site is also provided, along with a table with the age- and sex-specific all-cause mortality by 5-year age groups. Some sites also provide tables of age-specific fertility and migration rates.

The site profiles are sequenced, first according to geographic area, then by country alphabetically, and finally by site alphabetically. Hence, they appear in the following order:

East Africa
- Ethiopia — Butajira DSS
- Tanzania — Dar es Salaam DSS; Hai DSS; Ifakara DSS; Morogoro DSS; Rufiji DSS
- Zambia — Gwembe DSS

Southern Africa
- Mozambique — Manhiça DSS
- South Africa — Agincourt DSS; Dikgale DSS; Hlabisa DSS

West Africa
- Burkina Faso — Nouna DSS; Oubritenga DSS
- The Gambia — Farafenni DSS
- Ghana — Navrongo DSS
- Guinea-Bissau — Bandim DSS
- Senegal — Bandafassi DSS; Mlomp DSS; Niakhar DSS

Asia
- Bangladesh — Matlab DSS; Operations Research Project DSS
- Viet Nam — FilaBavi DSS

For quick reference, Table III.1 provides a matrix of key features of all the sites in these profiles.

Table III.1. Key features of INDEPTH DSS sites profiled in Part III of this volume.

DSS site	Chapter	DSS pop. (2000)	Residential status[a]	Start date	URI (months)	VA	GIS	SE status	Migration tracking	Data mgmt
East Africa										
Butajira, Ethiopia	8	40 000	R	1987	3	✔	✔	✔	✔	Custom dBase
Dar es Salaam, Tanzania	9	70 000	U	1992	6	✔	✔	✔	✔	Custom FoxPro
Hai, Tanzania	10	154 000	R,P	1992	12	✔	✔	✔	✔	Custom FoxPro
Ifakara, Tanzania	11	60 000	R	1996	4	✔	✔	✔	✔	Custom HRS
Morogoro, Tanzania	12	120 000	R,P	1992	12	✔	✔	✔	✔	Custom FoxPro
Rufiji, Tanzania	13	85 000	R	1998	4	✔	✔	✔	✔	Custom HRS
Gwembe, Zambia	14	10 000	R	1956	36	✗	✗	✔	✔	Custom dBase
Southern Africa										
Manhiça, Mozambique	15	36 000	R,P	1996	4	✔	✔	✔	✔	Custom HRS
Agincourt, South Africa	16	67 000	R	1992	12	✔	✔	✔	✔	Custom Access
Digkale, South Africa	17	8 000	P	1995	12	✗	✗	✗	✔	Custom Access
Hlabisa, South Africa	18	85 000	R,P,U	2000	4	✔	✔	✔	✔	Delphi 5, MS SQL
West Africa										
Nouna, Burkina Faso	19	55 000	R	1992	3	✔	✔	✔	✗	Custom HRS
Oubritenga, Burkina Faso	20	100 000	R	1993	12	✗	✗	✗	✗	Custom Epi
Farafenni, The Gambia	21	16 000	R	1981	3	✔	✔	✔	✔	Custom HRS
Navrongo, Ghana	22	141 000	R	1993	3	✔	✔	✔	✔	Custom HRS
Bandim, Guinea-Bissau	23	100 000	U,R	1978	3	✔	✔	✔	✔	Custom dBase
Bandafassi, Senegal	24	10 500	R	1970	12	✔	✗	✗	✔	Custom
Mlomp, Senegal	25	7 500	R	1985	12	✔	✗	✗	✔	Custom
Niakhar, Senegal	26	29 000	R	1962	3	✔	✗	✔	✔	Custom FoxPro
Asia										
Matlab cont.,[b] Bangladesh	27	107 000	R	1966	1	✔	✔	✔	✔	Custom Oracle
Matlab treat.,[c] Bangladesh	27	108 000	R	1966	1	✔	✔	✔	✔	Custom Oracle
ORP, Bangladesh	28	127 000	U,R	1982	3	✔	✗	✔	✔	Custom R-base
FilaBavi, Viet Nam	29	52 000	R	1999	3	✗	✔	✔	✔	Custom Access
Derived data (totals, ranges)		1 592 000	21R,4U,5P	1956–99	1–36	19/23	16/23	19/23	21/23	

Source: INDEPTH data.
Note: Most demographic indicators are from 1995–99, but see Part II, Chapter 6, or Part III, for exact dates for data for each site. Also, demographic indicators may differ here and in Part III, because the latter reports values from the most recent years or uses different denominators. GIS, geographic information system; HRS, household-registration system; mgmt, management; ORP, Operations Research Project; pop., population; SE, socioeconomic; URI, update-round interval; VA, verbal autopsy.
[a] P, peri-urban; R, rural; U, urban.
[b] Control area.
[c] Treatment area.

Dep. ratio (%)	SR (M/F × 100)	Avg. household size	TFR	CRNI (%)	MMR	IMR (%)	U5M rate[d]	U5M ratio[e]	U5M $_5q_0$[f]	CBR	CDR	ASCDR	e_0 F	e_0 M
103	94	NA	6.6	2.8	NA	67.8	28.0	119.7	119.3	39.7	11.4	12.4	57	56
59	98	3.8	NA	1.6	669	71.1	25.2	122.4	113.7	28.6	12.8	16.8	50	50
91	93	4.6	NA	1.5	368	67.1	17.6	97.9	91.7	25.7	10.9	10.0	63	56
87	97	5.0	4.8	2.1	NA	93.2	24.9	146.1	124.2	32.0	11.4	11.9	58	56
78	97	4.0	NA	0.6	1183	116.7	39.6	212.9	182.8	24.2	17.7	18.6	46	44
110	93	4.8	6.2	2.5	393	102.1	58.4	134.3	179.4	29.7	15.0	12.4	52	53
93	NA	NA	5.5	NA	NA	72.6	44.1	NA	183.0	NA	15.5	15.7	54	47
87	83	4.0	5.0	2.6	NA	78.5	30.2	128.6	148.4	40.1	14.4	13.8	58	47
79	93	6.4	3.0	1.9	230	44.0	10.0	51.0	51.0	25.2	6.4	6.5	69	63
74	96	6.3	1.9	1.5	NA	38.9	7.8	46.7	45.2	21.1	6.2	6.2	68	62
NA	90	7.0	NA	NA	NA	NA	NA	NA	NA	NA	NA	NA	NA	NA
110	100	8.0	6.6	2.5	NA	40.9	31.3	145.5	137.2	39.3	14.1	14.0	53	54
NA	88	NA	NA	2.1	NA	96.5	70.5	202.5	187.7	35.7	14.6	13.9	55	52
117	90	NA	6.8	2.1	424	74.7	38.6	186.0	170.1	35.5	14.7	14.5	55	51
84	89	10.0	4.1	1.4	NA	90.0	40.6	183.6	183.4	30.7	16.3	16.7	51	47
82	92	4.6	U 5.8 R 6.8	2.4	818	U102.0 R 128.0	57.4	256.0	226.3	51.8	28.4	30.0	39	36
92	96	14.6	6.5	3.0	826	125.5	58.4	225.7	253.3	51.4	21.8	19.4	48	45
69	104	6.3	4.0	1.2	436	45.2	19.2	94.0	88.7	22.1	10.1	9.7	65	60
104	98	10.4	7.0	2.6	575	81.2	48.5	200.0	208.8	NA	17.2	15.8	54	49
75	NA	5.1	3.6	2.0	NA	70.0	23.0	89.7	88.0	28.3	8.1	10.7	65	63
75	97	5.5	3.0	1.9	NA	50.6	15.2	66.9	62.5	25.8	7.0	9.0	67	67
71	99	5.4	2.9	1.8	NA	65.2	17.8	86.8	85.5	24.7	7.0	9.7	66	62
72	93	4.6	1.8	NA	NA	31.9	6.4	NA	NA	NA	NA	4.7	NA	NA
59–252	83–104	3.8–14.6	1.8–7.0	0.65–2.96	368–1183	31.9–128	5.3–70.5	12.1–256	32.3–253.3	21.1–51.8	5.3–28.4	4.7–30.0	46.1–81.35	44.4–71.1

Note: ASCDR, age-standardized crude death rate (annual number of deaths per 1000 population standardized using the INDEPTH African standard age structure for all African sites and Segi standard age structure [see Segi 1960] for all Asian sites), avg., average; CBR, crude birth rate (annual number of births per 1000 population); CDR, crude death rate (annual number of deaths per 1000 population); CRNI, crude rate of natural increase (crude birth rate minus crude death rate per 100; ignores migrations); Dep. ratio, dependency ratio (ratio of the sum of the populations <15 and >64 years old to the population 15–64 years old ×100); e_0, life expectancy at birth; F, female; IMR, infant mortality ratio (number of deaths in infants between birth and 1 year old per 1000 live births); M, male; MMR, maternal mortality ratio (number of pregnancy-related deaths in women 15–49 years old per 100 000 live births); NA, not available; SR, sex ratio; TFR, total fertility rate (average number of children per woman 14–49 years old); U5M, under-five mortality.

d Number of deaths in children under 5 years old per 1000 under-5 person–years.

e Number of deaths in children under 5 years old per 1000 live births.

f Probability of dying before reaching the age of 5 years per 1000 children.

Chapter 8

BUTAJIRA DSS, ETHIOPIA

Yemane Berhane[1] and Peter Byass[2]

Site description

Physical geography of the Butajira DSA

The Butajira Rural Health Programme (BRHP), centred on the Butajira DSS, is in Meskan and Mareko District, Gurage Zone, in the Southern Nations, Nationalities and Peoples Regional State in Ethiopia (Figure 8.1). The estimated area of the district is 797 km^2, of which Butajira covers about 9 km^2. The area is 130 km south of Addis Ababa and 50 km west of Zway in the Rift Valley, latitude 8.2°N and longitude 38.5°E. Climate varies from arid lowland areas at altitudes of around 1500 m above sea level (asl) (tropical climate) to cool mountainous areas of up to 3500 m asl (temperate climate). The main wet season occurs between June and October, with the remaining months predominantly dry. Daytime temperatures are typically 20–30°C, with nighttime temperatures falling close to freezing at higher altitudes. The lowland areas are drought prone and have been affected during the main droughts in Ethiopia.

Figure 8.1. Location of the Butajira DSS site, Ethiopia (monitored population, 40 000).

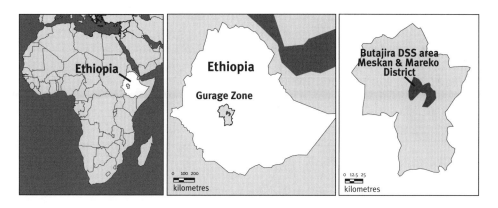

Population characteristics of the Butajira DSA

1 Department of Community Health, Faculty of Medicine, Addis Ababa University, Ethiopia.
2 Department of Public Health and Clinical Medicine, Umeå University, Sweden.

The district's population is currently an estimated 260 000, with a density of around 325 people/km². The DSA covers a sample within the district, following 10 communities initially sampled from the entire district, using a probability-proportional-to-size technique. The DSS population is currently an estimated 40 000 (in 2000). Nine of the 10 sites are rural, and 1 is located in Butajira.

The main ethnic group is Gurage, which is further divided into minor ethnic groups or tribes. The Meskan, Mareko, Sodo, Siliti, and Dobi are major tribal groups. Two-thirds of the people follow the Islamic religion, and orthodox Christianity is the second-dominant religion. The major language is Guragigna, with variations between tribal groups. Amharic, the national language, is widely spoken and is also an important written language. Only a minority of individuals, generally in the younger age groups and in the urban area, understand foreign languages such as English. The main occupations are farming in rural areas and small-scale business in town. The district has 30 schools: 1 technical school, 1 high school, and 28 primary schools. About 77% of the population is illiterate. Illiteracy is greater among females and the rural population.

Most houses in rural areas are round, thatched huts, built from timber and mud. In the town, housing is typically dense and crowded, usually with zinc roofs. The main water sources in rural areas are rivers and wells; in town, people have tap water, but it is not piped to every household. Sanitation in general is poor, and only a few houses have latrines. An all-weather gravel road connects Butajira with Addis Ababa, the capital, but other villages in the district are generally connected to the town only via dry-weather roads. Butajira has 24-hour electrical and telephone services, but neither extends to rural areas. The only health centre in the district is in Butajira, and it has so far provided the highest level of health care available, the nearest referral centre being some 100 km away. At present, a new district hospital is being constructed and commissioned in the town. A growing number of private clinics and dispensaries are also available in the district.

Health problems have been associated predominantly with infections and maternity, and difficult access to health care in the rural areas has often exacerbated the problems. Also, a trend has been observed toward a higher incidence of noncommunicable diseases.

The population has suffered from a number of events at the national level, including the long-term Ethiopian civil war (up to the defeat of the Mengistu regime in 1991) and the more recent border conflict with Eritrea. Although the study area had no direct involvement in these conflicts, conscription programs and the diversion of national resources to the military have had detrimental effects nationwide. Similarly, severe and recurring droughts have had considerable effects on rural populations at various times, particularly in lowland areas.

Butajira DSS procedures

Introduction to the Butajira DSS site

The BRHP was initiated in mid-1986 with a complete census of the 10 sampled *kebeles* (*kebele* is the smallest administrative unit in Ethiopia) in the District of Meskan and Mareko. Soon after, by January 1987, a DSS with continuous registration of vital events was initiated. The major aims were to develop and evaluate a system for continuous registration of births and deaths to generate valid data on fertility and mortality and provide a study base for essential health research and intervention (Berhane et al. 1999).

The BRHP DSS is primarily a collaborative research project undertaken by the Department of Community Health, Faculty of Medicine, Addis Ababa University, Ethiopia, and the Division of Epidemiology, Department of Public Health and Clinical Medicine, Umea University, Sweden. The collaboration started as a doctoral-study project (Shamebo 1993). Later, it grew into a departmental collaboration and included the development of the study-base infrastructure and involvement of a multi-disciplinary group of researchers. The original DSS population in 1987 was around 28 000 and grew over 10 years to about 37 000 active individuals, with more than 60 000 individuals involved at some time during this first 10 years of monitoring.

Studies in Butajira have been conducted in a set of nine randomly selected (probability-proportional-to-size technique) rural *kebeles* (known as "peasants' associations") and one urban *kebele* (the Urban Dwellers' Association). Monthly visits to each household have provided the data. The DSS operates as a dynamic open-cohort system. The individual person–years are aggregated to serve as denominators for calculation of various health and demographic indices. So far, three complete censuses of the population (in 1986, 1995, and 1999) have been done. The extent of similarity between the 1994 national census and the DSS database illustrates the quality of the continuous registration system. Currently, the surveillance interval is changing from monthly to quarterly. Custom-made software, based on the dBase system, is used to handle the data.

The BRHP registers births, deaths, marriages, new households, out- and in-migrations, and internal moves (migration within BRHP DSS *kebeles*). Household and environmental variables were measured during the censuses. The study base is now well established and is being used for other more focused studies on essential health problems of the country, using qualitative, as well as quantitative, research methods. So far, research on childhood respiratory illnesses, other infectious diseases, reproductive health, and mental health has been conducted using the study-base infrastructure.

The intensity and diversity of the research activities have also required a wider participation of multidisciplinary researchers. The participating researchers have backgrounds in obstetrics (Andersson 2000; Berhane 2000), pediatrics (Muhe 1994), epidemiology and biostatistics (Shamebo 1993), sociology, psychiatry (Alem 1997), nursing, and public health. At present, more than 50 field staff are working in the DSS.

This work has contributed to human-resource development and research capacity-building at the Faculty of Medicine, Addis Ababa University. Several training opportunities have been offered at masters and doctoral levels. The doctoral training is conducted in a sandwich model that allows researchers to stay close to their mother institutions and carry on their routine responsibilities. This model of training has also significantly reduced the risk of "brain drain," which may occur when people are sent for long-term training abroad. Doctoral training is offered by European universities, mainly by Umeå University, Sweden. The public health master's program is conducted by the Department of Community Health, Faculty of Medicine, Addis Ababa University.

Butajira DSS data collection and processing

The Butajira area was originally selected for the establishment of the DSS for several reasons. At 130 km from Addis Ababa, it was considered beyond the direct influence of the municipal area but not too far from the university. In the mid-1980s, civil war raged in northern Ethiopia — hence a location to the south was preferred in the interests of long-term continuity. The area also offered a diversity of developmental, geographic, ethnic, and religious parameters within a fairly discrete area. As time passed, the extent of this diversity and its major consequences for many population parameters became increasingly apparent.

Field procedures

INITIAL CENSUS — The initial census of the population in the selected villages was done in 1987 to obtain the baseline population and establish a system of DSS with continuous registration of vital and migratory events at household level. The total population was 28 780. Any adult member of the household >15 years old was eligible to respond in the monthly household interviews. These were carried out by a team of secondary-school graduate enumerators who were based in the *kebeles*. Each vital event was registered on a separate form at the household level. Basic demographic, social, housing-condition, and health-care-use characteristics were recorded for each household on its entry into the DSS and then during each reenumeration (Berhane et al. 1999).

REGULAR UPDATE ROUNDS — As it happened, the first overall update of the 1987 census was not done until 1995, which was, in retrospect, too long. A further update round was then conducted in 1999.

CONTINUOUS SURVEILLANCE — From the time of the 1987 census until 1999, continuous surveillance was carried out during monthly visits to each household. However, in the light of experience, both here and elsewhere, quarterly household visits were phased in during 1999 and 2000.

FIELD SUPERVISION AND QUALITY CONTROL — Data-quality-assurance mechanisms have been instituted at several points to ensure the integrity of the data. The most critical of these mechanisms is field supervision. Field supervisors daily supervise data collection and check each completed data form. They also make random visits to selected households each month, using a weekly distributed timetable. Research assistants supervise the data flow from the households to the computer system. They also check the data at the field level, for randomly selected households. Researchers work in the field to provide on-site technical assistance and guidance and check data quality. With the advent and easy availability of the global positioning system, mapping exercises at the household level have been carried out more recently.

Data management

Data for the DSS were initially entered as text strings, but the DSS has, since 1994, used software based on the dBase IV platform. As developed for Butajira, this program includes procedures for automatic consistency checking and has more sophisticated facilities for data management and retrieval. The indigenous calendar used in Ethiopia runs behind the international calendar by 2809 days and has 13 months in a year, and this has presented serious obstacles to using proprietary packages for longitudinal data.

Data are currently entered in Butajira, which allows any inconsistent questionnaires to be immediately sent back to the field. This is a significant improvement over earlier practice, which was to centralize data operations in Addis Ababa.

The site manipulates and analyzes data with dBase, Epi-Info, and the Cohort program, developed by Umeå University, which does person–year-based analyses of events in dynamic cohorts. National and international publications and scientific conferences have been the main routes to disseminate this information. Community feedback meetings have been held periodically.

Butajira DSS basic outputs

Demographic indicators

The study population increased from a baseline of 28 616 in 1987 to 37 323 at the beginning of 1997, suggesting a mean yearly growth rate of 2.7%. The explanation for the major difference in population growth between areas has been urbanization, along with a marked excess of births over deaths and net migration into the urban area.

Figure 8.2. Population pyramid for person–years observed at the Butajira DSS site, 1995–99.

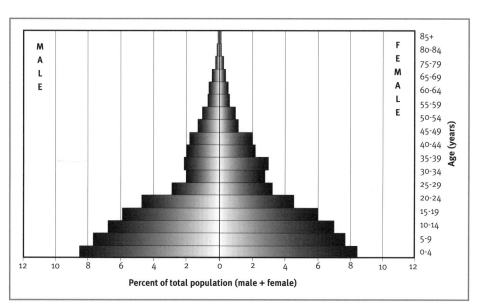

The population profile is typical for sub-Saharan Africa: 4.3% of person–years occur in the first year of life, 14.4% in the next 4 years, 29.9% in the 5–14 age group, 48.6% in the 15–64 age group, and only 2.8% in the ≥65 age group (Figure 8.2). The age-dependency ratio is thus 106%. The male–female ratio is 94%.

During 10 years of surveillance, 5143 deaths and 15 667 births were registered in the area, from a total of 336 074 person–years of follow-up. Thus, based on the observed total number of deaths in this study base, the crude mortality rate is 15.3 per 1000 person–years. A total of 71 004 person–years has been observed among women 15–44 years old, representing 2367 reproductive lifetimes and hence an overall fertility of 6.6 births/woman. The maternal mortality ratio has been estimated using several methods and is believed to be around 600 per 100 000 live births (Berhane et al. 2001).

Deaths among children <5 years old represent 48% of all mortality. Half of these deaths occurred during the first year of life, and 53% before 2 months. From the age-specific mortality rates we can estimate the cumulative mortality throughout life. Thus, among live births, an estimated 4.2% die during the first 2 months of life, 8.0% before 1 year, 16.6% before 5 years, 36% before 15 years, and 56% before 65 years. Substantial variations have occurred between areas with regard to under-five mortality, with rates ranging from 80 per 1000 person–years in the urban area to 219 per 1000 person–years in the lowlands. From the age-specific mortality rates, we estimate a current life expectancy at birth of 50.8 years — 49.3 years for males and 52.3 years for females.

Table 8.1 shows the age- and sex-specific all-cause mortality at the Butajira DSS site.

Table 8.1. Age- and sex-specific mortality at the Butajira DSS site, Ethiopia, 1995–99.

Age (years)	Deaths ($_nD_x$) Male	Female	Person–years observed ($_nPY_x$) Male	Female
<1	92	104	1340	1395
1–4	73	77	4863	4748
5–9	38	34	5608	5613
10–14	16	14	4944	5130
15–19	18	16	4292	4380
20–24	20	11	3464	3320
25–29	14	11	2082	2345
30–34	7	14	1448	2022
35–39	11	12	1541	2171
40–44	17	11	1436	1604
45–49	20	23	1314	1458
50–54	12	7	960	853
55–59	11	17	747	728
60–64	16	12	514	457
65–69	14	14	459	389
70–74	17	14	298	278
75–79	7	12	159	194
80–84	5	8	98	89
≥85	7	8	50	82
Births	2890			
CDR	11.44			
CBR	39.66			
CRNI	28.21			

Note: CBR, crude birth rate (actual number of births per 1000 population); CDR, crude death rate (actual number of deaths per 1000 population); CRNI, crude rate of natural increase (CBR minus CDR per 100; does not take into account migration); $_nD_x$, observed deaths between ages x and x+n; $_nPY_x$, observed person–years between ages x and x+n.

Acknowledgments

Our heart-felt gratitude goes, first of all, to the people of the Butajira site, who generously shared their personal information and experiences, and to the entire field staff, who diligently collected the data. We thank the health and administrative authorities in Butajira, Gurage Zone, and the Regional Health Bureau in Awassa for their facilitation of the fieldwork. We are very grateful to the Ethiopian Science and Technology Commission and the Swedish Agency for Research Cooperation with Developing Countries for generously funding the program since its establishment. Research, technical, and administrative staff at the Faculty of Medicine, Addis Ababa University, Ethiopia, and the Division of Epidemiology, Department of Public Health and Clinical Medicine, Umeå University, Sweden, are acknowledged for their all-round facilitation.

Chapter 9

DAR ES SALAAM DSS, TANZANIA

Robert Mswia, David Whiting, Gregory Kabadi, Honorati Masanja, and Philip Setel[1]

Site description

Physical geography of the Dar es Salaam DSA

The Dar es Salaam region, on the east coast of Tanzania, includes the municipalities of Ilala, Temeke, and Kinondoni (which constitute the city of Dar es Salaam) and a few outlying areas (Figure 9.1). It borders on the Indian Ocean to the east and, on all other sides, the coast region. In 1988, the estimated population of Dar es Salaam, according to a national census, was 1 360 865. But the city grew rapidly during the 1990s, and the current population of Dar es Salaam is estimated at 3 million. The area participating in surveillance covered eight "branches" in two municipal areas of Dar es Salaam: Temeke and Ilala.

Dar es Salaam is at sea level, and the DSS site lies between latitudes 6.82° and 6.89°S and longitudes 39.24° and 39.30°E. The climate is typically tropical, with hot weather throughout the year (range, about 26°–35°C) and two rainy seasons: short rains in November–December and long rains in March–May.

Figure 9.1. Location of the Dar es Salaam DSS site, Tanzania (monitored population, 70 000).

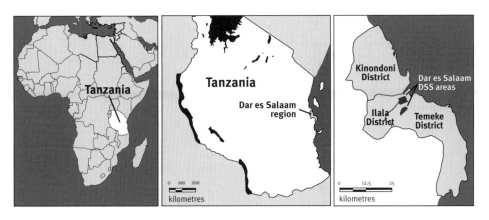

1 Adult Morbidity and Mortality Project, Tanzania.

Population characteristics of the Dar es Salaam DSA

Because socioeconomic status is important in the study of mortality differentials, three areas of the city — Ilala, Mtoni, and Keko — were chosen. These areas were thought best for the following reasons:

- Ilala, because it is an old planned part of the city, whose inhabitants are largely urbanized;

- Keko, because it is mixed socioeconomically, containing both people of higher socioeconomic status and government civil servants, living in reasonable accommodation; and

- Mtoni, because it is an area of fairly low socioeconomic status, whose citizens include a large proportion of the original inhabitants of the Dar es Salaam region, many leading a peri-urban or semirural life.

These three areas contain eight branches, with a total population of 69 304 (as of June 1999).

Originally, the Zaramo ethnic group inhabited the area that is now Dar es Salaam. During the 20th century, however, the population became a mix of many of the country's ethnic groups. Thus, the population in the DSA is a mixture of people from all parts of Tanzania. The majority of the population in the project area are Muslims (70%), and the remainder are Christians (30%).

The major language of people participating in the DSS is Kiswahili. A large portion of people in the DSA engage in small business or manual labour (both skilled and unskilled); and a few have office jobs.

Information on the highest level of education attained by individuals has been collected in both the census and the mortality-data survey, and the proportion of girls attending school is slightly higher than that of boys for all ages up to 14 years. Thereafter, this proportion drops significantly. From age 25, women with no formal education constitute a proportion two to three times greater than that of men. From age 30, significantly more men than women have completed primary and postprimary education.

The majority of people in Dar es Salaam live in low-cost rental housing, and the mean household size is 3.8. More than 70% of households occupy only one or two rooms. About 80% of households have tap water. Use of pit latrines is extensive (90%) in the Dar es Salaam DSA. It has both paved and unpaved roads, and all areas are well served with public transportation. The area has both public and private telecommunications. Electricity is available in these areas, mostly for domestic uses, such as lighting and cooking.

The Dar es Salaam region has one national and three municipal-government hospitals. People in the surveillance area make good use of all these facilities, although none is within the DSA itself. Two of the municipal hospitals, however, are within easy access to the study community, and the DSS population also has access to government health centres and dispensaries and to a number of private hospitals and dispensaries. The private hospitals are outside of the DSA, but some private dispensaries operate within the area.

Dar es Salaam DSS procedures

Introduction to the Dar es Salaam DSS site

DSS work is carried out in Dar es Salaam primarily to provide reliable population denominators for continuous cause-specific mortality monitoring. The demographic and mortality monitoring together provide municipal authorities with information on the burden of disease, health-facility use in the period before death, and population conditions. These data are used for evidence-based planning and evaluation of health services. The monitoring is an activity of the Tanzanian Ministry of Health and the municipal health-management team, as part of the Adult Morbidity and Mortality Project, phase 2 (AMMP-2). The goal of AMMP-2 is to decrease the morbidity and mortality stemming from conditions particularly likely to cause suffering and disadvantage among Tanzania's poor people, where these conditions are amenable to health-service interventions. To contribute to this goal, the project has aimed to strengthen evidence-based planning and development of cost-effective health services within the context of health-sector reform in project districts and in the Ministry of Health of Tanzania.

Demographic and mortality monitoring in AMMP-1 and -2 is carried out in Hai District (Kilimanjaro region) and Morogoro District (Morogoro region), as well as in Dar es Salaam (see Chapters 10 and 12). In 1992, when DSS work began, the Dar es Salaam DSA comprised seven urban branches, with a total population of 67 000. At the end of 1993, one more branch, with a population of 4500, was included in the monitoring to make a total population of 71 500. The population in the Dar es Salaam DSA has remained remarkably constant, despite considerable in- and out-migration each year. Although the initial focus was on adults, the system has been collecting data on people of all ages.

The DSS is incorporated into both national and district structures. In the Ministry of Health, the National Sentinel System assumes overall responsibility for using DSS to gather demographic and mortality data. This system also operates in the Hai, Morogoro, and Rufiji DSS sites. At the district level, surveillance work will become part of the routine systems of the district. Mortality monitoring will continue indefinitely, and DSS will continue as long as the district has no cost-effective alternative way of generating reliable population denominators.

The Dar es Salaam Public Health Service Delivery System is the primary local user of the data, and the Ministry of Health is the primary national user. Additional users of the data include

- The government's multisectoral National AIDS Control Programme;

- The Vice President's Office (which produces national poverty- and welfare-monitoring indicators);

- Ministry of Health initiatives for malaria control (for example, social marketing of insecticide-treated nets and the national malarial-drug policy);

- Nongovernmental organizations (for example, the Tanzania Public Health Association);

- Projects (for example, Dar es Salaam Urban Health Project);

- Donors (for assessment of health-sector performance);

- National Poverty Monitoring Group;

- Other sectors, such as the Ministry of Education, Bureau of Statistics, and Ministry of Labour and Youth Development; and

- Tanzanian and international researchers.

Dar es Salaam DSS data collection and processing

The initial population in the DSS approached the level that Hayes et al. (1989) suggested is best for the ascertainment of cause-specific mortality. As stated above, the Dar es Salaam areas were chosen to represent a range of urban living conditions, including variations in socioeconomic status and population density.

Field procedures

INITIAL CENSUS — An initial census was carried out in 1992, because neither vital registration nor the 1988 National Census provided an accurate basis for estimating population denominators. At first, a baseline census was taken to determine who was resident in each household under surveillance. A single form was used for each household.

REGULAR UPDATE ROUNDS — Subsequently, the population has been enumerated twice a year (May–June and October–November). In each update round, the information from the previous round is printed on new forms for each household. Each household is visited, and an adult member is interviewed. The enumerators verify and, where necessary, update existing data. When new households appear as a result of either migration into the area or splitting of existing households, they are registered on new-household forms. Key informants, such as local leaders, identify these households. Vital events (births and deaths) and migrations are recorded for each household. The following information is recorded for each individual: name, age, sex, relationship to head of household, main occupation, marital status, alcohol consumption and smoking habits, date of entry into the household, mode of entry, date of exit, mode of exit, and whether the individual's parents are alive. Recently, questions on religion have been added. Migration tracking is limited to recording the dates of entry into and exit from the area and the district of origin or destination; successive migrations of individuals into and out of the area are not linked. Thus, although it is possible to determine who is resident at any point in time (and therefore to calculate denominators), it is impossible to calculate the total time particular individuals spend in the DSA.

The DSS employs eight community-development workers as enumerators for the census-update rounds, and three clinical officers act as verbal-autopsy (VA) supervisors. The system also has community-based key informants, who report deaths to the VA supervisor on a regular basis. Whereas the census-update rounds take place twice annually, mortality monitoring, which provides information on probable causes of death, is continuous. Probable causes of death are determined using VA techniques.

CONTINUOUS MORTALITY SURVEILLANCE — The primary objective of the AMMP approach to DSS is to provide sentinel data on the burden of disease to inform health planning and priority-setting, and thus efforts are made to determine the cause of death for each person who dies in the area under surveillance. This is achieved by interviewing the relatives and caretakers of the deceased, using a short, standard interview schedule. Different forms are used for deaths among infants <31 days old, children between 31 days and <5 years old, and all persons ≥5 years old. The forms contain a section to identify the respondent, one to identify the deceased, an open-ended history section, a checklist of previously diagnosed conditions, a checklist of symptoms and their duration, a list of health services sought in the period leading up to the death, a residential history, and a summary of any confirmatory evidence, such as medical records or a death certificate. Trained health personnel complete the form after interviewing one or more of the deceased's relatives or caretakers. Wherever possible, the interview takes place within 6 weeks of the death.

Deaths are usually reported by community-based key informants, and in Dar es Salaam various individuals are used for this purpose. Key informants are chosen because of their awareness of events, such as deaths, in their communities. In addition, communities receive feedback in a newsletter; consequently, they perceive a benefit in participating in the surveillance system and actively report deaths to the key informants, thus making this a form of vital registration. Recently, each key informant from a village or area has been given a *turubai* (canvas tarpaulin) so that the bereaved families from the community can borrow it for funeral gatherings during the mourning period. This has enabled key informants to get information on a death that has occurred in his or her area and thus report it to the supervisor. The VA personnel meet the key informants on a regular basis to find out about new deaths that have occurred. They then meet with the relatives or caretaker of the deceased to verify that the death has occurred, then perform the VA.

Two physicians independently assign a cause of death. Until 1999, a modified version of ICD-10 was used. From 2000, a shorter, broader list of codes, developed by AMMP and the Ministry of Health, has been used. The diagnoses given by the two coders are compared, and discrepancies are given to a third coder. If all three coders disagree, the form is coded as "uncertain/unknown." Wherever possible, confirmatory evidence of the cause of death is obtained. This includes in- and out-patient records, death certificates, and burial permits.

Data management

During the census, a field supervisor reviews all completed forms and returns those with errors and inconsistencies to the enumerators for correction. Those passing inspection are sent to the data centre in Dar es Salaam and entered into a computer. All census forms with errors detected during data entry are logged and returned to the field for correction. Once the corrected forms are returned to the office, they are logged back in, and the problems are resolved.

Staff are trained to enter the data into microcomputers using a data-entry system designed specifically for the project in Microsoft FoxPro. They are instructed on how the census forms should be completed so that, in addition to the computer validation programs, they, too, can detect errors and inconsistencies. The validation programs range from simple range checks to checks for inconsistencies across household members, such as an individual identified as a "spouse" but with marital status recorded as "never married."

Several methods are employed to ensure data quality, including checks in the field and in the data-entry process. Supervisors visit a random sample of households to verify entries on the census forms and check that the census includes all the households visited and that no nonexistent households have been included. Following each census, reinterviews are also conducted of a sample of households for each enumerator. Because of the large amount of data collected in a single census, it is impossible to double enter all data for verification; instead, a 5–10% random sample is taken, and the forms are checked against the entered data.

At the end of each interview, the interviewers give each household a newsletter designed by the municipal health-management team and produced and distributed by the project for US $0.11 per household. It contains health-education messages and simplified presentations of results from the previous round. It shows that the DSS is part of the functioning of the district health system. The newsletter is designed to help the communities and their leaders better understand the areas where they live. In 1999, 94% of households reported receiving the newsletter, and 89% of households reported reading it.

Dar es Salaam DSS basic outputs

Demographic indicators

The primary outputs of the system are estimates of cause-specific mortality for all ages. As stated, the resident population of the DSS site is about 70 000. Average household size is 3.8. Male–female ratio is 100 : 102, with an age-dependency ratio of 59%. The main age group structures of the current population are as follows: those <1 year old account for 3.1%; 1–4 years old, 10.4%; 5–14 years old, 21.9%; 15–64 years old, 63.0%; and ≥65 years old, 1.6%. Between July 1992 and June 1999, the maternal mortality ratio was 669 per 100 000 live births.

The following migration figures reflect changes of residence of people on an annual basis and do not capture short-term movements between the enumeration rounds. In 1998–99, the surveillance area had an out-migration of 17 796 people. The region of destination was obtained for 15 124 of these: most (75%) migrated to another part of Dar es Salaam; the rest, to various parts of the country, except for 172 who moved to other countries outside Tanzania. During the same years, 16 581 people migrated to households within the surveillance area. The place of origin for 13 087 (79%) was determined: 68% migrated from areas within Dar es Salaam; the remainder came from other parts of Tanzania, except for 67 who came from other countries. As can be seen from the figures above, the population in the Dar es Salaam surveillance area is very dynamic. Dar es Salaam attracts young adults, and this can be seen in the shape of the population pyramid (Figure 9.2). The excess of females becomes obvious in the 15–19-year age group, whereas for males this occurs 5 years later.

Table 9.1 shows the age- and sex-specific all-cause mortality at the Dar es Salaam DSS site.

Figure 9.2. Population pyramid for person–years observed at the Dar es Salaam DSS site, Tanzania, 1995–99.

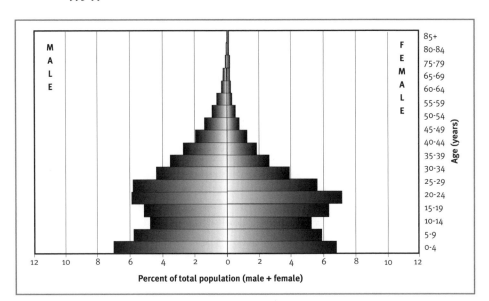

Table 9.1. Age- and sex-specific mortality at the Dar es Salaam DSS site, Tanzania, 1995–99.

Age (years)	Deaths ($_nD_x$) Male	Deaths ($_nD_x$) Female	Person–years observed ($_nPY_x$) Male	Person–years observed ($_nPY_x$) Female
<1	358	362	5 154	5 150
1–4	258	261	19 602	19 203
5–9	80	54	20 289	21 130
10–14	42	31	16 686	18 767
15–19	36	65	17 950	22 735
20–24	97	144	20 672	25 522
25–29	184	268	20 495	20 169
30–34	170	249	15 402	14 022
35–39	201	176	12 357	9 564
40–44	165	125	9 416	6 710
45–49	150	85	6 822	4 582
50–54	107	73	4 804	2 870
55–59	65	38	3 262	2 009
60–64	103	50	2 009	1 344
65–69	62	32	1 997	970
70–74	74	74	765	755
75–79	57	44	384	589
80–84	36	53	157	240
≥85	35	51	113	175
Births	10 122			
CDR	12.75			
CBR	28.59			
CRNI	15.84			

Note: CBR, crude birth rate (actual number of births per 1000 population); CDR, crude death rate (actual number of deaths per 1000 population); CRNI, crude rate of natural increase (CBR minus CDR per 100; does not take into account migration); $_nD_x$, observed deaths between ages x and $x+n$; $_nPY_x$, observed person–years between ages x and $x+n$.

In 2000, AMMP added questions to the census round to determine more detailed fertility and migration characteristics and their effects on the population structure. Preliminary analyses of the data indicated that a considerable amount of short-term migration occurred between census rounds. In addition, the age-specific fertility rates of those who migrated to Dar es Salaam were about half those of older residents. The in-migration of young adults, with lower levels of fertility, contributed to the "bulge" in the population pyramid in the 15–49 age group. These are preliminary data, and further analyses of these data are planned.

Acknowledgments

AMMP is a project of the Tanzania Ministry of Health, funded by the Department for International Development (DFID), United Kingdom. The project is implemented in partnership with the University of Newcastle upon Tyne, United Kingdom.

This chapter is, in part, an output of a project that DFID has funded for the benefit of Tanzania and other developing countries, and the views expressed are not necessarily those of DFID.

The AMMP team includes K.G.M.M. Alberti, Richard Amaro, Yusuf Hemed, Berlina Job, Gregory Kabadi, Judith Kahama, Joel Kalula, Ayoub Kibao, John Kissima, Henry Kitange, Regina Kutaga, Mary Lewanga, Frederic Macha, Haroun Machibya, Honorati Masanja, Louisa Masayanyika, Mkamba Mashombo, Godwill Massawe, Gabriel Masuki, Ali Mhina, Veronica Mkusa, Ades Moshy, Hamisi Mponezya, Robert Mswia, Deo Mtasiwa, Ferdinand Mugusi, Samuel Ngatunga, Mkay Nguluma, Peter Nkulila, Seif Rashid, J.J. Rubona, Asha Sankole, Daudi Simba, Philip Setel, Nigel Unwin, and David Whiting.

The AMMP team would like to acknowledge the municipal health-management team from Temeke and Ilala for their continued support and collaboration. We are also grateful for the contributions and efforts of AMMP support staff: Mariana Lugemwa, Dorothy Lyimo, Rukia Mwamtemi, Getrude Peter, Charles William, Mustapha Kahise, and Juma Mfinanga. Finally, we would like to express our sincere thanks to all those who live in the project area for their patience and cooperation.

Chapter 10

HAI DSS, TANZANIA

Robert Mswia, David Whiting, Gregory Kabadi, Honorati Masanja, and Philip Setel[1]

Site description

Physical geography of the Hai DSA

Hai District is on the slopes of Mount Kilimanjaro, in Kilimanjaro region, in northeast Tanzania (Figure 10.1). The district has an area of 13 000 km^2, spanning three ecological zones. Its lowland zone lies between 750 and 1000 m above sea level (asl), with scanty rainfall (about 325 mm a year), warm to hot temperatures, and sparse population density (about 70 people per km^2). The midland zone lies between 1000 and 1600 m asl and has higher rainfall (about 1560 mm a year), moderate temperatures, and higher population density (about 150–160 per km^2). The highland zone is above 1600 m asl and has heavy rainfall, cool temperatures, and mountain forests and grasslands. People do not live in this zone, but it constitutes the largest water reservoir (from rainfall and glacial runoff) and forest reserve in Kilimanjaro. Multiple springs and rivers flow from this zone and water both the midland and the lowland zones

Figure 10.1 Location of the Hai DSS site, Tanzania (monitored population, 154 000).

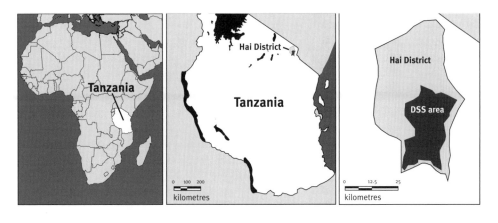

1 Adult Morbidity and Mortality Project, Tanzania.

before emptying into the Pangani River basin. The district has 4 administrative divisions, 11 wards, and 61 villages. The Hai DSS site lies between latitudes 3.13° and 3.46°S and longitudes 37.11° and 37.36°E, and it covers three of the four divisions of the district.

Population characteristics of the Hai DSA

As of 1999, the Hai DSS site has had a population of about 154 000, with an average annual rate of growth of 1.7% from 1992 through 1999. It has 36 000 households (rounded to nearest thousand), and the average household size is 4.6. A household is defined as "people eating from the same cooking pot." Many villages in the DSA are rural, and some are peri-urban. The main ethnic groups are Chagga and the Maasai. Major religious groups in the area are Christian (79%) and Muslim (20%). Indigenous languages are commonly spoken in the villages, although the national language, Kiswahili, is widely understood and spoken.

Agriculture, livestock keeping, dairy farming, commercial mining, and cottage industries are the main economic activities. At present, the district has 139 primary schools, with a total student population of 40 000. It has 13 secondary schools (both public and private), with 5000 pupils, and 5 postprimary technical schools, with 720 pupils. About 95% of school-age children attend school, and about 96% of the population is literate.

The district has 2 hospitals, 2 health centres, 39 dispensaries, and 61 village health posts. These provide curative, preventive, and health-promotion services. About 85% of children <5 years old are vaccinated against five major communicable diseases. Water is plentiful in the highland and midland zones, but it is often polluted with microbes, toxic minerals, and agricultural chemicals.

Wood is the main source of fuel. Because the population is growing rapidly, demand for fuelwood is rising sharply, and people are now encroaching on the highland forest reserve in Kilimanjaro National Park. Thirty-six of 61 villages have electricity, but the use of this source of energy is limited because of the cost. A few households use biogas (gas processed from waste products, such as cow dung and agricultural wastes).

Hai has a transportation infrastructure comprising 710 km of road and an international airport (Kilimanjaro International Airport). Most roads are unpaved, and they are often impassable for vehicles during the rainy season. Community-based data show that the main causes of death in Hai are HIV–AIDS, cancer, perinatal causes, acute febrile illness (including malaria), pneumonia, diarrheal diseases, injuries (both intentional and unintentional), malnutrition, and maternal causes.

Hai DSS procedures

Introduction to the Hai DSS site

DSS work is carried out in Hai to provide reliable population denominators for continuous monitoring of cause-specific mortality. Such demographic and mortality monitoring activities have together provided district authorities with information on the burden of disease, health-facility use in the period before death, and population conditions. These data are used for evidence-based planning and evaluation of health services. The monitoring is an activity of the Tanzanian Ministry of Health and the district health-management team, as part of the Adult Morbidity and Mortality Project, phase 2 (AMMP-2). The goal of AMMP-2 is to decrease the morbidity and mortality stemming from conditions particularly likely to cause suffering and disadvantage among Tanzania's poor people, where these conditions are amenable to health-service interventions. To contribute to this goal, the project has aimed to strengthen evidence-based planning and development of cost-effective health services within the context of health-sector reform in project districts and in the Ministry of Health in Tanzania.

AMMP was established in 1992 to provide information for the Tanzanian Ministry of Health, regarding the policy implications of adult morbidity and mortality in the country. Demographic and mortality monitoring in both phases of AMMP has been carried out in Temeke and Ilala districts (Dar es Salaam) and Morogoro rural district (Morogoro region), as well as in Hai District (see Chapters 9, 12). In 1992, the Hai project area had 51 rural villages, with a total population of 142 000. The population has grown to a current total of 154 000. Although the initial focus was on adults, the system now collects data on people of all ages.

As stated, the demographic and mortality monitoring began in 1992. Since then there has been one enumeration round each year. The DSS is now being incorporated into both national and district structures. In the Ministry of Health, the National Sentinel System has overall responsibility for using DSS to collect demographic and mortality data. Dar es Salaam and Morogoro rural sites are also becoming part of this sentinel system, and the Rufiji DSS site contributes data on cause-specific mortality to it. Monitoring work is expected to become part of the routine systems of the district. Mortality monitoring will continue indefinitely, and DSS will continue as long as the district has no cost-effective alternative for generating reliable population denominators.

Hai DSS data collection and processing

The size of the population in the DSS (when originally established) was intended to approximate the level that Hayes et al. (1989) suggested is best for ascertaining cause-specific mortality. Within the original set of three AMMP-supported areas (Hai, Dar es Salaam, Morogoro), Hai, a fairly affluent rural area, was chosen to represent a range of rural living conditions, including variations in socioeconomic status and population density.

The Hai District health-management team and the district council (through the office of the district executive director and the district social-services committee) are primary local users of the data. The Ministry of Health is the primary national user. Additional users of the data include

- The government's multisectoral National AIDS Control Programme;

- The Vice President's Office (which produces national poverty- and welfare-monitoring indicators);

- Ministry of Health initiatives for malaria control (for example, social marketing of insecticide-treated nets and the national malarial-drug policy);

- Nongovernmental organizations (for example, the Tanzania Public Health Association);

- Projects (for example, World Vision, Tanzania);

- Donors (for assessment of health-sector performance);

- National Poverty Monitoring Group;

- Other sectors, such as the Ministry of Education, Bureau of Statistics, and Ministry of Labour and Youth Development; and

- Tanzanian and international researchers.

Field procedures

INITIAL CENSUS AND REGULAR UPDATE ROUNDS — The initial census was carried out in 1992, starting with a baseline census to determine who was present in each household in the DSA. A single form was used for each household. Subsequently, the population has been enumerated once a year for an 8-week period beginning each July. Although the census-update rounds take place annually, mortality monitoring, which provides information on probable causes of death, is continuous throughout the year. Probable cause of death is determined using the verbal-autopsy (VA) technique. Fifty-six village members — mostly rural medical assistants, nurses, village health workers, and retired health personnel — are given a small amount of money to act as enumerators for the census-update rounds. They are also key informants who report deaths to the VA supervisory team on a regular basis. Five clinical-health officers from the district constitute the VA supervisory team. In each census round the information from the previous round is printed on new forms for each household. Each household is visited, and an adult member of the household is interviewed. The enumerators verify and, where necessary, update existing data. When new households appear as a result of either migration into the area or splitting of existing households (for example, through marriage), they are registered on new-household forms. The enumerators, with the help of 10 cell leaders (local branch leaders, who are in charge of 10 households and are supposed to know members of the branch), identify these households. Vital events (births and deaths) and migrations are recorded for each household. The following items of data are recorded for each individual during a household visit: name, age, sex, relationship to head of household, main occupation, marital status, drinking and smoking habits, date of entry into the household, mode of entry, date of exit, mode of exit, and whether the individual's parents are alive. Recently, questions on religion and residency were added. Migration tracking is limited to recording the date of entry into and exit from the area and the district of origin or destination;

successive migrations of individuals into and out of the area are not linked. It is possible therefore to determine who is resident at any point in time (and therefore to calculate denominators), but it is impossible to calculate the total time each individual has spent in the surveillance area.

CONTINUOUS MORTALITY SURVEILLANCE — The primary objective of the AMMP DSS is to provide sentinel data on the burden of disease to inform health planning and priority-setting. Therefore, an effort is made to determine the cause of death for each person who dies in the area. This is achieved by interviewing the relatives and caretakers of the deceased, using a short, standard interview schedule. Different forms are used for deaths of infants <31 days old, of children between 31 days and <5 years old, and of all persons ≥5 years old. The forms contain a section to identify the respondent, one to identify the deceased, an open-ended history section, a checklist of previously diagnosed conditions, a checklist of symptoms and their duration, a list of health services sought in the period leading up to the death, a residential history, and a summary of any confirmatory evidence, such as medical records or a death certificate. Trained health personnel complete the form after interviewing one or more of the deceased's relatives or caretakers. Wherever possible, the interview takes place within 6 weeks of the death. Deaths are usually reported by the community-based key informants mentioned above. These individuals have been chosen because of their awareness of events in their communities and the likelihood that they will know of any deaths that occur. In addition, communities receive feedback in a newsletter; consequently, they perceive a benefit in participating in the surveillance system and actively report deaths to the key informants. Recently, each key informant from a village or area has been given a *turubai* (canvas tarpaulin) so that bereaved families from the community can borrow it for funeral gatherings. This has enabled key informants to get information on deaths that occur in their area and report them to the supervisor. The personnel who perform the VAs meet with the key informants on a regular basis to find out about new deaths. They then arrange to meet with the relatives or caretakers of the deceased to verify that the death has occurred, then perform the VA.

Two physicians independently assign a cause of death. Until 1999, a modified version of ICD-10 was used. From 2000, AMMP began to use a shorter, broader list of codes. The diagnoses given by the two coders are compared, and discrepancies are given to a third coder. If all three coders disagree, the form is coded as "unknown." Wherever possible, confirmatory evidence of the cause of death is obtained. This includes in- and out-patient records, a death certificate, or a burial permit.

Data management

Enumerators meet weekly with their supervisors during a census to assess progress and solve the various problems the enumerators encounter. In addition, during the census, a field supervisor reviews all completed forms and returns those with errors or inconsistencies to the enumerators for correction. Those that pass inspection are sent to the data centre in Dar es Salaam and entered into a computer. All census forms with errors detected during data entry are logged and returned to the field for correction. Once the corrected forms are returned to the office, they are logged back in, and the problems are resolved. Staff are trained to enter data into microcomputers using a data-entry system designed specifically for the project in Microsoft FoxPro. They are instructed on how the census forms should be completed so that they, too, in addition to the computer validation programs, can detect errors and inconsistencies. The validation programs include simple range checks and checks for inconsistencies across household members, such as an individual identified as a "spouse" but with marital status recorded as "never married."

Several methods are employed to ensure data quality, including checks in the field and the data-entry process. Supervisors visit a random sample of households to verify entries on the census forms and check that the census includes all the households visited but no nonexistent households. Following each census, reinterviews are also conducted of a sample of households for each enumerator. Because of the large amounts of data collected in a single census, it is impossible to double enter all data for verification; instead, a 5–10% random sample is taken and the forms are checked against the captured data.

The interviewers give each household a newsletter at the end of each interview. It is produced and distributed for US $0.08 per household and contains health-education messages and simplified presentations of results from the previous round. It demonstrates that the DSS is part of the functioning of the district health system. The newsletter is designed to help the communities and their leaders better understand the areas where they live. In 1999, 95% of households reported receiving the newsletter, and 81% of households reported reading it.

Hai DSS basic outputs

Demographic indicators

The primary outputs of the system are estimates of cause-specific mortality for all ages. The DSS has a current population of 154 000, with an annual growth rate of 1.7%. Average household size is 4.6. The male-to-female ratio is 100 : 108, with an age-dependency ratio of 91%. The main age-group structures of the current population are as follows: those <1 year old account for 2.7% of the entire population participating in the DSS; 1–4 years old, 11.1%; 5–14 years old, 27.7%; 15–64 years old, 52.4%; and ≥65 years old, 6.1% (Figure 10.2). Between July 1992 and June 1999, the maternal mortality ratio was 368 per 100 000 live births.

The figures presented below reflect change of residence on an annual basis and do not capture short-term movements between the enumeration rounds. In the year 1998–99, the DSA had an out-migration of 14 951 people. The region of destination was obtained for 12 855 of these people. The most common destination (48%) was another part of Hai, whereas 10% migrated to Dar es Salaam, the commercial centre of Tanzania. The remainder migrated to other parts of Tanzania, except for a few who migrated internationally (mostly to Kenya). Also in that year, 16 575 people migrated to households within the DSA. The place of origin for 73% of them was determined: 53% migrated from areas within Hai, and 686 (5.6% of those who gave a place of origin) came from Dar es Salaam. The remainder came from other parts of Tanzania, except for 88, who came from 10 other countries, mainly Kenya.

Table 10.1 shows the age- and sex-specific all-cause mortality at the Hai DSS site.

Figure 10.2. Population pyramid for person–years observed at the Hai DSS site, Tanzania, 1995–99.

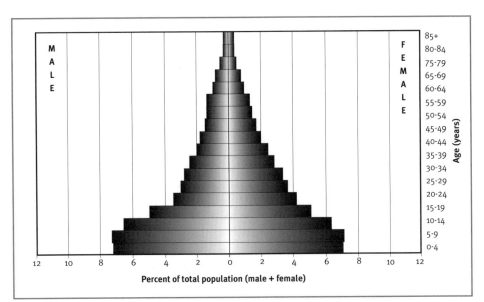

Table 10.1. Age- and sex-specific mortality at the Hai DSS site, Tanzania, 1995–99.

Age (years)	Deaths ($_nD_x$)		Person–years observed ($_nPY_x$)	
	Male	Female	Male	Female
<1	699	587	9 999	10 000
1–4	297	293	43 648	43 160
5–9	161	118	54 209	53 555
10–14	79	61	48 642	47 642
15–19	94	56	36 738	38 453
20–24	110	150	25 682	31 591
25–29	164	236	22 076	27 682
30–34	252	268	20 518	25 263
35–39	272	211	18 068	21 215
40–44	236	171	14 725	18 479
45–49	215	126	12 219	13 965
50–54	197	105	10 877	12 920
55–59	154	115	10 084	11 229
60–64	221	122	10 048	10 030
65–69	211	133	7 186	7 266
70–74	247	146	5 917	5 879
75–79	225	145	3 867	3 859
80–84	182	161	2 407	2 867
≥85	412	474	2 239	2 661
Births	10 122			
CDR	12.75			
CBR	28.59			
CRNI	15.84			

Note: CBR, crude birth rate (actual number of births per 1000 population); CDR, crude death rate (actual number of deaths per 1000 population); CRNI, crude rate of natural increase (CBR minus CDR per 100; does not take into account migration); $_nD_x$, observed deaths between ages x and $x+n$; $_nPY_x$, observed person–years between ages x and $x+n$.

Acknowledgments

AMMP is a project of the Tanzania Ministry of Health, funded by the Department for International Development (DFID), United Kingdom. The project is implemented in partnership with the University of Newcastle upon Tyne, United Kingdom.

This chapter is an output of a project that DFID funded for the benefit of Tanzania and other developing countries, and the views expressed are not necessarily those of DFID.

The AMMP team includes K.G.M.M. Alberti, Richard Amaro, Yusuf Hemed, Berlina Job, Gregory Kabadi, Judith Kahama, Joel Kalula, Ayoub Kibao, John Kissima, Henry Kitange, Regina Kutaga, Mary Lewanga, Frederic Macha, Haroun Machibya, Honorati Masanja, Louisa Masayanyika, Mkamba Mashombo, Godwill Massawe, Gabriel Masuki, Ali Mhina, Veronica Mkusa, Ades Moshy, Hamisi Mponezya, Robert Mswia, Deo Mtasiwa, Ferdinand Mugusi, Samuel Ngatunga, Mkay Nguluma, Peter Nkulila, Seif Rashid, J.J. Rubona, Asha Sankole, Daudi Simba, Philip Setel, Nigel Unwin, and David Whiting.

The AMMP team would like to acknowledge the district health-management team from Hai for their continued support and collaboration. We are also grateful for the contributions and efforts made by the AMMP support staff: Mariana Lugemwa, Dorothy Lyimo, Rukia Mwamtemi, Getrude Peter, Charles William, Mustapha Kahise, and Juma Mfinanga. Finally, we would like to express our sincere thanks to all those who live in the project area for their patience and cooperation.

Chapter 11

IFAKARA DSS, TANZANIA

*Joanna Armstrong Schellenberg,[1,2] Oscar Mukasa,[1] Salim Abdulla,[1] Tanya Marchant,[1]
Christian Lengeler,[2] Nassor Kikumbih,[1] Hassan Mshinda,[1] and Rose Nathan[1]*

Site description

Physical geography of the Ifakara DSA

The Ifakara DSS (latitudes 8°00′–8°35′S, longitudes 35°58′–36°48′E, altitude 270–1000 m above sea level) includes 25 villages of Kilombero and Ulanga districts, in the Morogoro region of southwest Tanzania, about 320 km from Dar es Salaam (Figure 11.1). The area covers 80 km × 18 km in Kilombero District and 40 km × 25 km in Ulanga District, making a total of 2400 km² of Guinea savannah in the floodplain of the Kilombero River, which divides the two districts. The Udzungwa Mountains lie to the northwest. The area has a rainy season from November to May, but rain may fall in any month of the year. Annual rainfall is 1200–1800 mm, and the annual mean temperature is 26°C.

Figure 11.1. Location of the Ifakara DSS site, Tanzania (monitored population, 60 000).

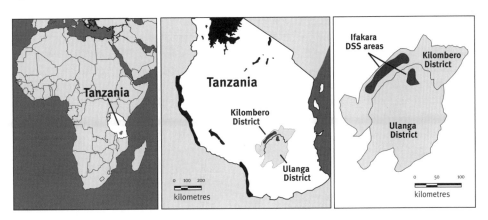

1 Ifakora Health Research and Development Centre, Tanzania.
2 Swiss Tropical Institute, Switzerland.

Population characteristics of the Ifakara DSA

The DSA has a population of 60 000 people, living in 12 000 scattered rural house-holds. Its population density is 25 people/km². It has a wide mix of ethnic groups, including Wandamba, Wapogoro, Wabena, Wambunga, and Wahehe. About 40% of the population is Muslim; and 60%, Christian. Although most people speak the language of their own ethnic group, the national language, Swahili, is widely spoken.

The most common occupations are subsistence farming, fishing, and small-scale trading; and rice and maize are the predominant food crops. All villages have government primary schools. The median age at enrollment in school is 8.75 years. Literacy rates among adults are 88% for men and 69% for women. Most local houses have mud walls and thatched roofs, but up to one-third have brick walls and corrugated iron roofs. Most families have a second house known as a *shamba* house (farmhouse), where they stay during the planting and harvesting seasons. The most common sources of water are shallow wells, open wells, and rivers.

The site has no paved roads, and some villages are cut off for parts of the year as a result of flooding. Limited seasonal bus service runs up to three times each day between the towns of Ifakara, Mahenge, and Malinyi. The Tazara railway links the towns of Ifakara and Mlimba. The site has no telephone service, and most houses have no electricity. Catholic missionary stations in some villages are connected by a radio-call network.

The public health system comprises a network of village health workers, health posts, dispensaries, health centres, and hospitals, offering a varying quality of care. In Ifakara, the capital of Kilombero, the main hospital is a large, well-equipped mission-designated district hospital. The hospital in Mahenge, the Ulanga District capital, has more limited facilities. The mother and child health services are well developed, and vaccination coverage is high, with 74% of children in Kilombero and 63% of children in Ulanga receiving measles vaccines by the time they are 1 year old. Use of health services is also fairly high: 49% of children <5 years old who were reported sick in Kilombero in a 2-week period were taken to a health facility. Use of health facilities is slightly lower in Ulanga, with 39% of sick children being taken to a health facility.

According to health services and local people, malaria is the foremost health problem for both adults and children (Tanner et al. 1991). Malaria transmission from *Plasmodium falciparum* is intense and perennial, despite marked seasonality in mosquito densities, which peak with the rains. *Anopheles gambiae* and *Anopheles funestus* are the main vectors, with an estimated 200–300 infective bites/person a year occurring in rural areas close to Ifakara (Smith et al. 1993). Life-threatening malaria occurs largely in children and commonly in those <1 year old (Schellenberg et al. 1999). Anemia is extremely common: 86% of children <5 years old have some level of anemia (Hb < 11 g/dL), and 9% of children aged 6–11 months have life-threatening anemia (Hb < 5 g/dL). The largest single cause of this anemia is malaria (Menendez et al. 1997).

In 1997, median monthly household expenditure varied from US $77 to US $96, depending on the season, of which about 75% is for food.

In January–May 1999, part of the area suffered a famine, during which emergency food aid was distributed by the government, the World Food Programme, and local nongovernmental organizations. Since mid-1997 a social-marketing program for insecticide-treated mosquito nets to control malaria has been ongoing in Kilombero and Ulanga. The nets are popular, with 54% of children <5 years old using a net and

37% using an ever-treated net. However, most nets are not treated regularly: only 13% of children <5 years old sleep under a recently treated mosquito net.

Ifakara DSS procedures

Introduction to the Ifakara DSS site

The original aim of the DSS was to provide a framework to evaluate a social-marketing program for treated mosquito nets (Armstrong Schellenberg et al. 1999). The current aims are

- To collect accurate information on health and survival;

- To facilitate use of this information to improve health at district and national levels; and

- To provide a framework for population-based health research relevant to local health priorities and needs.

The DSS started in 1996, with a population of 52 000. The current population (end of 1999) is 60 000. Each household is visited every 4 months, to collect information on pregnancies, births, deaths, and migrations, using the household-registration system (HRS) developed originally in Navrongo, Ghana (Binka et al. 1999). Between household visits, key informants report births and deaths as they occur. No verbal autopsy (VA) questionnaires were used until 2000, although deaths among children born in 1998 and 1999 were followed up with an open question on the events leading up to the child's death. Educational level, roofing type, and a brief checklist of household possessions are assessed annually. Additional surveys of samples of the population have covered perceptions of malaria, its treatment, and its prevention; household expenditures; willingness to pay for treated mosquito nets; fertility; child fostering; an evaluation of a discount-voucher system for treated mosquito nets; and the effect of treated nets on child survival, malaria, and anemia.

The DSS team currently employs 39 full-time staff: 22 interviewers, 8 supervisors, 2 assistant field managers, 3 data entry clerks, a filing clerk, a driver, a data manager, and a field manager. This team works under the overall coordination of a demographer or epidemiologist. In addition, at the subvillage level, 104 key informants chosen by village leaders are paid a small allowance for every event they report. The interviewers live in the villages where they work, using bicycles for transportation. Supervisors also live in the DSA and hold weekly meetings with managers and data-management staff in Ifakara. Supervisors use motorbikes for transportation. All field staff attend monthly meetings in Ifakara, and key informants attend meetings every 4 months in the DSA.

The Ifakara DSS is a unit within the Ifakara Health Research and Development Centre, which is an independent Tanzanian trust. Its current scientific partners include the Swiss Tropical Institute (STI), the US Centers for Disease Control (CDC), the Tanzanian Ministry of Health, the International Development Research Centre, the Tanzania Essential Health Interventions Project, the Adult Morbidity and Mortality Project, and the World Health Organization (WHO). Funding for the DSS is provided by the Swiss Agency for Development and Co-operation (SDC), CDC, WHO, STI, and the Swiss National Science Foundation (SNSF).

Outputs of the DSS are disseminated locally through a community newsletter (delivered to all households every round) and through meetings with community leaders. Results are also made available to district health-management teams in printed form and through their attendance at district health-planning meetings.

Ifakara DSS data collection and processing

The area was originally selected as a rural area, including parts of two districts. It had an initial target population of about 50 000 people for the evaluation of the social-marketing program for malaria control using treated nets.

Field procedures

INITIAL CENSUS — A baseline census was carried out from September to December 1996. It noted people's names, sex, dates of birth, and relationships within the household, made sketch maps of household locations, and recorded the rough locations of any *shamba* houses.

REGULAR UPDATE ROUNDS — Since January 1997 every household has been visited every 4 months by a DSS interviewer, who updates the census record by asking an adult member of the household about in- and out-migrations, pregnancies, births, and deaths. Bereavement interviews (the VAs) on all deaths were introduced in September 2000. A field supervisor carries out these interviews.

CONTINUOUS SURVEILLANCE — Village-based reporters in each *kitongoji* (subvillage) are a source of information on births and deaths between the visits every 4 months. They record all such events in a notebook. This information is checked and transcribed on a standard form every month by a field supervisor. Village reporters are paid a small sum of money for each event they report and for meeting with their supervisor each month.

FIELD SUPERVISION AND QUALITY CONTROL — Every week, supervisors revisit a randomly selected 10% of the households visited by DSS interviewers and repeat the interview. At the time of these interviews, supervisors do not have access to the original data but use a copy that contains a random number of deliberate errors they should detect and correct. Supervisors also carry out accompanied interviews with a convenience sample of two households for every interviewer every week. Assistant field managers and field managers also carry out spot checks on every interviewer and supervisor at least once each round. They check from a random starting point that every neighbouring household has been registered. Information from the village-based reporters is checked against that from the DSS interviewers.

Data management

All forms are brought to Ifakara, where they are logged by a filing clerk before being processed by the data clerks, who update the databases for every household visit and every event (pregnancy, birth, death, or migration) detected during household visits. Data from each week's work is entered into the HRS database and processed before the following week's field meeting. Checking programs are run, and any inconsistencies or

Figure 11.2. Population pyramid for person–years observed at the Ifakara DSS site, Tanzania, 1997–99.

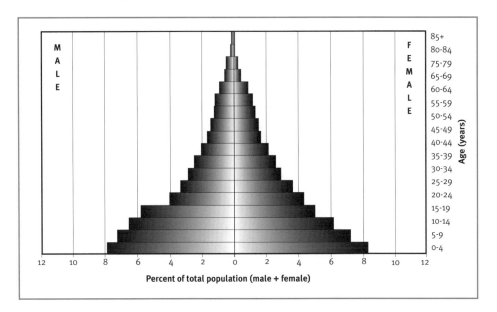

queries are referred back to the field team for correction within 2 weeks of the original interview.

Population, mortality, and fertility data are sent to village leaders every year (more often if requested). Summary information is disseminated to each household in the DSA through a community newsletter. Feedback is given to district-level health workers at semiannual meetings. DSS results reach national and international levels through technical reports and publications.

Ifakara DSS basic outputs

Demographic indicators

Three percent of the population is <1 year old; 16%, 0–4 years old; 26%, 5–14 years old; 53%, 15–64 years old; and 4%, ≥65 years old (Figure 11.2). The age-dependency ratio is 87%, and 51% of the population is female, giving a sex ratio of 97 males for every 100 females. The total fertility is estimated at 4.8 births per woman. During 1999, the infant mortality rate was 90 per 1000 live births, and mortality in children 1–4 years old was 12.9 per 1000 per year. Average household size is 5.0, and 81% of house-hold heads are male. The population is highly mobile, with most families moving to the *shamba* areas for a few weeks at a time, depending on the farming season.

Table 11.1 shows the age- and sex-specific all-cause mortality at the Ifakara DSS site.

Table 11.1. Age- and sex-specific mortality at the Ifakara DSS site, Tanzania, 1997–99.

Age (years)	Death s ($_nD_x$) Male	Death s ($_nD_x$) Female	Person–years observed ($_nPY_x$) Male	Person–years observed ($_nPY_x$) Female
<1	218	258	2 718	2 829
1–4	133	137	9 830	10 540
5–9	29	39	11 525	11 657
10–14	12	16	10 368	9 995
15–19	19	22	9 180	8 119
20–24	25	29	6 385	7 014
25–29	32	37	5 237	5 940
30–34	47	39	4 492	4 768
35–39	46	26	3 896	4 249
40–44	36	29	3 182	3 495
45–49	29	22	2 569	2 762
50–54	36	26	2 225	2 542
55–59	51	28	1 854	2 226
60–64	37	38	1 754	1 970
65–69	36	37	1 315	1 517
70–74	44	42	813	797
75–79	47	35	677	507
80–84	19	18	214	220
≥85	21	17	132	126
Births	5 106			
CDR	11.35			
CBR	31.98			
CRNI	20.63			

Note: CBR, crude birth rate (actual number of births per 1000 population); CDR, crude death rate (actual number of deaths per 1000 population); CRNI, crude rate of natural increase (CBR minus CDR per 100; does not take into account migration); $_nD_x$, observed deaths between ages x and $x+n$; $_nPY_x$, observed person–years between ages x and $x+n$.

Acknowledgments

We wish to thank the residents of the DSA; Dr Lwilla and Dr Mbena, district medical officers of Kilombero and Ulanga districts; and the field and data-room staff of the Ifakara DSS. We also thank SDC, CDC, WHO, STI, and SNSF for financial support.

Chapter 12

MOROGORO DSS, TANZANIA

Robert Mswia, Gregory Kabadi, David Whiting, Honorati Masanja, and Philip Setel[1]

Site description

Physical geography of the Morogoro DSA

Morogoro District is situated in Morogoro region, about 180 km from Dar es Salaam. Morogoro has a low population density and mixed topography, which includes mountains and plains (Figure 12.1). It covers an area of 19 250 km^2 and has 10 administrative divisions, divided into 43 wards, each of these divided into 215 registered villages. The Morogoro rural DSS site lies between latitudes 6.60° and 7.29°S and longitudes 37.35° and 38.30°E. The surveillance area covers 61 of the 215 registered villages. These are in three divisions — Ngerengere, Kingolwira, and Mlali. The villages cover a wide area, including the lowlands and slopes of the Uluguru mountain range. The most isolated villages (Kidunda and Usungura) are close to the Selous Game Reserve, about 160 km away from district headquarters.

Figure 12.1. Location of the Morogoro DSS site, Tanzania (monitored population, 120 000).

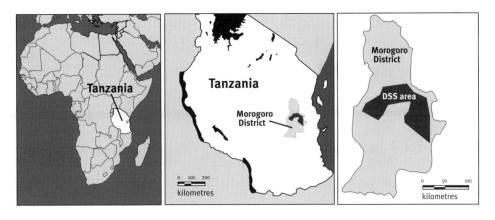

[1] Adult Morbidity and Mortality Project, Tanzania.

Population characteristics of the Morogoro DSA

Currently, the surveillance area has a population of 120 000, with an annual growth rate of 3.6%. The current number of households is 31 000, and the average household size is 4.0. A household is defined as "people eating from the same cooking pot." About 18% are single-person households. The area is generally poor, rural, and is among the 50% most deprived regions in Tanzania, according to the poverty and welfare indicators for 1999 of the Vice President's Office. The main ethnic groups are the Luguru, Sagara, and Pogoro. The population participating in surveillance, however, comprises a wide mixture of ethnic groups. The religious groups in the area are Muslims (57%), Christians (41%), and others (2%). Indigenous languages are commonly spoken in the villages, but the national language, Kiswahili, is widely understood and spoken.

The main occupation of people of all ages in the area is farming, including 45.2% of males and 52.7% of females. The proportion of girls attending school is slightly higher than that of boys for all ages up to 14 years. The proportion of people from age 15 stating that they had no formal education is 65% for women but only 35% for men.

About 40% of the households in the Morogoro DSS use tap water (34.8% public tap, 2.7% neighbour's tap, and 3.2% own tap); 32.3%, river or rain water; and 26.9%, wells. More than 90% use pit latrines. Less than 1% of the households in the project area use electricity or gas as the main cooking fuel. The majority (90%) use firewood, and the remainder use kerosene stoves or charcoal for cooking. Some of the villages in Morogoro surveillance area have access to electricity, especially those along the main roads and those with health facilities.

Transportation in the district is mainly by road. The roads from Dar es Salaam to Dodoma and Iringa pass through the district. Most of the other roads are unsealed and difficult to travel along during the rainy season. Morogoro District has 3 hospitals, 6 health centres, and 81 dispensaries.

The main causes of death in the area are acute febrile illness (including malaria), diarrheal diseases, HIV–AIDS, injuries (both intentional and unintentional), anemia, pulmonary TB, and malnutrition.

Morogoro DSS procedures

Introduction to the Morogoro DSS site

DSS work is carried out in Morogoro to provide reliable population denominators for continuous cause-specific mortality surveillance. The demographic and mortality monitoring provides district authorities with information on the burden of disease, health-facility use in the period before death, and population conditions. These data are used for evidence-based planning and evaluation of health services. The monitoring is an activity of the Tanzanian Ministry of Health and the district health-management team, as part of the Adult Morbidity and Mortality Project, phase 2 (AMMP-2). The goal of AMMP-2 is to decrease the morbidity and mortality stemming from conditions particularly likely to cause suffering and disadvantage among Tanzania's poor people, where these conditions are amenable to health-service interventions. To contribute to this goal, the project aims to strengthen evidence-based planning and development of cost-effective health services within the context of health-sector reform in project districts and the Ministry of Health in Tanzania.

Demographic and mortality surveillance in both phases of AMMP has been carried out in Hai District (Kilimanjaro region) and Dar es Salaam, as well as in Morogoro (see Chapters 9 and 10). In 1992, the DSS site in Morogoro had a population of 99 000, but it has since grown to a current total of 120 000. Whereas the initial focus was on adult health, the system now collects data on people of all ages.

Demographic and mortality surveillance began in 1992. Since then the DSS has had one enumeration round each year. The system is incorporated into both national and district structures. In the Ministry of Health, the National Sentinel System assumes overall responsibility for ascertaining a national picture of the burden of disease, using the DSS to gather demographic and mortality data. The Hai and Dar es Salaam sites are also becoming a part of this sentinel system, and for the time being the Rufiji site contributes cause-specific mortality data. Surveillance work will become part of the routine systems of the district. Mortality surveillance will continue indefinitely, and the DSS will continue as long as the site is without a cost-effective alternative for gathering reliable population denominators.

Morogoro DSS data collection and processing

The size of the population in the DSS approached the level that Hayes et al. (1989) suggested is best for the ascertainment of cause-specific mortality. Within the original set of three AMMP-supported areas, Morogoro was chosen to represent poor rural living conditions and low population density.

Field procedures

INITIAL CENSUS — Because the 1988 national census did not provide an accurate basis for estimating population denominators, an initial census round was carried out in 1992. The baseline census was taken to determine who was present in each household under surveillance. Since then the population has been enumerated once a year for an 8-week period beginning each August. Whereas the census-update rounds take place annually, mortality surveillance to provide information on probable causes of death is continuous. Probable cause of death is determined using the verbal-autopsy (VA) technique. About 86 villagers, most of them village health workers and primary-school teachers, are paid a small remuneration for acting as enumerators for the census-update rounds and as key informants to report deaths to the VA supervisory team. Four clinical-health officers from the district constitute the VA supervisory team.

REGULAR UPDATE ROUNDS — In subsequent census rounds, information from the previous round is printed on new forms for each household. Each household is visited, and an adult member of the household is interviewed. The enumerators verify and, where necessary, update existing data. When new households appear as a result of either migration into the area or splitting of existing households (for example, through marriage), they are registered on new-household forms. Vital events (births and deaths) and migrations are recorded for each household. The following items of data are recorded for each individual during a household visit: name, age, sex, relationship to head of household, main occupation, marital status, alcohol consumption and smoking habits, date of entry into the household, mode of entry, date of exit, mode of exit, and whether his or her parents are alive. Recently, questions on religion have been added to increase knowledge of the social characteristics of the population. Migration tracking is limited to recording the date of entry into and exit from the area and the district of origin or destination; successive migrations of individuals into and out of the area are not linked. It is thus possible to determine who is resident at any point in time (and therefore to calculate denominators) but not to calculate the total time each individual has spent in the surveillance area.

CONTINUOUS MORTALITY SURVEILLANCE — The primary objective of the AMMP approach to DSS is to inform health planning and priority-setting by providing sentinel data on the burden of disease. Therefore, an effort is made to determine the cause of death for each resident. This is achieved by interviewing the relatives and caretakers of deceased people, using a short, standard interview schedule. Different forms are used for deaths of infants <31 days old, of children between 31 days and <5 years old, and of all persons ≥5 years old. The forms contain a section to identify the respondent, another to identify the deceased, an open-ended history section, a checklist of previously diagnosed conditions, a checklist of symptoms and their duration, a list of health services sought in the period leading to the death, a residential history, and a summary of any confirmatory evidence, such as medical records or a death certificate. The form is completed by trained health personnel, who interview one or more relatives or caretakers. Wherever possible, the interview takes place within 6 weeks of the date of death. Deaths are usually reported by community-based key informants. The key informants are chosen because of their awareness of events in their community; that is, they are likely to hear of deaths that occur. In addition, the communities receive feedback in a newsletter; they consequently perceive a benefit from taking part in the surveillance system and actively report deaths to the key informants. The personnel who perform the VAs meet with the key informants on a regular basis to find out about new deaths. They then arrange to meet with the relatives or caretakers of the deceased to verify the death and then perform the VA. Two physicians independently assign a cause of death. Until 1999, a modified version of ICD-10 was used. From 2000, a shorter, broader list of codes, developed by AMMP, has been used. The diagnoses given by the two coders are compared, and discrepancies are given to a third coder. If all three coders disagree, the cause of death is coded as "unknown." As noted, confirmatory evidence of the cause of death is obtained, whenever possible.

Data management

During the census a field supervisor reviews all completed forms, and those with errors or inconsistencies are returned to the enumerators for correction. Those that pass inspection are sent to the data centre in Dar es Salaam and entered into a computer. All census forms with errors detected during data entry are logged and returned to the field for correction. Once the corrected forms are returned to the office, they are logged back in, and the problems are resolved.

Staff are trained to enter data into microcomputers using a data-entry system designed specifically for the project in Microsoft FoxPro. They are instructed on the correct completion of the census forms so that they, too, in addition to the computer validation programs, can detect errors or inconsistencies. The validation programs include simple range checks and checks for inconsistencies across household members, such as an individual identified as a "spouse" but with a marital status recorded as "never married."

Several methods are employed to ensure data quality, including checks in the field and data-entry processes. Supervisors visit a random sample of households to verify entries on the census forms to check that all households visited have been included in the census and that no nonexistent households have been included. Following each census, reinterviews are conducted of a sample of households for each enumerator. Because of the large amount of data collected during a single census, it is impossible to double enter all data for verification; instead, a 5–10% random sample is taken, and the forms are checked against the captured data.

Each household is given a newsletter at the end of each interview. This newsletter is produced and distributed at a cost of about US $0.10 per household and contains health-education messages and simplified presentations of results from the previous round. The newsletter demonstrates that the DSS is part of the functioning of the district-health system and is designed to help the communities and their leaders better understand the areas where they live. In 1998, 94% of households reported receiving the newsletter, and 65% reported reading it.

Morogoro DSS basic outputs

Demographic indicators

The primary outputs of the system are estimates of cause-specific mortality for all ages. The DSS shows that the current population of the surveillance area is 120 000 and has an annual growth rate of 3.6%. The proportions of the population in the various age groups are as follows: <1 year old, 2.6%; 1–4 years old, 9.7%; 5–14 years old, 26.4%; 15–64 years old, 56.3%; and ≥65 years old, 5.0%. The ratio of males to females is 100 : 103, and the age-dependency ratio is 78.6%. The infant mortality rate is 99.7 per 1000 live births, and the under-five mortality rate is 39.6 per 1000. The maternal mortality rate is 1183 per 100 000 live births for the period between July 1992 and June 1999. The average household size is 4.0 with a headship of 73% males and 27% females.

The shape of the population pyramid (Figure 12.2) in the two rural Tanzanian districts, based on AMMP census techniques, shows a narrowing in the base over time; that is, the proportion of the population <5 years old is less than expected, assuming "typical" developing-country conditions of high-fertility and a growing population. This narrowing effect may be due to real factors or to the under-enumeration of infants and young children in the annual census round, or to both. Some possible contributing factors would be rapidly declining fertility (as a result of both HIV–AIDS and so-called secular trends) and higher child mortality (perhaps partly a result of the HIV–AIDS pandemic). In addition, the narrowing effect is most pronounced in villages along the major east–west highway, suggesting that part of the explanation may be the mobility of young people in these areas. If this aspect of the population structure is an artifact of under-ascertainment of infants, our estimates of infant mortality will be too high. If need be, this could be corrected using indirect methods.

Table 12.1 shows the age- and sex-specific all-cause mortality at the Morogoro DSS site.

Figure 12.2. Population pyramid of person–years observed in the Morogoro DSS site, Tanzania, 1995–99.

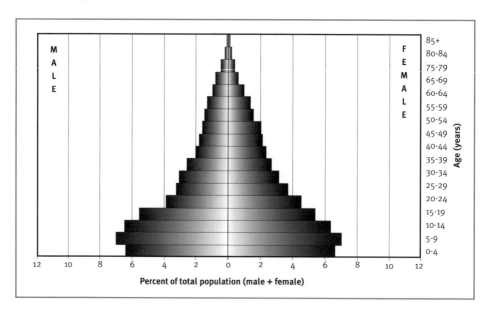

Table 12.1. Age- and sex-specific mortality at the Morogoro DSS site, Tanzania, 1995–99.

Age (years)	Death s ($_nD_x$)		Person–years observed ($_nPY_x$)	
	Male	Female	Male	Female
<1	725	795	6 403	6 585
1–4	648	604	27 974	29 075
5–9	227	210	37 856	37 882
10–14	91	84	34 925	34 064
15–19	104	117	29 781	28 958
20–24	127	220	20 814	24 299
25–29	239	334	17 289	19 878
30–34	246	313	16 442	16 906
35–39	249	270	13 795	14 413
40–44	262	183	10 864	12 606
45–49	273	178	9 735	11 389
50–54	232	149	8 666	10 869
55–59	206	145	8 002	8 392
60–64	244	178	7 066	7 345
65–69	268	194	5 304	5 125
70–74	272	179	4 329	3 221
75–79	210	135	2 616	2 049
80–84	131	160	1 238	984
≥85	177	169	632	513
Births	13 021			
CDR	17.74			
CBR	24.19			
CRNI	6.45			

Note: CBR, crude birth rate (actual number of births per 1000 population); CDR, crude death rate (actual number of deaths per 1000 population); CRNI, crude rate of natural increase (CBR minus CDR per 100; does not take into account migration); $_nD_x$, observed deaths between ages x and $x+n$; $_nPY_x$, observed person–years between ages x and $x+n$.

Migration depends on the time used to define migration events. The following figures reflect changes of residence on an annual basis and do not capture short-term movements between the enumeration rounds. During 1998–99, 10 896 people migrated out of the surveillance area. The region of destination was obtained for 7887 of these: most (65%) migrated to another part of Morogoro, and 15% migrated to Dar es Salaam, the commercial centre of Tanzania. The rest migrated to various parts of the country, except for 13 people who migrated to other countries. During the same years, 15 585 people migrated to households within the surveillance area. The place of origin for 11 298 (72.4%) was determined: a similar proportion (67%) migrated from areas within Morogoro, and 809 (7.2% of those who gave a place of origin) came from Dar es Salaam; the rest came from various other parts of Tanzania, and just 4 came from other countries.

Acknowledgments

AMMP is a project of the Tanzania Ministry of Health, funded by the Department for International Development (DFID), United Kingdom. The project is implemented in partnership with the University of Newcastle upon Tyne, United Kingdom.

This chapter is, in part, an output of a project that DFID has funded for the benefit of Tanzania and other developing countries, and the views expressed are not necessarily those of DFID.

The AMMP team includes K.G.M.M. Alberti, Richard Amaro, Yusuf Hemed, Berlina Job, Gregory Kabadi, Judith Kahama, Joel Kalula, Ayoub Kibao, John Kissima, Henry Kitange, Regina Kutaga, Mary Lewanga, Frederic Macha, Haroun Machibya, Honorati Masanja, Louisa Masayanyika, Mkamba Mashombo, Godwill Massawe, Gabriel Masuki, Ali Mhina, Veronica Mkusa, Ades Moshy, Hamisi Mponezya, Robert Mswia, Deo Mtasiwa, Ferdinand Mugusi, Samuel Ngatunga, Mkay Nguluma, Peter Nkulila, Seif Rashid, J.J. Rubona, Asha Sankole, Daudi Simba, Philip Setel, Nigel Unwin, and David Whiting.

The AMMP team would like to acknowledge the district health-management team from Morogoro for its continued support and collaboration. We are also grateful for the contributions and efforts of the AMMP support staff: Mariana Lugemwa, Dorothy Lyimo, Rukia Mwamtemi, Getrude Peter, Charles William, Mustapha Kahise, and Juma Mfinanga. Finally, we would like to express our sincere thanks to all those who live in the project area for their patience and cooperation.

Chapter 13

Rufiji DSS, Tanzania

Eleuther Mwageni, Devota Momburi, Zaharani Juma, Mohamed Irema, Honorati Masanja, and the Tanzania Essential Health Interventions Project and Adult Morbidity and Mortality Project teams

Site description

Physical geography of the Rufiji DSA

The Rufiji DSA extends between latitudes 7.47° and 8.03°S and longitudes 38.62° and 39.17°E. The Rufiji DSS is in Rufiji District, Tanzania, about 178 km south of Dar es Salaam (Figure 13.1). Rufiji is one of the six districts of the coast region, the others being Bagamoyo, Kibaha, Kisarawe, Mafia, and Mkuranga. Rufiji, in the south, has 6 divisions, with 19 wards, divided into 94 registered villages and 385 hamlets. The district covers an area of about 14 500 km². The Rufiji DSS operates in 6 contiguous wards and 31 villages (about 60 km long × 30 km wide) and covers an area of 1813 km².

Figure 13.1. Location of the Rufiji DSS site, Tanzania (monitored population, 85 000).

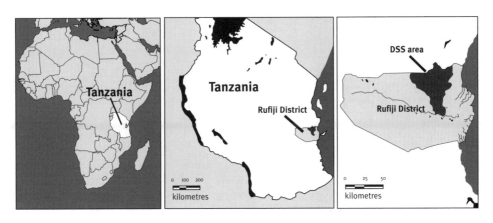

Rufiji has a mean altitude of <500 m above sea level. Its vegetation is mainly tropical forest and grassland. The district has hot weather throughout the year and two rainy seasons: short rains (October–December) and long rains (February–May). The average annual precipitation in the district is 800–1000 mm. A prominent feature of the district is the Rufiji River, with its large floodplain and delta, the most extensive in the country. Mangrove forests flank the tributaries of the delta. The river, from which the district takes its name, divides the district geographically into roughly equal halves. The district is also a gateway to Selous Game Reserve, which has a variety of wild animals, such as zebras, buffalo, hartebeest, monkeys, lions, hyenas, warthogs, and elephants.

Population characteristics of the Rufiji DSA

Rufiji has a population of about 182 000, of which 85 000 (about 47% of the district) is under surveillance. The population densities for the district and for the surveillance area are $12.5/km^2$ and $46/km^2$, respectively. The mean household size for the whole district is about 5.0 (TBS 1994). The district is largely rural, but the population is clustered around Utete (district headquarters), Ikwiriri, Kibiti, and Bungu townships (see "Rufiji DSS basic outputs," below, for DSS-generated demographics).

Rufiji District is home to several ethnic groups. The largest of these is the Ndengereko, who, according to oral tradition, are the original inhabitants of the area; other groups include the Matumbi, Nyagatwa (concentrated in the delta area), Ngindo, Pogoro, and Makonde. The majority of the people are Muslims, with a few Christians and followers of indigenous religions. In addition to local languages, Kiswahili is widely spoken; English is not commonly used in the area.

The majority of the people in Rufiji are subsistence farmers. Farming areas are often set some distance from the family home to take advantage of periodically flooded alluvial soils. With temporary houses located on farmland, this means that some households are often split geographically for up to 4 months of the year. Major crops include cassava, maize, rice, millet, sesame, coconut, and cashew nuts. Fruit such as mangoes, oranges, pineapples, papaya, and jackfruit are also grown. Some residents are involved in fishing or small-scale commercial activities, such as selling wood products (for example, timber, furniture, and carvings).

Each village has at least one primary school (with standard grades 1–7). The district has four secondary schools (three government and one private), of which two are located in the DSA. A Folk Development College — a postprimary polytechnic — is located in Ikwiriri township. According to the 1988 population census (TBS 1994), more males (66%) than females (34%)are literate in the district.

Most villages in the surveillance area have a central place for shops and a market. The dwellings are simple, comprising a mixture of huts with walls made of mud and wooden poles, with thatched or corrugated roofs, as well as conventional brick houses in the townships. In the Rufiji floodplain, *dungus* (traditional shelters on stilts built to deal with flooding) are a common feature. Tap-water supply is very limited, and the majority of people rely on communal boreholes or use natural-spring or river water for domestic purposes — a few use harvested rainwater. The DSA's main transportation route is the north–south Dar es Salaam – Lindi and Mtwara trunk road, half of which is paved; and the other, unsealed. Unpaved feeder roads and tracks link most of the villages to this trunk road. Telephone facilities in the district are located in the three townships. The district is not connected to the national electric grid, but Ikwiriri township has 24-hour diesel-generated electric power from the national electric-supply company. Other places that have electricity depend on private generators.

The district has 55 health facilities: 2 hospitals (1 government and 1 mission), 5 government health centres, 44 government dispensaries, and 4 nongovernment dispensaries. A private dispensary based at Kibiti offers the services of a mobile clinic in some parts of the district. Over-the-counter drugs are available from many private shops and kiosks in the villages. Many people also obtain services from traditional healers, including traditional birth attendants. Malaria and waterborne diseases, such as cholera and diarrhea, are the major health problems in the area, according to both the health services and local people. Major causes of mortality include acute febrile illnesses (including malaria), acute lower-respiratory infections, tuberculosis, AIDS, and perinatal illnesses. Immunization coverage ranges from 85% for BCG (tuberculosis) to 66% for measles in children 12–23 months old. About 89% of the population lives within 5 km of a formal health facility. All villages and health facilities in the district have been positioned using GPS and mapped in a GIS database of district health resources.

Rufiji DSS procedures

Introduction to the Rufiji DSS site

The objectives of the Rufiji DSS are to provide sentinel data for health policy and planning and to monitor the impact of health reforms. Data and experiences from the Rufiji DSS are being assessed for their use in assisting district health-management teams, policymakers, and planners to make more appropriate resource allocations to improve the health situation in the district and the country as a whole. With the Adult Morbidity and Mortality Project (AMMP), experiences from the Rufiji DSS are also informing the development of methods for the National Sentinel System, which monitors the burden of disease in Tanzania. The Rufiji DSS commenced field operations in November 1998.

The Rufiji project employs the DSS to collect health-status and demographic data. The DSS approach involves a continuous surveillance of households and members within households in cycles or intervals, known in the Rufiji DSS as "rounds," of 4 months each. Members (or residents) of the Rufiji DSS are individuals who have resided in the surveillance area for a period of the previous 4 months. The Rufiji DSS collects information on demographic, household, socioeconomic, and environmental characteristics of the population. Verbal autopsies (VAs) conducted on all Rufiji DSS-registered deaths, using specific standard questionnaires, determine cause of death. The VA instruments and coding procedures used in the Rufiji DSS are identical to those used by AMMP.

The Rufiji DSS has a team of 52 people, who are entirely district based. The staff, headed by a station manager, is organized into three groups: field (field manager, 7 enumerator supervisors, 3 VA supervisors, 4 migration supervisors, and 25 enumerators); data (data manager, data assistant, filing clerk, and 3 data-entry clerks); and support (accountant, secretary, driver and mechanic, cleaner, and security guard). Most fieldworkers are deployed throughout the DSA, whereas the data and support teams are based in the field station in Ikwiriri township, south of the DSA.

The Rufiji DSS also has access to about 118 key informants. These are community leaders, whose responsibilities are to assist the field staff in reporting births or deaths in their respective areas and sometimes in finding prospective households for inclusion in the DSS.

The project is comanaged by the Tanzania Essential Health Intervention Project (TEHIP) (funded by the International Development Research Centre, Canada) and AMMP (funded by the Department for International Development, United Kingdom). Both TEHIP and AMMP are projects under the auspices of the Tanzania Ministry of Health. AMMP is implemented in partnership with the University of Newcastle upon Tyne (United Kingdom).

The local district health-management team, the Tanzania Ministry of Health, and national and international collaborative research-and-development projects are the main consumers of Rufiji DSS data.

Rufiji DSS data collection and processing

Field procedures

MAPPING — The Rufiji DSS employed a nonrandomized, purposive technique in selecting the wards under surveillance. It covers the total population in the six contiguous wards of Bungu, Ikwiriri, Kibiti, Mchukwi, Mgomba, and Umwe and operates exclusively to the north of the Rufiji River, which flows along a roughly west–east axis through the district. This side of the river is home to the majority of the population and is more easily accessible throughout the year, whereas communities south of the river, as well as those in the delta, may be inaccessible for varying periods during the long rains. The Rufiji DSS targeted an initial population of 70 000, which was set to provide mortality data similar to those from other DSS sites in the AMMP (see Hayes et al. 1989 and Chapters 9, 10, and 12). Given an average household size of 4–5, it was estimated that the DSS would need to include 14 000–17 500 households. All villages have been positioned using GPS. Mapping of households is planned.

INITIAL CENSUS — The Rufiji DSS data collection began with enumerators conducting an initial census in the sampled area to establish the baseline population. This population forms the foundation for establishing a longitudinal DSS and provides background data on the population. The census data are obtained using standard questionnaires with both closed- and open-ended questions. The enumerators collect data on household (household head, relation to household head), demographic (age, sex), socioeconomic (education, occupation), and environmental (source of drinking water and sanitation facility) conditions. For purposes of identity, each registered household and person is given a unique number to distinguish the household within its village and the individual within his or her household. The unique number for each individual is known as the "permanent ID" and comprises IDs of the village and household and the number for the individual within the household.

REGULAR UPDATE ROUNDS — Longitudinal data collection of demographic, household, socioeconomic, and environmental characteristics is maintained through subsequent update rounds. These rounds take 4 months to complete; the day after one round finishes the next round begins, and households are visited in sequence. Update rounds are undertaken to maintain accurate denominators for estimation of age, sex, and cause-specific death rates. In their periodic visits, enumerators register new people found in the households. These include unregistered individuals who could have been missed during the initial census. During the rounds the enumerators verify the status of each household and individual, using the household-registration books (HRBs), and, if necessary, change their records. The enumerators make all alterations in the respective HRBs, in conjunction with filling in a changes form.

CONTINUOUS SURVEILLANCE — The Rufiji DSS involves the continuous recording of vital events within households and among members over time. These events, recorded by enumerators using specific event forms, include births, deaths, pregnancies, pregnancy outcomes, marital-status changes, and migrations (in and out of the surveillance area). In addition, lay key informants assist the enumerators by independently recording births and deaths in their hamlets.

VA interviews on all DSS-registered deaths are conducted by VA supervisors, using specific standard questionnaires for deaths of infants <31 days old; children between 31 days and <5 years old; and all persons ≥5 years old. The interviews are held with one of the adult relatives of the deceased (preferably a caretaker) well informed of the sequence of events leading up to the death. VA supervisors conduct interviews within 2 months of the report of a death and use any available documents, such as a death certificate or prescriptions, to obtain confirmatory evidence about the cause of death from the last health facility the deceased visited before dying. Such evidence, however, is often unavailable. The completed questionnaires are then coded independently by two physicians, according to a list of causes of death, based on the 10th revision of the International Classification of Diseases. A third physician is asked to independently code the cause of death in the case of discordant results. Where there are three discordant codes, the cause is registered as "unknown."

SUPERVISION AND QUALITY ASSURANCE — The field manager supervises all field operations and spends about 60% of the time supervising field activities and the remainder in the field station's office. On completion of interviews or household visits, field supervisors randomly select and revisit 3–5% of the households interviewed or updated by the enumerators, for quality control. Errors noted are communicated immediately to enumerators or brought up for discussion during the regular bimonthly field-staff meetings.

Data management

The Rufiji DSS data-collection process uses a variety of forms. These forms include baseline census, event, changes, HRBs, and VA questionnaires. A reliable mechanism is in place to ensure smooth production and flow of these forms between the field and the DSS data centre. The DSS filing clerk is responsible for ensuring production and distribution of the forms to the field staff. On completion of the data collection, the supervisors or the filing clerk take the forms to the Rufiji DSS data centre, where the forms are registered by the filing clerk before data entry.

Data management of the Rufiji DSS uses standard, public-domain household-registration system (HRS) computer software, with built-in reporting and checking routines (Indome et al. 1995). The HRS is capable of maintaining a consistent record of vital events occurring among people in a fixed geographic area and generating up-to-date registration books for field use. Once enumerators have completed their interviews, the data are taken to the Rufiji DSS data centre for entry, and the data entered are then printed in loose sheets or forms, known as HRBs. The filing clerk systematically arranges the HRBs by household and hamlet to facilitate the fieldwork and household interview. The HRB is printed so that it can be used in three rounds of interviews. Likewise, completed VA forms are double entered in the DSS data centre, the differences are reconciled, and then the forms are dispatched for physician coding and returned to the DSS data centre for final processing.

The software for data entry has a built-in series of logical checks and menu-driven procedures to maintain the consistency of the event data with data in the database. For example, the HRS will disallow data entry of a pregnancy of a male resident. To optimize quality, field activities are performed in conjunction with data operations. Completed forms from the field are taken to the DSS data centre for data entry. Errors noted during data entry are verified, reported to the field supervisors for diagnosis, and then corrected both in the field and at the DSS data centre.

The HRS software is also used for data analysis. The software can compute basic demographic rates, such as fertility, mortality, in- and out-migration, and person–year denominators. If all the field and data protocols are followed, fully edited and cleaned data should result at the end of each 4-month round. The data can be used to describe characteristics of the population — such as age, sex, marital and parental relations, and household headship — and the dynamics of birth, death, migration, and nuptiality. The addition of the mortality surveillance using the VA allows the generation of cause-specific mortality rates and other measures of disease burden (such as years of life lost) for all ages and both sexes. The findings obtained are presented to the community in simple tables or graphics through biannual newsletters issued to every household in the surveillance area. In addition, TEHIP reprocesses the findings into intervention-addressable shares of the burden of disease, before they are given, in graphical format, to the Rufiji District health-management teams and the Ministry of Health.

Rufiji DSS basic outputs

Demographic indicators

The Rufiji DSA now has a population of about 85 000 and an annual population growth rate of 2.3%. This means the population in the DSA will take about three decades to double. The age and sex composition of the area is presented in the population pyramid in Figure 13.2. The pyramid reveals a broad base that tapers toward the older ages, indicating that the population is young. The population structure is as follows: <1 year old, 2.7%; 0–4 years old, 16%; 5–14 years old, 30%; 15–64 years old, 46%; and ≥65 years old, 8%. The male–female ratio is 92.7 : 100. The DSA has more females (52%) than males (48%). The age-dependency ratio is 110. The total fertility rate is 6.2 children per woman 15–49 years old. The infant-mortality rate is 102.1 per 1000 live births. The under-five mortality ratio is 133 per 1000 live births. The under-five mortality rate is 32.7 per 1000 children. Average household size is 4.8. Males are more likely to be heads of households (73%) and educated (57%) than females (27% and 43%, respectively), and 26% of the population has migrated out of, or into, the DSA.

Figure 13.2. Population pyramid for person–years observed at the Rufiji DSS site, Tanzania, 1999.

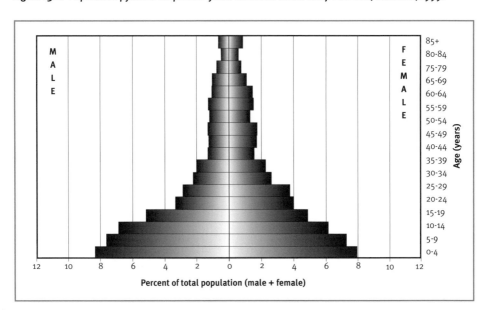

Table 13.1. Age- and sex-specific mortality at the Rufiji DSS site, Tanzania, 1999.

Age (years)	Death s ($_nD_x$)		Person–years observed ($_nPY_x$)	
	Male	Female	Male	Female
<1	130	156	794	787
1–4	49	41	5090	4847
5–9	16	11	5376	5164
10–14	6	12	4861	4348
15–19	7	7	3615	3448
20–24	2	18	2339	2804
25–29	6	26	2000	2676
30–34	15	21	1553	1862
35–39	17	22	1415	1595
40–44	10	12	912	1117
45–49	15	10	862	1226
50–54	13	13	826	1235
55–59	18	14	836	933
60–64	25	13	884	1078
65–69	17	28	729	1030
70–74	25	24	706	772
75–79	35	24	522	527
80–84	28	31	328	414
≥85	66	77	444	608
Births	2800			
CDR	15.02			
CBR	39.68			
CRNI	24.66			

Note: CBR, crude birth rate (actual number of births per 1000 population); CDR, crude death rate (actual number of deaths per 1000 population); CRNI, crude rate of natural increase (CBR minus CDR per 100; does not take into account migration); $_nD_x$, observed deaths between ages x and $x+n$; $_nPY_x$, observed person–years between ages x and $x+n$.

Table 13.2. Age-specific fertility rate at the Rufiji DSS site, Tanzania, 1999.

Age group (years)	Person–years	Births (*n*)	Fertility rate per 1000
15–19	3 415.5	562	164.5
20–24	2 804.2	692	246.8
25–29	2 648.8	636	240.1
30–34	1 861.0	401	215.5
35–39	1 598.5	296	185.2
40–44	1 119.8	115	102.7
45–49	1 231.4	98	79.6
GFR (15–49)	14 679.3	2 800	190.7
TFR	6.2		

Note: GFR, general fertility rate; TFR, total fertility rate.

Out-migration exceeds in-migration in the DSA. The propensity to migrate into the DSA is higher among females (57%) than males (43%). These percentages are the same for out-migration.

All-causes mortality data for the Rufiji DSS are summarized in Table 13.1. The table reveals that mortality in the DSA is fairly high. The mortality pattern is U shaped, indicating high death rates among children (<5 years old) and adults ≥65 years old. Variations occur in the mortality-age profile between men and women, with women 20–44 years old having higher probabilities of dying than men.

The age-specific fertility rates (ASFRs) and total fertility rate of the DSA are presented in Table 13.2. The ASFRs show a regular feature, with a childbearing peak occurring among women 20–24 years old and fertility levels declining thereafter. ASFR distributions can be classified into three broad groups: early-peak type (20–24 age group), late-peak type (25–29 age group), and broad-peak type (where ASFRs in the 20–24 and 25–29 age groups differ slightly) (Kpedekpo 1982). One notes that fertility levels in the Rufiji DSS are of the early-peak type. This indicates that in the DSA women marry or begin childbearing early in life.

Acknowledgments

This work is supported in part by a grant from the International Development Research Centre (IDRC), Canada, through TEHIP, in collaboration with the Tanzanian Ministry of Health. It is also an output of AMMP. AMMP is a project of the Tanzanian Ministry of Health, funded by the Department for International Development (DFID), United Kingdom, and implemented in partnership with the University of Newcastle upon Tyne, United Kingdom. The views expressed are not necessarily those of the Ministry of Health, IDRC, or DFID.

The Rufiji DSS team includes Ali N. Mangara, Amina S. Mtumbuka, Amiri B. Msati, Antonia M. Shayo, Asha Juma Mzoa, Athumani M. Mwinyihija, Baraka R. Bashir, Cecilia R. Makwaia, Denis Navakongwe, Devota B. Momburi, Eleuther Mwageni, Ephrem Mapunda, Fikiri M. Mtandatu, Fredrick A. Swilla, Grace A. Massawe, Hamisi A. Milandu, Hamisi Sodangu, Hashim M. Kalungo, Hermenegilda D. Mtena, Jafari A.

Mpwapwa, Jane I. Masumai, Julieth L. Kulanga, Kahema I. Nassoro, Kulwa L. Francis, Liberati M. Kahumba, Makala M. Mbura, Manitu M. Malekano, Maua H. Msango, Mohamed Y. Kitambulio, Moshi B. Kitingi, Muhidin B. Mlanzi, Mwajuma N. Mkundi, Mwanate A. Dyandumbo, Mzuzuri Mrisho, Nivone Kikaho, Nuhu A. Kihambwe, Omari S. Matimbwa, Omari S. Mkumba, Omari S. Mnete, Peter S. Ndali, Priscilla F. Mlay, Ramadhani Makutika, Said H. Putta, Sharifa O. Sobo, Sihaba S. Ngabunzwa, Subilaga A. Mwaisela, Tabley N. Tangale, Tumu Nindi, Uwesu Mohamed, Wabishi M. Nyangalilo, Yahya K. Mkilindi, and Zaharan Juma.

The Rufiji DSS team wishes to acknowledge the financial, technical, management, and administrative support of TEHIP (Don de Savigny, Harun Kasale, Robert Kilala, Victor Lihendeko, Conrad Mbuya, Godfrey Munna, Graham Reid, and Elimamba Tenga) and AMMP (Yusuf Hemed, Regina Kutaga, Honorati Masanja, Hamisi Mponezya, Robert Mswia, Ferdinand Mugusi, Philip Setel, and David Whiting). We also wish to express our gratitude to INDEPTH and the Navrongo Health Research Centre, Ministry of Health, Ghana, and in particular, Fred Binka, Felix Kondayire, Pierre Ngom, and Peter Wontuo for their technical exchange visits and support in establishing the Rufiji DSS. Finally, we are grateful for the continuing collaboration with the Rufiji District council, the Rufiji District health-management team, the district medical officer, Dr Saidi Mkikima, and the entire population in the Rufiji DSA for their continued support and collaboration.

Chapter 14

Gwembe DSS, Zambia

Gwembe Tonga Research Project

Site description

The Gwembe Tonga Research Project (GTRP) was initiated in 1956 by Elizabeth Colson and Thayer Scudder to study the impact of resettlement associated with the creation of Lake Kariba. Initially, seven villages were chosen as intensive study sites, but as the study progressed the number was reduced to four. Two of the four villages, Sinafala and Siameja, moved relatively short distances and were relocated near or a few kilometres away from Lake Kariba. The other two villages, Mazulu and Musulumba, had to move about 160 km downstream to a site below the dam.

Physical geography of the Gwembe DSA

The primary portion of the Gwembe Tonga DSS study area is located between latitudes 16° and 18°S and longitudes 26° and 29°E in the Southern Province of Zambia (Figure 14.1). The study area encompasses four study villages (and many other villages not in the study) each covering an area of several square kilometres. The villages are scattered for 300 km along the length of the Gwembe Valley, a relatively low-lying

Figure 14.1. Location of the Gwembe Tonga DSS site, Zambia (monitored population, 15 000).

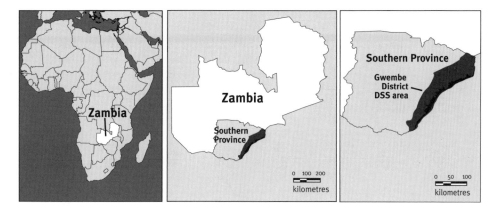

semi-arid area with an average elevation of about 400–500 m above sea level. The Gwembe Valley contains the Zambezi River, and, after 1958, Lake Kariba, which resulted from the construction of the Kariba Dam. Rainfall occurs between October and March and is variable. Small droughts and yearly periods of hunger during the rainy season are more common than not. Temperatures range from near 0°C at night during the cold season (June–August) to 40°C and above during the hot, wet season (November–March). Between August and November, it is hot and dry.

In addition to the rural villages in the Gwembe Valley, the Gwembe Tonga DSS follows migrants and emigrants to the urban areas of Lusaka and Ndola and also to a rural frontier settlement area called Chikanta, located on the plateau several hundred kilometres northwest of the Gwembe Valley study area.

Population characteristics of the Gwembe DSA

Over the more than 40 years since the study began, 15 000 people have been observed, and 10 000 of them were still alive in 1995, the last date, at the time of writing, for which analysis was carried out. The population density varies considerably from high-density villages and urban settings to fairly low-density rural areas.

The main ethnic group inhabiting the study area is the Gwembe Tonga, who practice various indigenous religions, various forms of Christianity, and combinations of the two. Most of the study population is engaged in subsistence and small-scale cash-crop agriculture, but a minority obtain jobs in the rural areas. Many young people migrate to urban areas to seek wage labour, and there is some circular local migration to access seasonal wage labour available with large commercial farming enterprises. Almost all people inhabiting the study area have access to primary education and, if they can afford it, secondary education as well. Few can complete secondary education, and very few move on to tertiary education.

Access to the villages varies: two are readily accessible via tarred and short dirt roads; and two are much less accessible, via poor-quality dirt roads only. Homes are generally built of mud brick and have thatch roofing. In the rural areas, water is provided from shallow wells, the Zambezi River, Lake Kariba, and, in rare instances, boreholes. The urban water supply comes mainly from boreholes and the Kafue River. Most water is of poor quality. None of the rural villages have electricity, although some structures do.

All villages have a clinic within or nearby, but the service varies considerably because of inadequate staff and supplies. There are district hospitals of reasonable quality, although access can be difficult, depending on the season. Additionally, the cost of medical treatment at the hospitals is a burden to most villagers, especially since the International Monetary Fund's (IMF's) structural adjustment in 1992. Immunization programs have been fairly reliable and reasonably successful, but exact figures cannot be quoted. Perinatal clinics operate weekly or biweekly in most of the villages. The villagers themselves rate hunger as their primary health problem, followed by malaria, dysentery, and HIV.

Since the study began, in 1956, the population has faced forced relocation, several measles and cholera epidemics, the war for Zimbabwean independence (waged in part where the population lives), the economic downturn that began in the 1970s, severe droughts in the early 1980s and mid-1990s, the IMF's structural-adjustment programs, and now the HIV–AIDS epidemic, which began having an impact during the early 1990s.

Gwembe DSS procedures

Introduction to the Gwembe DSS site

The Gwembe Tonga Research Project was designed to document the way of life of the Gwembe Tonga before they were forcibly relocated to make space for Lake Kariba in 1956 and to document their adaptation to the new situation after they were relocated in 1958. The study was designed and initiated by anthropologists Elizabeth Colson and Thayer Scudder and was largely conceived as an investigation into social change and adaptation. Although the core focus has always been on social and socioeconomic issues, significant components have been added in the areas of nutrition, growth, development processes, and demography.

Gwembe DSS data collection and processing

Field procedures

INITIAL CENSUS — The initial census was conducted in 1956, and it enumerated the entire population of the four villages remaining in the study: Mazulu, Musulumba, Siameja,[1] and Sinafala.

REGULAR UPDATE ROUNDS — Until 1995, data were collected at roughly 3-year intervals by complete enumerations that updated information on the original population, all of its descendents, and those who had married someone descending from the original population. As a result of the anthropologists' methodology — recording accurate genealogies for their work — the study population consists of all the original inhabitants of the four villages plus all their direct descendents and those who have married into their families. Hence, this is a genealogically defined sample predominantly. In addition to the genealogically defined group, the study also includes a relatively small number of people who have moved permanently into the geographical and social boundaries of the village but are not directly related to anyone in the original enumeration.

CONTINUOUS SURVEILLANCE — Starting during the 1970s, local informants in each village have kept records of vital events between the major updates and kept daily diaries describing a range of activities in the village.[2] Since 1995 a more typical data-collection system has been initiated, consisting of event-specific questionnaires. From 1995 on, two interviewers in each village[3] have been employed full time to record all vital, nuptial, and migration events and to administer a long questionnaire, once each year, to

---

1 The initial enumeration of Siameja captured roughly half of the original population of that village, and it is that half that has been followed ever since.

2 The local informants in Siameja began recording information later than those in the other three villages.

3 There is only one permanent interviewer in Siameja.

elicit a range of socioeconomic indicators. Additionally, the prices of a large range of daily consumables are recorded on a quarterly basis. These will be used to construct a local price index to correct monetary transactions for local inflation.

The current questionnaires are designed to record information on birth, death, migration, initiation of marital union, marital separation, resumption of marital union, divorce, end of marital union through death, marriage payment, annual socioeconomic interview, and quarterly price index information.

The interviewers use a genealogical list to identify individuals and locate their individual ID numbers (names are not permanent identifiers). In addition, one or two long-term employees keep daily diaries describing a range of activities in the village, with particular emphasis on the proceedings of village court cases.

Data management

In each village, a supervisor oversees the operation, and someone from the GTRP senior staff visits the villages twice a year to resupply the questionnaires, collect the completed ones, and pay the research assistants.

Until 1995, all data management was handled by the two senior anthropologists, Elizabeth Colson and Thayer Scudder. They recorded everything in ASCII text files, using an ingenious coding mechanism to relate individuals in the genealogy, and between 1992 and 1997 those files were converted to a relational database. At the same time, event-driven questionnaires, designed to work with the relational organization of the data, were introduced.

Data quality is assured through multiple reinterviews and continuous data collection, with checking and rechecking of recorded data at each subsequent interview. Data quality is measured by analyzing patterns in event counts, age reporting, and trends and comparing these patterns with those of neighbouring populations and standard models.

Data analysis relies on a collection of custom-designed relational-database tools, and the use of statistical techniques for the analysis of longitudinal data. The first work to come from the demographic analysis of the data is a basic analysis of the demographic history of the population (Clark et al. 1995).

Gwembe DSS basic outputs

Demographic indicators

Between 1957 and 1995, the Gwembe Tonga DSS recorded 82 000 person–years of exposure for males and 94 000 person–years of exposure for females. For males, 22% of those were lived by children aged 5 years and younger and 51% by children aged 15 years or younger. For females, the corresponding figures were 20% and 50%. This information is displayed graphically in Figure 14.2 as a population pyramid.

During 1991–95, mortality was fairly high. During that period, roughly 1 in 10 newborns died before reaching 1 year old, and only 8 of 10 newborns survived to their fifth birthday. For adults, 6 of 10 men or women who lived to age 20 survived to age 50. Over that same period, the two sexes combined generated a crude death rate of 25 per 1000 (24 per 1000 when standardized using the Segi [1960] age standard). This is

Figure 14.2. Population pyramid for person–years observed at the Gwembe Tonga DSS site, Zambia, 1957–95.

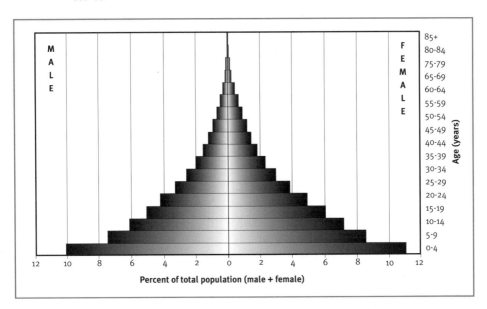

high in comparison with the developed world, but only moderately high compared with other developing regions. Over the duration of the study, the life expectancy at birth rose from 38 years for both men and women in 1957–61 to 52 years for men and 58 years for women in 1982–86, then fell back to 46 years for men and 50 years for women in 1992–95. The recent reduction in life expectancy at birth reflects the impact of HIV–AIDS and the deterioration of the economy and the health-care system in Zambia.

The total fertility rate peaked during the period of 1972–76 at a level of 7 children per woman and subsequently fell to a level of about 4 children per woman during the period of 1992–95. The married total fertility rate peaked at a little more than 10 children per woman in the 1972–76 period and fell to just over 6 children per woman in 1992–95. In both cases, the decline was mediated by a substantial reduction in age-specific fertility rates for women between 20 and 39 years old, with a slightly greater reduction for women between 30 and 39 years old.

Tables 14.1 and 14.2 contain age-specific mortality and fertility rates calculated over the period of 1957–95. They do not reveal the changes that have taken place over time, but they do provide good measures of the average age-specific rates during the entire period over which data have been collected.

Table 14.1. Age- and sex-specific mortality at the Gwembe Tonga DSS site, Zambia, 1957–95.

Age (years)	Observed deaths ($_nD_x$) Male	Female	Observed person–years ($_nPY_x$) Male	Female	Observed mortality rate ($_nM_x$) Male	Female
0	473	404	4 281	4 494	110.49	89.90
1–4	386	366	13 399	14 728	28.81	24.85
5–9	88	82	13 112	14 968	6.71	5.48
10–14	32	27	10 724	12 546	2.98	2.15
15–19	16	17	8 904	10 616	1.80	1.60
20–24	15	27	7 326	8 562	2.05	3.15
25–29	26	26	5 773	6 714	4.50	3.87
30–34	32	30	4 564	5 270	7.01	5.69
35–39	36	19	3 508	4 127	10.26	4.60
40–44	28	24	2 774	3 248	10.09	7.39
45–49	18	14	2 146	2 555	8.39	5.48
50–54	28	25	1 670	2 083	16.77	12.00
55–59	21	16	1 207	1 571	17.40	10.18
60–64	30	17	863	1 152	34.76	14.76
65–69	15	28	536	742	27.99	37.74
70–74	17	27	334	410	50.90	65.85
75–79	11	10	198	199	55.56	50.25
80–84	4	18	107	108	37.38	166.67
85–89	9	5	65	34	138.46	147.06
90–94	5	2	31	11	161.29	181.82
95–99	1	1	7	3	142.86	333.33

Note: $_nD_x$, observed deaths between ages x and $x+n$; $_nM_x$, observed mortality rate for ages x and $x+n$; $_nPY_x$, observed person–years between ages x and $x+n$.

Table 14.2. Female age-specific fertility rates at the Gwembe Tonga DSS site, 1957–95.

Age (years)	Total (per 1000)	Married (per 1000)
10–14	3.08	177.22
15–19	117.58	369.11
20–24	256.92	330.13
25–29	240.17	285.57
30–34	215.26	259.05
35–39	172.06	206.98
40–44	81.12	100.21
45–49	17.49	22.82
50–54	0.50	0.81
TFR (15–49)	5.50	7.87

Note: Rates reflect annual hazards of giving birth. TFR, total fertility rate for women 15–49 years old.

Acknowledgments

The 15 000 people of Gwembe Tonga who have contributed their time and patience to the creation of the Gwembe Demographic Database deserve primary acknowledgment and thanks.

Elizabeth Colson and Thayer Scudder collected and did the original coding and input all the data presented here. They have been supported over the years by numerous organizations, to which we are thankful. Material presented in this chapter has been made possible through the support of the National Science Foundation of the United States, the William Penn Foundation, the Fulbright International Scholarship Program of the United States, and the National Institute on Aging of the National Institutes of Health of the United States. We are grateful to INDEPTH for making it possible to contribute these data to this monograph on mortality.

Chapter 15

MANHIÇA DSS, MOZAMBIQUE

P.L. Alonso, F. Saúte, J.J. Aponte, F.X. Gómez-Olivé, A. Nhacolo, R. Thomson,
E. Macete, F. Abacassamo, P.J. Ventura, X. Bosch, C. Menéndez, and M. Dgedge[1]

Site description

Physical geography of the Manhiça DSA

The Manhiça DSA is in the district of Manhiça (Maputo Province) in southern Mozambique at latitude 25°24′S and longitude 32°48′E (Figure 15.1). It lies at an average altitude of 50 m above sea level and covers an area of 100 km². The district has two distinct zones: the fertile lowlands, which comprise the floodplains of the Incomati River, are sparsely inhabited, and are subject to intensive sugar cane and fruit farming; and an escarpment of moderate height, which gives rise to a flat plateau on which virtually the entire DSA is situated. The area has two distinct seasons. The warm season is between November and April, when most of the rains fall (annual rainfall during 1998 was 1100 mm); a cool, dry season lasts for the rest of the year.

Figure 15.1. Location of the Manhiça DSS site, Mozambique (monitored population, 36 000).

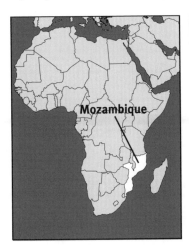  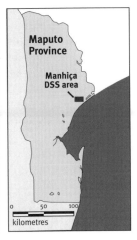

---

[1] Manhiça Health Research Centre.

Population characteristics of the Manhiça DSA

The town of Manhiça and the surrounding villages have a population of about 36 600 inhabitants, with a density of 360 inhabitants/km². The population is peri-urban and rural. People of the area are mainly Xironga and Xichangana, and their languages are often termed Ronga and Changana. The two dominant religions are Islam and Christianity. The people of the DSA are mostly subsistence farmers and workers in an agricultural cooperative that grows sugarcane, bananas, and rice. Workers also operate a large sugarcane-processing factory. An increasing number of small traders are establishing shops and businesses along the busy road that transects the district from north to south. There are 10 primary schools in the study area (6768 students and 85 teachers) and 1 secondary school (1492 students and 32 teachers). The rate of illiteracy is higher among females, at 47%, than among males, at 24%. Whereas 66% of men and 49% of women have primary education, only 9% of men and 4% of women have secondary education; and less than 1% of both men and women have gone beyond their secondary education.

Villages in this area typically comprise a loose conglomeration of compounds separated by garden plots and grazing land. Houses are simple, with walls typically made of cane, with thatched or corrugated roofs. In towns, houses are often grouped into family compounds and surrounded by grass fences. Towns grew substantially during the civil war in the 1980s as displaced people looked for refuge. After the end of the war, few inhabitants returned to their original homes, and displaced settlements have now been integrated into towns. Water comes mainly from community wells, although some households have their own wells. Some areas have community-run pumps. Both wells and pumps are supervised and chlorinated regularly by the District Water and Sanitation Department. The Maputo–Beira road and the Maputo–Xai railroad cross the area from north to south. With the exception of the (small) centre of the town of Manhiça, which has an erratic public-electricity service, the rest of the area relies on more traditional systems for lighting.

Centro de Investigação em Saúde de Manhiça (CISM, Manhiça health research centre) is in the centre of the study area. This 80-bed health facility includes a busy outpatient clinic, a maternity and child-care unit with an expanded immunization program and nutritional services, and a 24-hour emergency room. A smaller, 10-bed health centre is located 6 km south of the village of Manhiça. Malaria, acute respiratory infection, and malnutrition remain the most important causes of illness and death in children <5 years old.

Mozambique is recovering from a long period of war, including the independence wars against the Portuguese colonial power and the more recent civil armed conflict. The country still ranks as one of the poorest in the world, with an estimated per capita income of less than US $300. Although mild flooding of the alluvial plains of the rivers that cross southern Mozambique is not uncommon, the devastation caused by the large-scale floods of February 2000 had not been experienced for the last 30 years.

Manhiça DSS procedures

Introduction to the Manhiça DSS site

The overall objective of the Manhiça DSS site is to create a demographic platform to contribute to the research infrastructure of CISM. Its specific objectives are

- To describe the health profile of a rural population in southern Mozambique and thereby help identify priority research issues and inform policy;

- To describe in detail the epidemiology and burden of disease associated with malaria and acute respiratory infections; and

- To create a platform to help implement and evaluate new control strategies.

The first census was carried out in the second half of 1996, registering a total of 33 500 inhabitants in the area. Currently, the total population under surveillance is around 36 600. The DSS was set up in the area immediately after the first enumeration and was based on the household-registration system (HRS), with some modifications. Update rounds are conducted every 4 months. During these rounds, every household is visited, and all vital events and changes of residency are recorded. Vital events include all births and deaths of the registered resident population in the study area. A resident is defined as any person who lives in the study area and expects to stay for at least the next 3 months. Should a resident leave the study area for 3 months or more, he or she is regarded as a migrant.

A number of field surveys have been carried out to define the epidemiology of malaria. These have included both cross-sectional surveys of children, adults, and pregnant women and cohort studies. The DSS site also has the natural catchment population of the Manhiça District hospital. Since late 1996, it has had a 24-hour hospital monitoring system that identifies all children attending the hospital from the study area and characterizes the morbidity patterns of this rural population.

The DSS operates under the direction of an epidemiologist and a junior demographer. A team of two supervisors and eight fieldworkers assists them. Researchers from CISM and others from the Ministry of Health and the School of Medicine at Eduardo Mondlane University are the main users of this facility.

Manhiça DSS data collection and processing

The selection of the site was made in early 1995. A suitable place to establish a peripheral research centre to investigate priority health issues of rural populations with access to a district hospital was sought. A balance between the rural settings and the logistic and supply needs of a sophisticated research centre had to be achieved. The town of Manhiça and its surrounding population, only 80 km from Maputo on good roads, was the optimum choice. Finally, the available data indicated that malaria was hyperendemic in the area, and therefore the site had potential for studies of malaria.

Field procedures

MAPPING — Airphotos of the area, available from the National Cartographic Institute, were digitized by the Catalan Cartographic Institute. The main geographic landmarks, including the Incomati River, the national road, and the railroad, were georeferenced. All households of the area were systematically numerated, and their position was determined using a GPS with differential correction. These data were then down-loaded on the digitized photographs. The limits of the neighbourhoods were designed on the map, using the numbering of the households already positioned.

INITIAL CENSUS — The initial census was carried out from August to October 1996. After meetings with the community leaders, the census team was scheduled to visit the zones included in the DSS. For each zone, the chief of zone indicated which houses belonged to that zone. All households were numerated and then mapped using GPS, and every single person received a permanent ID number. For the households, information about the type of construction, number of constructions, and availability of a kitchen and toilet in the household was collected. Information collected on individuals included date of birth, parents, marital status, relationship with the chief of the household, and education level.

REGULAR UPDATE ROUNDS — Update rounds, where the fieldworkers visit all houses, are carried out every 4 months. In addition, the supervisors visit the chiefs of the zones every 2 weeks to collect information on vital events. Informal visits to other community key informants are done while doing the fieldwork.

Out- and in-migrations are registered, as well as destinations and origins. When the migration occurs within the study area the person receives a localization number related to the new house where he or she is going to live. A new in-migrant receives an ID number. As the ID number is permanent, a former resident of the area who rein-migrates receives a localization number.

CONTINUOUS SURVEILLANCE — The two field supervisors carry out daily visits at both CISM and Maragra's Maternity, where all deliveries of the last 24 hours are registered. The baby and its mother are then visited at home, weekly until the baby is 1 month old. Two supervisors with motorbikes, supported by a large network of key community informants, identify all vital events in the study area and maintain a pregnancy register every week. The supervisors, with the objective of collecting demographic information, carry out regular fortnightly visits to the chief of the zones. Every 6 months, specially trained medical students of Eduardo Mondlane University in Maputo carry out verbal autopsies (VAs) of all deaths occurring among children <15 years old.

SUPERVISION AND QUALITY CONTROL — The DSS undertakes two types of supervision: field and computer supervision. The field supervision comprises random visits to households already visited by the fieldworker during the previous 24 hours to check the information collected by the fieldworker. Computer quality control consists of weekly comparisons between data recorded by the fieldworker in the census book and the information available on the computer. Moreover, once a year, a direct comparison is made of all information entered into the computer and information recorded by the fieldworkers in the census book.

Data management

Paper processing is used for all information collected. Information is registered in the fieldworkers' household registration book and on precoded questionnaires, which are then processed at the computer centre. The researchers carry out weekly spot checks of the forms to discover any incompleteness of information and inconsistencies. The forms are then transferred to the data-management unit, where they are recorded and issued with a unique ID serial number. Once a questionnaire is entered into the computer, it is then sequenced and stored according to the type of demographic event.

Five working stations with an uninterruptible power supply are linked to a server with Windows NT 4.0 and Windows 95 environment. Specific software written in Visual FoxPro 5.0 is used for data entry and cleaning. This software is based on the HRS. It has a built-in series of logical checks and procedures to maintain the consistency and referential integrity of the databases. Standardized data-management procedures include systematic double entry of all forms by two data clerks. Inconsistencies are listed and corrected, based on the form information. Once the two entries are made consistent, the first entry is copied to a different folder accessible to researchers as "read only." The main server contains a mirror disk to produce continuous backup. Moreover, a weekly backup is made onto a CD. All databases are transferred to STATA software for analyses.

Data quality control is assured through weekly checks using Visual FoxPro. These checks produce lists of inconsistencies, which are then corrected in the field by supervisors.

Demographic rates, such as fertility, mortality, and in- and out-migration, are calculated at the end of each round. The fieldworkers use VA to estimate specific mortality rates among individuals <15 years old. Merged with the hospital monitoring system, the DSS allows estimations of community-based morbidity rates. This information is accessible to the Ministry of Health.

Manhiça DSS basic outputs

Demographic indicators

The Manhiça population in mid-1999 reached 34 526: 4% are <1 year old; 13%, 0–4 years old; 26%, 5–14 years old; 51%, 15–64 years old; and 5%, ≥65 years old (Figure 15.2). Table 15.1 shows age- and sex-specific mortality at the DSS site. The infant-mortality rate is 78.5 per 1000 live births, and the under-five mortality rate is 130 per 1000. The age-dependency ratio is 0.87. The sex ratio is 83, and the total fertility rate is 5 (Table 15.2). Average household size is 4.0. Female-headed households account for 35%; and male, 65%. Primary school was attended by 76.4% of males and 53% of females ≥15 years old.

Figure 15.2. Population pyramid for person–years observed at the Manhiça DSS site, Mozambique, 1998–99.

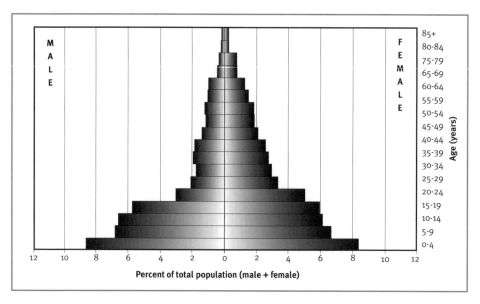

Percent of total population (male + female)

Table 15.1. Age- and sex-specific mortality at the Manhiça DSS site, Mozambique, 1998–99.

Age (years)	Death s ($_nD_x$)		Person–years observed ($_nPY_x$)	
	Male	Female	Male	Female
<1	119	77	1308	1247
1–4	81	70	4486	4450
5–9	11	15	4561	4547
10–14	12	6	4429	4201
15–19	12	11	3828	4068
20–24	6	23	1991	3460
25–29	13	17	1357	2321
30–34	25	15	1128	2050
35–39	22	9	1257	1908
40–44	30	11	1204	1765
45–49	17	17	893	1449
50–54	20	16	730	1298
55–59	32	34	777	1279
60–64	26	25	664	1041
65–69	27	20	627	885
70–74	14	28	262	554
75–79	15	32	199	532
80–84	9	17	94	207
≥85	17	22	85	202
Births	2698			
CDR	14.45			
CBR	40.06			
CRNI	25.61			

Note: CBR, crude birth rate (actual number of births per 1000 population); CDR, crude death rate (actual number of deaths per 1000 population); CRNI, crude rate of natural increase (CBR minus CDR per 100; does not take into account migration); $_nD_x$, observed deaths between ages x and $x+n$; $_nPY_x$, observed person–years between ages x and $x+n$.

Table 15.2. Age-specific fertility rates at the Manhiça DSS, Mozambique, 1998.

Age group (years)	Females	Births	Age-specific fertility rate
15–19	1975	281	0.1442
20–24	1648	373	0.2264
25–29	1122	244	0.2174
30–34	1001	188	0.1878
35–39	924	138	0.1494
40–44	854	46	0.0538
45–50	705	10	0.0142
TFR	5		

Note: TFR, total fertility rate.

Acknowledgments

The Spanish Agency for International Cooperation funds the running costs of CISM. During 1999, various studies were funded by 13 sources, including the World Health Organization, United Nations Children's Fund, INDEPTH, Hospital Clinic of Barcelona (University of Barcelona, Spain), the Spanish Ministry of Health, and Eduardo Mondlane University, Mozambique. CISM is the first peripheral research centre of the Mozambican Ministry of Health. It is being developed under the premises of the cooperation program between Mozambique and Spain. A collaborative agreement, further developed between the Ministry of Health, the Maputo School of Medicine at Eduardo Mondlane University, and the Hospital Clinic of Barcelona, ensures the running of the centre.

Chapter 16

AGINCOURT DSS, SOUTH AFRICA

Mark Collinson,[1] Obed Mokoena,[1] Niko Mgiba,[1] Kathleen Kahn,[1] Stephen Tollman,[1] Michel Garenne,[2] Kobus Herbst,[3] Elizabeth Malomane,[4] and Sheona Shackleton[1]

Site description

Physical geography of the Agincourt DSA

The Agincourt DSS is situated about 500 km northeast of Johannesburg in the Agincourt subdistrict of the Bushbuckridge region, Northern Province (Figure 16.1). Until 1994, the site was in a "homeland," or bantustan area. The site extends between latitudes 24°50′ and 24°56′S and longitudes 31°08′ and 31°25′E. The altitude is 400–600 m above sea level. The field site, with 21 village communities, covers 390 km² and measures 38 km × 16 km at its widest points.

The geoecological zone is semi-arid savanna, better suited to game farming and low-density cattle farming than to crop cultivation. Low average rainfall is common, with mean rainfall ranging from 700 to 550 mm in the western and eastern parts of the site. In addition, a high variability in interseasonal rainfall patterns renders the

Figure 16.1. Location of the Agincourt DSS site, South Africa (monitored population, 66 800).

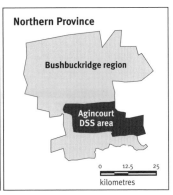

[1] University of Witwatersrand, South Africa.

[2] French Center for Population and Development (CEPED).

[3] Africa Centre for Population Studies and Reproductive Health.

[4] Northern Province Department of Health, South Africa.

area vulnerable to drought. Some 80% of the rain falls during the summer months of November–March. The area is affected by drought on average every 3.5 years, and even when rainfall is normal it is insufficient to fully supply the domestic-water or irrigation needs of the area. The area experiences hot summer and mild winter months. The temperature range is 12°–40°C in summer and 5°–27°C in winter.

Population characteristics of the Agincourt DSA

The total DSS population is 66 840, with 10 500 households and a population density of 172 persons/km^2. The male–female ratio for the total population is 0.929. The setting is rural in terms of distance from urban centres and lack of infrastructure. The main ethnic group is Shangaan, although Mozambicans, originally refugees, constitute more than a quarter (29%) of the total population. Both groups are Shangaan-speaking, and the Mozambicans are culturally affiliated with the South African host population. The area has mainstream Christian churches and independent African churches, and many people hold a mixture of indigenous and Christian beliefs.

Unemployment is estimated at 40–50%. Formal-sector employment involves migrant men who work in the mines, in the manufacturing and service industries of larger towns, and on nearby game and commercial farms and timber plantations. Women make up an increasing proportion of the migrant-labour population. Another source of local employment is the public sector. Informal-sector activities are widespread, and they include food- and fruit-vending. Pensions are an important source of income for many families. Female-headed households constitute 32% of all households (Tollman et al. 1995).

Almost all villages have at least one primary school, and 14 of the 21 villages have a secondary school. More than 40% of adults 25–59 years old have received no formal schooling. Six percent have completed secondary school, and only 3% have proceeded to some form of postsecondary education. Of those 15–24 years old, almost all have attended primary school, but only 46% have made the transition to secondary school. Although 85% of those 10–14 years old were enrolled in primary school, age of enrollment is frequently delayed. Adult female literacy (56%) is somewhat lower than adult male literacy (62%) (Tollman et al. 1995).

Various types of housing are found, ranging from traditional mud huts to brick dwellings with tin or tiled roofs. Stands are generally too small to support subsistence agriculture, and crops grown merely supplement the family diet. Water is pumped via purification plants, in some cases only to the main reservoirs in the villages. In other cases, water is harvested from wells dug mainly in riverbeds, and in rare cases from boreholes. Women or children collect water manually, usually in 25-L drums, and transport it either by wheelbarrow or on the head. Water shortage poses a serious problem in most villages. Levels of household sanitation are poor, and pit toilets of varying effectiveness are the norm. All roads are unpaved. Public transportation is limited to privately owned minibus taxis. Although seriously lacking, electricity and telephone services are benefiting from recent development initiatives.

The DSS site has a health centre and five satellite clinics, all staffed by nurses. A restricted number of drugs are dispensed from each of these primary-care facilities, and the health centre has a small laboratory, able to perform a limited number of diagnostic tests. An ambulance is based at the health centre. All services are free, and they include child health, family planning, antenatal care, delivery and postpartum care, minor ailments, and chronic-disease treatments. Although waiting times are long, most of these services are underused. A contributing factor in this is poor drug supply. Referrals are to two district hospitals, each about 25 km from the health centre. The main health problems revealed by verbal-autopsy (VA) analysis are diarrhea, kwashiorkor, and AIDS in children <5 years old; accidents, violence, and AIDS in the 15–49 age group; and chronic degenerative diseases, mainly cardiac, cerebrovascular, liver, and malignant diseases, among those ≥50 years old (Kahn et al. 1999; Tollman et al. 1999; Garenne, Tollman, Kahn, and Gear 2000). Seasonal malaria is evident. A high rate of adolescent fertility occurs in the midst of escalating HIV sero-prevalence (Garenne, Tollman, and Kahn 2000).

Forced relocation of communities under the apartheid regime (in the 1940–60 period) and the formation of ethnically divided homelands in the 1970s had a significant impact on the social, economic, and demographic profile of the population. The government of the time sought to massively exploit the labour in rural South Africa while simultaneously restricting development. Homeland governments were given hegemonic powers, with dubious results. Although poorly organized and managed, homeland health services rested on a network of mission hospitals and clinics and were thus less fragmented than their urban counterparts. This led to their having a more comfortable fit with South Africa's new decentralized, district-based health system. As a result, densely settled rural villages with cash-based economies and males 20–59 years old largely absent from the permanent population became the pattern of settlement. Recent changes in government have affected movement patterns. With more freedom of movement people tend to move to rural towns. Along paved roads through these rural areas, the rural towns are becoming development nodes.

Agincourt DSS procedures

Introduction to the Agincourt DSS site

The original objectives of the Agincourt study were (Tollman 1999)

1. To provide essential information on the demography, health status, and fertility status of the Agincourt community, as a basis for the improved formulation, implementation, and assessment of district-level programs;

2. To serve as a sentinel field site providing accurate information on the population dynamics of rural communities in South Africa, to inform the evolution of rural health and development policy; and

3. To provide the capacity and a database to support more advanced community-based studies and field trials in the future.

The current primary objective relates directly to objective 3, namely, to provide a research infrastructure and longitudinal database for a range of community-based studies on the burden of disease, health-systems interventions, and social–household–community dynamics, to inform decentralized health and social policy.

The Agincourt baseline census was conducted in 1992. The original population monitored was 57 509 individuals in 8896 households. By 1999 this had increased to 66 840 individuals in 10 500 households. VAs and maternity histories were introduced in 1993. A partnership between the Agincourt DSS, the study communities, and the local health services was established and is carefully nurtured (Tollman et al. 1995).

The Agincourt DSS data are updated every 12 months. Residents are defined as either "permanent" (resident in the study site for ≥6 months in the preceding year) or "migrant" (resident in the study area for <6 months but nevertheless regarding the Agincourt area as "home"). A VA is conducted in the vernacular on all deaths by a trained lay fieldworker and assessed by medical practitioners (Kahn et al. 2000). The software system contains a relational database, constructed in Microsoft Access 2000. The main demographic, health, and socioeconomic variables measured routinely by the DSS include births, deaths, in- and out-migrations, household relationships, resident status, refugee status, education, and antenatal and delivery health-seeking practices. In the DSS update of 1999, information on chronic cough was collected for a study on active case-finding for tuberculosis. In 2000, information on labour-force participation in the formal and informal sectors was collected; for 2001, a module describing the burden of disabilities was planned.

The Agincourt DSS is the foundation for the Agincourt Health and Population Programme (AHPP), a research initiative of the University of Witwatersrand. It is housed within the Health Systems Development Unit of the Faculty of Health Sciences. AHPP has strong ties to the Northern Province Department of Health and the Bushbuckridge regional and district health services. The core management team comprises the AHPP leader, senior researcher, field-research manager, and site manager. The DSS field team comprises 4 supervisors, 20 fieldworkers, 1 VA supervisor, and 4 VA fieldworkers, all employed on contract for the duration of data collection. In 2000, a part-time data-form checker was employed. The data-capture team comprises a supervisor and two data typists.

Work is under way within AHPP to address a portfolio of clinical, public-health, population, and social challenges, including

- Changing patterns of mortality, fertility, and migration;

- Increasing circulatory disease and interpersonal violence among adults;

- Estimation of the burden of respiratory syncytial virus and investigation of persisting kwashiorkor among children <5 years old;

- Links between the health and population status of former refugees (Mozambicans) and their livelihood strategies;

- Household and community dynamics, in particular, resource flows, adaptive strategies, and the consequences of aging and adult death on the household;

- Labour migration and its impact on men's sexual behaviour and use of contraception; and

- Evaluation of public service and adolescent-oriented interventions against HIV–AIDS and TB.

Community feedback and dialogue are integral to the Agincourt research process. Information from the DSS and related research initiatives is communicated to the study communities through printed "village fact sheets" and through ad hoc community meetings. This facilitates community involvement in local health action and related development activities. Information is regularly discussed with district and regional health-service managers and senior officials of the Northern Province and national Department of Health.

Agincourt DSS data collection and processing

Several factors influenced the choice of the Agincourt field site, in particular

- Its location, some distance from any tar road or township settlement;

- The presence of a health centre, with its satellite clinics and its potential to function as a referral network;

- The need to develop rational referral patterns, delinked from constraints imposed by homeland boundaries; and

- The presence of large numbers of Mozambicans, displaced by the recent civil war.

Field procedures

MAPPING — Hand-drawn maps of each village were made for the initial census in 1992. These included roads, dwellings, and other reference landmarks, such as railway lines, power lines, shops, churches, and soccer fields. Since then village maps have been updated each year through both specific fieldwork exercises and routine correction and updating during census fieldwork. The maps make it possible for any member of the team to return to a particular household without risk of confusion.

INITIAL CENSUS AND REGULAR UPDATE ROUNDS — Six census rounds have been completed to date (1992 baseline, 1993–94, 1995, 1997, 1999, 2000). Rounds are conducted in the dry season, that is, July–November. A fieldworker interviews the best respondent available at the time of the visit. Individual information is checked for every household member. All events that have occurred since the previous census are recorded, and any status observations are updated. Where possible, questions are directed to particular household members; for example, maternity-history or pregnancy-outcome questions are directed to the woman involved. If appropriate respondents are unavailable, the fieldworkers undertake revisits, usually during evenings and on weekends, with a limit placed at two revisits per household. From the second round onwards, a VA has been conducted on every death to determine the most probable cause. VAs are conducted concurrently with the census, but with a separate team of fieldworkers who are dedicated to VA interviews only.

In 1999, with the aim of increasing the speed of data collection, the field team was expanded to 4 supervisors, 20 fieldworkers, 1 VA supervisor, and 4 VA fieldworkers. The team operates out of five field offices, provided by clinics or community members at no charge.

SUPERVISION AND QUALITY CONTROL — To ensure data quality, supervised visits and random duplicate visits are conducted. For supervised visits, the supervisor goes into the field with the fieldworker and observes a number of interviews. After each interview, constructive feedback is given to the fieldworker, with the aim of improving interview technique. Random duplicate visits are conducted by the supervisor on 2% of the population. After a careful explanation is given, the entire interview is conducted again; differences between the first and second interviews are identified; and possible reasons for these are determined. From these data, quality can be assessed, and error rates can be computed.

Furthermore, form-checking occurs in a structured system at four levels of the field organization. The checks become more detailed as the form progresses through the system. An error is returned to the fieldworker for correction, and, where necessary, a revisit is done. Supervisors keep track of forms, using printed checklists.

Data management

Existing details of each household are printed on the census forms. The fieldworker checks this information, and, in addition, status fields are updated for each household member. Separate event forms are used for pregnancy outcomes, deaths, migrations, and maternity histories and are only completed if one of these events occurred in the intercensal period. Death forms are completed in duplicate, so that one copy can be passed on to the VA team. The forms from each interview are stapled together in a predetermined order. Supervision-checklist forms allow for the monitoring of data collection from each dwelling.

When a form has left the field and passed all quality checks it is captured on a software system. Currently, data are captured using simultaneous data entry on three computers connected to a network, writing to a database on a server. The software system is a "relational" database, currently held in Microsoft Access 2000. A custom-made data-entry program has been developed that sits on top of the Access database and, by mirroring the format of the data forms, provides an easy-to-use interface between the user and the database. The database consists of related tables that store different aspects of the data. The main table is the "Individual" table, which stores key information on all individuals encountered. The "Residence" table provides information on individual residence episodes, indicating how and when a person entered and exited a particular location in the field site. A "Memberships" table records information on how and when an individual entered and exited a particular household (that is, a social grouping, defined as people "eating from the same pot"). The system contains tables for each event category — "Births," "Deaths," "Migrations," and "Maternity histories" — and an "Observations" table records information about each interview. In addition, a range of status-observation tables record information about individuals updated at various frequencies during census rounds. These include "Residence status" (updated in rounds 1–6), "Education status" (rounds 1 and 4), "Cough status" (round 5), and "Labour status" (round 6).

The system incorporates built-in validation checks. Implausible data (such as a date of death occurring before a date of birth) are prevented from entering the database. When these errors occur, the form is put to one side, reviewed by the data manager, and, when necessary, returned to the team supervisor for resolution. Unusual, though possible, data (such as a delivery by a woman >50 years old) are also flagged by the system and reviewed by the data manager. As data are entered, computer checks are done to look for invalid codes, missing values, inconsistencies within and between records, incorrect spellings of place names, and duplicate entries. A useful data-quality check after a census is a comparison of the villages of origin of "internal" in-migrants with destinations of internal out-migrants, as well as a review of demographic trends.

Basic analyses are done to produce village fact sheets, community-feedback information, sampling frames, and denominator information. Further data-cleaning and demographic analyses are conducted to produce reliable population data. A monograph of the "baseline" findings was produced in 1994, and all findings of specific scientific or policy interest are published in local and international peer-reviewed journals. Presentations are made to policymakers at subdistrict, district, regional, provincial, and national levels.

Agincourt DSS basic outputs

Demographic indicators

The total *(de jure)* population was 66 840 in 1999. Of these, the permanent population (resident in the site for more than 6 months of the preceding year) was 56 566. The sex ratio (male–female) in the total population was 0.929, falling to 0.712 in the permanent population 15–49 years old. The age structure in the total population at the end of 1999 was as follows: 2.3% were <1 year old; 12.0%, 0–4 years old; 27.6%, 5–14 years old; 55.9%, 15–64 years old; and 4.5%, ≥65 years old (Figure 16.2). The total fertility rate (TFR) was 2.72 in 1999 (Table 16.1). The proportion of female-headed households was 32%. The age-dependency ratio was 0.79. The infant mortality rate was 43.0 per 1000 live births among males and 45.1 per 1000 live births among girls. Mean household size was 6.4, and the adult literacy rate[5] in females was 56% and in males 62%.

Migration monitoring is conducted by recording data on individuals moving into or out of a household between census rounds (Table 16.2). Moves are classified as internal if they have their origin and destination within the DSS site villages; otherwise they are classified as external moves. The place of origin or destination, date of the move, and reason for its occurrence are captured for each move.

---

[5] Computed as the percentage of persons ≥15 years old with at least 4 years of formal schooling.

Figure 16.2. Population pyramid for person–years observed at the Agincourt DSS site, South Africa, 1995–99.

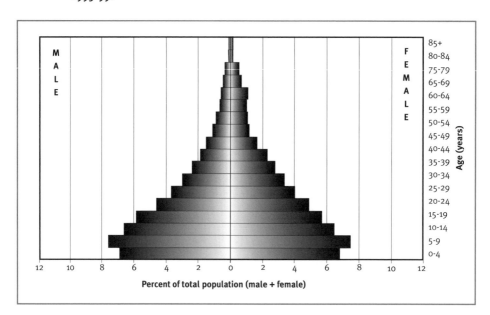

Table 16.1. Age-specific fertility rates at the Agincourt DSS site, South Africa, by 2-year periods, 1992–99.

Age group (years)	1992–93			1994–95			1996–97			1998–99		
	PYs	Births	ASFR	PYs	Births	ASFR	PYs	Births	ASFR	PYs	Births	ASFR
12–14	2661	34	0.0128	3354	44	0.0131	3418	39	0.0114	2887	24	0.0083
15–19	5622	649	0.1154	7323	729	0.0996	7447	754	0.1012	6360	496	0.0780
20–24	4912	717	0.1460	6303	800	0.1269	6449	807	0.1251	5476	647	0.1181
25–29	4100	619	0.1510	5183	678	0.1308	5245	606	0.1155	4497	517	0.1150
30–34	3337	421	0.1261	4468	535	0.1198	4488	487	0.1085	3638	361	0.0992
35–39	2736	297	0.1086	3476	333	0.0958	3630	308	0.0848	3191	252	0.0790
40–44	2066	139	0.0673	2882	144	0.0500	3028	165	0.0545	2528	135	0.0534
45–49	1381	26	0.0188	1839	45	0.0245	2126	40	0.0188	2034	28	0.0138
TFR		3.70			3.28			3.08			2.81	

Note: ASFR, age-specific fertility rate; PYs, person–years; TFR, total fertility rate.

Demographic trends

A profound decline has occurred in TFR, from around 6 births per woman in 1970–74 to 2.72 births per woman in 1999 (Garenne, Tollman, and Kahn 2000). Mortality had been declining for some time, until about 1993. Since 1994 an increase in mortality in three age groups has been documented: young adults 20–49 years old (both sexes), children 0–4 years old (both sexes), and older adult women 50–64 years old (male mortality continues to decline in this age group) (Table 16.3). Migration trends show a net population loss, as a result of an excess of external out-migration over external in-migration (about 1% of the population per year). The main focus for departures has been nearby towns, in particular Mkhuhlu. This move toward Mkhuhlu was particularly strong in the 1994–95 period (Collinson et al. 2000).

Table 16.2. Out- and in-migration rates by age at the Agincourt DSS site, South Africa, 1992-99.

Age group (years)	Person–years	Out-migrations (n)	Out-migration rate	In-migrations (n)	In-migration rate
0–4	69 147	4 552	0.066	4 691	0.068
5–9	71 115	4 981	0.070	4 068	0.057
10–14	61 705	3 785	0.061	3 016	0.049
15–19	53 345	3 817	0.072	3 350	0.063
20–24	44 278	3 675	0.083	3 191	0.072
25–29	35 871	3 167	0.088	2 491	0.069
30–34	29 593	2 263	0.076	1 774	0.060
35–39	23 822	1 435	0.060	1 113	0.047
40–44	19 097	923	0.048	708	0.037
45–49	14 271	587	0.041	426	0.030
50–54	10 541	409	0.039	290	0.028
55–59	9 217	358	0.039	319	0.035
60–64	8 272	292	0.035	270	0.033
65–69	7 524	237	0.031	219	0.029
70–74	5 464	220	0.040	152	0.028
75–79	3 508	147	0.042	105	0.030
80–84	1 408	76	0.054	45	0.032
≥85	1 116	54	0.048	58	0.052

Table 16.3. Age- and sex-specific mortality at the Agincourt DSS site, South Africa, 1995–99.

Age (years)	Deaths ($_nD_x$) Male	Female	Person–years observed ($_nPY_x$) Male	Female
<1	59	65	3 877	3 866
1–4	76	75	17 147	17 093
5–9	14	19	23 175	23 002
10–14	14	12	20 119	19 943
15–19	16	18	17 741	17 494
20–24	32	30	14 014	15 098
25–29	46	30	11 122	12 356
30–34	53	36	9 027	10 365
35–39	61	37	7 198	8 572
40–44	44	36	5 634	7 025
45–49	69	20	4 559	5 111
50–54	48	22	3 322	3 572
55–59	56	19	2 697	3 285
60–64	41	48	1 980	3 132
65–69	56	63	1 733	3 351
70–74	58	66	1 352	2 086
75–79	70	65	1 021	1 583
80–84	29	33	415	507
≥85	27	40	292	479
Births	7 326			
CDR	5.27			
CBR	24.07			
CRNI	18.80			

Note: CBR, crude birth rate (actual number of births per 1000 population); CDR, crude death rate (actual number of deaths per 1000 population); CRNI, crude rate of natural increase (CBR minus CDR per 100; does not take into account migration); $_nD_x$, observed deaths between ages x and $x+n$; $_nPY_x$, observed person–years between ages x and $x+n$.

Acknowledgments

The Agincourt team is indebted to the communities of Bushbuckridge and to the Northern Province Department of Health for their partnership, support, and ongoing contributions to these efforts. We also acknowledge, with pleasure, the encouragement and support of the Wellcome Trust, United Kindom, Andrew W. Mellon Foundation, United States, University of Witwatersrand, South Africa, Anglo American Chairman's Fund, South Africa, the European Union, and the Henry J. Kaiser Family Foundation, United States.

Chapter 17

DIKGALE DSS, SOUTH AFRICA

Marianne Alberts and Sandy Burger[1]

Site description

Physical geography of the Dikgale DSA

The Dikgale DSS site is located in the central region of Mankweng District, Northern Province, South Africa, about 40 km from Pietersburg, the capital of the Northern Province, and 15 km from the University of the North (Figure 17.1). The site covers an area of 71 km^2 and is 6 km $\times$ 10.8 km. It is situated between latitudes 23.46° and 23.48°S and longitudes 29.42° and 29.47°E and lies at an average altitude of 1400 m above sea level. Each village has a central residential area comprising demarcated housing stands, with communal grazing land some distance away. The geoecological zone is open woodland–steppe, with continental climate, and the temperature ranges from an average minimum of 6°C in winter to an average maximum of 26°C in summer. The average rainfall is 401–500 mm, with most of the rain falling between November and April. Droughts are common and, together with seasonality, play a major role in the availability of fresh produce.

Figure 17.1. Location of the Dikgale DSS site, South Africa (monitored population, 7900).

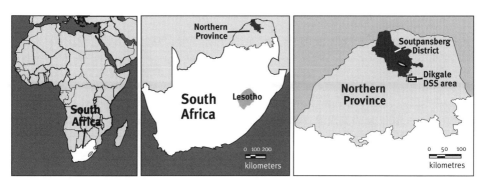

[1] University of the North, South Africa.

Population characteristics of the Dikgale DSA

The total population comprises 7956 people, with a population density of 116 inhabitants/km^2. The site is peri-urban, and the main ethnic group is Pedi. Most of the inhabitants belong to the Moria Zionist Church, which has a combination of Christian and indigenous beliefs, while others belong to the Lutheran or Anglican churches. The language spoken by all inhabitants of the site is Northern Sotho.

A large proportion of adults are migrant workers, whereas others work as farm labourers on neighbouring farms or as domestic workers in nearby towns. Many are pensioners. The unemployment rate in the area is high.

There are four primary schools and three secondary schools in the DSA. In all schools, the classrooms are overcrowded, and few educational amenities are available. Most children attend primary school, and the adult literacy rate is 79.8 and 73.6% in males and females, respectively.

Dwelling units consist of a mixture of shacks, traditional mud huts, and conventional brick houses. A few households have water taps in their yards, but most must fetch water from taps situated at strategic points in the villages. Most households have a pit latrine in their yards, but they have no organized waste disposal. Infrastructure in the villages is poor, and none of the roads is tarred. A bus service is available mornings and evenings during weekdays.

Free health care is given at a primary health-care clinic in the field site to children <6 years old, pregnant women, and the elderly. The service provided by the clinic includes family planning, antenatal care, growth monitoring and immunization in children, and management of patients with chronic diseases. Mankweng Hospital, situated 15–20 km from the field site, serves as a referral hospital.

Both infectious and noninfectious diseases are prevalent in the area. According to records kept at the clinic, the main health problems in children are respiratory and gastrointestinal diseases. Undernutrition is common, and the growth of a large proportion of children is stunted. From a survey undertaken in the DSS site, the health problems in adults include type-2 diabetes, hypertension, iron overload, and obesity.

Dikgale DSS procedures

Introduction to the Dikgale DSS site

The broad aim of the Dikgale DSS is to provide information to improve the health of the people of Northern Province and to assist the local government in developing an effective health-care policy. As no accurate data were available on the prevalence of diseases in rural and peri-urban areas of the Northern Province, the initial objective of the DSS was to establish a field site to assess the incidence and prevalence of diseases.

Community leaders in Dikgale were approached regarding the possibility of conducting research on health status, and their cooperation was obtained. The site was subsequently established, and the first census was undertaken from August to November 1995. At that time, the population was 8001, but it decreased to 7956 by 1998. Every year an update is undertaken. A distinction is made between the total population in the study area, which comprises all who regard their home as being in the area, and the permanent population, which consists of those resident in the area for ≥6 months in the year preceding the census update.

Demographic variables measured routinely include births, migrations, and deaths. Maternity histories are also conducted. Several special surveys have also been undertaken to determine the prevalence of specific diseases and disorders, such as iron and vitamin-A status in preschool children, vision defects, and the prevalence of noninfectious diseases in the adult population.

An office for the use of the fieldworkers is located in the field site. The coordinator of the Dikgale DSS is a staff member of the University of the North. Data collected at the DSS site are regularly forwarded to the Department of Health, Northern Province.

Dikgale DSS data collection and processing

The Dikgale DSS site was chosen because of its proximity to the University of the North and because of the presence at the site of a primary health-care clinic.

Field procedures

MAPPING — The fieldworkers constructed a sketch map of each village, with all roads and landmarks, such as schools and shops, indicated. They gave each household a number.

INITIAL CENSUS — The initial census was undertaken during August–November 1995. Fieldworkers visited each household and recorded the name, age, and education of each household member.

REGULAR UPDATE ROUNDS — Updates occur annually. During the update, fieldworkers visit each household with a printout of the census form. Any changes that have occurred since the last visit are recorded on the form.

A full maternity history is taken from each woman in the household who has had a child. Particulars pertaining to date of birth, gender, and live or stillbirths are entered on the maternity-history form. All births that occurred since the last visit are recorded, along with birth weight, site of delivery, and use of contraceptives. Death forms are completed for each death. Migration inquiries include information on origin or destination and reasons for the change of locality.

SUPERVISION AND QUALITY CONTROL — The field site is visited regularly, and quality checks are carried out by coordinators on a random sample of 2.5% of households. Any problems encountered are discussed and solved.

Data management

The forms that have been completed by the fieldworkers are checked manually before being processed. All data are entered into a custom-designed Access database program. The program contains checks to limit entry errors. A series of validation routines are run; corrections are made with reference to the raw data; and return visits to the field are made, where indicated.

Data analysis is done in Microsoft Excel. Reports are produced on a regular basis and forwarded to the community and local authorities.

Figure 17.2. Population pyramid for person–years observed at the Dikgale DSS site, South Africa, 1995–99.

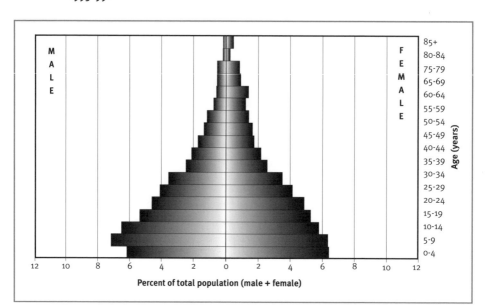

Dikgale DSS basic outputs

Demographic indicators

The population in 1998 was 7956, and the proportion of the population <1 year old was 1.6%; 1–4 years old, 11.25%; 5–14 years old, 25.68%; 15–64 years old, 57.33%; and ≥65 years, 5.74% (Figure 17.2). The age-dependency ratio is 0.74; the sex ratio, 0.96; and the infant mortality rate, 38.9 per 1000 live births. The average household size is 6.33, and the household headship is 58% male and 42% female. The percentage of people aged ≥15 years who are literate is 79.8% for males and 73.6% for females.

Migration surveys are undertaken every year and indicate a complex pattern of migration. Most movement takes place either within the same village or to another village at the DSS site or to a neighbouring village. Very few move to urban areas. The largest proportion of subjects either leaving or in-migrating occurs in the age group of 0–24 years. Few subjects >40 years old move away from their homes.

Table 17.1 shows the age- and sex-specific all-case mortality at the Dikgale DSS site.

Table 17.1. Age- and sex-specific mortality at the Dikgale DSS site, South Africa, 1995–99.

Age (years)	Deaths ($_nD_x$) Male	Deaths ($_nD_x$) Female	Person–years observed ($_nPY_x$) Male	Person–years observed ($_nPY_x$) Female
0–4	16	12	1744	1852
5–9	1	2	2026	1830
10–14	2	1	1835	1666
15–19	5	1	1507	1521
20–24	0	1	1301	1403
25–29	2	8	1146	1195
30–34	7	2	994	1014
35–39	5	5	687	740
40–44	7	2	588	632
45–49	5	2	477	508
50–54	8	3	368	486
55–59	7	6	316	412
60–64	2	5	197	359
65–69	4	4	147	407
70–74	5	4	133	265
75–79	11	11	135	245
80–84	5	3	37	83
≥85	4	16	39	135
Births	599			
CDR	6.47			
CBR	21.07			
CRNI	14.60			

Note: CBR, crude birth rate (actual number of births per 1000 population); CDR, crude death rate (actual number of deaths per 1000 population); CRNI, crude rate of natural increase (CBR minus CDR per 100; does not take into account migration); $_nD_x$, observed deaths between ages x and $x+n$; $_nPY_x$, observed person–years between ages x and $x+n$.

Acknowledgments

The project was funded by the Norwegian Universities Committee for Development Research and Education.

The Dikgale DSS team includes the following staff: M. Mogashoa, E. Makhura, S. Makgato, and S. Mokokoane. Colleagues include S. Tollman, Department of Community Health, University of Witwatersrand, South Africa, M. Garenne, Centre français sur la population et le développement, Paris, France, K. Herbst, Department of Community Health, Medical University of South Africa, South Africa, and J. Sundby, Department of Medical Anthropology, Oslo University, Norway.

Chapter 18

HLABISA DSS, SOUTH AFRICA

Geoff Solarsh, Justus Benzler, Vicky Hosegood, Frank Tanser, and Annemie Vanneste[1]

Site description

Physical geography of the Hlabisa DSA

Hlabisa health district is located in northern KwaZulu-Natal, South Africa, and covers an area of 1430 km^2 (Figure 18.1). Altitude ranges from 20 to 500 m above sea level. The terrain is flat to undulating, to mountainous, and vegetation ranges from sparse grassland to thick forest. The DSS site is located between latitudes 28.18° and 28.47°S and longitudes 31.97° and 32.38°E.

Figure 18.1. Location of the Hlabisa DSS site, South Africa (monitored population, 85 000).

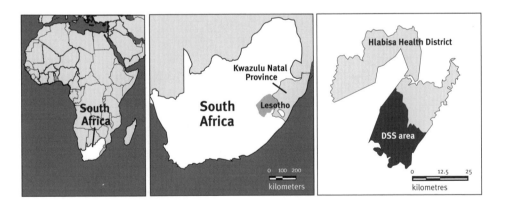

1 Africa Centre Demographic Information System, Africa Centre for Population Studies and Reproductive Health (University of Natal, University of Durban-Westville, and Medical Research Council of South Africa), South Africa.

Population characteristics of the Hlabisa DSA

The Hlabisa District is one of many official rural magisterial districts in KwaZulu-Natal. Before the political transition in 1994, this district formed part of the KwaZulu home-land and was coterminous with the Hlabisa health ward, an integrated and semi-autonomous unit of the homeland health system. It was built around a community, or nonspecialist, hospital, from which comprehensive primary health-care services were administered and supervised through a radiating network of fixed and mobile clinics. After the political transition, the KwaZulu homeland was dismantled, and all services were reorganized into a three-tier national health system, with national-, provincial-, and district-level responsibilities. Although the districts are in a state of transition, the Hlabisa health subdistrict is largely coterminous with the previous Hlabisa health ward and still functions as a semiautonomous and integrated health system at the district level. This site, therefore, constitutes a functional unit of the national health system and provides a representative district health-system model for the implementation of national health policies and programs.

The resident population of 210 000 is Zulu speaking and predominantly rural, although the district has pockets of urban and peri-urban populations in the south-east, near the market town of Mtubatuba. It is made up of four tribal areas, each under the local authority of a tribal chief, or *inkosi*. Although residents of the tribal area owe allegiance to, and fall under the local jurisdiction of, the chief, they are not necessarily members of his traditional clan or tribe. No data are yet available on reli-gion, but the majority of people are considered Christians.

Unlike in many other parts of Africa, where homesteads are clustered in clearly identifiable villages, rural populations in KwaZulu-Natal live in scattered multigenera-tional homesteads of varying size (1–100 people). The area is characterized by large variations in population density (0–6500 people per km^2). There is substantial circula-tory migration between the district and commercial and industrial centres, at varying distances from the Hlabisa District, and, to a lesser extent, between the district and remote rural areas in the hinterland. This is largely driven by the need for employ-ment and educational opportunities. Wide differentials also appear in living stan-dards, literacy rates, and access to electricity and clean water, although overall social and environmental conditions are substantially better than in many other countries in sub-Saharan Africa. Annual per capita income is US $1730, the literacy rate is 69%, and life expectancy at the beginning of the AIDS epidemic averaged 63 years. South African populations show substantial demographic and epidemiological variability, reflecting regional and ethnic differences and, in the final analysis, vast differentials in social and economic conditions.

The health infrastructure in the Hlabisa District is typical of many other rural health districts in KwaZulu-Natal and, to a lesser extent, elsewhere in South Africa. The central fixed health facility in the district is a community hospital, run by general-ist medical practitioners and nurses. It provides a wide range of curative and emer-gency services, including surgical and obstetrical care and the usual range of primary health-care services offered at fixed clinics. Scattered throughout the district are 12 fixed nurse-run clinics, providing routine prenatal, natal, and postnatal care; family planning, preventive child-health services (including immunizations); treatment for TB, sexually transmitted diseases, and noncommunicable diseases, such as diabetes and hypertension; and treatment of a wide range of minor complaints. All conditions considered to exceed the capacity or skill of the resident nurses are referred to the hospital. These clinics are supervised from the hospital and are visited biweekly by a medical doctor from the hospital.

In those parts of the district not covered by fixed clinics, mobile health services are provided on a 2–4-week basis at defined points. The level and range of services offered are similar to those offered at the fixed clinics, but the mobile clinics are unable to offer deliveries or any other forms of treatment or care requiring short-term stay or admission. Community health workers cover about half of the homesteads in the district and are largely responsible for nutritional and general health promotion in these households, supervised home care, and, where necessary, referral to clinic or hospital.

Clinics are generally well used, with about 95% of pregnant women attending an antenatal clinic at least once during their pregnancies and up to 80% of children achieving full primary vaccination, that is, up to and including a measles vaccination. Substantial use is also made of the medical services offered by private practitioners in Mtubatuba and at private clinics farther afield in the towns of Empangeni and Richard's Bay.

Hlabisa DSS procedures

Introduction to the Hlabisa DSS site

In 1991, MRC established a research station at Hlabisa hospital as a rural research unit of the national Centre for Epidemiological Research in South Africa. The presence of this productive MRC unit was probably the most important factor in the selection of the Hlabisa District for the Africa Centre for Population Studies and Reproductive Health.

The Africa Centre for Population Studies and Reproductive Health was established in April 1997 and moved into the Hlabisa District in November 1997. Since then residential and office infrastructures have been established, the entire health district has been mapped, and the DSS has been set up in the southeastern section of the district. Other projects have also been set up during this period, including studies to determine the effect of exclusive breastfeeding on mother-to-child transmission (MTCT) of HIV and another to determine the effect of male labour migration on HIV infection of nonmigrant partners.

The demographic surveillance area is based in the tribal area of Mpukunyoni, the most populous and least mountainous part of the Hlabisa District, and includes the township of Kwamsane. It is about 435 km^2 in area and is sharply demarcated by the hard boundaries of large perennial rivers, nature reserves, forestry areas, and commercial farmland on all but its northern boundary. As a result, the area is a fairly discrete and well-circumscribed geographical unit, allowing clear definition of the survey population. Although we do not yet have the data to show it, we fully expect the surveillance population to be representative of rural populations in KwaZulu-Natal and, to a lesser extent, of rural black populations elsewhere in the country.

The objectives of the Hlabisa DSS are

- To describe the demographic, social, and health impacts of a rapidly spreading HIV epidemic in a population going through the health transition;

- To assess the ameliorating effect of various intervention strategies on the march of the epidemic;

- To measure the burden of disease, including that of HIV–AIDS, on this population;
- To describe patterns and determinants of health-service use and their impacts on demographic and health outcomes; and

- To provide infrastructural and methodological support for a number of related reproductive-health research projects within the same population, including
  - Sampling frames at household and individual levels,
  - Explanatory and confounding variables for distal outcomes,
  - Linkage of health-facility and household data sets,
  - Linkage of data sets from various projects, and
  - Project management and logistical planning within a population setting.

The total population of the Hlabisa District was estimated at 210 000 in the last national census (1996). The DSS population is now expected to include 70 000 residents and an additional 15 000 nonresidents who are considered part of the 11 000 registered households in the DSA. This number falls within the recommended range for DSSs and is a sufficient sample size to generate most key demographic rates besides maternal mortality. We cater to nonresident members in the DSS, because of the large numbers of migrants who regularly return home, contribute significantly to the financial resources of households, and, because they often return home to give birth or to die, will contribute to both mortality and fertility estimates.

Formal data collection began in 2000, and, at the time of writing, the first annual data set is not yet complete.

The DSS in the Hlabisa site is a foundation project of the Africa Centre for Population Studies and Reproductive Health, an international research centre based in the Hlabisa health district. The Africa Centre was established in 1997 as a consortium between two universities — the University of Natal and the University of Durban-Westville — and the Medical Research Council (MRC) of South Africa. It has been funded through a generous 5-year grant from the Wellcome Trust in the United Kingdom.

The DSS, specifically, will generate demographic, social, and economic trends in a population going through the health transition and concurrently experiencing the complex effects of a rampant HIV epidemic. It will also provide a platform and framework for a wide range of smaller research projects concerned with household and family dynamics, microeconomic policy and programs, and burden-of-disease assessments, including HIV and noncommunicable diseases. These data will be of extreme importance to provincial and national health planners in South Africa. They will also be very important for anyone interested in modelling the impact of the HIV epidemic in rural African populations throughout the subcontinent. The DSS will be intimately integrated into a mother-and-child cohort of 2000 mother–child pairs and therefore uniquely positioned to evaluate interventions to reduce MTCT of HIV and other interventions in early childhood. In relation to the three participating institutions the DSS also provides a very important source of data for the construction of community-based curricula for population studies, reproductive health, and child health relevant to undergraduate and postgraduate trainees. A strong commitment to community-based and service-oriented education at these institutions creates many opportunities for these linkages, and some initial steps have already been taken toward the development of these programs.

Hlabisa DSS data collection and processing

Field procedures

MAPPING — The entire DSS data set is georeferenced and is linked to programs with cartographic functions and the capacity for complex spatial analysis. This GIS, a key component of the larger demographic-information system, comprises a series of geographical layers of the district — including magisterial and nature-reserve boundaries, roads, and rivers — and covers about 500 facilities and 26 000 homesteads, 10 000 of which are under continuous demographic surveillance. Extensive use was made of differential GPS units (accuracy of <2 m) in setting up the DSS. Fourteen fieldworkers and 3 supervisors were trained in the use of differential GPS. The fieldworkers were divided into four teams (three mapping teams of four members each and one backup team of two members). Each mapping team was assigned a supervisor and given a portion of the district to map and a set of maps covering the district. The maps, based on recent aerial photographs, contained the estimated positions of all homesteads and facilities in the district. The supervisors were responsible for coordinating the movements of the fieldworkers.

Data dictionaries, which restricted data entry to a unique block of 5000 numbers, were uploaded to each fieldworker's hand-held GPS unit. The data dictionaries allowed the fieldworkers to collect all attribute data, using the GPS units — thereby obviating the use of all forms. Tags bearing the unique ID numbers of the homesteads were affixed and information about the homestead was collected only if a senior resident of the homestead was present and in a position to provide permission for the homestead to be mapped. The backup team was responsible for visiting absentee homesteads and collecting the associated attribute data and affixing tags. Once the fieldworkers returned from the field, the data were downloaded to computers. Differential correction occurred the next day.

The area is socially and physically heterogeneous, and the population is dispersed throughout the DSS site. This presented numerous problems for the equitable distribution of work among fieldworkers. A fuzzy-logic model within a GIS was therefore used to ergonomically define 48 fieldworker areas and thereby equitably distribute the workload. The GIS procedure for doing this was described in Tanser (2000).

Future GIS research will focus on the geographic analysis of the demographic and health data collected by the DSS down to homestead level (once these data are available). In particular, it is hoped that HIV status will be geographically linked to homestead data so that researchers can explore patterns of HIV in the DSS site and possible models to explain the distribution.

INITIAL CENSUS — The Africa Centre for Population Studies and Reproductive Health, only recently established, commenced its first round of visits to all homesteads in the DSS site in February 2000. The population within the circumscribed DSS site is the study sample, and data collection covers an observation period starting 1 January 2000. In the first round, a complete census of all homesteads (places of residence), households (social groups), and individuals has been conducted. Baseline data collection has included descriptive characteristics of homesteads and households, demographic attributes of all individuals, and detailed pregnancy and reproductive histories from all women of reproductive age.

REGULAR UPDATE ROUNDS — Continuous registration and updates of all new and existing homesteads, households, and individuals occurs during each round of data collection. All homesteads in the DSA are visited every 4 months to register new individuals and households, update demographic variables on registered individuals and households, and record all births, deaths, and migrations. Reproductive-health questionnaires are completed on all women of reproductive age (15–49 years) who were not registered in previous rounds or were not previously eligible for this baseline questionnaire. In subsequent update rounds, all demographic events and changes in the status of all homesteads, households, and individuals in the surveillance area are recorded. Additional modules dealing with subjects such as household socioeconomic status, health-related conditions, HIV sero-prevalence, or disability may be added on to routine updates as the need arises. Monitoring will continue for a minimum of 5 years, but it will almost certainly be extended if the research program is productive.

Baseline surveys on all women of reproductive age will be conducted throughout the duration of the project. Household socioeconomic questionnaires are expected to be administered annually at all homesteads in the DSS site. Other surveys, such as disability and HIV sero-prevalence surveys, are likely to be conducted in the future as the need arises. At present, no biological samples or direct measurements are taken as part of DSS activities.

CONTINUOUS SURVEILLANCE — Births and deaths are recorded and related data are regularly updated as above. Deaths are reported as part of the regular notification of vital events. Every death notification triggers a separate visit by a verbal-autopsy (VA) nurse, who administers a standard three-part VA questionnaire to determine the likely cause of death.

SUPERVISION AND QUALITY ASSURANCE — Supervisors check all questionnaires when they come out of the field, and serial subsamples are further checked by managers at various levels. Supervisors make weekly quality-control visits to at least 5% of homesteads visited by fieldworkers in the preceding period, to validate interview findings. During the first 2–4 weeks of each round, supervisors accompany each of their fieldworkers on weekly supervised visits to take any opportunity to support and correct interviewing-technique difficulties or misconceptions as early as possible. Additional, unannounced spot checks are made in the case of weak or unreliable fieldworkers.

Data management

Data are also collected at homestead and household levels from a hierarchy of key informants, with highest priority given to those with the greatest knowledge of other household members. Individual data are collected preferentially from the individual concerned, but in his or her absence they are collected from the best-informed key informant. In the case of reproductive-health questionnaires, all information is collected directly from the woman herself. All questionnaires are entered into a large relational Access database, using a customized front end (programed in Delphi 5) specifically developed for the Africa Centre for Population Studies and Reproductive Health.

Figure 18.2. Population pyramid of person–years (both resident and nonresident) observed at the Hlabisa DSS, South Africa, 2000.

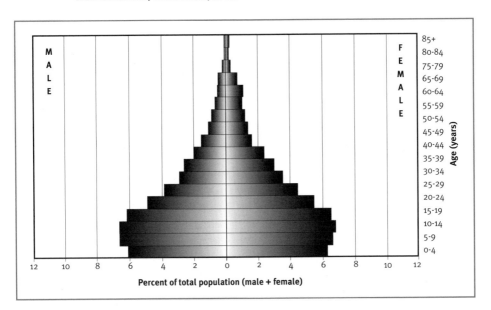

Data are single punched in two shifts of six data capturers each and subjected, in the data-entry program, to a series of checks of validity and consistency. All questionnaires with evident errors or omissions are returned to the field for correction, and those that are free of errors are archived after data capture. All errors that cannot be corrected by supervisors are returned to fieldworkers for revisits and corrections.

The core data set will be routinely analyzed and form the subject of regular annual reports, which will be widely disseminated in hard copy and on the Internet. The core data set will be exclusively available to the Africa Centre's investigators and their collaborators for a limited period (still to be defined) but will thereafter be made available in anonymized form to a larger audience for secondary analysis. Substudies built on the DSS core data will be encouraged, be the property of the investigators, and be made available to the scientific community through peer-reviewed literature. A final policy on data-sharing and dissemination has not yet been drafted, but the above principles are likely to apply.

Hlabisa DSS basic outputs

Demographic indicators

Actual DSS monitoring began in 2000, and the first annual data set was not yet complete at the time of writing. Hence, no indicators can be provided for the moment. A population period for 2000 is shown in Figure 18.2.

Acknowledgments

The Africa Centre for Population Studies and Reproductive Health was established through a large core grant from the Wellcome Trust in the United Kingdom for a minimum period of 5 years. Since then additional funding has been obtained from the National Institutes of Health in the United States. Additional funders — such as the Centre for International Migration, a German governmental aid organization supporting human capacity development in developing countries — have made important contributions to funding for the work of expatriate scientists.

The DSS team would like to specially acknowledge the support we have received throughout the DSS-development process from Dr Robert Howells, the program leader, and from Dr Wendy Ewart, the program officer responsible for the Population Studies Programme at the Wellcome Trust. Wendy's unflagging optimism and belief in the abilities of this team went a long way to sustaining us through the many demanding challenges of setting up a DSS while concurrently establishing a new research field site. We believe the support we received went far beyond anything we could have expected from the representatives of a large international funder.

An important formative influence in the development of the Hlabisa DSS has come from the DSS model provided by the Navrongo Health Research Centre. We are aware of the important contributions to this model provided by Fred Binka and Jim Phillips and wish to thank them for hosting us at Navrongo and for sharing their experience so freely. Important elements of the system design were also influenced by the Nouna DSS in Burkina Faso. We are grateful to Michel Garenne for much support for the theoretical background.

We are also grateful to Steve Tollman and the team at Agincourt in South Africa who have supported us through many different phases of this project and have generously shared important ideas and resources from the Agincourt team.

A team of social, medical, and population scientists from the participating institutions assisted with the pilot studies that laid down the definitions and concepts on which the DSS has been based. In particular, we wish to thank Eleanor Preston-Whyte, Tessa Marcus, Mark Lurie, and Abby Harrison for their assistance.

Special mention must be made of the continuous and critical nurturing role of Dudu Biyela, the community liaison manager of the Africa Centre. Dudu helped us to take our first halting steps into the Hlabisa community and watched over us through every twist and turn in our relationship with it. The position of "mother" of the Hlabisa DSS is not reflected in our staffing structure or as a budgetary line item, but a few of us know to whom this role belongs and how deservedly it has been earned.

Finally and most importantly, we wish to recognize the important services and essential contributions of all members of the 80-strong DSS team responsible for the diverse tasks and functions that make a system of this kind run efficiently and enable high-quality data to be generated.

Chapter 19

NOUNA DSS, BURKINA FASO

Yazoumé Yé, Aboubakary Sanou, Adjima Gbangou, and Bocar Kouyaté[1]

Site description

Physical geography of the Nouna DSA

The DSS site of the Centre de recherche en santé de Nouna (CRSN, Nouna Health Research Center) is in the Nouna health district in northwest Burkina Faso, 300 km from the capital, Ouagadougou (Figure 19.1). The Nouna area is a dry orchard savannah, populated almost exclusively with subsistence farmers of various ethnic groups. The area has a sub-Saharan climate, with a mean annual rainfall of 796 mm (range 483–1083 mm) over the past five decades.

Figure 19.1. Location of the Nouna DSS site, Burkina Faso (monitored population, 55 000).

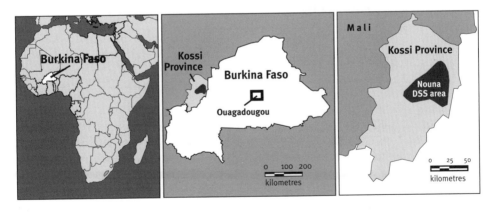

Population characteristics of the Nouna DSA

The Nouna DSS site has a population of about 55 000, settled over 1775 km². The density of the population is about 30.98 individuals per km². The population is rural and semiurban (essentially living in Nouna town). The main ethnic groups are the Marka, Bwaba, Samo, Mossi, and Foulani. Dioula language is widely and commonly spoken, permitting communication between all the various ethnic groups. People are mostly farmers or cattle keepers, which both have low economic status.

Schools have been there since 1935, yet most children do not attend. Some attend Quranic school. More than 80% of the population is illiterate.

Houses are generally clustered. But some villages have more dispersed farming houses around a principal settlement. Wells are the main water source; however, fewer than half the people of the town of Nouna have piped water.

The whole district is difficult to access during the rainy season, when the unpaved road leading to its centre becomes impassable. The town of Nouna is linked to the rest of the country by telephone but has an inadequate system of public transportation. A source of electricity serves the town 19 hours a day.

The district has 1 district hospital, 1 medical centre, and 15 peripheral health centres. The population of the DSS site is in an area with four peripheral health centres and the district hospital. The health-care-financing system is based on user fees for the occasional patient looking for modern care. Acute respiratory infection, malaria, and diarrhea are the main health problems.

The historic-events calendar includes the two wars against Mali, in 1974 and 1985, and the cholera epidemic in Nouna in 1971.

Nouna DSS procedures

Introduction to the Nouna DSS site

CRSN started in the early 1990s as Projet recherche action pour améliorer les soins de santé (action research project to improve health care), a collaborative project between the Department of Tropical Hygiene and Public Health, the University of Heidelberg, and the Ministry of Health, Burkina Faso. The main objectives were to

- Conceptualize and lead multidisciplinary field-based health-research projects relevant to national health policy;

- Disseminate results of the research to promote health-sector reforms;

- Contribute to capacity-building in health research; and

- Provide the Ministry of Health with data for health policy and planning.

The Nouna DSS of CRSN has conducted regular population censuses since 1992 (baseline of 26 000 individuals), maintained a vital-events-registration system, and performed routine verbal-autopsy (VA) interviews. The DSS covers a total population of about 55 000, living in 41 villages and — as of 2000 — the town of Nouna. The DSS team comprises one demographer, one research assistant, one database specialist, one GIS specialist, three field supervisors, seven interviewers, five data-entry clerks, one data-entry supervisor, and two archivists.

Nouna DSS data collection and processing

Field procedures

INITIAL CENSUS — The baseline census took place in 1992, during which demographic information was collected on all individuals in the study area. The baseline census for the suburban part took place in January 2000.

REGULAR UPDATE ROUNDS — Two further censuses were done in 1994 and 1998, to check and update information from previous censuses. Census update rounds are planned for every 2 years to supplement the vital-events registration and produce a clear picture of the study population at certain fixed points in time.

Previously programed as a monthly activity, the vital-event registration has collected data every 3 months from all households of the DSS since January 2000. Previously, an interviewer visited the key informant of each village to obtain information about any vital events. Now, the seven interviewers visit each household to inquire about all members previously registered or actually living in the household and identify all new vital events since the previous visits. Data are collected on births, deaths, pregnancies, and migration in or out of the household, including all dates related to these events. A VA is conducted after the interviewer confirms a death, but no sooner than 3 months after the death has occurred. The form used includes ID information retrieved from the DSS. The completed questionnaires are coded by two physicians. Where the diagnoses are different, a third physician gives an independent assessment. A cause of death is determined if at least two of the medical doctors agree; otherwise, the cause is classified as "unknown."

SUPERVISION AND QUALITY CONTROL — To reduce errors, interviewers use preprinted database registration forms for data collection. Three field supervisors safeguard the quality of the collected data in the field, employing a number of approaches. Supervisors examine the questionnaires in the field to check if the data collected by the interviewer make sense. They observe the interviewers during supervised interviews, giving feedback at the end. The supervisor repeats a 5–10% sample of completed questionnaires to verify the information. In addition, a number of blind-control interviews are conducted, during which the supervisor collects the data again and compares these with the data from the interviewer. Finally, the supervisor reads and corrects each questionnaire at the office before giving it to the data-entry clerks.

Data management

The Nouna DSS currently uses a custom-designed database, based on Microsoft Access, but this will change soon to Household Registration Software, version 2. The database can register longitudinal information and check data consistency. It includes information from both the vital-event registration and the census. Once interviewers fill in questionnaires, their forms are checked by field supervisors and sent to an archivist. The archivist sends the questionnaires to the data-entry team, which comprises one database manager, one data-entry supervisor, and five data-entry clerks. During data entry, questionnaires with missing or unclear information are sent back to the field supervisors and, if necessary, the interviewers for correction, via the data-entry supervisor, or via the database manager in the case of complicated problems.

The database team and the field team work closely together, so most problems are resolved quickly.

Checking data consistency is done in two steps:

1. *Controlled data entry* — The data-entry program is developed to prevent errors by applying user-friendly data-entry masks, including easy-to-enter codes, two data-entry modes (read only and modify), and automatic attribution of individual IDs. It also has automatic validation and verification of household and individual IDs, using message boxes for warnings.

2. *Manual supervision* — As data are entered into several computers, the data supervisor merges all the files into one single database. After the merging, specified variables are reviewed by listing and verification of all the households and individuals entered (check for completeness) and by searching all variables for invalid values (this includes syntactic tests to check whether entered values are allowed and semantic tests to compare two variables with some logic relation). Further validation is carried out through duplicate data entry of 5% of all questionnaires by the data-entry supervisor.

Nouna DSS basic outputs

Demographic indicators

The following describes the 1998 data set. The population count was 30 886 individuals, distributed in the following main age-group structure: 0–4 years old, 18.3%; 5–15 years old, 29.9%; 15–64 years old, 47.7%; and ≥65 years old, 4.1% (Figure 19.2). Females constitute 50.1% of this population. The annual growth rate is 1.5%, with a fertility rate of 6.6. Most of the indicators present a similar picture to the 1996 national census, with no significant difference. The mean household size is 8, and the age-dependency ratio is 109.8. Migration is dominated by internal movement and to some extent by external movement from the centre of the country to the river borders of this zone.

Table 19.1 shows the age- and sex-specific all-cause mortality at the Nouna DSS site.

Acknowledgments

We gratefully acknowledge all the help received from the University of Heidelberg, the Karl Sauerborn Foundation, and the European Union to run our DSS since 1992. We also thank our study-area population for being open and available for our long and repetitive questions.

Figure 19.2. Population pyramid for person–years observed at the Nouna DSS site, Burkina Faso, 1995–98.

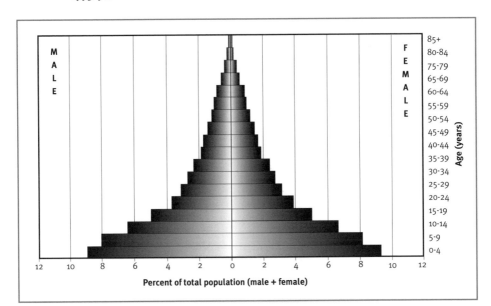

Table 19.1. Age- and sex-specific mortality at the Nouna DSS site, Burnina Faso, 1995–98.

Age (years)	Deaths ($_nD_x$)		Person–years observed ($_nPY_x$)	
	Male	Female	Male	Female
<1	78	110	2221	2504
1–4	238	242	8218	8423
5–9	85	67	9408	9593
10–14	30	31	7484	7829
15–19	21	30	5791	5904
20–24	27	20	4304	4544
25–29	20	25	3632	3736
30–34	21	16	3135	3230
35–39	18	15	2688	2832
40–44	19	22	2154	2219
45–49	21	19	1979	1993
50–54	14	24	1659	1727
55–59	24	30	1359	1422
60–64	35	35	1170	1144
65–69	29	47	977	1016
70–74	38	36	651	656
75–79	31	44	411	439
80–84	30	21	229	227
≥85	12	25	114	132
Births	4602			
CDR	14.08			
CBR	39.28			
CRNI	25.20			

Note: CBR, crude birth rate (actual number of births per 1000 population); CDR, crude death rate (actual number of deaths per 1000 population); CRNI, crude rate of natural increase (CBR minus CDR per 100; does not take into account migration); $_nD_x$, observed deaths between ages x and $x+n$; $_nPY_x$, observed person–years between ages x and $x+n$.

Chapter 20

Oubritenga DSS, Burkina Faso

Diadier Amadou Diallo,[1] Simon Cousens,[2] Aphonse Rouamba,[1] Nadine Cuzin-Ouattara,[1] Edith Iboudo-Sanogo,[1] Annette Habluetzel,[3] and Fulvio Esposito[3]

Site description

Physical geography of the Oubritenga DSA

The DSS site of the Centre national de recherche et de formation sur le paludisme (CNRFP, National Centre for Research and Training on Malaria) is in the Province of Oubritenga, north of Ouagadougou, in Burkina Faso, and involves 158 villages (Figure 20.1). The area covered is about 1000 km², about one-third of the health district. The health district covers all of the Province of Oubritenga and two departments of the Province of Kadiogo. The DSS site is 38 km × 34 km and lies between latitudes 12°28′ and 12°47′N and longitudes 1°13′ and 1°32′W. The climate is characteristic of a Sudan savannah area, with a dry, cool season from November to February, a dry, hot season from March to May, and a rainy season from June to October. The mean annual rainfall is about 650 mm, and the average annual temperature ranges between 23° and 33°C. A large and permanent reservoir lies within the area.

Figure 20.1. Location of the Oubritenga DSS site, Burkina Faso (monitored population, 99 700).

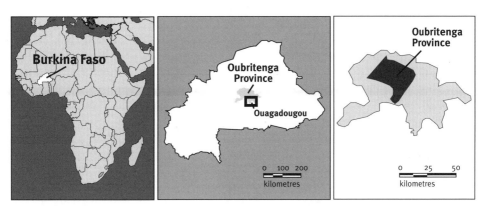

[1] Centre national de recherche et de formation sur le paludisme, Burkina Faso.

[2] University of Camerrno, Italy.

[3] London School of Hygiene and Tropical Medicine, UK.

Population characteristics of the Oubritenga DSA

Only populations living in rural settings were enrolled in the DSS; therefore, the peri-urban population from the district capital was not included. Even though children less than 59 months old are the population of interest, all age groups are followed up. Population density is about 100 inhabitants/km^2. Of the more than 60 ethnic groups in Burkina Faso, only 2 of these live in the DSS site. More than 98% of the residents belong to the Mossi, the largest single ethnic group in Burkina Faso, and the remaining 2% belong to the Fulani. The main religions in the area are Islam, Christianity, and local animist traditions. Moore is the language spoken by at least 98% of the population. As in most of the rural areas in Burkina Faso, the great majority of population of the DSS site lives by subsistence farming. Millet, sorghum, peanuts, and beans represent the main crops. In the dry season, villages close to water reservoirs practice market gardening. Formal education is provided in 49 primary schools and 5 secondary schools in the DSA. About 88% of the population >15 years old has received no education at all, 3% have some level of literacy in local languages, and 9% have attended primary school or beyond.

Villages range in size from 10 to 200 dispersed compounds, with an average village comprising about 60 compounds. Compounds are surrounded by walls and separated from each other by fields. A typical compound encloses, on average, three or four round huts and two rectangular houses made of mud bricks. Round huts are covered with conical thatched roofs, and rectangular houses are covered with corrugated iron or mud. Adult males have their own houses, often equipped with local beds, and women live in separate houses with their children and sleep on mats laid on the floor. On average, 10–12 people live in a compound. Generally, villages have some access to safe water, as most of them are equipped with at least one drilled well. Latrine coverage, on the other hand, is very low. None of the 158 villages in the study area has access to electricity or telecommunications.

Access to the DSS site is possible via two main roads — one paved and one unpaved — delimiting its western and eastern boundaries, respectively. Interconnecting unpaved roads within the DSS site are quite good and allow access to most of the villages, except in periods of unusually heavy rain, which may render some villages unreachable for a few days. A railway linking Ouagadougou to a northern city crosses the site.

The whole province of Oubritenga has 1 district hospital and 32 governmental health centres and dispensaries. Of these, the district hospital and 10 health centres and dispensaries are in the DSA. However, people can also go to other health facilities at the periphery of the DSS site. Consultations are free, but patients pay for any drugs prescribed. They can find essential drug depots in 23 of the health facilities. However, the extent to which all these facilities are used by the communities is questionable, as use of health facilities in rural areas is low.

Several intervention programs have been implemented in the district, with support from a wide range of partners. One of the major interventions is the implementation of insecticide-treated curtains (ITCs). Half of the DSA was equipped with ITCs in mid-1994, and the other half was equipped in mid-1996. Other intervention programs have been carried out at the district level by the district health-management team. These programs include an expanded immunization program, reproductive health, nutrition, water and sanitation, and community information and education.

Data from the health district indicate that in 1997 BCG (bacillus Calmette-Guérin) vaccine coverage was 77.5%; DPT, 53.3%; and measles, 52%. Data from the same source indicate that the most important causes of death in the district are malaria, acute respiratory infections, and diarrhea. Measles and meningitis are also among the important causes of death, with year-to-year variations.

Since the beginning of the DSS two major epidemics have occurred in the site, measles and meningoccocal meningitis, both in 1996.

Oubritenga DSS procedures

Introduction to the Oubritenga DSS site

Originally, the DSS was set up to assess the impact of ITCs on all-cause child mortality. It was one of four settings in Africa that hosted large-scale trials of insecticide-treated materials, initiated and supported by UNDP/World Bank/WHO Special Programme for Research and Training in Tropical Diseases. Over 2 years (1994–96) of implementation of the ITC trial, a 15% reduction in mortality was observed in children 6–59 months old (Habluetzel et al. 1997). From mid-1996 to 1999, the objective has shifted to studying issues in sustaining the initial impact of ITCs on child mortality.

At the first census in 1993, the DSS site had 88 807 inhabitants. At the most recent census, held in mid-1999, the population had increased to 99 705. Seventy-nine additional villages, neighbouring the DSS site and totaling about 65 000 inhabitants, were enumerated in 1999, and they will be included in the DSS (data not available yet).

Since 1993 annual census rounds have been performed to collect basic demographic information. In addition, from 1993 to 1996, a continuous DSS has been in place in all villages. Each village is visited once every 3 weeks. At each census or continuous DSS visit, births, deaths, and migrations occurring between the previous census or visit and the ongoing one are registered, including the date on which each event occurred. Pregnancies are also registered. Deaths of newborns are registered if the child was alive at birth. Any person living in the study area for at least 6 months is considered resident, but people leaving their villages for >6 months are considered migrants.

Apart from monitoring child mortality, research activities undertaken in the DSA have focused mainly on malaria transmission and malaria morbidity studies. Ascertainment of cause of death was conducted between 1994 and 1996, using structured and unstructured verbal-autopsy questionnaires. Socioeconomic surveys were conducted between 1995 and 1996 to estimate household income and help respond to issues related to the communities' willingness to pay for ITCs.

The nearest village within the DSS site is about 10 km from CNRFP, and the most distant village is about 50 km away. The current DSS team includes 1 geographer, 3 drivers, 6 supervisors, and 18 enumerators (for the census). Since 1996 the six fieldworkers responsible for continuous surveillance have not been part of the team.

Oubritenga DSS data collection and processing

The DSS site was selected to host the ITC trial, with approval from the health and administrative authorities of Burkina Faso. The main reason for its selection was the ease of access. Other aspects also favoured the selection of the site, such as past contacts between CNRFP research staff and some of the communities and epidemiological considerations.

Field procedures

MAPPING — Details of the DSS methods were published elsewhere (Diallo et al. 1996). In brief, in 1993 CNRFP identified 158 villages, using GPS to obtain each village's coordinates. Each village has a code, and then each compound was given a number, which was painted on the wall. Households from each compound were also numbered, and individuals in a household received a registration number. A unique ID number was then created for each individual, using four codes: village, compound, household, and registration order number.

INITIAL CENSUS AND UPDATE ROUNDS — Since 1993 annual census rounds have been performed. At each of these, enumerators use preprinted "roll calls," generated from a computerized database. Three teams of enumerators depart every morning from CNRFP by car to make door-to-door visits. Each enumerator is trained to check all completed forms before leaving a compound. At the end of the day, forms from each team are gathered and checked by the team supervisors, and any discrepancies are corrected in the field the same day, before the forms are sent to the data-management office. Forms undergo a further thorough check by a team of three people in the data-management office. Those not properly completed are returned to the team supervisors the following morning for correction at the relevant compound.

CONTINUOUS SURVEILLANCE — Between 1993 and 1996, continuous demographic monitoring was performed in all villages by a team of trained fieldworkers equipped with motorbikes. Six fieldworkers were recruited and trained to perform the continuous DSS, using community key informants. Each fieldworker was responsible for 24–29 villages. Continuous DSS monitoring was stopped in 1996 because it added very little information to vital events captured during the census updates. A comparison between the census and the continuous demographic system was published by Diallo et al. (1996).

SUPERVISION AND QUALITY CONTROL — Quality control of information collected by enumerators is assessed through repeat visits performed by team supervisors in randomly selected compounds. Any major difference on reported information is checked by a third person.

Data management

Roll calls are printed for each village, using a dBase program. All roll calls completed during the census are sent to the data-management office, where they are kept until data collection is complete and all data have been entered and cleaned. Two data clerks, using Epi Info Version 6.0, are in charge of data entry. Computers operate on a local network.

Any discrepancy found during data entry is reported to the data manager and checked back to the field. Double entry is the standard procedure for all the data. Files are systematically validated and cleaned before they are merged into one single file, from which back-up copies are made and kept at different locations.

Stata 5.0 software is currently used for data analysis. Mortality rates are calculated by age and sex, using number of deaths as the numerator and person–years at risk as the denominator. Subsequent rounds of censuses have been used to disseminate results to the study communities. Annual reports are disseminated to local health and administrative authorities, including the district health-management team, and to the funding agency. Scientific publications and international meetings are the channels for dissemination of results to the scientific community.

Oubritenga DSS basic outputs

Demographic indicators

Of the 99 705 inhabitants at the 1999 census, 46.8% were males and 53.2% were females. The population <5 years old constitutes 18.5% of the total; those 5–14 years old, 30.9%; those 15–64 years, 45.7%; and those ≥65 years old, only 4.9% (Figure 20.2). Thus, this population is fairly young, with about half being less than 15 years old.

Crude mortality rates for males in all age groups together were 24.2/1000, 17.1/1000, 18.7/1000, 11.5/1000, and 14.9/1000 in 1994, 1995, 1996, 1997, and 1998, respectively. Crude mortality rates for females in these years were 19.9/1000, 14.0/1000, 15.8/1000, 10.1/1000, and 13.7/1000. These figures indicate a higher male than female mortality. Female mortality appeared to be higher than male mortality only for those between 15 and 24 years old, and this might be due to maternal mortality. In 1997, mortality was very low compared with the other periods.

Age-specific mortality data (Table 20.1) indicate higher infant mortality (males and females together), with 180.1/1000, 142.0/1000, and 121.4/1000 for the first 3 years, respectively. In 1997 and 1998, mortality figures in the same age group declined noticeably (69.5/1000 and 84.9/1000, respectively). Mortality rates for children 1–4 years old were 32.4/1000, 23.2/1000, 31.1/1000, 19.4/1000, and 28.3/1000 in 1994, 1995, 1996, 1997, and 1998, respectively, whereas under-five mortality rates were 65.6/1000, 49.8/1000, 51.4/1000, 30.6/1000, and 41.5/1000 for the same years. It is important to stress that child-mortality figures should be interpreted with caution, as malaria-control intervention was implemented from 1994 to 1999. From 1994 to mid-1996, half of the DSA was covered with ITCs, and they completely covered the DSS site from mid-1996 to 1999.

Figure 20.2. Population pyramid of person–years observed for the Oubritenga DSS Site, Burkina Faso, 1995–98.

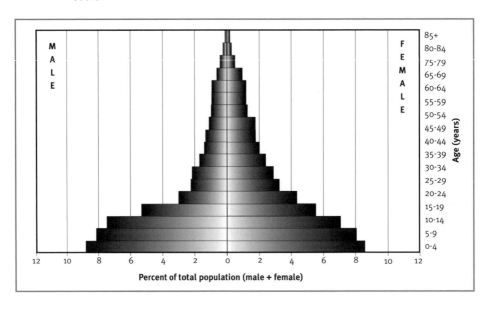

Table 20.1. Age- and sex-specific mortality at the Oubritenga DSS site, Burkina Faso, 1995–98.

Age (years)	Death s ($_nD_x$) Male	Female	Person–years observed ($_nPY_x$) Male	Female
<1	882	765	8 035	7 829
1–4	876	935	34 175	33 206
5–9	189	145	38 961	38 667
10–14	82	61	35 857	33 928
15–19	62	94	25 399	26 582
20–24	39	83	14 117	20 811
25–29	72	78	10 603	15 542
30–34	88	78	10 302	13 805
35–39	77	64	8 098	11 483
40–44	57	68	6 692	9 590
45–49	70	59	6 265	8 458
50–54	67	81	5 330	8 364
55–59	87	64	4 671	6 000
60–64	94	87	4 531	5 571
65–69	185	153	4 483	5 550
70–74	169	226	3 096	4 426
75–79	173	169	2 032	2 283
80–84	147	104	1 127	1 169
≥85	101	136	519	759
Births	17 070			
CDR	14.57			
CBR	35.69			
CRNI	21.12			

Note: CBR, crude birth rate (actual number of births per 1000 population); CDR, crude death rate (actual number of deaths per 1000 population); CRNI, crude rate of natural increase (CBR minus CDR per 100; does not take into account migration); $_nD_x$, observed deaths between ages x and $x+n$; $_nPY_x$, observed person–years between ages x and $x+n$.

Acknowledgments

We thank the population of the study villages for their cooperation and support throughout the period of this study, the Burkina Faso Ministry of Health, the director of health of the Oubritenga Province, and the director of CNRFP, Dr Seydou Ouili, for assistance in the implementation of the study. We thank the DSS team for their contributions to various aspects of the demographic monitoring. We are also indebted to the staff of CNRFP, without whom this study would not have been possible. This investigation received financial support from the United Nations Development Programme, World Bank, and World Health Organization's Special Programme for Research and Training in Tropical Diseases, the European Commission (International Cooperation–Developing Countries, Directorate General XII), the Danish Agency for International Development, and the Ministry for University and Scientific Research of Italy, which formed part of a program of activities run by CNRFP under the bilateral-cooperation agreement between Burkina Faso and the Italian Direzione Generale per la Cooperazione allo Sviluppo (Directorate-General for Development Co-operation), Ministry of Foreign Affairs.

Chapter 21

Farafenni DSS, The Gambia

Amy A. Ratcliffe, Allan G. Hill, Pierre Gomez, and Gijs Walraven[1]

Site description

Physical geography of the Farafenni DSA

The Gambia is the smallest continental country in Africa, with a land area of just 10 360 km² (480 km from east to west and on average 48 km from north to south) and a total population of 1.4 million in July 2000 (Figure 21.1). It is surrounded by Senegal, with which it once shared a short-lived federation ("Senegambia"), from 1982 to 1989. The town of Farafenni is on the north bank of the Gambia River, about 170 km inland from the capital, Banjul. The main road between Dakar and the Casamance crosses the Gambia River at Farafenni, which has a ferry suitable for heavy vehicles. The average annual rainfall, measured at the Farafenni field station in 1989–99, was 683 mm, but the relative variability is large (22.6%), with amounts in the 11-year period ranging from 515 mm in 1991 to 1000 mm in 1999. The Gambia has a single rainy season, extending from June to October, with peak rains in August. The vegetation is dry savannah, with scattered trees, but in the rainy season, grasses and bushes grow strongly. Rice is cultivated in the river bottoms and in the upland areas where millet, sorghum, and other cereals are the staple food crops.

Figure 21.1. Location of the Farafenni DSS site, The Gambia (monitored population, 16 000).

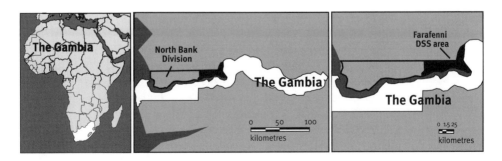

[1] UK Medical Research Council, The Gambia.

Population characteristics of the Farafenni DSA

The surveillance site is located in a rural area between latitudes 13° and 14°N and longitudes 15° and 16°W and comprises 40 small villages, extending 32 km to the east and 22 km to the west of the town of Farafenni (1993 population, 21 000). The population of the 40 villages has been studied by the UK Medical Research Council (MRC) since October 1981. The villages were originally selected for the study of malaria interventions requiring little previous use of antimalarials, which meant that larger villages and those within about 10 km of the town of Farafenni were excluded (see below).

By mid-1999, the surveillance population included 16 202 residents of rural villages ranging in size from 40 to 1221 inhabitants. Three main ethnic and linguistic groups are represented in the study area: Mandinka (43%), Wollof (36%), and Fula (20%). Nearly all of the residents are Muslim. Farming is the primary occupation of most residents, both male and female. In a 1998 survey, men were asked about their main occupations: 92% said farming, 12% said a trade or craft, and 9% said some form of trading or commerce. The population is poor. In June–July 1996, a survey of household heads revealed that only 61% had radios, 44% slept on iron or wooden beds, 35% had carts, and 40% still had homes with thatched roofs (Hill et al. 1996). Nine primary schools serve the study area, but only four are located in study villages. Many children have to walk up to 5 km to school, which restricts school attendance. In a 1998 survey, just 10% of the men ≥18 years old and 3% of the women 15–54 years old had ever attended school. In a 2000 survey of household heads, only 54% of households with school-age children reported any children attending school.

Villages are organized into compounds containing up to 149 people, with an average of 18 persons overall. A compound is based on an extended family unit, headed by a senior man. Residents might include the head's brothers or sons and their and his own wives and children. Polygyny is widespread: 40% of married men were polygynous in 1998, with an average 2.6 wives each. Co-wives very often reside in the same compound, together with their children. Additional compound residents include distant relatives or nonfamily members, such as foster children or Quranic scholars. Compounds consist of a group of buildings bordered by some kind of fence. Most houses are constructed of mud-brick walls, with either thatched or corrugated-metal roofs; cement buildings are rare. Kitchens and other buildings are more commonly made from *krinting* (woven lattice work) and thatch. Water is usually gathered from a common pump well (82% of compounds), but 12% of compounds still rely on traditional wells, with buckets and ropes. The pump wells became a common feature of most villages after the late 1980s. Most compounds do not have standard latrines, but some have a simple hole in the ground that is used by adults more often than children. None of the villages has electricity.

A single graded road runs east–west on the north bank of the river from the eastern part of the country, through Farafenni to Barra on the coast, the crossing point for Banjul on the opposite shore. Unimproved tracks link this road to the villages. An intermittent public bus service began in 1986, along the main north-bank road. Most villagers walk to Farafenni, but horse and donkey carts and a few privately owned bush taxis provide transport to the town, especially on market day (Sunday in Farafenni). The study villages have no telephones, but three of the nearby larger villages not in the surveillance system have public payphones.

Village-based primary health care was begun in The Gambia in 1981 (Greenwood et al. 1990a, b). A health centre was established in the town of Farafenni in 1983, and in 1998 it was upgraded to become the third hospital in the country. The hospital has 155 beds and provides essential medical, pediatric, obstetric, gynecological, surgical, and ophthalmic services. Before these services were available in Farafenni, patients had to be transported to the Royal Victoria Hospital in Banjul, using the ferry and an ambulance or bus service. In the early 1980s, the health centre was staffed by a team of two to four physicians from China, but at present, MRC physicians and Cuban doctors support the hospital's clinical services. At two dispensaries closer to the study villages, patients can be seen and referred to Farafenni. The town has a few private dispensaries and pharmacies. Eight paid community-health nurses (CHNs) serve the area and supervise the volunteer traditional birth attendants (TBAs) and village health workers (VHWs), who form the base of the primary health-care (PHC) program. CHNs manage maternal- and child-health (MCH) clinics, including five monthly mobile clinics in study villages and two static weekly clinics accessible to residents of the study area. All villages with a population of more than 400 persons are eligible to become PHC villages, with a resident TBA and a VHW, but this depends on the level of commitment and organization of each village. Fifteen of the 40 villages within the Farafenni DSS have been designated PHC villages. Full details of The Gambia's PHC system were published by GTG (1981) and Hill et al. (2000).

The district health-management team, with support from MRC physicians, maintains weekly clinics in two larger villages, one to the east and the other to the west of Farafenni. The MRC fieldworkers use referral forms to encourage needy residents of the study area to attend these clinics. User fees are charged for all these public-health services. Mothers may use maternal- and child (under-five)-health services after buying a child-health or antenatal card for 5 dalasi (in 2001, 15.45 Gambian dalasi [GMD] = 1 United States dollar [USD]). The clinic fee for children 5–14 years old is 1 dalasi; and for adults, 5 dalasi. Admission fees at the hospital for adults (free for children <5 years old and pregnant women) are 25 dalasi a week, and for major operations, the fee is 50 dalasi.

Immunization levels in the study area are fairly high: 88% of children had received BCG vaccine by 1 year old; 75%, DPT3 by 2 years old; and 64%, measles vaccine by 2 years old (unpublished data). Virtually all women in the study area who delivered babies in 1998 had received some antenatal care, with the mean number of visits at 3.5 for each woman. The first visit occurred fairly late in the pregnancy, on average at 5.7 months. Twenty percent of all deliveries in 1998 were attended by a health professional, 51% by a TBA, and 25% by a relative, but 4% of the women delivered "on their own."

Based on preliminary reviews of verbal autopsies (VAs) for 1998 and 1999, the most frequent cause of death in infants was acute respiratory infection (ARI), whereas in children 1–4 years old it was malaria. These two conditions accounted for about half of the deaths in children <12 years old. Other leading causes of death were acute gastroenteritis, malnutrition, anemia, and septicemia. For adults, major causes of death during 1999 were ARI, gastroenteritis, tuberculosis, cardiovascular disease, and malignancies. Maternal mortality is still an important cause of death in women of reproductive age. Very few AIDS deaths have been reported.

The MRC Farafenni field station is currently a base for work on malaria, trachoma, noncommunicable diseases, male and female fertility, and reproductive health. Although not all of the work conducted at the station involves the surveillance villages, very often research projects include at least one of the study villages. Additional data can be readily added to the surveillance data, as all studies use the permanent ID number for individuals.

Farafenni DSS procedures

Introduction to the Farafenni DSS site

Since October 1981 MRC has maintained the Farafenni DSS as a surveillance site for both demographic and health data. At its inception, the primary objective of the project was to monitor the impact of the Gambian PHC program on outcomes of pregnancy and child survival. Surveillance of births and deaths began in April 1982, after the completion of the original census. The 16 larger villages of the area joined the PHC program in early 1983. Another MRC objective was to monitor malaria morbidity and mortality within the area and consider ways to link malaria interventions with the PHC program. Large villages and towns with drug sellers and access to drugs in 1981 were thus excluded from the study area, as antimalarial drugs were available outside the government system.

The site has been used to answer a range of scientific questions, and a search of the literature using the names of the main investigators quickly reveals more than 100 published papers and reports. Here, we refer to just a few key publications to provide an introduction to some of the research output from the site. The initial work on malaria prophylaxis is summarized by Greenwood et al. (1989). The ability of village health workers to provide this prophylaxis was examined by Menon, Snow, et al. (1990). Later work included studies of chloroquine resistance (Allen et al. 1990; Menon, Otoo, et al. 1990). Work in the early 1990s was mainly on issues such as malaria prophylaxis and iron supplementation in pregnancy (Greenwood et al. 1994; Menendez, Todd, Alonso, Francis, et al. 1994; Menendez, Todd, Alonso, Lulat et al. 1994). More work on the effectiveness of impregnated bednets and treatment of malaria was conducted in the Farafenni villages (Müller et al. 1996). Over the last few years, much of the malaria work has focused on reduction of *Plasmodium falciparum* malaria transmission (Targett et al. 2001; von Seidlein et al. 2001). The progress of the PHC program was evaluated using the study villages (Greenwood et al. 1990a, b) and was looked at in greater detail by Hill et al. (1998) and Hill et al. (2000). In 1992 and 1994 studies were conducted on fertility and its proximate, as well as its cultural, determinants (Bledsoe et al. 1994; Bledsoe et al. 1998). In the mid- and late 1990s, a new focus for work in the study villages was adult health. A comparative study of noncommunicable disease among adults in Banjul and the study villages was completed in 1997 (van der Sande et al. 2000; Nyan et al. 2001a, b; van der Sande et al. 2001; Walraven, Nyan et al. 2001). The MRC reproductive-health program included a major field study using interview, clinical, and laboratory methods, covering about half of the resident female population of reproductive age (Walraven, Scherf et al. 2001). Maternal mortality was examined by Greenwood et al. (1987), Graham et al. (1989), Greenwood et al. (1990a), and more recently by Walraven et al. (2000). The program included a demographic study of the fertility and reproduction of men in 1998–99 (Ratcliffe et al. 2000).

Ongoing intervention projects include studies of

- Postpartum hemorrhage;

- Influence of type of menstrual hygiene ("traditional" versus "modern") on abnormal vaginal flora and infections;

- Better postpartum care, with special attention for anemia, family planning, hygiene, and breastfeeding; and

- Fly control and diarrhea and trachoma (Emerson et al. 1999).

Work is also ongoing on human papilloma virus and cervical dysplasia, chlamydia infection and infertility, and fertility dynamics.

Farafenni DSS data collection and processing

The surveillance system was originally set up to follow the population of young children, rather than monitoring the demography of the general population. Since then the surveillance has expanded to include information on all residents of the study area, adults and children. In 1986, one village withdrew, after a misunderstanding about the collection of blood samples for a cross-sectional survey.

In 1998, the surveillance system was converted to the household-registration system (HRS) originally developed for use in Navrongo, Ghana. New field- and data-management procedures were implemented at conversion, as described below. Before the HRS, censuses were conducted biennially, and data were collected on an ongoing basis through village recorders (citizens of the villages), with regular visits from fieldworkers. Since 1998 fieldworkers have visited each compound to collect data on vital events, at least once every 3 months. The most recent census was conducted in 2000.

Field procedures

MAPPING — Maps of the villages were last revised in 1998. New compounds are added to the maps as changes are observed during the census rounds every 3 months. The latitude and longitude of all villages and compounds have been established using hand-held GPS devices. Work is under way to link these coordinates with other maps, including those available from satellite photography.

INITIAL CENSUS — The initial census was begun in October 1981, but it is impossible to identify the population originally enumerated, because until April 1989 the census was updated without archiving.

Censuses are conducted in the study area biennially. During these censuses, fieldworkers visit every compound to verify and update information on all residents. Fieldworkers use a roster of all current residents and previous residents who have migrated. New residents are added after it has been established that they are not temporary visitors. Since the inception of HRS one census has been conducted, in 2000. This census was different from the normal HRS rounds every 3 months in that the HRS team of fieldworkers was expanded, and this enlarged team worked together with the field supervisor in each village.

REGULAR UPDATE ROUNDS — Since the conversion to the HRS three fieldworkers have been responsible for the surveillance, under the direction of a field supervisor. Each fieldworker is responsible for updating a specific set of villages in which they are resident. Fieldwork is organized into a series of 3-month periods, called rounds. Fieldworkers visit each compound at least once in every round. Working from a list of all residents for each compound, the fieldworkers verify and update the recorded information with the compound head or another senior adult. These printed lists are organized by village and are filed in binders that the fieldworkers take with them to the field. These lists are updated and reprinted each year.

Village recorders who were originally responsible for reporting vital events for their villages are still involved in the fieldwork. They continue to provide a useful point of contact for the fieldworkers and help with outreach and sensitization, explaining new studies and passing on research findings to the villagers.

CONTINUOUS SURVEILLANCE — All deaths, births, migration within or beyond the study area, pregnancies, and marriages are recorded during the rounds that are made every 3 months. The files on individuals also include information on their enumerated parents and husband (if married). Pregnancies are followed for outcomes of miscarriage, still- or live birth, and more complete coverage of neonatal deaths. Information on pregnancies is collected from TBAs, MCH clinics, and regular updating rounds. Marriages are recorded for women because of the complexity of recording data on several wives for polygynous men. Men can be linked to their wives easily within the HRS system. VAs are conducted for all deaths. Children's deaths have been followed with VAs since 1998. Deaths of women of reproductive age as far back as 1993 were studied in 1998. All deaths of adults are also followed with a VA. Socioeconomic surveys were conducted in 1996 and 2000. Often a round will include some additional questions to complement the basic surveillance. Recently, this included a set of questions on perceptions of mortality change since the early 1980s.

FIELD SUPERVISION AND QUALITY CONTROL — Weekly meetings are held with the senior staff responsible for the HRS and the field- and data-management team to sort out queries and procedural issues. Errors identified during data entry and checking using the HRS are referred to the fieldworkers for resolution during the succeeding week.

Data management and analysis

At the outset, the data were recorded in paper ledgers organized by compound. Snow and Rowan converted the older ledgers to dBase II computer files, readable on BBC Torch, and then on IBM personal computers running dBase III. The initial numbering system was based on the Matlab, Bangladesh, system, with all compounds numbered sequentially from 1 to more than 900. In 1992, the compounds were remapped and renumbered, replacing the old survey number with a new survey number that included village, compound, and personal identifiers arranged in a hierarchical sequence.

Starting in 1989, the data were saved in a "frozen" census every March 31. For the period before the frozen-census files were archived, it is impossible to calculate the person–years accurately, although data on birth and death events are available from April 1982 onwards. Vital rates for this earlier period have to be taken from published reports. As the census years begin on 1 April each year, nine frozen-census rounds occurred from 1989 to 1997, and these provide the raw data for estimating birth and death rates for this period. These flat files can be linked, but before conversion to HRS, this was cumbersome and time-consuming, and the calculation of person–years of exposure remained problematic because of the lack of detail on the dates of migration. The routine surveillance was checked every 2 years by conducting a full reenumeration of the entire study site, and this enumeration often led to corrections in the older data and thus to some minor changes in the resulting annual rates.

In 1998, full conversion to HRS was completed. The detailed conversion tasks required close examination of the quality and consistency of the archived data. Dates of death, for example, were compared with the status variable "dead" to reveal inconsistencies. The discrete census files in dBase were cleaned and linked chronologically before the conversion to HRS. The decision was made to merge the frozen-census fields backwards from the 1997 frozen census, on the assumption that the most recent data were the most accurate (MacLeod 1998). After being merged, the data were rechecked for missing or impossible codes, and corrections were made, as necessary. The number of changes was not large, but they took many hours to check, both in the office and in the field. The final merged files contained information on 30 460 individuals, recorded since 1981. Some complex checks were applied using SAS software to deal with residents missing in one census and recorded in a subsequent enumeration or vice versa. The late recording of some vital events, missed by fieldworkers but picked up during a reenumeration, still poses a challenge for analysts eager to calculate rates based on true person–years of exposure.

After careful merging and checking of the archived data — the "legacy" data in HRS parlance — the original dBase fields were converted to the data sets used in HRS. The HRS version in use in Farafenni was modified, and this included the conversion of the older variable names to new names used in HRS. Several new variables were not on the original dBase fields and had to be collected from the field (husband's ID, pregnancy outcome) or inferred from other variables (household status, migration types).

All these tasks were accomplished in 1998 and since then, both the office and field procedures are driven by the demands of HRS. Within FoxPro, files can be easily constructed to link individuals to their relatives or other members of social groups, such as a compound. The moves of individuals in and out of the study area several times in a single year can now be properly recorded, whereas the previous system was only able to record one migration event in a census year. The HRS includes extensive data validation and consistency checks even at the data-entry stage.

Individuals are considered eligible for enumeration if they expect to be resident in the study area for at least 6 months and are present during the rainy season. A seven-digit permanent ID number uniquely identifies all individuals, including information on their village and compound of enumeration, as well as a unique personal identifier. Information on individuals includes name, sex, ethnicity, date of birth, parents' ID (if parents were enumerated), village, compound, and household of residence, residency status, and date of status change. The IDs of husbands are linked to those of their wives. Individual village (*alkalo*), compound, and household heads are also designated. Pregnancies and pregnancy outcomes are recorded.

All updates are recorded directly on the lists of individuals that the fieldworkers take to the field. The field supervisor checks these lists. The data-entry clerk responsible for the HRS checks every entry and is responsible for all queries. All data are now entered directly into the HRS. Internal validity checks are performed at the data-entry stage. Back-up copies are made frequently.

Queries are sent back weekly to the field through the field supervisor. During reenumeration, major discrepancies are reviewed, and changes are made if appropriate. Any proposed changes to individual records not associated with a demographic event (such as name or birth-date changes or deletion of suspected duplicated records of individuals) are submitted by fieldworkers as a "petition for change," and these are considered using information from the field and the history recorded in the HRS.

Data analysis is performed by senior scientists attached to the relevant unit. The programs in the HRS are useful for basic rates and ratios, but additional analysis with SAS or SPSS software is needed for more detailed work. The FoxPro system greatly facilitates the construction of flat files for these analyses. Results are shared at village meetings, meetings with local health workers, and seminars with policymakers. Analyses are submitted for publication in peer-reviewed journals, and findings are presented at international conferences and meetings.

Farafenni DSS basic outputs

Demographic indicators

The mid-year population for 1999 was 16 202. Of this population, 17.4% were <5 years old; 29.1%, 5–14 years old; 49.2%, 15–64; and 4.3%, ≥65 years old (Figure 21.2). The age-dependency ratio was 1.17, with 52% of the population <15 or ≥65 years old. The sex ratio was 0.90. The total fertility rate for 1993–98 for women was estimated at 6.8 in a 1998 cross-sectional survey (Ratcliffe et al. 2000). For the period 1995–99, the mortality rate for infants was 74.3/1000, and that for children 1–4 years old was 40.2/1000 (Table 21.1). The maternal mortality ratio for the years 1993–98 was 424 per 100 000 live births (Walraven et al. 2000). In 1999, household heads were identified, but information on relationships to household heads and residence in households was not available.

Trends in infant, child, and maternal mortality

A recent analysis has considered the trends in infant and child mortality over a 15-year period, using data from the demographic surveillance history. Comparisons were made between PHC and non-PHC villages. This analysis indicated a marked improvement in infant and under-five mortality in both sets of villages. Infant mortality dropped from 134/1000 in 1982–83 to 69/1000 in 1992–94 in the PHC villages and from 155/1000 to 91/1000 in the non-PHC villages over the same period. The mortality rates for children 1–4 years old dropped from 42/1000 in 1982–83 to 28/1000 in 1992–94 in the PHC villages and from 45/1000 to 38/1000 in the non-PHC villages over the same period. Since 1994, when support for the PHC services was reduced, infant mortality in the PHC villages has risen to 89/1000, and mortality of children 1–4 years old has converged to 34/1000 in both sets of villages. The trend toward lower mortality for infants and children in the area is clear. The impact of PHC is also notable, with impacts on the mortality of children 1–4 years old in the PHC villages strongest during the 1980s. This seemed to flag after support for PHC was reduced in 1994 (data for 1982–83 are from Greenwood et al. [1990b]; other data are from Hill et al. [2000]).

Figure 21.2. Population pyramid of person–years observed at the Farafenni DSS site, The Gambia, 1995–99.

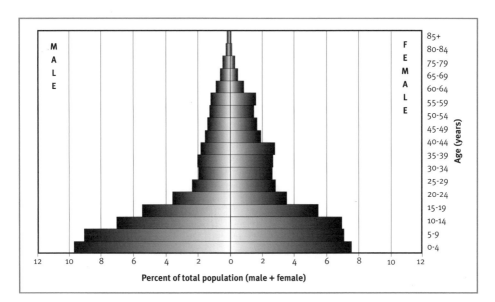

Table 21.1. Age- and sex-specific mortality at the Farafenni DSS site, The Gambia, 1995-99.

Age (years)	Death s ($_nD_x$)		Person–years observed ($_nPY_x$)	
	Male	Female	Male	Female
<1	113	104	1585	1497
1–4	185	139	6205	4729
5–9	40	40	7284	5852
10–14	25	14	5645	5730
15–19	10	15	4348	4525
20–24	11	13	2838	2949
25–29	3	10	1848	2378
30–34	9	14	1517	2205
35–39	15	12	1585	2239
40–44	19	11	1420	2327
45–49	14	12	1204	1616
50–54	26	13	1071	1425
55–59	19	20	954	1269
60–64	35	35	913	1372
65–69	36	27	635	750
70–74	28	24	424	444
75–79	27	23	296	298
80–84	20	14	147	135
≥85	15	11	107	107
Births	2907			
CDR	14.67			
CBR	35.51			
CRNI	20.84			

Note: CBR, crude birth rate (actual number of births per 1000 population); CDR, crude death rate (actual number of deaths per 1000 population); CRNI, crude rate of natural increase (CBR minus CDR per 100; does not take into account migration); $_nD_x$, observed deaths between ages x and $x+n$; $_nPY_x$, observed person–years between ages x and $x+n$.

In the 1980s, three studies used the surveillance system to estimate the level of maternal mortality in the region. In the first study, between April 1982 and March 1983, all pregnancies in the area were followed prospectively, and the maternal mortality ratio was estimated at 2362 per 100 000 live births (with wide confidence intervals, as a result of small sample size) (Greenwood et al. 1987). In the second study, a reproductive-age mortality survey of all deaths in women between April 1984 and March 1987 estimated a maternal mortality ratio of 1091 per 100 000 live births (Greenwood et al. 1990a). The third study, conducted in the fall of 1987, was a field trial of the sisterhood method in six of the villages in the Farafenni surveillance area, and it documented a maternal mortality ratio of 1005 per 100 000 live births for the mid-1970s (Graham et al. 1989). During the 1993–98 period, 74 female deaths were recorded among women 15–49 years old, and 18 were classified as maternal deaths (25.7%). In the same period, 4245 live births occurred, corresponding to a maternal mortality ratio of 424 per 100 000 live births, less than half the levels reported from studies in the 1980s. The level of maternal mortality has decreased in both PHC villages (with trained TBAs) and non-PHC villages (with no trained TBAs), with the two sets of villages showing no significant difference. Although impossible to ascertain with certainty, the decrease is probably related to a combination of increased availability of essential obstetric care, improved transport, and increased communication (Walraven et al. 2000).

Men's and women's fertility rates and experiences with reproduction

The first detailed survey on fertility in 1992 revealed that the total fertility rate for women 15–54 years old was 7.5 births for the period 1987–92. Then, only 9% of women used any form of contraception, and only 5% used a modern method (pill, condom, or injectable) (Bledsoe et al. 1994; Bledsoe et al. 1998). The fertility rates from the 1998 sample survey of 1621 women indicated slightly lower fertility without a major change in contraceptive use (with 8.4% of sexually active women using modern methods in 1998).

A study of male fertility and the strategies available for men to achieve reproduction was undertaken in 1998 in the Farafenni DSA: 1315 men ≥18 years old and 1621 women 15–54 years old from 21 of the study villages were interviewed to construct marriage and pregnancy histories; 110 men were interviewed about the circumstances around their marriages and divorce; and life-history, qualitative interviews were conducted with 15 men. Polygyny is widespread throughout the study area, with 40% of the married men and 54% of the married women living in polygynous unions. The reproductive experiences of men and women are vastly different. In 1993–98, before the survey, men achieved a total fertility rate of 12.0, whereas women's total fertility rate was 6.8. Married men's fertility desires for themselves and for their wives were also very different: for themselves, they desired a total of 15.2 children, but for each of their wives, they desired only 7.3. In qualitative interviews, many men explained that they considered fertility outside of their direct control, but they mentioned specific actions they might take to increase chances of achieving higher fertility. These were prayer, resolution of health problems, and marriage. Marriage is an important reproductive strategy for men in that it increases the chances of having many children and brings productive, adult women into their families. This study illustrates the importance of studying gender with fertility. Men's experiences are unique, but the intentions and interests of men cannot be included in studies of fertility that focus only on female outcomes (Ratcliffe et al. 2000).

Acknowledgments

The Farafenni DSS site is supported by MRC, but many other funders have contributed to its success. For the demography, in particular, we have to thank the Rockefeller Foundation, the Andrew Mellon Foundation, and the then UK Overseas Development Administration (now the Department for International Development) through a grant to the London School of Hygiene and Tropical Medicine. We thank the many individuals who over many years have contributed to the establishment and development of the surveillance system at Farafenni, especially the previous heads of station, who supported the system when financial constraints and political changes made the work more difficult. The heads of station include Andrew K. Bradley (1981–84), Robert Snow (1985–87), Aron Menon (1986–88), Pedro Alonso (1988–90), Steven Allen (1990), Steve Lindsay (1991–92), Umberto D'Alessandro (1992–94), and Olaf Müller (1994–95). We would like to thank many other people who over many years contributed to the establishment and development of the surveillance system at Farafenni, especially Bill MacLeod and Bruce Macleod. The continued interest of the former director of MRC (Brian Greenwood) and that of the current director (Keith McAdam) have been important in the maintenance of the system. We acknowledge with particular gratitude the contributions of the current Farafenni DSS field staff: Louie Loppy, Ousman Bah, Malick Njie, and Tumani Trawally.

Chapter 22

Navrongo DSS, Ghana

Philomena Nyarko,[1] Peter Wontuo,[1] Alex Nazzar,[1] Jim Phillips,[2] Pierre Ngom,[3] and Fred Binka[1]

Site description

Physical geography of the Navrongo DSA

The Navrongo DSS site is in the Kassena-Nankana District of the Upper East region of Ghana (Figure 22.1). The district lies between latitudes 10°30′ and 11°00′N and longitudes 1°00′ and 1°30′W and covers an area of 1675 km² along the Ghana–Burkina Faso border. It measures roughly 55 km × 50 km and has an altitude of 200–400 m above sea level. The land is fairly flat, and passing through it from Burkina Faso is the White Volta River, which feeds Lake Volta (the world's largest artificial lake) in the Volta region, south of Ghana.

Figure 22.1. Location of the Navrongo DSS site, Ghana (monitored population, 141 000).

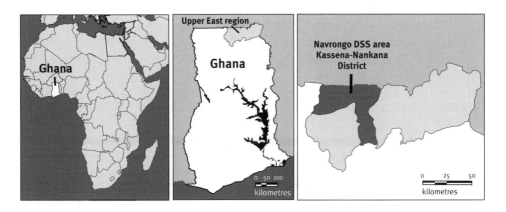

[1] Navrongo Health Research Centre, Navrongo, Ghana.

[2] Policy Research Division, Population Council, New York, United States.

[3] African Population and Health Research Centre, Nairobi, Kenya.

Located in the Guinea savannah belt, the district is typically Sahelian (hot and dry), with the vegetation consisting mostly of semi-arid grassland interspersed with short trees. The region has two main seasons, wet and dry. The wet season extends from April to October, with the heaviest rainfall mainly occurring between June and October. The mean annual rainfall is 1365 mm, but the highest level is recorded in August. Similarly, the dry season is subdivided into the *harmattan* (November–mid-February) and the dry hot season (mid-February–April). Monthly temperatures range from 20° to 40°C, with the mean minimum and maximum temperatures estimated at 22.8° and 34.4°C, respectively, for 1999.

Population characteristics of the Navrongo DSA

The population of Kassena-Nankana on 1 July 1999 was 140 881, which is slightly less than 1% of Ghana's population and about 15% of the total population of the Upper East region. The population density is 84 individuals/km². The district is largely rural, with only 9.5% living in urban quarters. The population comprises two distinct ethno-linguistic groups: the Kassena (49%) and the Nankani (46%). The Builsa and migrants belonging to other ethnic groups constitute the remainder (5%). The main languages spoken are Kassim and Nankam, with Buili spoken by most of the minority tribe. Despite the linguistic distinction, the population is in many respects a homogeneous group, with a common culture. The district has 10 traditional paramount chiefdoms and has traditional forms of village organization, leadership, and governance. At both the village level and the family level, communities have a strong traditional social structure, which influences economic and social behaviour. Male dominance is strong, constraining the autonomy of women and limiting their health decisions. For example, curative and preventive health care may not be sought without the permission of the husband or, in his absence, the head of the compound (Binka et al. 1994).

The main religious faith is animism, but Christianity is gradually becoming more prominent, especially among women (Debpuur et al. 2000). Currently, about 33% of the people are Christian, 5% are Muslim, and the rest profess the indigenous religion. However, the dominant animist faith guides daily life, economic decisions, health beliefs, and practices. This reliance on indigenous medicine hampers the use of health services.

Lack of a communication system, a road network, and electricity in the district also impacts adversely on the health of the population. Subsistence agriculture is the mainstay of the district's economy, complemented to some extent by retail trading. About 90% of the people are farmers. The major agricultural products are groundnuts, millet, guinea corn, rice, sorghum, sweet potatoes, beans, and tomatoes. Rearing of cattle, goats, sheep, pigs, and fowl, including guinea fowl, also forms part of the agricultural activities. Unfortunately, the rainfall pattern limits food cultivation to a single growing season; and even though the Tono irrigation dam and a few dugout wells supply water for dry-season farming, the major crop during this time is tomato. Weather conditions in the district can be very severe, with occasional floods or droughts and poor harvests as a result. This situation has given rise to a net annual out-migration for some time now. Nutritional problems are therefore common, aggravating the mortality impacts of infectious-disease morbidity, and poverty and economic isolation complicate efforts to improve health conditions in the district (Binka et al. 1999).

The district has 77 primary schools, 35 junior secondary schools, 5 senior secondary schools, 1 training college, and 2 vocational institutions. It also accommodates the Faculty for Integrated Development Studies of the University for Development Studies, which focuses on integrated science. Also, the Catholic mission manages an orphanage.

About 89% of the houses in the district are mud huts with thatched roofs. The rest, which are built with cement blocks, are mostly found in the urban area. Almost two-thirds (65%) of the roofs are constructed with straw. Zinc sheets are used for the remaining 35%. The main sources of water in Kassena-Nankana are streams, wells, and boreholes. In a few urban houses, however, pipelines have been installed to provide treated water. Similarly, only 7% of the compounds have access to properly constructed toilet facilities, suggesting that as many as 93% of households use the bushes in their immediate surroundings. For those compounds with toilet facilities, two-thirds use either Kumasi ventilated improved pit, pan, or pit latrines, and the rest use water closets.

The district has a hospital, four health centres, and four clinics in selected communities. These static health-delivery points are complemented by community-based service delivery in all but the eastern part of the district, which serves as an experimental control cell. As part of the Ghana Ministry of Health policy, free health services are available for all children <5 years old and to all people ≥70 years old. In 1999, the district's immunization coverage for children 12–23 months old was 80%; for BCG (bacillus Calmette-Guérin), 72%; for Polio3, 70%; for DPT3; and for measles, 63%. The major causes of morbidity in the district are malaria, gastroenteritis, and acute respiratory infections. The district also has a high prevalence of cerebrospinal meningitis, with the peak season being March to April. Although improved delivery of family-planning services is one of the objectives of the Navrongo community-health and family-planning (CHFP) project, only 10% of married women in the district use the service.

Navrongo DSS procedures

Introduction to the Navrongo DSS site

The Navrongo DSS uses a longitudinal household-registration system (HRS), set up in July 1993 by the Navrongo Health Research Centre (NHRC) to support research on the determinants of morbidity, mortality, and fertility in an area typical of Ghana's rural savannah zone. The Navrongo DSS routinely updates vital events (births, deaths, migration, marriages, and pregnancies) in all of about 14 200 compounds within the study area. Where a death has occurred, the compound is revisited to obtain information on the circumstances leading to the death. These verbal postmortems are conducted using different schedules for children and adults. In addition to the vital events, educational attainment and vaccination coverage within the population are annually monitored.

The DSS started with a baseline census of the rural district in 1993, followed by compound visits at 90-day cycles to monitor demographic events. The baseline survey included a socioeconomic module, which lists compound possessions and the materials used in constructing the building. In the last quarter of 1995, DSS activities were extended to include Navrongo, the only urban area in the district. To qualify as a member of a compound, a person should have been resident in the compound for at least 3 months, except for a newborn baby whose mother is already a compound member. The initial DSS covered about 125 000 people, but with the addition of the urban area the population has increased to almost 141 000. Detailed information on fertility and child health is obtained through the annual panel survey of a sample of DSS compounds. The HRS is the computing software used for processing and analyzing the Navrongo DSS database. The initial DOS software (HRS1) has been upgraded to a Windows version (HRS2). The HRS system allows for data entry, editing, validation, and calculation of age- and sex-specific demographic rates and life tables.

The field and data-processing operations of the Navrongo DSS are managed by a team comprising a demographer, two research assistants, two principal field supervisors, a data manager, and a data assistant. The team coordinates the activities of the 26 fieldworkers and 12 field supervisors, who are responsible for field data collection, as well as the 2 filing clerks and 3 data-entry clerks who receive and process the field instruments. The fieldworkers are expected to visit and interview all compounds within their work area. The 12 field supervisors, in contrast, are responsible for conducting verbal autopsies (VAs), carrying out quality checks, resolving queries, and pairing migrants. Training, planning, supervision, and coordination of field activities are undertaken by the two principal supervisors, the two research assistants, and the demographer.

The field data collection and processing are mainly supported by funds from the Rockefeller Foundation, with technical assistance from the Population Council. Data are used to compile reports for the Ghana Ministry of Health, which is the major consumer of the Navrongo DSS data. Lessons learned from the Navrongo CHFP project through the DSS and the panel surveys have, for example, activated a process of extending the new health-delivery approach implemented in this district to the country as a whole. Other institutions that have also benefited from the Navrongo DSS database are the universities and other educational and research institutions.

Navrongo DSS data collection and processing

The Navrongo DSS evolved from an earlier study of Kassena-Nankana in 1989 by the Department of Community Health of the Kwame Nkrumah University of Science and Technology and the London School of Hygiene and Tropical Medicine, with support from the Ghana Ministry of Health and the UK Overseas Development Administration (now the Department for International Development). This study, popularly called the Ghana vitamin-A supplementation trial (VAST), included continuous demographic and health surveys of resident members of the study compounds, with the aim of helping to evaluate the effect of vitamin-A supplementation to children <5 years old. When VAST came to an end in 1992, NHRC was established to shed more light on the health problems in northern Ghana and help find practical solutions to them. The NHRC thus used and built on existing VAST resources. In 1993, the DSS was reorganized, with respect to its coverage and content, and formally set up as the Navrongo DSS to serve as a basis for assessing the mortality effects of insecticide-treated bednets. The bednet study was concurrent with the factorial experiment on the fertility and mortality impacts of NHRC's CHFP project, which has been in operation to date.

Field procedures

INITIAL CENSUS — The baseline census provided basic demographic data on all residents as of 1 July 1993. Other information gathered includes that on family relationships, compound possessions, and characteristics of the residential structure. For DSS purposes, Kassena-Nankana is divided into five zones. These are further subdivided into 21 subzones and 244 clusters. On average, 9 contiguous clusters are assigned to each of the 26 fieldworkers to enhance fieldwork and reduce costs. To track the population, each fieldworker is expected to visit, and update demographic information on, 15 compounds every day. The main data-collection instruments used for the routine recording and updating of vital events are compound-registration books (CRBs) and event forms. CRBs are field registers containing basic demographic information on all compounds in a cluster. Where a cluster has more than 99 compounds, an additional CRB is used. An event form is also filled out for each recorded event.

REGULAR UPDATE ROUNDS — All vital demographic events occurring within the district are updated through regular visits to each compound every 90 days. During these compound visits, new events are registered. Pregnancies recorded earlier are also monitored during these quarterly visits, until the pregnancies are terminated. This is to help improve on birth and death reporting, in particular by capturing neonatal deaths. For every vital event that is recorded, detailed information is collected using the appropriate event-registration form. VAs on deaths of any of those registered with the Navrongo DSS are also conducted to obtain information on the circumstances leading to the death. Trained field supervisors visit each of the compounds where a death has been reported and administer the appropriate VA questionnaire to the closest relative of the deceased. Three medical doctors independently code these questionnaires to determine the probable cause of death. Where at least two of the doctors agree on one diagnosis, it is accepted as the cause of death. When they disagree, the case is coded as "undetermined" and is set aside for further discussion.

Apart from the event updates, the first quarter of each year is devoted to updating information on the educational attainment of those aged 6 years or more and the last quarter of the year is used to collect data on the vaccination status of children younger than 2 years.

CONTINUOUS SURVEILLANCE — Vital demographic events, including in- and out-migrations, marriages, pregnancies, births, and deaths, are continuously monitored through quarterly updates. In addition to the routine collection of data by fieldworkers, the Navrongo DSS has recruited a number of voluntary community key informants (CKIs) to record all pregnancies, births, and child deaths that occur in their localities during the intervals between interviewer visits to compounds. Currently, 170 CKIs work within the district. Two field supervisors are assigned to visit the CKIs in their homes every 2 weeks to collect the information they have gathered over the period. These data supplement what the Navrongo DSS fieldworkers collect during their regular visits to the compounds every 90 days.

FIELD SUPERVISION AND QUALITY CONTROL — For each round of data collection, quality assurance is achieved through reinterviewing a 3% random sample of compounds, conducted by a quality control supervisor. Other field checks include the reinterviewing of some of the compounds already covered by the fieldworker, random reviews of CRBs and event forms for inconsistencies and omissions, and observation of field interviews. Procedures employed at the office level include the assessment of the work progress of field staff at weekly meetings and a week's retraining of interviewers at the end of each round of data collection.

The Navrongo DSS also has a mechanism for pairing internal migrants, to avoid double counting and to minimize loss to follow up on. This process of pairing migrants is aided by issuing identity cards to all compound members. The identity cards are meant to improve the reporting of event dates and facilitate the linking of migrants to their previous records. To avoid familiarity with the respondents and forestall any attempts to manipulate data, the field staff do not work in the same clusters for more than two consecutive rounds. Improvement in event capture is also achieved through the voluntary activities of CKIs, who for a token fee record births, deaths, and pregnancies in their communities during the interval between interviewer visits.

Data management

Every fortnight, each fieldworker submits all completed CRBs and event forms to the filing clerks. These records are then carefully documented and sent to the data-entry clerks, who upddate the database, using the HRS data-entry system.

A data manager, a data assistant, and three data-entry clerks carry out the data-processing operations of the Navrongo DSS. Each of these personnel has a different level of access to operate the database. A successful entry into the system allows for data to be added, edited, or deleted. Other forms of data manipulation, such as validation and report generation, can also be carried out, depending on the level of access. Until July 2000, the DOS-based HRS1 software was used to process and analyze the Navrongo DSS data. Currently, data-processing is done using HRS2, an upgrade of HRS1. This software operates in Windows (using Visual FoxPro) and has a number of improved features, including its flexibility in specifying constraints on the legal values for a data-entry field, database triggers to help make the appropriate changes in other related tables to maintain consistency, and use of one ID specification for referencing all data-entry forms, thus making data management easier (Ngom et al. 1999).

The functional components of the HRS2 software comprise data entry, validation, reports and output, visit register, and utilities. The data-entry option permits the entry, deleting, and editing of both baseline compound information and longitudinal data, and the validation procedure allows for logical-consistency checks on subsets of compounds and their members. The reports-and-output option is used to generate key demographic rates, population distribution, and life tables. The visit-register procedure is used to print the CRBs, which are used to record information during field visits. Finally, the utilities function is used by the data manager to add new user IDs, set interview-round information, and generate reconciliation reports to help follow up on unreported pregnancy outcomes and unmatched internal migrants, among others.

When CRBs and event forms are returned to the computer centre at the weekly zonal meetings for fieldworkers, it takes 1 or 2 days to have them sorted and distributed to the data-entry clerks. Data entry and validation take about 1 week.

The HRS system has built-in validation programs, which help to maintain consistency in the database. Computer operations are organized to correspond to the interviewing cycle so that information that fails the HRS logical checks is printed with the relevant error message for field reconciliation. On the other hand, records that pass the logical tests are archived into the database. Thus, each round generates fully edited and cleaned data before a new cycle begins. The updated information is used

Figure 22.2. Population pyramid for person–years observed at the Navrongo DSS site, Ghana, 1995–99.

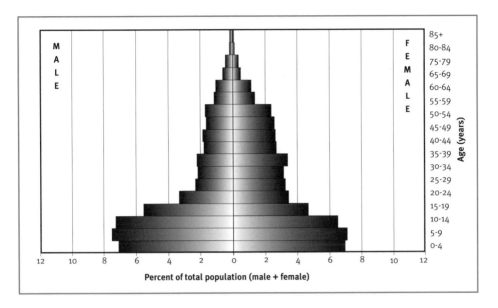

to generate new CRBs for the next round's compound visits, and the old ones are archived by the filing clerks for future reference.

Analysis of the data is achieved using FoxPro and STATA software. Most of the output from the Navrongo DSS is compiled as reports and circulated to the Ghana Ministry of Health, the sponsors, and other interested bodies. Regular dissemination seminars are also organized for visitors to NHRC and institutions making specific requests. Occasionally, *durbars* (traditional gatherings organized by community leaders to build consensus on community issues) are convened to share the findings with the chiefs and subjects of the various paramouncies within the district.

Navrongo DSS basic outputs

Demographic indicators

In 1999, Kassena-Nankana registered a population of 140 881. The population is quite young, with about 41% <15 years old (Figure 22.2). The broad age distribution is as follows: 0–4 years old, 13.1%; 5–14 years old, 28.0%; 15–64 years old, 54.2%; and ≥65 years old, 4.7%. These figures imply an age-dependency ratio of 84%. Females constitute 53% of the population, giving a sex ratio of 89 males per 100 females. Educational attainment in the district is quite low. In general, about two-thirds (65.5%) of the population ≥15 years old have received no formal education, and only 8.2% have attained senior secondary or higher levels of schooling. The distribution by sex indicates that more females (74.6%) tend to be uneducated than males (54.4%). Similarly, current school attendance among those 6–25 years old is lower for females (48%) than males (54%). Overall, about 55% of all the population ≥6 years old has never been to school.

Table 22.1. Age- and sex-specific mortality at the Navrongo DSS site, Ghana, 1995–99.

Age (years)	Deaths $(_nD_x)$ Male	Female	Person–years observed $(_nPY_x)$ Male	Female	Observed mortality rate $(_nM_x)$ Male	Female
<1	1 160	1 130	10 107	10 241	114.77	110.34
1–4	858	738	38 795	38 364	22.12	19.24
5–9	243	197	51 644	49 662	4.71	3.97
10–14	164	122	50 035	45 385	3.28	2.69
15–19	117	76	37 926	32 598	3.08	2.33
20–24	87	97	22 522	23 960	3.86	4.05
25–29	99	132	15 415	22 666	6.42	5.82
30–34	145	167	14 669	21 913	9.88	7.62
35–39	172	137	15 006	23 658	11.46	5.79
40–44	227	150	12 138	18 833	18.70	7.96
45–49	255	195	12 502	18 382	20.40	10.61
50–54	286	313	11 099	18 091	25.77	17.30
55–59	385	443	11 409	16 672	33.75	26.57
60–64	348	339	7 522	9 513	46.26	35.64
65–69	404	479	6 812	8 024	59.31	59.70
70–74	253	320	3 869	3 522	65.39	90.86
75–79	293	279	2 728	2 558	107.40	109.07
80–84	115	101	1 076	743	106.88	135.94
≥85	149	103	943	677	158.01	152.14
Births	20 462					
CDR	16.31					
CBR	29.58					
CRNI	13.28					

Note: CBR, crude birth rate (actual number of births per 1000 population); CDR, crude death rate (actual number of deaths per 1000 population); CRNI, crude rate of natural increase (CBR minus CDR per 100; does not take into account migration); $_nD_x$, observed deaths between ages x and $x+n$; $_nM_x$, ratio of deaths to person–years lived; $_nPY_x$, observed person–years between ages x and $x+n$.

In the Navrongo DSS, the compound is the unit of observation, and the compound has an average of 10 members. A compound is defined as a traditional multi-roomed house, which is usually walled together and stands alone from other housing structures. It houses one family unit, which could include several generations, and is recognized by the name of its head. Males dominate the headships of these compounds, with females heading only 10.2%. In 1999, the population recorded a crude death rate of 14.1 per 1000 and a crude birth rate of 28.0 per 1000 person–years, suggesting a crude rate of natural increase of 13.9%. The total fertility rate for the same year was 4.1 for each woman.

Mortality in Kassena-Nankana is very high. The infant and under-five mortality rates for 1999 are estimated at 90 per 1000 live births and 150 per 1000 children <5 years old, respectively. Life expectancy at birth is 52.6 years. Generally, males in the district have a shorter life span (49.9 years) than females (54.8 years). For the period 1995–99, the crude death rate was 17.7 per 1000 person–years for males and 15.1 per 1000 person–years for females (Table 22.1). The age pattern of mortality for each sex is, as expected, curvilinear, with children and adults being the most vulnerable. At all ages, males generally have higher mortality rates than females, but the differentials are much larger for those ≥35 years old.

A trend assessment indicates that between 1994–96 and 1997–99, the age-standardized death rate declined from 20.8 per 1000 to 19.6 per 1000 for males and from 19.7 per 1000 to 16.5 per 1000 for females. Infant mortality rate for the period of 1997–99 is estimated at 106.1 per 1000 live births for males and 99.7 per 1000 live births for females, a decline from a level of 124.5 per 1000 live births for male infants and 125.7 per 1000 live births for female infants within the period 1994–96. Although these figures are far above those recorded at the national level, the registered improvements in survival may have resulted from the participatory approach to health-service delivery launched within the district by NHRC, as well as the various health interventions put in place as part of the research activities of NHRC. Obviously, females recorded the highest decline in mortality of the period under consideration.

Similarly, the fertility rate has declined from 4.7 births per woman to 4.2 births per woman between 1994–96 and 1997–99 (Table 22.2).

Migration figures for the district show that the population is highly mobile. For the period 1997–99, the district had a net out-migration of 12.0 per 1000 person–years. Migration is concentrated among young adults 15–29 years old (Tables 22.3 and 22.4).

Table 22.2. Age-specific fertility rates, Kassena-Nankana District, Ghana, 1994–99.

Age (years)	Fertility rates	
	1994–96	1997–99
15–19	80.2	68.3
20–24	210.4	176.8
25–29	212.9	191.5
30–34	194.3	174.3
35–39	142.5	125.9
40–44	76.1	68.1
45–49	27.6	26.5
TFR (15–49)	4.7	4.2

Note: TFR, total fertility rate.

Table 22.3. Age-specific in-migration rates, Kassena-Nankana District, Ghana, 1994–99.

Age (years)	In-migration rates	
	1994–96	1997–99
0–4	80.7	89.9
5–9	66.8	75.3
10–14	67.9	75.8
15–19	128.9	139.9
20–24	176.9	187.1
25–29	146.3	156.9
30–34	86.2	110.3
35–39	60.3	70.3
40–44	43.7	55.9
45–49	31.4	40.4
50–54	25.3	26.8
55–59	18.5	20.2
60–64	17.3	21.3
≥65	25.6	34.0

Table 22.4. Age-specific out-migration rates, Kassena-
Nankana District, Ghana, 1994–99.

Age (years)	Out-migration rates	
	1994–96	1997–99
0–4	75.2	94.3
5–9	74.5	76.0
10–14	96.5	91.5
15–19	187.4	199.5
20–24	217.9	218.9
25–29	158.2	171.9
30–34	97.6	109.8
35–39	61.9	71.9
40–44	46.5	51.9
45–49	30.7	37.1
50–54	19.8	29.3
55–59	16.9	21.9
60–64	15.8	22.2
≥65	20.9	27.5

Acknowledgments

NHRC acknowledges, with sincere gratitude, the financial support of the Rockefeller Foundation for the overall running of the Navrongo DSS. The DSS was developed in collaboration with Bruce MacLeod of the University of Southern Maine. Development work was funded by the Mellon Foundation, the Population Council, the Thrasher Foundation, and the Finnish International Development Assistance. Finally, we are most grateful to our mother institution, the Ministry of Health, and the people of the Kassena-Nankana District for their immense assistance and cooperation in the implementation of the DSS.

Chapter 23

Bandim DSS, Guinea-Bissau

Morten Sodemann, Henrik Jensen, Amabelia Rodrigues, Tomé Cá, and Peter Aaby[1]

Site description

Physical geography of the Bandim DSA

The Bandim DSS is located in a suburban area of the capital Bissau in Guinea-Bissau, West Africa, a former Portuguese colony, which was liberated in 1974, after a violent war (Figure 23.1). The study area comprises five suburbs of the capital and a mobile rural unit. These areas are situated at latitude 12.00°N and longitude 15.00°W. Total population of the country is about 1.3 million. The climate is subtropical. Mangrove vegetation covers the banks along the many rivers. The southern and northern parts are mainly forest, and the rest of the country is wooded savannah, much of which is under cultivation with rice fields and crops like peanuts, maize, and manioc. The rainy season, with its high humidity, lasts from June to October. Temperatures range from 20° to 36°C.

Figure 23.1. Location of the Bandim DSS site, Guinea-Bissau (monitored population, 100 000).

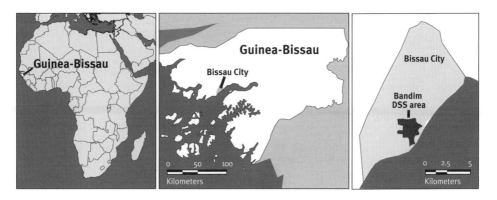

[1] Bandim Project, Guinea-Bissau Ministry of Health, Guinea-Bissau.

Population characteristics of the Bandim DSA

The DSS has a population of more than 100 000, which is partly suburban and partly rural. Public water supply is available for some 35% of the population in the capital only, and drinking water is not boiled. The area has no public sewerage system, and all latrines are pit latrines. Major economic activities include small-scale agriculture and petty trading, with a large proportion of the population engaged only seasonally in selling cashew nuts, cashew wine, palm oil, fruits, vegetables, or rice. Smaller domestic animals sleep inside the house. Houses are made of mud bricks, and roofs are either thatched or covered with corrugated iron. The public sector has 36 000 employees, and the majority of these are soldiers. Schools are primarily public, but in recent years a growing number of small private schools have appeared. In 1994, 25.6% of males and 45.1% of females >10 years old had no school education. The literacy rate is 13.0% in rural areas and 35.2% in urban areas. In the urban areas, the Pepel is the largest ethnic group (38%), followed by the Manjaco (15%) and various Muslim ethnic groups, mainly Fula and Mandinga (12.4%). In rural areas, Fula (25.8%) is the largest single ethnic group, followed by Pepel (22.7%), Mandinga (19.4%), and Balanta (18.4%). In urban areas, most people speak Criolo. An increasing number of private clinics, hospital-like institutions, and pharmacies have distorted the health structure over the past decade. The study area has two health centres; one, built by the project, has a six-bed maternity ward and a laboratory. The capital has only one pediatric ward, which facilitates follow-up of children from the study area during and after hospitalization. Of the children who died in Bandim in 1993, 49% were hospitalized, and 90% were seen by a physician or nurse before dying. Thirty-two percent of children with diarrhea were brought to a health facility, according to a 1993 survey. In 1995, measles-vaccination coverage in the urban area was 83.8% among children <2 years old. Acute and persistent diarrhea accounts for the majority of childhood morbidity and mortality. HIV-2 infection is still more prevalent than HIV-1. Including double infections, the HIV-1 prevalence was about 5% in 1999. Cholera epidemics were observed for the first time in 1987, and again in 1994 and 1997.

Bandim DSS procedures

Introduction to the Bandim DSS site

After independence in 1974 an extremely high under-five mortality rate (around 500/1000 person–years observed) prompted the Ministry of Health to approach the Swedish Agency for Research Cooperation with Developing Countries to organize a study to define nutritional priorities in preventive health care. The nutrition and child-health study was initiated in 1978, and a census was carried out, with a subsequent anthropometric survey and organization of antenatal care for all women found pregnant during the census. All new pregnancies were registered, together with births, deaths, and migrations. This became the basis for the ongoing registration of the population in the Bandim suburb. Distinct ecological zones were selected, and regular rural population surveys, covering five regions, were initiated in the interior. A number of other suburban communities have been added over the years (Bandim 2 and Belem in 1984, Mindará in 1994, and Cuntum in 1999), and in 1990 a follow-up cluster survey of rural women of fertile age was initiated in five rural areas. In 1993, the

Bandim project took over the administration of a community study in the Caio sector, Cacheu region, which had previously been administered from the Medical Research Council (MRC) of the United Kingdom laboratories in The Gambia. Besides close relations with the MRC in The Gambia, the Bandim project has collaborated with the Institut de recherche pour le développement (IRD, institute for development research; formerly ORMSTOM) in Senegal since 1983.

An armed conflict between rebel soldiers and the government started on 7 June 1998 with involvement of troops from Senegal and Guinea-Conakry. Several outbreaks of fighting and consecutive attempts to establish cease-fires followed, until the final cease-fire was established in February 1999 after the arrival of a joint African peace-keeping force. During this period, the majority of the inhabitants of the study area fled to a village outside Bissau. It was possible to carry out a census with subsequent follow-up during the period of national conflict, and it has been possible to follow people after their return to the study area.

The central features of the research in Bandim are the attempts to follow long-term consequences of various infections, health conditions, and interventions. Main areas of research are determinants of measles mortality, evaluation of various measles-vaccination schemes, long-term consequences of measles infection, crowding and health, epidemiology and control of diarrheal and respiratory diseases, management of childhood illnesses, impact of breastfeeding and weaning on morbidity and survival, risk factors for hospitalization, immunological determinants of child survival (T-lymphocyte subsets, thymus growth, and delayed hypersensitivity), maternal mortality, epidemiology of HIV-2 and other retroviruses, and epidemiology and control of tuberculosis.

The Bandim DSS covers a population of 75 000 in five suburbs, nearly 30% of the population of Bissau, the capital. The rural population covered is 28 000 in five regions, and the survey of women of fertile age comprises 25 000 women. The study is presently monitoring nearly 12% of all births in Guinea-Bissau, with around 6000 registered births each year.

The site headquarters are situated in the Bandim suburban area of Bissau, where the main study population is found. A mobile team based in Bandim carries out the rural surveys. The project has 100 field assistants, 55 medical doctors, nurses, and laboratory technicians, and 8–10 expatriate academics. The administration consists of an administrator, an accountant, a secretary, and three drivers. The site has a contract of collaboration with the Ministry of Health but a status like that of a nongovernmental organization project, with full financial and managerial autonomy. It has close financial and training relations with the National Health Laboratory, where most immunological and biochemical analyses are carried out.

Continuous registration of all measles cases in the study area since 1978 has suggested innovative ideas about the epidemiology of the disease, as well as its long-term consequences. As a consequence of the focus on maternal and child health, the database system fully relates information on all vital events to anthropometry, vaccination status, morbidity, and nutritional aspects, as well as hospitalizations and diagnosis. Special features include a focus on registration and monthly follow-up of pregnancies; and 14 years of continuous morbidity surveillance (diarrheal and respiratory diseases).

The project has no core funding but relies on funding from many different organizations including the Danish International Development Agency (DANIDA). A number of specialized studies have independent funding from the Danish Research Council (measles, diarrhea, viral infections, respiratory infections, and HIV-2), MRC

(HIV-2), European Union (measles, diarrhea, and HIV-2), and NOVO (RSV epidemiology and sonography).

Research results have been disseminated through international journals and national conferences on specific issues or in advisory groups at national and international levels (for example, the World Health Organization).

Bandim DSS data collection and processing

Field procedures

MAPPING — Mapping was done by hand and has now been transferred to a GIS-based system (MAP-INFO) in 1995. Spatial analyses have been done on cases of diarrhea and measles epidemics.

INITIAL CENSUS — The first census was done in 1978. Over the years a number of censuses have been carried out in Bissau (1981, 1986, 1988, 1993, 1995, 1997, and 1999) and in some of the rural areas to keep track of the population and document family structure. In each census, information is collected on names, date of birth or age, sex, household status, family relation, ethnic group, civil status, level of schooling, use of bednets, use of common bed, and type of work.

REGULAR UPDATE ROUNDS — Partly as a result of the population's being increasingly mobile after economic liberalization, censuses have now become an annual event in the Bissau districts, as well as in the Caio sector. Migrations are tracked within the study area; in certain studies, migrations are tracked outside the study area as well.

CONTINUOUS SURVEILLANCE — With a historical focus on maternal and childhood health, registration during pregnancy has been a key element of the data-collection system. Field assistants visit all households once a month to enquire about new pregnancies and register women who have already given birth. In the urban districts, children are followed up every 3 months from birth until they are 3 years old age (since 1999, until they are 5 years old). The interval between routine visits in the rural areas is 6 months. Often children are followed more closely, owing to the specificity of the studies, such as weekly morbidity surveys of respiratory and diarrheal diseases. Information is gathered on anthropometry (weight, height, and arm circumference), immunizations, feeding and breastfeeding, infections and hospitalization, various socioeconomic indicators, and migrations and deaths. In Bissau, data on hospitalization of children from the study area are collected routinely at the hospital. Sources of data are primarily household members, such as mothers or caretakers.

Death certification is done by a brief verbal-autopsy (VA)-like questionnaire conducted by one or two specialized field assistants usually 2 weeks to 3 months after the death (one questionnaire for children and a different one for adults). Expatriate and national medical doctors carried out more thorough VA surveys in 1987, 1993, and 1999.

SUPERVISION AND QUALITY ASSURANCE — One supervisor is assigned for each 2–3 field assistants, and the same supervisor is responsible for questionnaire-checking and data entry. Each assistant is supervised weekly in the field. Temporal analysis of assistant bias is carried out every 3 months.

Figure 23.2. Population pyramid of person–years observed at the Bandim DSS site, Guinea-Bissau, 1995–97.

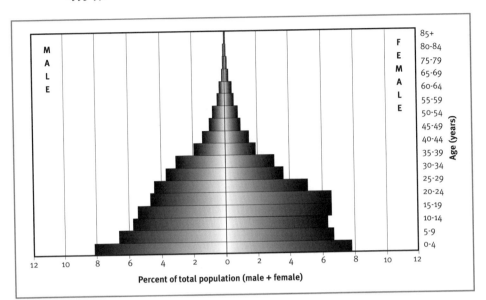

Data management

Data are entered using laptops into a menu-based dBase program designed specifically for the Bandim site. The database program has built-in control and validation features. Once a month, a report of inconsistent or missing information is printed out for correction. Each supervisor checks questionnaires before data entry. National supervisors and expatriates carry out field supervision.

Bandim DSS basic outputs

Demographic indicators

The Bandim DSS site has more than 100 000 people under continuous surveillance (75 000 urban and 28 000 rural). Three percent are infants; 13%, <5 years old; 25%, 5–14 years old; 57%, 15–64 years old; and 2%, ≥65 years old (Figure 23.2). The age-dependency ratio is 82, and the sex ratio is 0.92. The total fertility rate for women 15–49 years old is 5.8 for urban and 6.8 for rural. The infant mortality rate is 102 per 1000 live births in the urban areas and 128 per 1000 live births in rural areas. The under-five mortality ratio is 256 per 1000 live births. The maternal mortality ratio is 818 per 100 000 live births. Table 23.1 shows the age- and sex-specific all-cause mortality at the Bandim site. The average household size is 4.57, and 67.1% of males and 40.7% of females ≥15 years old are literate.

Table 23.1. Age- and sex-specific mortality at the Bandim DSS site, Guinea-Bissau, 1995–97.

Age (years)	Death s ($_nD_x$)		Person–years observed ($_nPY_x$)	
	Male	Female	Male	Female
<1	306	264	2518	2429
1–4	236	219	6644	6249
5–9	47	40	3702	3919
10–14	21	17	3153	3561
15–19	15	10	2831	3456
20–24	17	27	2441	3613
25–29	29	31	2278	2723
30–34	30	29	2094	2065
35–39	27	24	1676	1643
40–44	41	29	1163	1046
45–49	41	28	772	822
50–54	25	23	581	538
55–59	34	32	501	455
60–64	29	24	276	282
65–69	29	13	195	240
70–74	17	17	104	140
75–79	19	11	106	72
80–84	7	9	40	42
≥85	5	8	25	36
CDR	28.4			
CBR	51.8			
CRNI	23.4			

Note: CBR, crude birth rate (actual number of births per 1000 population); CDR, crude death rate (actual number of deaths per 1000 population); CRNI, crude rate of natural increase (CBR minus CDR per 100; does not take into account migration); $_nD_x$, observed deaths between ages x and $x+n$; $_nPY_x$, observed person–years between ages x and $x+n$.

Acknowledgments

The Bandim site has close relations with the MRC in The Gambia and has collaborated with IRD in Senegal since 1983. The site is a division of the Danish epidemiology science centre, Statens Seruminstiut. The main donors include DANIDA, the Danish Council for Development Research, and the Science and Technology for Development Programme of the European Community. We are grateful to these collaborators and donors, whose support has constituted a backbone to the site. Supervisors and field assistants are invaluable to any demographic and health-survey site. Without their care and interest in collecting the best information there would be no site.

Chapter 24

BANDAFASSI DSS, SENEGAL

Gilles Pison,[1] Emmanuelle Guyavarch,[1] and Cheikh Sokhna[2]

Site description

Physical geography of the Bandafassi DSA

The Bandafassi area is in Senegal, between latitudes 12°46′ and 12°30′N and longitudes 12°16′ and 12°31′E, at an altitude of 60–426 m above sea level (Figure 24.1). It is about 500 km from the capital, Dakar, in the region of Tambacounda and the Département of Kedougou, eastern Senegal, near the borders of Senegal, Mali, and Guinea. The site covers about half the Arrondissement of Bandafassi. The Bandafassi area is 25 km × by 25 km wide and has an area of 600 km².

The ecological zone is Sudan savannah. The area has a rainy season from June to October and a dry season from November to May, and it had an average rainfall of 1097 mm a year during 1984–95.

Figure 24.1. Location of the Bandafassi DSS site, Senegal (monitored population, 10 500).

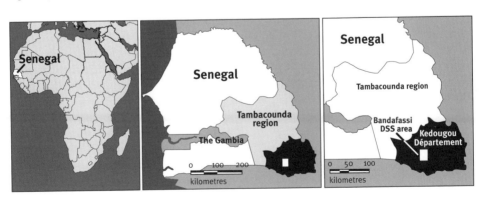

1 Institut national d'études démographiques, Paris, France.

2 Université Cheikh Anta Diop (Cheikh Anta Diop University [University of Dakar]), Institut de recherche pour le développement, Dakar, Senegal.

Population characteristics of the Bandafassi DSA

On 1 January 2000, the Bandafassi site had a population of 10 509. The population density is low, about 18 inhabitants/km2 in 42 villages. The villages are small (240 inhabitants on average), and some are divided into hamlets. Three ethnic groups live in distinct villages:

- Bedik (25% of the population), who have their own language, which is related to the Mande linguistic group;

- Mandinka (16% of the population); and

- Fula Bande (59% of the population), culturally very close to the subgroup of Guinea.

The Fula and a minority of the Mandinka are Muslims, whereas the majority of the Mandinka and the Bedik are animists, with a few Christians.

The area is rural, and the main economic activities are cultivation of cereals (sorghum, maize, and rice), peanuts, and cotton and cattle-breeding. Part of the young male population migrates seasonally to cities or other rural areas of the country.

Ten villages have primary schools, but seven have only one teacher. Secondary schools are in the cities of Kedougou (25 km away) and Tambacounda (250 km away). In 2000, 26% of women 15–29 years old and 10% of those 30–44 years old had been to school for at least 1 year.

The residential unit is a compound housing the members (15 on average) of an extended patrilineal family. A compound usually contains one hut for each ever-married woman and sometimes additional huts for unmarried adult sons and for the head of the compound. Polygyny is frequent: there are 180 married women for each 100 married men. When a man has several wives, each one has her own hut, close to those of the others. Children sleep in their mother's hut until they are about 15 years old. Teenage girls leave the compound to marry, and boys build small huts to sleep in, often with age-mates. Older children may sleep in the huts of old or childless women in the compound, even if their mother lives in her own hut (Pison 1982).

The vast majority of dwellings are huts with thatched roofs. Water is taken from rivers, backwater, wells, or bore holes. Most compounds have no toilet facilities, and no one has electricity. The area is one of the most remote in Senegal, 700 km from the national capital, Dakar, and 250 km from the regional capital, Tambacounda, with poor local roads, often impassable during the rainy season, which lasts half of the year. The closest hospital where a caesarian section can be performed is in Tambacounda.

The area has one public-health post, in the village of Bandafassi, and this is run by a nurse. The area is divided into two sectors: in the southern sector, immunizations are given at the public-health post of Bandafassi and by the nurse who travels by motorbike to vaccinate children in more remote villages; and in the northern sector, a nurse from the Catholic mission in Kedougou visits each village several times a year to vaccinate and examine children and mothers. Before 1987 when the national immunization program (expanded immunization program) reached the area for the first time, vaccination coverage was almost zero. In 1992, full vaccination was given to 39% of children 12–35 months old.

Bandafassi DSS procedures

Introduction to the Bandafassi DSS site

The original objective of the Bandafassi project (in 1970) was to measure survival rates in various genotype subgroups of a population (comparing, for example, persons with the gene responsible for drepanocytosis [gene S] and those without it). Genotypes were determined from blood samples; survival rates were estimated from the follow-up of individuals with a known genotype over several years. Regular updates of demographic information on births, deaths, marriages, and migrations was done for the entire Bandafassi area. The original objective was rapidly abandoned and the project became a demographic and health project, whose main objectives were to study the demographic and health situation of a West African population with very high mortality levels, to observe changes over time, and to examine the factors involved (Pison et al. 1997).

The baseline survey was organized at various dates in the villages of the various subpopulations of the Bandafassi area: in 1970, for the Mandinka (1095 inhabitants at that time); 1975, for the Fula (3701 inhabitants); and 1980, for the Bedik (1818 inhabitants). In 1975 and 1980, as mentioned above, the newly enumerated subpopulation was added to the population already being followed up. The total population increased from 6577 inhabitants at the beginning of 1980 to 10 509 inhabitants at the beginning of 2000.

The Bandafassi studies are managed by a team of researchers from several institutions based in Senegal and France, with several doctoral students from both countries working on the project. In France, the main institution involved is the Institut national d'études démographiques (national institute for demographic studies). In Senegal, the institutions involved are the Unité de paludologie afro-tropicale from the Institut de recherche pour le développement, the Programme national de lutte contre le SIDA (national program for the fight against AIDS) of the Ministry of Health, and the Cheikh Anta Diop University (University of Dakar), whose several students work on the project.

Bandafassi DSS data collection and processing

Field procedures

INITIAL CENSUS — The first operation was a census, followed by several surveys to improve the information of the census and collect other data needed for subsequent studies. These included an age survey to estimate ages of adults and children or improve the unreliable data collected on these during the census. An indirect method was used, based on the classification of the village population by birth rank (Pison 1980). It also included a genealogical survey to collect genealogies up to known ascendants and down to living collateral relatives. One use of the genealogies in the project is to get detailed information on the relationships between members of a compound, in particular the relationship of each one to the head of the compound (Pison 1985). Finally, a union- and birth-histories survey was conducted for adult men and women.

At the census, a person was considered a member of the compound if the head of the compound declared it to be so. This definition was broad and resulted in a *de jure* population under study. Thereafter, a criterion was used to decide whether and when a person was to be excluded or included in the population.

A person is considered to exit from the study population by either death or out-migration. Part of the population of Bandafassi engages in seasonal migrations, with seasonal migrants sometimes remaining 1 or 2 years outside the area before returning. A person who was absent from three successive yearly rounds, without returning in between, is regarded as having emigrated and no longer resident in the study population at the date of the third round. Because of this definition, some vital events for the study occur outside its immediate area. Some births, for example, occur to women classified in the study population but physically absent at the time of delivery, and these births are registered and included in the calculation of rates, although information on them is less accurate. There are special exit criteria for babies born outside; namely, they are considered to have become emigrants on the same dates as their mothers.

A new person is considered to have entered the study population either through birth to a woman of the study population or through in-migration. Information on in-migrants is collected when the list of compounds of a village is checked ("Are there new compounds or new families who settled since the last visit?") or when the list of members of a compound is checked ("Are there new persons in the compound since the last visit?"). Some in-migrants are villagers who left the area several years before and were excluded from the study population. Information is collected to determine in which compound they were previously registered, to match new and old information.

Information is routinely collected on movements from one compound to another within the study area. Some categories of the population, such as older widows or orphans, frequently move for short periods of time and live in between several compounds. These people may be considered members of all the compounds or of none of them. As a consequence, their movements are not always declared.

REGULAR UPDATE ROUNDS — The Bandafassi DSS is a multiround demographic surveillance, with annual rounds. Once each year, in February and March, all villages and hamlets are visited, and information on events occurring since the last visit is collected. This is done in three steps. First, the list of people present in each compound at the preceding visit is checked, and information is obtained on new births, marriages, migrations, deaths, and current pregnancies. Information is provided by the head of the compound or key informants in the village or hamlet. Not all compounds are visited systematically, as experience indicates that villages are small enough that information on vital events is common knowledge and that a well-chosen informant can accurately provide such basic information. The information on events is recorded directly on the nominative list.

CONTINUOUS SURVEILLANCE — For each death identified in the first step of the surveillance, information on its cause is obtained from a close relative of the dead person (usually the mother in case of a child death) through a verbal-autopsy (VA) questionnaire. This questionnaire was introduced in 1985; before then, simple questions were asked, such as "Why did the person die?," "Of what disease?" Since 1985, detailed VAs have been performed, but only for the deaths of children <15 years old.

Other information not part of routine census has been collected at various times, including for studies on immunization, parasitological status, resistance to

Figure 24.2. Population pyramid for person–years observed at the Bandafassi DSS site, Senegal, 1995–99.

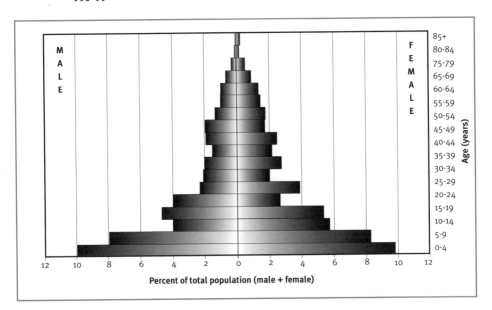

sexually transmitted diseases, and malaria (Enel and Pison 1992; Enel et al. 1993; Enel, Lagarde et al. 1994; Enel, Pison et al. 1994; Lagarde et al. 1995; Lagarde et al. 1996a, b, 1997, 1998; Diop et al. 2000; Lagarde et al. 2000), as well as studies on contraceptive prevalence, breastfeeding, and nutrition.

Data management

Information collected during the baseline and follow-up surveys has been coded and stored in databases designed in the 1970s and 1980s, with some adaptations since then. The information collected during each annual survey is processed in two steps: it is entered into laptops with state-of-the-art software during the surveillance; thereafter, the information is verified and added to the database, using PostgreSQL software.

Bandafassi DSS basic outputs

Demographic indicators

The total (*de jure*) population is 10 509. The sex ratio in the total population was 0.96. The age structure in the total population was as follows: 4.0% was <1 year old; 17.2%, 0–4 years old; 26.5%, 5–14 years old; 52.0%, 15–64 years old; and 4.3%, ≥65 years old (Figure 24.2). The total fertility rate was 6.5. The dependency ratio was 0.923. The infant mortality rate was 135/1000 live births. Mean household size was 14.6, and the adult literacy rate among females was 7% in 2000. Life expectancy at birth was 48 years for females and 45 years for males. The maternal mortality ratio for the period 1988–97 was 826 per 100 000 live births.

Table 24.1 shows the age- and sex-specific all-cause mortality for the site.

Table 24.1. Age- and sex-specific mortality at the Bandafassi DSS site, Senegal, 1995–99.

Age (years)	Death s ($_nD_x$)		Person–years observed ($_nPY_x$)	
	Male	Female	Male	Female
<1	145	120	949	953
1–4	118	96	3192	3106
5–9	12	25	3304	3423
10–14	6	12	1632	2368
15–19	10	10	1936	2213
20–24	10	7	1633	1095
25–29	4	12	947	1599
30–34	7	8	863	829
35–39	11	10	831	1129
40–44	6	4	628	888
45–49	8	8	796	1022
50–54	12	11	803	715
55–59	15	15	546	723
60–64	12	15	407	595
65–69	28	25	398	549
70–74	26	20	265	362
75–79	10	22	125	212
80–84	11	14	49	68
≥85	3	13	27	102
Births	2122			
CDR	21.82			
CBR	51.40			
CRNI	29.57			

Note: CBR, crude birth rate (actual number of births per 1000 population); CDR, crude death rate (actual number of deaths per 1000 population); CRNI, crude rate of natural increase (CBR minus CDR per 100; does not take into account migration); $_nD_x$, observed deaths between ages x and $x+n$; $_nPY_x$, observed person–years between ages x and $x+n$.

Fertility and child-mortality trends

The total fertility rate has not changed over the last 20 years: it was 6.4 children per woman on average in 1980–89 and 6.5 in 1990–99 (Table 24.2). In Mlomp (another rural site in Senegal), in contrast, total fertility declined rather rapidly, from 5.3 children per woman in 1985–89 to 4.3 in 1990–94 and 3.6 in 1995–99 (see Chapter 25).

Trends in child mortality also differ between these two sites. In Bandafassi, child mortality was very high, and it has decreased over the surveillance period: under-five mortality rate ($_5q_0$) was 470 per 1000 in 1976–79, 351 per 1000 in 1980–89, and 254 per 1000 in 1990–99. In Mlomp, on the contrary, child mortality, although comparatively low, has not diminished: under-five mortality rate ($_5q_0$) was 87 per 1000 in 1985–89, 124 per 1000 in 1990–94, and 100 per 1000 in 1995–99.

Table 24.2. Age-specific fertility rates at the Bandafassi DSS site, Senegal, 1985–99.

Age (years)	1985–89			1990–94			1995–99		
	PY	Births	Births/PY (×1000)	PY	Births	Births/PY (×1000)	PY	Births	Births/PY (×1000)
10–14	1083.16	21	19.39	3977.91	35	8.80	5342.05	10	1.87
15–19	984.97	252	255.85	3544.45	721	203.42	4107.66	722	175.77
20–24	727.38	237	325.83	3155.35	986	312.48	3457.14	1057	305.74
25–29	655.82	167	254.64	2770.06	784	283.03	3034.63	917	302.18
30–34	582.39	127	218.07	2321.57	536	230.88	2816.70	741	263.07
35–39	507.70	82	161.51	2110.57	311	147.35	2517.00	417	165.67
40–44	404.15	32	79.18	1833.36	124	67.64	2186.44	149	68.15
45–49	496.33	8	16.12	1604.81	24	14.96	1943.47	29	14.92
50–54	400.50	5	12.48	1589.15	8	5.03	1645.55	4	2.43

Note: PY, person–years.

Acknowledgments

The following institutions have provided financial support to the Bandafassi and Mlomp DSS projects: Institut national d'études démographiques, Agence national de recherches sur le SIDA, Institut français de recherche pour le développement, European Community, World Health Organization, Institut national de la santé et de la recherche médicale (national institute of health and medical research), and Centre national de la recherche scientifique (national centre for scientific research), Muséum national d'histoire naturelle (national museum of natural history).

Chapter 25

Mlomp DSS, Senegal

Gilles Pison,[1] Abdoulaye Wade,[2] Alexis Gabadinho,[1] and Catherine Enel[1]

Site description

Physical geography of the Mlomp DSA

The Mlomp DSS site, about 500 km from the capital, Dakar, in Senegal, lies between latitudes 12°36' and 12°32'N and longitudes 16°33' and 16°37'E, at an altitude ranging from 0 to 20 m above sea level (Figure 25.1). It is in the region of Ziguinchor, Département of Oussouye, in southwest Senegal, near the border between Senegal and Guinea-Bissau. It covers about half the Arrondissement of Loudia-Ouolof. The Mlomp DSS site is about 11 km × 7 km and has an area of 70 km². Villages are households grouped in a circle with a 3-km diameter and surrounded by lands that are flooded during the rainy season and cultivated for rice.

Figure 25.1. Location of the Mlomp DSS site, Senegal (monitored population, 6200).

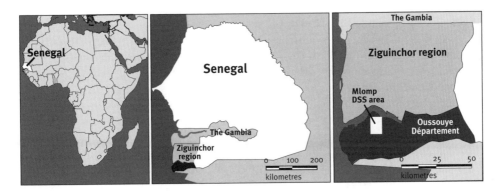

1 Institut national d'études démographiques (national institute for demographic studies), Paris, France.

2 Programme national de lutte contre le SIDA (national program for the fight against AIDS), Dakar, Senegal.

The site is in a Guinea savannah and mangrove ecological zone. The area has a rainy season from June to October and a dry season from November to May and had an average rainfall of 1230 mm a year during 1984–95.

Population characteristics of the Mlomp DSA

The Mlomp DSS site had a population of 7591 on 1 January 2000 and a population density of 108 inhabitants/km^2. It has 11 villages. Most people belong to the Diola ethnic group and are animists, with a large minority of Christians and a few Muslims. People speak Diola, and most also speak Oulof, the main national language in Senegal, and French, the teaching language at school. The area is rural, and rice cultivation is the main economic activity. The majority of the adult population engages in seasonal migrations. The residential unit is a household housing a family of 6.3 persons on average, and polygyny is rare.

The first school opened in 1949; two other primary schools, in 1960 and 1972; and a secondary school, in 1985. That year 17% of women ≥15 years old had been to school for at least 1 year compared with 53% of girls 7–14 years old.

Most dwellings are of mud. Houses are covered with thatched roofs (66% of houses in 1990) or corrugated iron (33%). A large majority of them (74%) have no toilet facilities; the rest (26%) have pit latrines. Water is from wells. No one has electricity. The area is 10 km from the small city of Oussouye and 50 km from the regional capital, Ziguinchor. Ziguinchor has the closest hospital where a caesarian section can be performed. Local tar roads are passable most of the year.

A nongovernmental health centre, run by French Roman Catholic nurses, was opened in 1961 in the centre of the area. It is well supplied with medicines and equipped to perform simple laboratory tests. The village also runs a maternity clinic, opened in 1968, close to the health centre. The proportion of deliveries occurring at a maternity facility increased from 50% in 1961 to >95% in 1970 (Enel et al. 1993). Most of the children (99%) are correctly vaccinated with measles, yellow fever, BCG (bacillus Calmette-Guérin), and diphtheria–pertussis–tetanus–polio vaccines (as recommended by the expanded immunization program) (Pison, Trape, et al. 1993).

In the 1970s and 1980s, anthropometry surveys with monthly visits for children <5 years old were conducted (the age limit was reduced to 3 years old in 1985). Most children were enrolled in this program (94% in 1989). Since 1989 the program has continued, but with diminishing coverage, as parents have no longer been receiving supplementary food for themselves and their children.

Malaria surveys carried out in the 1960s indicated that malaria was mesoendemic. An antimalaria program was started in 1975, promoting regular intake of chloroquine for everyone during the rainy season. Families were also encouraged to keep a stock of chloroquine at home and treat any case of fever with this drug. Until 1989, this program reduced the parasite rate in children during the rainy season to <10%. Following the emergence of chloroquine resistance in 1990, the parasite rate in children rose sharply, reaching 46% in 1992 and 51% in 1994. Chloroquine resistance (measured in vivo) progressed from 36% in 1991 to 46% in 1995 (Trape et al. 1998).

Serological surveys conducted in 1990 and 1995 showed an HIV seroprevalence close to 1% among individuals ≥20 years old and an annual incidence rate of 1 per 1000 each year during the period 1990–95 (Le Guenno et al. 1992; Diop et al. 2000).

One particular feature of Mlomp is seasonal migration (Enel and Pison 1992; Pison, Le Guenno et al. 1993; Enel, Pison et al. 1994): the majority of the adult population is absent for more than half of the year (7 months on average). Eighty percent of unmarried women 15–24 years old are employed as house servants in the main cities of Senegal and The Gambia; once married, women usually stay at home all year round. Eighty percent of men 20–40 years old migrate and continue to migrate after marriage and until of advanced age. The proportion of migrants diminishes among those ≥40 years old, however, and is <50% among those ≥60 years old. Middle-aged men migrate to harvest palm wine in other villages of the same region, or in other regions, or near the main cities of Senegal or The Gambia. Younger men migrate to fish.

Mlomp DSS procedures

Introduction to the Mlomp DSS site

When the Mlomp project started in 1985, Senegal already had two rural areas under long-term demographic and epidemiological surveillance: Bandafassi, in the southeast, where surveillance started in 1970; and Niakhar, in the west centre, where surveillance started in 1962. As in Bandafassi, the Mlomp project's main objective was to study the demographic and health situation of an African rural population to observe changes over time and examine the factors involved (Pison, Trape et al. 1993). The Mlomp site is in the southwest Casamance region of Senegal, a region with historic, economic, and ethnic patterns very different from those of the other sites and consequently providing the opportunity to better cover the diversity of demographic and epidemiological situations in the country.

The baseline survey, conducted in Mlomp in late 1984 and early 1985, found a population of 6218. The extent of the area under surveillance has not changed, but the population had increased to 7591 by the beginning of 2000.

The Mlomp studies are managed by a team of researchers from several institutions based in Senegal and France, and several doctoral students from both countries work in the projects. In France, the main institution involved is the Institut national d'études démographiques (national institute for demographic studies) in Paris. In Senegal, the institutions involved are the Unité de paludologie afro-tropicale (organization for the study of tropical African malaria) from the Institut de recherche pour le développement (institute for development research), the Programme national de lutte contre le SIDA (national program for the fight against AIDS) of the Ministry of Health, and Cheikh Anta Diop University (University of Dakar), which has several students working in the project.

Mlomp DSS data collection and processing

Field procedures

INITIAL CENSUS — The initial census was followed by several surveys designed to improve the information of the census and collect other data needed for subsequent studies. These included an age survey to estimate ages of adults and children or improve the unreliable data collected on these during the census. It also included a genealogical survey to collect genealogies, going up to known ascendants and down to living collateral relatives. One use of the genealogies in the project is to get detailed information on the relationships between members of a compound and in particular the relationship of each one to the head of the compound (Pison 1985). Finally, a union- and birth-histories survey was conducted for adult men and women.

At the census, a person was considered a member of the compound if the head of the compound declared it to be so. This definition was broad and resulted in a *de jure* population under study. Thereafter, a criterion was used to decide whether and when a person was to be excluded or included in the population.

A person was considered to exit from the study population through either death or emigration. Part of the population of Mlomp engages in seasonal migration, with seasonal migrants sometimes remaining 1 or 2 years outside the area before returning. A person who is absent for two successive yearly rounds, without returning in between, is regarded as having emigrated and no longer resident in the study population at the date of the second round. This definition results in the inclusion of some vital events that occur outside the study area. Some births, for example, occur to women classified in the study population but physically absent at the time of delivery, and these births are registered and included in the calculation of rates, although information on them is less accurate. Special exit criteria apply to babies born outside the study area: they are considered emigrants on the same date as their mother.

A new person enters the study population either through birth to a woman of the study population or through immigration. Information on immigrants is collected when the list of compounds of a village is checked ("Are there new compounds or new families who settled since the last visit?") or when the list of members of a compound is checked ("Are there new persons in the compound since the last visit?"). Some immigrants are villagers who left the area several years before and were excluded from the study population. Information is collected to determine in which compound they were previously registered, to match the new and old information.

Information is routinely collected on movements from one compound to another within the study area. Some categories of the population, such as older widows or orphans, frequently move for short periods of time and live in between several compounds, and they may be considered members of these compounds or of none. As a consequence, their movements are not always declared.

REGULAR UPDATE ROUNDS — The Mlomp DSS is a multiround demographic surveillance, with annual rounds. Once each year, in February and March, all compounds are visited, and information on events occurring since the last visit is collected. This is done in three steps. First, the list of people present in each compound at the preceding visit is checked, and information is obtained on new births, marriages, migrations, deaths, and current pregnancies. Information is provided by the head of the compound or key informants in the village or hamlet. The information on events is recorded directly on the nominative list.

CONTINUOUS SURVEILLANCE — Information provided by local registers is matched with that collected independently during the surveillance. Information from registers with fair quality is used to systematically correct errors and complete the information collected at the yearly rounds. These are maternity-clinic registers (for prenatal visits and deliveries), civil and parish registers (for births), and dispensary or hospital registers (for death, growth monitoring, and vaccinations). The local dispensary collaborates with the research project, and one completes several registers, in particular a death register. Although the local registers rarely cover the entire population and are sometimes subject to errors, using them improves the quality and the precision of data. Verbal autopsies (VAs) have been performed for all deaths since the beginning of the study. For each death identified in the first step of the annual surveillance, information on its cause is obtained from a close relative of the dead person, usually the mother in the case of a child's death, using a VA questionnaire.

Other information not part of the routine data has been collected at various times. These included serological, parasitological, or resistance surveys for sexually transmitted disease and malaria studies (Enel and Pison 1992; Enel, Lagarde et al. 1994; Enel, Pison et al. 1994; Lagarde et al. 1995; Lagarde et al. 1996a, b, 1997, 1998; Diop et al. 2000; Lagarde et al. 2000); and contraceptive-prevalence, breastfeeding, and nutritional surveys.

Data management and analysis

Information collected during the baseline and follow-up surveys has been coded and stored in databases designed in the 1970s and 1980s, with some adaptations since then. The information collected during each annual surveillance is processed in two steps: in the villages, it is entered into laptops, with state-of-the-art software, during the surveillance; thereafter, the information is verified and added to the database, using PostgreSQL software.

Mlomp DSS basic outputs

Demographic indicators

The total (*de jure*) population is 7591 (population size on 1 January 2000). The sex ratio in the total population was 1.04. The age structure in the total population was as follows: 1.7% was <1 year old; 9.8%, 0–4 years old; 23.3%, 5–14 years old; 59.3%, 15–64 years old; and 7.6%, ≥65 years old. The total fertility rate was 4.0. The dependency ratio was 0.687. The infant mortality rate was 59/1000. The mean household size was 6.3, and the adult literacy rate in females was 17% in 1985. Life expectancy at birth for females was 64 years and for males was 56 years. The maternal mortality ratio for the period 1985–98 was 436 per 100 000 live births.

Fertility and child-mortality trends

In Mlomp, the total fertility (Table 25.1) declined rather rapidly from 5.3 children per woman in 1985–89 to 4.3 in 1990–94 and 3.6 in 1995–99. In Bandafassi (see Chapter 24), in contrast, the total fertility rate has not changed over the last 20 years: it was 6.4 children per woman on average during the period 1980–89 and 6.5 during the period 1990–99.

Trends in child mortality also differ between these two sites. In Mlomp, child mortality, although comparatively low, has not decreased: under-five mortality rate ($_5q_0$) was 87 per 1000 in 1985–89, 124 per 1000 in 1990–94, and 100 per 1000 in 1995–99.

Table 25.2 shows the age- and sex-specific all-cause mortality at the Mlomp site.

Table 25.1. Age-specific fertility rates at the Mlomp DSS site, Senegal, 1985–99.

Age (years)	1985–89			1990–94			1995–99		
	PY	Births	Births/PY (× 1000)	PY	Births	Births/PY (× 1000)	PY	Births	Births/PY (× 1000)
10–14	2146.94	3	1.40	2419.41	1	0.41	2213.92	1	0.45
15–19	2044.72	76	37.17	2215.70	76	34.30	2493.85	83	33.28
20–24	1532.74	187	122.00	1835.06	229	124.79	1947.26	199	102.19
25–29	789.01	159	201.52	1231.62	189	153.46	1440.96	208	144.35
30–34	537.74	146	271.51	693.27	135	194.73	984.57	178	180.79
35–39	562.38	143	254.28	487.66	100	205.06	631.37	100	158.39
40–44	529.44	81	152.99	539.55	68	126.03	491.84	46	93.53
45–49	716.07	19	26.53	517.40	14	27.06	535.50	3	5.60
50–54	672.50	1	1.49	699.31	0	0.00	525.16	1	1.90

Note: PY, person–years.

Table 25.2. Age- and sex-specific mortality at the Mlomp DSS site, Senegal, 1995–99.

Age (years)	Deaths ($_nD_x$) Male	Female	Person–years observed ($_nPY_x$) Male	Female
<1	18	19	361	372
1–4	17	23	1551	1717
5–9	7	7	2097	2076
10–14	4	1	2298	2209
15–19	5	0	2417	2488
20–24	4	4	2097	1943
25–29	5	3	1884	1438
30–34	3	1	1187	982
35–39	8	2	824	630
40–44	2	2	558	491
45–49	7	6	491	534
50–54	5	1	484	524
55–59	9	7	719	665
60–64	10	13	664	620
65–69	20	5	509	569
70–74	25	20	408	433
75–79	30	22	221	293
80–84	7	23	38	143
≥85	9	20	38	78
Births	819			
CDR	10.09			
CBR	22.10			
CRNI	12.01			

Note: CBR, crude birth rate (actual number of births per 1000 population); CDR, crude death rate (actual number of deaths per 1000 population); CRNI, crude rate of natural increase (CBR minus CDR per 100; does not take into account migration); $_nD_x$, observed deaths between ages x and $x+n$; $_nPY_x$, observed person–years between ages x and $x+n$.

Age structure

The age pyramid of the Mlomp population on 1 January 2000 is affected by two troughs (Figure 25.2). The first is for those 40–59 years old; it corresponds to individuals who were born during the period 1940–60. Two factors have contributed to this trough. First, during World War II a large proportion of young adult men were enrolled in the French army; as a result, fewer marriages and births occurred during that period. Second, the emigration to cities may have increased with the generations born in 1940 and after. The second trough is at the base of the pyramid. It is a result of the recent fertility decline, which has been very rapid in the Mlomp community.

Figure 25.2. Population pyramid for the observed population at the Mlomp DSS site, Senegal, 1 Jan 2000.

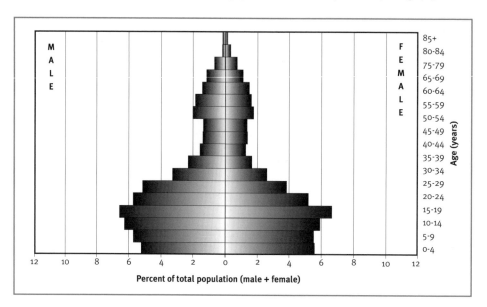

Acknowledgments

The following institutions have provided financial support to the Bandafassi and Mlomp projects: Institut national d'études démographiques (national institute for demographic studies), Agence national de recherches sur le SIDA (national agency for research on AIDS), Institut français de recherche pour le développement (French institute for development research), European Community, World Health Organization, Institut national de la santé et de la recherche médicale (national institute for health and medical research), and Centre national de la recherche scientifique (national centre for scientific research), Muséum national d'histoire naturelle (national museum of natural history).

Chapter 26

NIAKHAR DSS, SENEGAL

Valérie Delaunay, Adama Marra, Pierre Levi, and Jean-François Etard[1]

Site description

Physical geography of the Niakhar DSA

The study zone of Niakhar is in Senegal, at latitude 14.5°N and longitude 16.5°W (Figure 26.1). It is in the Département of Fatick, region of Fatick (Sine-Saloum), 135 km east of Dakar. The study zone is about 15 km × 15 km and covers 230 km². The climate is continental Sudanic sahelian, with temperatures ranging from 24°C in December–January to 30°C in May–June. For 30 years, the region has suffered from drought. Rainfall decreased from 808 mm a year in 1921–67, to 520 mm in 1968–87, and to 463 mm in 1988–98.

Population characteristics of the Niakhar DSA

From 1962 to 1966, sixty-five villages were surveyed annually. The study zone was then reduced to 8 villages until 1983, when it was extended to include 22 more villages, forming the current study zone of 30 villages. Eight of these have been under demographic surveillance for 38 years; and 22, for 17 years. The Niakhar area had a population of 30 215, as of 1 January 2000, with a high population density of about

Figure 26.1. Location of the Niakhar DSS site, Senegal (monitored population, 29 000).

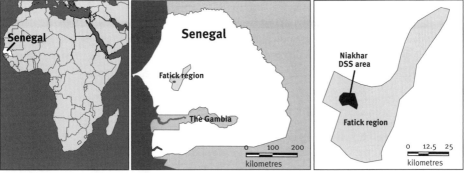

[1] Institut de recherche pour le développement (institute for development research), Senegal.

131 inhabitants/km^2. Demographic surveillance covers 30 villages of varying sizes: 60 individuals in Darou (the smallest) and 3150 in Toucar (the biggest); three other villages have more than 2000 individuals. The area is rural, but the three largest villages are more "urbanized," with health facilities, weekly market, daily buses to Dakar, and several shops. The Sereer ethnic group constitutes 96.5% of the population. Other ethnic groups are Wolof (1.4%), Toucouleur (1.1%), and Laobe (0.6%), with Peuhl, Moorish, Soce, and Diola making up the remainder (0.5%). Islam is the most-declared religion (74.5%); Christians constitute 22.4% of the population (19.9%, Roman Catholic; 2.6%, Protestant); and indigenous religion is declared by only 2.6%, although indigenous practices are very prevalent and observed in each family. The dominant language is Sereer, but many people speak Wolof.

The population lives traditionally on one food crop (millet), one cash crop (groundnuts), and cattle-raising. To cope with the agricultural crisis in Sahel and the demographic pressure (85 people/km^2 in 1966, 131 people/km^2 in 2000), new activities arose: predominantly, meat production and temporary migration to urban centres. Participation in formal education is very low: 59% of men and 80% of women 15–24 years old have no education. The first school opened in 1951, and the area now has nine public and two private schools.

The residential unit is the compound, which comprises one or more households, together with some members of the extended, patrilineal family. Traditional houses are huts (one for each ever-married woman and additional huts for unmarried adults). Modern structures, using concrete and corrugated iron, tend to replace traditional houses (43% of households have at least one corrugated iron roof). The availability of boreholes and drinking fountains has increased over the past several decades: 60% of the households now have access to tap water. The use of latrines is more recent: only 22% of the households have access to sanitation. The area has no electricity. The only paved roads are 15–30 km away from the villages, but several daily bus or taxi services to Dakar are available.

There are three health dispensaries within the study zone (the first opened in 1953, the last in 1983) and two outside it, providing basic services to the study population. These services include curative care, immunization, prenatal care, delivery, oral-rehydration therapy, and malnutrition management. The expanded program on immunization started between 1982 and 1984. At the department level, the proportion of fully immunized children among those 12–23 months old was 33%, and this was only 23% in January 2000. At the regional level, this coverage reached 61% in 1990 and decreased to 51% in 1991. Measles- and pertussis-vaccine trials resulted in a significant increase in immunization coverage within the study zone between 1987 and 1997.

Outbreaks of cholera occurred in 1985, 1987, and 1996, and a large meningococcal meningitis outbreak hit the population in 1998. Roughly half of the under-five mortality is due to diarrheal diseases, acute respiratory illness, and malnutrition; a quarter, to malaria.

Niakhar DSS procedures

Introduction to the Niakhar DSS site

The original objective of the Niakhar DSS site, in 1962, was to obtain reliable demographic and epidemiological data on a rural African population. Current objectives are to obtain a long-term assessment of demographic indicators, a basis for biomedical and social-sciences research, and continuous epidemiological surveillance. The Niakhar DSS has institutional affiliation with the Institut de recherche pour le développement (IRD, institute for development research; formerly ORSTOM).

The DSS has had several periods:

- 1962–66 — 65 villages had yearly surveys;

- 1967–83 — 8 villages had yearly surveys;

- 1984–86 — 30 villages had yearly surveys;

- 1987–97 — 30 villages had weekly surveys; and

- Since 1997 — 30 villages have had quarterly surveys.

Surveys are now conducted in February, May, August, and November every year. Between successive rounds, collected data are entered, checked, and used for updating the database. Migration data are probably the most difficult to collect, as they depend on the rule for residence used in the registry system. In- and out-migrations are counted after 6 months of presence or absence. Exceptions to this general rule concern temporary-work migrants, who are resident if they come back to the village for at least 1 month in the year; absent workers, who have their family (wife and children) in the village; and absent scholars who are considered resident within their family. Verbal autopsies (VAs) were completed for all deaths registered until 1997 and for deaths of those <55 years old thereafter.

The DSS routinely measures information on pregnancies, births, abortions (spontaneous), stillbirths, weaning, migrations, changes of marital status, immunizations, and cases of measles and whooping cough. Economic variables are measured using specific surveys on education, household equipment, and breeding and agricultural activities. Specific studies have been conducted on fertility, health-seeking behaviour, malaria, sexually transmitted diseases–HIV, anthropometric measures, and maternal mortality.

The project has five fieldworkers, three supervisors, three data-entry clerks, and two computer scientists. The Niakhar DSS system is geographically distributed between Niakhar and Dakar. Five fieldworkers visit the compounds, and two supervisors collect the completed questionnaires and bring them to the office in Niakhar on a daily basis, where they are checked. Questionnaires are then sent to Dakar for coding, data entry, updating, tabulation, and analysis. Main consumers of the Niakhar DSS data are researchers. However, results from demographic and epidemiological surveillance are regularly fed back to the local authorities, and in case of a potential disease outbreak the Ministry of Health is immediately alerted.

Niakhar DSS data collection and processing

Field procedures

INITIAL CENSUS — The initial census was conducted of 8 villages in 1962 and a further 22 villages in 1983. It comprised identification of the resident population and an abridged birth history for women (number of live births and deaths of children).

CONTINUOUS SURVEILLANCE — Data are currently collected on a quarterly basis. The local team involved in the data collection comprises five fieldworkers, two supervisors, and one head of station. They visit each compound every 3 months. Complete lists of people resident in the household and compound are produced each year. This list contains information on absence (date and reason), pregnancy if not terminated, spouses, etc. Specific spaces are provided to record information on the events occurring since the last visit. Spaces for three visits are available. Fieldworkers use these lists to ask questions about pregnancy, birth, stillbirth, death, migration, weaning, change in marital status, vaccination, measles, and whooping cough. To obtain accurate answers, concerned persons are interviewed personally; if they are absent or too young, a well-informed relative is interviewed. Until 1997, VAs were conducted for all deaths, and since then only for the deaths of people <55 years old. When a death occurs, the fieldworker interviews relatives of the deceased and completes a questionnaire with the identification of the person and the history and symptoms of the illness. The questionnaire is then read by two physicians, who each attribute a diagnosis. Where the two physicians disagree, a group of physicians gather to reach agreement on a diagnosis. The World Health Organization's ICD-9 is used for coding the most likely underlying cause of death.

FIELD SUPERVISION AND QUALITY ASSURANCE — After each day of data collection, the supervision team does consistency controls and registration of information. To make sure that all compounds were actually visited, some of them are revisited at random.

Data management

In Dakar, lists of people resident are checked, and some information is coded. An application program is used to enter, check, and save data in permanent files, which are processed to calculate all relevant statistics on the population. A menu is presented with these choices: data entry, data-checking, file-updating, browsing through files, or production of statistics.

Errors that appear in the data-processing step are corrected where possible; where not, the questionnaires are returned to the field.

Depending on the needs of epidemiologists and demographers, file extractions are done to present data according to a specific format for analysis. Reports on demographic and epidemiological data are produced for the local and national authorities. An analysis report is produced every 3 years.

Niakhar DSS basic outputs

On 1 January 2000, the population of the study area was 30 215. The population is very young: 46% are <15 years old (16.7% are 0–4 years old; 29.0%, 5–14 years old) (Figure 26.2). Children <1 year old constitute 3.9% of the population; the elderly, 5.1%. The age-dependency ratio is 1.04, and the sex ratio is 0.98 : 1.

In 1997, the average household size was 10.4, and the average compound size was 15.8. Although unusual in this society, 6.1% of households had a women as head.

Table 26.1 shows age- and sex-specific all-cause mortality for 1995–98, and Table 26.2 compares these data with those for 1984–88 and 1989–94. Demographic indicators for all three periods are presented in Table 26.3.

Figure 26.2. Population pyramid for person–years observed at the Niakhar DSS site, Senegal, 1995–98.

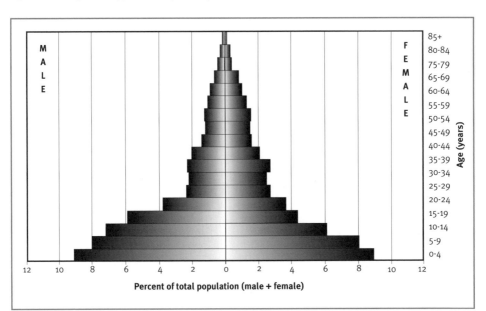

Table 26.1. Age- and sex-specific mortality at the Niakhar DSS site, Senegal, 1995–99.

Age (years)	Death s ($_nD_x$)		Person–years observed ($_nPY_x$)	
	Male	Female	Male	Female
<1	271	208	2 920	2 826
1–4	393	337	10 205	10 155
5–9	91	80	11 549	11 664
10–14	36	27	10 304	8 771
15–19	25	19	8 330	6 253
20–24	20	18	5 216	5 192
25–29	18	17	3 319	4 028
30–34	10	13	3 165	3 731
35–39	24	13	3 304	3 977
40–44	19	17	2 789	2 995
45–49	18	23	1 998	2 371
50–54	29	20	1 698	2 263
55–59	31	27	1 768	2 275
60–64	51	36	1 499	1 893
65–69	57	44	1 242	1 506
70–74	53	60	875	1 210
75–79	48	44	582	603
80–84	43	59	375	472
≥85	47	50	192	308
Births	5 997			
CDR	16.66			
CBR	41.70			
CRNI	2.5			

Note: CBR, crude birth rate (actual number of births per 1000 population); CDR, crude death rate (actual number of deaths per 1000 population); CRNI, crude rate of natural increase (CBR minus CDR per 100; does not take into account migration); $_nD_x$, observed deaths between ages x and $x+n$; $_nPY_x$, observed person–years between ages x and $x+n$.

Table 26.2. Historical age- and sex-specific all-cause mortality at the Niakhar DSS site, Senegal, 1984–98.

Age (years)	1984–88 Males			1984–88 Females			1989–93 Males			1989–93 Females			1994–98 Males			1994–98 Females		
	PY	Deaths	Death rate	PY	Deaths	Death rate	PY	Deaths	Death rate	PY	Deaths	Death rate	PY	Deaths	Death rate	PY	Deaths	Death rate
<1	2 791	369	132.2	2 757	306	111.0	2 815	262	93.1	2 757	205	74.4	2 920	271	92.8	2 826	208	73.6
1–4	9 115	436	47.8	8 877	402	45.3	9 983	350	35.1	10 103	333	33.0	10 205	393	38.5	10 155	337	33.2
5–9	9 747	48	4.9	9 485	46	4.8	11 105	68	6.1	10 921	52	4.8	11 549	91	7.9	11 664	80	6.9
10–14	7 476	19	2.5	6 829	14	2.1	9 579	19	2.0	7 722	16	2.1	10 304	36	3.5	8 771	27	3.1
15–19	5 248	15	2.9	4 631	8	1.7	7 268	19	2.6	5 325	16	3.0	8 330	25	3.0	6 253	19	3.0
20–24	4 032	12	3.0	4 618	20	4.3	4 165	21	5.0	4 329	18	4.2	5 216	20	3.8	5 192	18	3.5
25–29	3 847	26	6.8	4 590	23	5.0	3 189	16	5.0	4 021	9	2.2	3 319	18	5.4	4 028	17	4.2
30–34	3 490	25	7.2	3 597	15	4.2	3 271	9	2.8	4 042	19	4.7	3 165	10	3.2	3 731	13	3.5
35–39	2 414	15	6.2	2 679	18	6.7	3 257	20	6.1	3 558	15	4.2	3 304	24	7.3	3 977	13	3.3
40–44	1 944	20	10.3	2 450	12	4.9	2 273	10	4.4	2 560	20	7.8	2 789	19	6.8	2 995	17	5.7
45–49	1 991	20	10.0	2 517	29	11.5	1 836	18	9.8	2 324	16	6.9	1 998	18	9.0	2 371	23	9.7
50–54	1 817	32	17.6	2 299	27	11.7	1 807	18	10.0	2 359	16	6.8	1 698	29	17.1	2 263	20	8.8
55–59	1 597	39	24.4	1 920	37	19.3	1 720	28	16.3	2 144	26	12.1	1 768	31	17.5	2 275	27	11.9
60–64	1 266	30	23.7	1 667	37	22.2	1 506	29	19.3	1 779	35	19.7	1 499	51	34.0	1 893	36	19.0
65–69	1 057	52	49.2	1 170	48	41.0	1 134	40	35.3	1 478	45	30.4	1 242	57	45.9	1 506	44	29.2
70–74	805	56	69.6	986	56	56.8	867	52	60.0	978	52	53.2	875	53	60.6	1 210	60	49.6
75–79	509	50	98.2	630	48	76.2	546	43	78.8	660	48	72.7	582	48	82.5	603	44	73.0
80–84	287	50	174.2	414	39	94.2	315	40	127.0	435	49	112.6	375	43	114.7	472	59	125.0
≥85	207	54	260.9	342	59	172.5	198	39	197.0	320	75	234.4	192	47	244.79	308	50	162.3
CDR (s.e.)	59 690	1 368	22.9	62 458	1 244	19.9	66 834	1 101	16.4	67 815	1 065	15.7	71 330	1 284	18.0	72 493	1 112	15.3
ASDR (Segi) (s.e.)			20.6			17.2			15.4			13.9			17.7			14.0

Note: ASDR (Segi), age-specific death rate adjusted using the standard world population of Segi (1960); CDR, crude death rate (actual number of deaths per 1000 population); PY, person–years.

Table 26.3. Trends in demographic indicators at the Niakhar DSS site, Senegal, 1984–98.

Demographic indicator	1984–88	1989–93	1994–98
Total fertility rate	7.9	7.7	7.0
Neonatal mortality rate per 1000 live births	57	38	31
Infant mortality rate	122	86	79
Under-five mortality rate	282	196	200
Annual birth rate	47	46	42
Annual death rate	17	16	15
Annual out-migration rate	59	51	47
Annual in-migration rate	40	37	36
Natural annual population growth rate	3.22	2.98	2.61
Real annual population growth rate	1.28	1.64	1.51

	1984–97
Maternal mortality ratio (maternal deaths per 100 000 live births)	516 (ICD-9 definition) 575 (ICD-10 definition)

Note: ICD, International Classification of Diseases.

Acknowledgments

We thank the whole study population of Niakhar for their participation and welcome. We are grateful to Dr Pierre Cantrelle and Dr Michel Garenne for having initiated this longitudinal study. We thank all the staff of the Population and Health Laboratory from IRD, Dakar, who contributed to the data collection and management, particularly Ernest Faye, who has been coordinating the fieldwork for many years. We are most grateful to the late Dr Anouch Chahnazarian, who actively participated in the study design and initial data analyses.

We thank the subprefect of the district of Niakhar, the chief medical officers of Fatick and of the region of Fatick, and all the medical staff of health facilities in Niakhar, Ngayokhem, Toucar, and Diohine.

We thank all the staff, present and past, working for the Niakhar project: Peter Aaby, Agnès Adjamagbo, the late Jean-Pierre Beau, Charles Becker, Laurent Bouvier, Christophe Busquet, Pierre Cantrelle, Laurence Chabirand, Badara Cissé, René Collignon, Marème Dia, Waly Diafatte, Aïda Diagne, Aldiouma Diallo, Joseph Diatte, Samba Diatte, Latyr Diome, Abdou Diouf, Djibril Diouf, Pape Niokhor Diouf, Saliou Diouf, Samba Diouf, Raphaël Dogue, Jean-René Durand, Bassirou Fall, Alassane Faye, Aldiouma Faye, Ernest Faye, Gabriel Faye, Latyr Faye, Ousmane Faye, the late Carine Fenech, Jean-Yves Gagnepain, Belco Kodio, Jean-Yves Le Hesran, André Lericollais, Diaga Loum, Lissa Manga, Jean-François Molez, Emile Ndiaye, Emilie Ndiaye, Fatou Ndiaye, Malick Ndiaye, Michel Ndiaye, Ousmane Ndiaye, Prosper Ndiaye, Tofène Ndiaye, Etienne N'Dong, Antoine Ndour, Marie-Pierre Préziosi, Vincent Robert, Dominique Roquet, Philippe Royan, Badara Samb, Binta Sane, Marie Sane, Moussa Sarr, Tidiane Sène, Gilbert Senghor, Aminata Simaga, François Simondon, Kirsten Simondon, Cheikh Sokhna, Pierre Tine, Jean-François Trape, Florence Waïtzenegger-Lalou, and Ablaye Yam.

Funding sources have changed during the period of the DSS: IRD and United Nations Fund for Population Activities between 1962 and 1966; IRD between 1967 and 1983; IRD and the European Economic Community between 1984 and 1986; IRD, the Task Force for Child Survival, and Pasteur Mérieux SV between 1987 and 1997; IRD, to date.

Chapter 27

MATLAB DSS, BANGLADESH

Abdur Razzaque and Peter Kim Streatfield[1]

Site description

Physical geography of the Matlab DSA

Matlab *Upazila* (lower district) is in Chandpur District in Bangladesh. It is located about 55 km southeast of the capital, Dhaka, at latitude 23.38°N and longitude 90.72°E (Figure 27.1). The total DSA is 184 km^2. The climate is subtropical, with three seasons: monsoon, cool–dry, and hot–dry. The average annual rainfall of 2159 mm is concentrated in the monsoon season, extending from June through September. Being flat and low lying, the DSA is subject to annual flooding by the many canals and rivers that cross the region.

Figure 27.1. Location of the Matlab DSS site, Bangladesh (monitored population, 215 000).

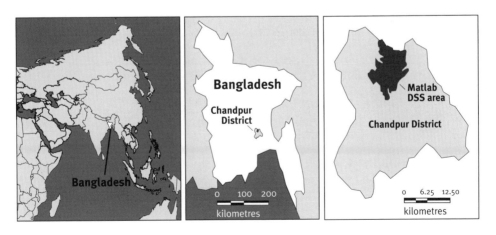

1 International Centre for Diarrhoeal Disease Research, Bangladesh.

Population characteristics of the Matlab DSA

In the 1996 census, 212 328 individuals were counted, yielding a population density of about 1100 individuals/km^2 residing in 142 villages. The area is typical of many rural and riverine-delta areas of Bangladesh. Almost 90% of the population are Muslim, and the great majority of the remainder are Hindu. All of them speak Bangla. The principal economic activities are agriculture and fishing, and the latter is primarily a Hindu occupation. In 1974, the illiterate constituted 65% in the treatment area and 69% in the comparison area, decreasing to 40% in 1996. For most dwellings, roof material is tin (95%), and in 30% of dwellings tin is also used for wall material. Use of tube wells for drinking water is common (95%), but use of this water for cooking and bathing is negligible (2–6%). Sanitary-latrine use is low (20%), and most people use an open latrine. Travel within Matlab *Upazila* and between the villages is mostly by foot, rickshaw, or country boats, particularly during the monsoon season. In 1974, those with a hurricane lamp constituted 60% of households, a figure that increased to about 90% in 1996, and ownership of a radio increased from 10% to 40% during the same period. The Matlab *Upazila* has two hospitals, located in the headquarters. In addition, the government runs about 10 union-level (lower *Upazila*) health centres, and the International Centre for Diarrhoeal Disease Research, Bangladesh (ICDDR,B), runs four health centres in the treatment area. Immunization coverage is more than 90% in the treatment area but about 50% in the comparison area. Matlab is considered an endemic cholera zone.

Matlab DSS procedures

Introduction to the Matlab DSS site

The fundamental mission of ICDDR,B is to develop and disseminate solutions to major world health and population problems, with emphasis on simple and cost-effective prevention and management.

The objectives of the project are as follows:

- To provide a small-area registration system that is suitable for assessing the effectiveness, safety, and acceptability of maternal and child-health and family-planning interventions;

- To undertake research on diarrheal diseases and the measurement of fertility and mortality and their determinants; and

- To develop a demographic field site for training program planners, researchers, and implementors.

The DSS has been operating in Matlab since 1966. At the onset, 132 villages were included in the system, and 101 villages were added in 1968. The *dais* (traditional birth attendants, mostly illiterate elderly women) were responsible for detecting the event, through weekly household visits. The health assistant (HA), accompanied by the *dai*, visited the household every 6 weeks to record the events on a standard registration form. A major modification in the field structure and program activities occurred in October 1977, when the DSA contracted: 84 villages (120 000 population) were no longer included, but 149 villages (173 443 population) were retained. The family-planning and health-services project was then launched in 70 villages (treatment area), covering a population of 88 925; the remaining 79 villages, with a population of 84 518, were considered the comparison area. At the introduction of the program, all *dais* of the treatment and comparison areas were replaced by female community-health workers (CHWs with at least seventh grade education) recruited from the same locality. The 1982 census covered the entire population of 149 villages, but the project was reduced to 142 villages in 1993, after river erosion forced 7 villages out of the comparison area. However, most of these people resettled in nearby villages of the DSA.

The surveillance system covers all households of the DSS villages. A typical village consists of several *baris* (groups of houses around a central courtyard), which function as the economic and social unit. Data are collected only from "regular residents," individuals residing in the DSA permanently or continuously for at least 6 months. Cause-of-death data have been collected since the beginning of the project and have improved over time.

Births, deaths, and migrations (in- and out-) have been recorded since 1966, but enumeration of marital unions and dissolution began only in 1975. The recording of intervillage movement has continued since the 1982 census, but the recording of split households and changes in household head began only after the 1993 census.

Health data have gradually been collected in the treatment area since 1977, and collection has recently been introduced in the comparison area, using what is known as the record-keeping system (RKS). The health data cover currently married women of reproductive age (reproductive status, contraception, tetanus, etc.) and children <5 years old (immunization, diarrhea, acute lower respiratory infection, breastfeeding, etc.). GIS data have been collected in the DSA since 1993. Since July 1998 the three projects (DSS, RKS, and GIS) have been brought under a single administration and termed the health and demographic surveillance system (HDSS). The system also collects socioeconomic data, and such data are available for 1974, 1982, and 1996.

Matlab DSS data collection and processing

Field procedures

INITIAL CENSUS AND REGULAR UPDATE ROUNDS — The DSS has been in operation in Matlab since the initial census of 1966.

Until very recently (end of 1998 in the comparison area and end of 1999 in the treatment area), CHWs detected DSS events through monthly household visits. HAs, accompanied by the CHWs (every 6 weeks), were responsible for recording the events on the standard registration form, and senior health assistants (SHAs) were the supervisors. Today, CHWs not only detect DSS events, they also record the events on standard registration forms through monthly household visits. Field research assistants (FRAs, previously HAs) are the supervisors, and the tier of SHAs has been abolished. In contrast, CHWs have collected the RKS data since its inception in 1977 in the treatment area and February 2000 in the comparison area. CHW household coverage differs in the two areas: 20–25 households are visited each day in the treatment area; and 50–55 households each day, in the comparison area. This difference in coverage is due to the fact that the CHWs provide health services to mothers and children <5 years old in the treatment area through a fixed-site clinic, whereas in the comparison area they simply advise the client to go to the government health facility. Until the 1982 census, a single ID number was used for each individual. However, at the time of the 1982 census, a dual-numbering system (current and registration) was introduced. The current ID number identifies the current location (village 1–3, household 4–7, and individual 8–9), and the registration number (phase 1–1, village 2–4, household 5–8, and individual 9–10) is permanent for each individual. The population is updated through the monthly rounds using the 1982 census as a base population. However, periodic censuses are conducted mainly to check the accuracy of the database and collect socioeconomic data.

CONTINUOUS SURVEILLANCE — During the household visit, a CHW inquires about demographic events that have occurred since the last visit and updates or collects health data for the RKS. The respondent can be any responsible member of the household for all DSS events other than pregnancy outcome. Pregnancy- and health-related information is usually collected from the mother. Special forms are used to record DSS data, and record-keeping books (RKBs) are used to record health data. Since 1986 a modified version of the ICD-9 has been introduced to code the cause of death on verbal-autopsy forms. The emphasis is on symptoms and events preceding death. Coding, which was previously done by the fieldworkers, is now done by a medical assistant. This person also makes independent field visits (10–15% of cases) where needed to clarify cause of death.

SUPERVISION AND QUALITY CONTROL — In the field, 91 CHWs (treatment area: 57 regular and 4 for leave vacancy; comparison area: 24 regular and 6 for leave vacancy) collect data through monthly household visits, supervised by 12 FRAs. The field manager and three assistants supervise overall field activities. Until very recently, staff members who worked within the system did field-level data-quality checks. However, a quality-control team has formed, comprising two FRAs. The Dhaka HDSS staff supervise the quality-control work under the head of the Matlab Health and Research Programme. The quality-control staff make random household visits to assess data quality.

Data management

CHWs bring completed event forms fortnightly to the subcentre, where they are checked by the FRAs. The FRAs then take the filled-in forms to the Matlab office, where they are used to update census volumes and then passed on to the computer unit for data entry. Until very recently, RKBs of the treatment area were brought to a subcentre meeting, where the data were first copied to a coding sheet by coders and then brought to the computer unit at the Matlab office. However, RKS data from the treatment and comparison areas are now being entered directly from the RKB to the computer at the Matlab office. Oracle database-management software has been used to develop data entry and database maintenance, using a Windows NT (network) environment. The Matlab HDSS office has eight data-entry technicians and two programing staff, but the Dhaka office has three programing and five data-management staff. The Dhaka office does data processing and database maintenance, using Developer 2000 in an Oracle environment and with a Unix operating system. Client tools of Oracle, Developer-2000, Microsoft Access, Excel, and SPSS are used to access data from the Oracle database. Microsoft Excel and Word are used for reporting.

Data entry at Matlab includes range and consistency checks in interactive mode. Validation of current ID and registration numbers, date of birth, sex, and out-migration status is done during entry. Subsequently, when data are loaded into the master database, consistency checks with the longitudinal data are done in Dhaka.

Yearly reports are regularly published and circulated among interested scientists, researchers, policy planners, and program managers within and outside the country. HDSS data are used extensively in papers prepared for scientific journals. The project also provides a sampling frame for all studies undertaken in the Matlab area.

Matlab DSS basic outputs

Demographic indicators

According to the *de jure* definition, 212 328 individuals were included in the 1996 census — 104 718 males and 107 610 females — yielding a sex ratio of 97.3. The age-specific fertility rates and total fertility rate of the treatment and comparison areas are shown in Table 27.1. The age pyramids of the population for the treatment and comparison areas both reflect a fertility transition well under way, with fewer children <5 years old than 5–9 years old (Figures 27.2 and 27.3). In fact, 2.4% of the population is <1 year old; 12%, <5 years old; 26%, 5–14 years old; 57.4%, 15–64 years old; and 4.5%, ≥65 years old. The population of both areas is young: 36% is <15 years old in the treatment area, compared with 40% in the comparison area. The population 15–49 years old constitutes 49% in the treatment area, compared with 46% in the comparison area. In 1974, in the treatment area, household size was 5.9, declining to 5.1 in 1996, and the figures in the comparison area were 5.8 and 5.5, respectively. About 80% of the households are headed by a male, and the remainder by a female. Nearly two-thirds of the male- and female-headed households belong to two generations (64% versus 58%).

Table 27.1. Age-specific fertility rates and total fertility rates in the treatment and comparison areas of the Matlab DSS site, Bangladesh, 1998.

Age (years)	Treatment area			Comparison area		
	Births	Women	Rate	Births	Women	Rate
15–19	302	5 415	55.8	334	5 438	61.4
20–24	903	5 123	176.3	933	4 470	208.7
25–29	796	4 497	177.0	852	4 037	211.0
30–34	584	4 462	130.9	565	3 885	145.4
35–39	198	3 850	51.4	268	3 360	79.8
40–44	38	2 827	13.4	41	2 551	16.1
45–49	6	2 178	2.8	5	1 904	2.6
All ages	2 827	28 352	99.7	2 998	25 645	116.9
TFR		3 038			3 625	

Note: TFR, total fertility rate.

Figure 27.2 Population pyramid for person–years observed in the treatment area of the Matlab DSS site, Bangladesh, 1998.

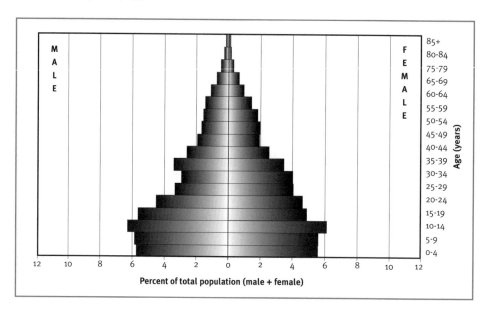

Figure 27.3. Population pyramid for person–years observed in the comparison area of the Matlab DSS site, Bangaldesh, 1998.

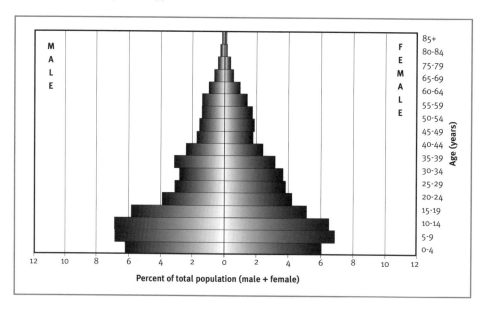

In 1988 and 1998, the crude death rate (per 1000 population) in the treatment area was higher for males than for females and has declined from 9.2 to 7.3 for males and 8.3 to 6.7 for females. In 1988, mortality in children <1 year old was found to be similar for males and females but in 1998 was higher for females than males (Table 27.2). The rate has declined from 81.6 to 45.6 for males and from 80.0 to 55.5 for females. A significant decline in mortality has also been observed among children 1–4 years old (from 6.0 to 4.0 for males and from 9.3 to 5.3 for females). In 1988, females had higher mortality than males. However, the difference has been small in recent years. A decline in mortality rate has been observed in all other age categories, but the magnitude of decline was small in most cases. Among those 15–39 years old, female mortality has usually been higher than that for males, but the reverse occurs among those 40–64 years old.

The level of mortality is higher in the comparison than in the treatment area; however, the pattern was similar in the two areas, with a few exceptions. In 1988, for example, crude death rate in the comparison area was higher for females than for males, and in both the periods (1988 and 1998) mortality in children <1 year old was found to be higher for females than for males (Table 27.3). The crude death rate has declined from 10.7 to 8.7 for males and from 11.3 to 7.5 for females. Mortality in children <1 year old has declined from 92.5 to 62.6 for males and from 100.5 to 78.2 for females. A significant decline in mortality rate has also been observed in those 1–4 years old, from 11.2 to 6.0 for males and from 17.7 to 5.5 for females. A decline in mortality rate has been observed in all other age categories, but the magnitude of decline was again small in most cases. In those 15–39 years old, female mortality was usually higher than male mortality, but this was reversed in those 40–64 years old. In both areas and in both periods, however, age-standardized death rates were found to be exactly similar to the crude death rate.

During the study period, a significant decline in mortality has been observed in both the treatment and the comparison areas,[2] with the decline marked more in those <5 years old than in those in other age groups. However, the level of mortality was higher in the comparison area than in the treatment area. ICDDR,B has been maintaining a health-intervention program in the treatment area[3] that targets mothers and children <5 years old, and it has been successful in reducing mortality of this vulnerable group. The decline in mortality in the comparison area, as well as in the other parts of Bangladesh, is mainly due to the government's commitment to improving the health status of the population and the country's acceptance of the Alma Ata declaration of primary health care for all. To achieve this goal, the government of Bangladesh has established various institutional-level service facilities[4] since the 1980s.

The overall crude death rate has been higher for males than females in both the areas, except in 1988 in the comparison area. Higher life expectancy for females than males was first observed in this population in the mid-1980s, and the pattern has been maintained, with some fluctuations. Such a mortality pattern is an indication of overall socioeconomic improvement and reduction of sex discrimination.

In 1988, among children <1 or 1–4 years old, mortality was usually higher for girls than for boys, but in 1998 this difference disappeared among children 1–4 years old. Higher mortality for boys than girls <1 year old (neonatal period) is mainly due to biological factors, whereas for children 1–4 years old it is mainly due to behavioural factors. However, with the decline in mortality, girls benefited more than boys in term of survival.

---

2 These two areas have similar socioeconomic conditions, but they differ in access to health services. Theoretically, government health programs exist in both areas, but in practice they mainly operate in the comparison area.

3 CHWs offer a choice of methods for contraception, motivate and counsel mothers on family planning, monitor and manage adverse effects, administer expanded immunization-program vaccines, provide acute respiratory-infection management, promote oral rehydration, distribute vitamin-A capsules, provide nutritional education, refer malnourished children, and distribute safe-delivery kits and iron tablets to pregnant women. They refer severely sick mothers or children to the subcentre or clinic.

4 These include maternal and child-welfare centres in urban and suburban areas, the *Upazila* health complex at the *Upazila* level, and family-welfare centres at the union level. The government has also established health-service facilities at rural dispensaries and satellite clinics. In addition, both oral-rehydration therapy for diarrhea management and immunization against the six major childhood diseases are actively promoted.

Table 27.2. Age- and sex-specific mortality in the treatment area of the Matlab DSS site, Bangladesh, 1998.

Age (years)	Death s ($_nD_x$) Male	Death s ($_nD_x$) Female	Person–years observed ($_nPY_x$) Male	Person–years observed ($_nPY_x$) Female
<1	64	79	1308	1268
1–4	20	26	4973	4912
5–9	9	3	6397	6211
10–14	4	6	6870	6784
15–19	5	4	6166	5415
20–24	3	7	4908	5123
25–29	2	4	3614	4497
30–34	4	12	3172	4462
35–39	4	8	3675	3850
40–44	12	7	2779	2827
45–49	11	6	2084	2178
50–54	20	12	1789	2213
55–59	34	23	1678	2041
60–64	39	25	1557	1608
65–69	41	42	1166	1079
70–74	39	37	761	735
75–79	33	38	454	374
80–84	26	16	247	170
≥85	22	17	135	93
Births	2827			
CDR	6.97			
CBR	25.80			
CRNI	18.83			

Note: CBR, crude birth rate (actual number of births per 1000 population); CDR, crude death rate (actual number of deaths per 1000 population); CRNI, crude rate of natural increase (CBR minus CDR per 100; does not take into account migration); $_nD_x$, observed deaths between ages x and $x+n$; $_nPY_x$, observed person–years between ages x and $x+n$.

Table 27.3. Age- and sex-specific mortality in the comparison area of the Matlab DSS site, Bangladesh, 1998.

Age (years)	Death s ($_nD_x$) Male	Death s ($_nD_x$) Female	Person–years observed ($_nPY_x$) Male	Person–years observed ($_nPY_x$) Female
<1	98	112	1420	1323
1–4	31	28	5155	5101
5–9	9	5	7274	7268
10–14	9	7	7295	6915
15–19	7	4	6146	5438
20–24	3	10	4095	4470
25–29	5	4	3243	4037
30–34	4	9	2949	3885
35–39	12	6	3279	3360
40–44	11	9	2506	2551
45–49	6	3	1796	1904
50–54	14	15	1613	1982
55–59	28	13	1476	1842
60–64	43	26	1442	1512
65–69	44	28	1016	1038
70–74	36	36	647	595
75–79	44	36	406	388
80–84	25	28	190	144
≥85	24	25	113	86
Births	2998			
CDR	8.09			
CBR	28.31			
CRNI	20.22			

Note: CBR, crude birth rate (actual number of births per 1000 population); CDR, crude death rate (actual number of deaths per 1000 population); CRNI, crude rate of natural increase (CBR minus CDR per 100; does not take into account migration); $_nD_x$, observed deaths between ages x and $x+n$; $_nPY_x$, observed person–years between ages x and $x+n$.

Acknowledgments

The Department for International Development in the United Kingdom has supported the project since 1992. Partial support has also come from ICDDR,B's core fund. ICDDR,B is supported by countries and agencies that share its concern for the health problems of developing countries. Current donors include

- The aid agencies of Australia, Bangladesh, Belgium, Canada, China, Germany, Japan, the Netherlands, Norway, Republic of Korea, Saudi Arabia, Sweden, Switzerland, the United Kingdom, and the United States;

- International organizations, including the Arab Gulf Fund, Asian Development Bank, European Union, International Atomic Energy Centre, United Nations Children's Fund, United Nations Development Programme, United Nations Population Fund, and World Health Organization;

- Private foundations, including Child Health Foundation, Ford Foundation, Population Council, Rockefeller Foundation, and the Sasakawa Foundation; and

- Private organizations, including the American Express Bank, Bayer AG, CARE, Family Health International, Helen Keller International, Johns Hopkins University, Procter and Gamble, RAND Corporation, SANDOZ, Swiss Red Cross, and the University of California at Davis.

Chapter 28

ORP DSS, BANGLADESH

ABM Khorshed Alam Mozumder and Mian Bazle Hussain[1]

Site description

Physical geography of the ORP DSA

The Operations Research Project (ORP) DSS has field sites in four parts of Bangladesh (Figure 28.1). Two of the three rural ORP DSAs, Mirsarai and Patiya, are in Chittagong Division, southeast Bangladesh; the other rural site, Abhoynagar, is in Khulna Division, southwest Bangladesh. The only urban ORP DSS site is in Dhaka. The ORP DSS rural sites cover 1864 km^2, and the urban site covers 46 km^2.

Figure 28.1. Location of the ORP DSS sites, Bangladesh (monitored population, 127 000).

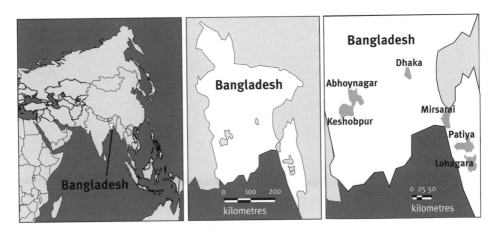

---

1 Centre for Health and Population Research, International Centre for Diarrhoeal Disease Research, Dhaka, Bangladesh.

Population characteristics of the ORP DSA

The majority of the population is Muslim (86%), followed by Hindu (13%), and the rest is Buddhist and Christian. One-third of males and more than two-thirds of females >6 years old have no education. Agriculture is the most important sector of the nation's economy. Cultivation is the primary occupation of people in the rural sample area. More than 80% of the women are housewives. In the urban ORP DSA, women head about 13% of households. Demolition of the slums in the urban setting by the City Corporation affects the study population from time to time.

The ORP rural areas have 1067 individuals/km^2, and the ORP urban area has 32 500/km^2. The average household size is 5.4. Currently married women of reproductive age (CMWRA) constitute 18% of the total population; and children <5 years old, 11.6%. Variations in population and family size were also distinct among the three rural and one urban ORP DSS site.

ORP DSS procedures

Introduction to the ORP DSS site

In 1997, ORP was set up as a follow-up to the Maternal Child Health and Family Planning (MCH–FP) extension projects (rural and urban) to undertake operations research for the entire National Integrated Population and Health Program, funded by the United States Agency for International Development (USAID) in Bangladesh. The MCH–FP extension projects set up the DSS, which in 1982 was known as the sample registration system. In 1997, both rural and urban DSS sites were merged to form the ORP DSS. The total number of households covered in the ORP DSS is 23 624, with a total population of 126 747 in 1999. The DSS has operated in Abhoynagar since 1982, Mirsarai since 1995, Patiya since 1998, and Dhaka since 1995.

The objectives of the ORP are

- To design and test efficient, effective, and sustainable health and family-planning service-delivery systems in the public and nongovernmental organization sectors;

- To monitor the progress of field tests and interventions;

- To provide feedback to the project management;

- To generate basic data; and

- To review and recommend changes affecting health and population policy.

ORP DSS data collection and processing

Field procedures

INITIAL CENSUS — The project adopted different sampling designs for the rural and urban settings. For rural areas, the design was a stratified two-stage sampling; initially, unions (administrative subunits in Bangladesh, with a population of about 20 000–30 000) were stratified, and then they were randomly selected from each stratum. Households served as the second-stage sampling units. A systematic random sampling technique was applied to select the sample households. In the urban area, a cluster sampling design was followed. All households, ranging between 40 and 50 of a selected cluster, were included in the ORP DSS. Among sample households, an enumeration was carried out to identify all household members, collect basic socioeconomic and demographic information about each, and assign a unique ID number to each individual in the DSS population. A separate in-depth baseline (knowledge, attitude, and practice) survey augmented existing data on each household.

REGULAR UPDATE ROUNDS — One female interviewer visits each household at regular 90-day intervals to collect data on demographic and programatic events. Such events include pregnancy termination, deaths, in- and out-migration, marital-status change, use of family-planning method, and immunization status of children and women. Incidence of acute respiratory infection (ARI) and diarrhea are also updated in each round. The interviews are carried out, with reproductive-aged female members of the household being the respondents of choice. One interviewer is assigned 15–20 households/day, covering an average of 800–900 households during the typical 90-day round. Currently, a total of 77 staff members conduct data processing and field interviews in 23 624 households. Interviews are conducted in households listed in the household-record book (HRB). The information is obtained for usual members or residents of the household, those who have lived (or intended to live) at the place of enumeration for a period of 2 months or more of the last 3 months (that is, the "reference period"). All information is recorded in the HRB, not on a form. The interviewers return the HRB to the computer section of the field on a weekly basis.

In addition to recording the mortality data in the HRB, interviewers also complete a separate death form for each death, in which detailed information is recorded (verbal autopsy) on symptoms before the death. This death form is sent to a qualified doctor for an appropriate diagnosis code, and thereafter for computer entry.

SUPERVISION AND QUALITY ASSURANCE — All interviewers receive 2 weeks of training before commencing interviews. They are also provided with an instruction manual detailing the interview proceedings. Each interviewer checks his or her work for completeness and accuracy before submitting it to the supervisor. Errors and inconsistencies are returned to the field for correction. Checking the "linkability of events" — the logical consistency of each event with the past household history — is most important. Checking identifies births where no mother is present, deaths of nonresidents, marriages of nonresidents, in-migrants who are already present, out-migrants who are nonresidents, and any ID code that does not match a corresponding individual.

To ensure maximum reliability and validity of data, an intensive but simple supervision procedure is adopted. This supervision procedure includes the following measures:

- *Supervised interviews* — Periodically, interviewers are observed by the supervisor while performing their field interviews. Supervisors assist them with any problems they have with the system and evaluate their understanding of the concepts and procedures.

- *Spot check* — In addition, supervisors make surprise visits to all teams in the field 1 day a week to examine their work, behaviour with the respondents, interview techniques, and ability to record information. The supervisor immediately explains and assists with any identified mistakes. At least 5% of interviews are spot-checked by the supervisor.

- *Reinterviews* — Supervisors conduct repeat interviews with some of the same households previously interviewed. Supervisors compare reinterview responses with those collected by interviewers, identify differences, and try to determine reasons for the differences. The reinterview also verifies that the correct sample of households was visited and determines the accuracy of events reported. Five percent of the households are randomly selected for reinterview in each 90-day round. Interviewers do not know beforehand which households are included for reinterview. Errors are discussed, and appropriate concepts and procedures are reviewed at monthly staff meetings.

- *Editing in the field office* — Editing and coding are done in the field office. Problems identified during editing are communicated to the supervisor, and the respective interviewers are asked to solve the problem. This may require going back to the household to collect the correct data. Editing and coding errors are discussed at the monthly staff meetings to prevent their recurrence.

- *Computer feedback* — Computer checks on ranges and consistencies produce error messages. Interviewers and field supervisors correct the errors.

Data management

Information from the HRB is entered into personal computers at the respective field sites. A personal computer relational database-management system in Rbase has been developed to update collected data and generate the needed tabulation. This system is basically an online, interactive database information system. Data consistency and integrity are processed to maintain the quality of data. Data-processing software check the logical integrity of an event against all available data on each sample individual and household. Ranges and logical checks have been incorporated into the software. Error reports containing identification of household members are given to interviewers to check with the respective household. Eight databases are maintained to store, process, and update data.

Standard reports of contraceptive-prevalence rates and worker–client-contact rates are prepared quarterly, and demographic rates are produced annually. The database design includes computerizing the interview date and date of movement of individual members into or out of households. This permits immediate calculation of the population at risk of vital events at any given point in time. Report preparation occurs routinely throughout the year. More important, however, are the special intervention-based studies that use ORP demographic data. Work files are extracted from the database for microlevel analysis of the data.

ORP DSS basic output

Demographic indicators

ORP DSS collects and generates information on demographic and programmatic variables and their covariates. Demographic indicators include pregnancy outcomes (type, date, attendant, place, and last menstruation date), death (date, place, and consultation before death), and marital-status change (type and date). The system also records information on the change of relationship to head of household. Programmatic indicators include use of family-planning method, type of method, source of family-planning method, reason for discontinuation or switching, and contact of CMWRA with the service provider at the doorstep and the static clinic. CMWRA's knowledge and use of static clinics are recorded. The ORP DSS also records information on immunization status by type and age of children. The ORP DSS also generates tetanus-toxoid information and the incidence of ARI and diarrhea among children <5 years old within 7 days of the interview date.

Table 28.1 shows age- and sex-specific all-cause mortality at the ORP DSS sites. Figure 28.2 is a population pyramid illustrating the age structure of the population at the sites.

Table 28.1. Age- and sex-specific mortality at the ORP DSS sites, Bangladesh, 1999.

Age (years)	Deaths ($_nD_x$) Male	Deaths ($_nD_x$) Female	Person–years observed ($_nPY_x$) Male	Person–years observed ($_nPY_x$) Female
<1	108	82	1380	1391
1–4	27	36	5748	5682
5–9	7	7	7558	7228
10–14	4	5	8094	7679
15–19	7	15	6938	7184
20–24	9	11	4826	5617
25–29	9	12	4090	4749
30–34	5	6	3691	4091
35–39	3	7	3609	3703
40–44	11	8	3153	2895
45–49	18	9	2576	2289
50–54	19	12	1891	1635
55–59	27	16	1425	1460
60–64	40	28	1236	1262
65–69	153	122	2354	2307
Births	2913			
CDR	7.00			
CBR	24.70			
CRNI	17.74			

Note: CBR, crude birth rate (actual number of births per 1000 population); CDR, crude death rate (actual number of deaths per 1000 population); CRNI, crude rate of natural increase (CBR minus CDR per 100; does not take into account migration); $_nD_x$, observed deaths between ages x and $x+n$; $_nPY_x$, observed person–years between ages x and $x+n$.

Figure 28.2. Population pyramid for person–years observed at the ORP DSS sites, Bangladesh, 1999.

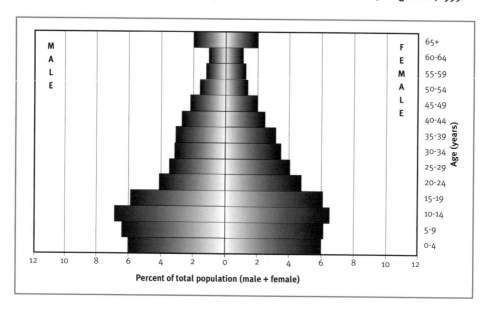

Percent of total population (male + female)

Acknowledgments

ORP — a project of the International Centre for Diarrhoeal Disease Research, Bangladesh (ICDDR,B), Centre for Health and Population Research — works in collaboration with the Ministry of Health and Family Welfare of the Government of the People's Republic of Bangladesh and is supported by USAID (under Cooperative Agreement No. 388-A-00-97-00032-00 with the ICDDR,B).

The Centre is supported by the following countries, donor agencies, and others who share its concern for the health and population problems of developing countries:

- *Aid agencies* — Governments of Australia, Bangladesh, Belgium, Canada, European Union, Japan, the Netherlands, Norway, Saudi Arabia, Sri Lanka, Sweden, Switzerland, the United Kingdom, and the United States;

- *UN agencies* — International Atomic Energy Agency, Joint United Nations Programme on HIV–AIDS, United Nations Children's Fund, and World Health Organization;

- *International organizations* — CARE Bangladesh, International Center for Research on Women, International Development Research Centre, Swiss Red Cross, and World Bank;

- *Foundations* — Ford Foundation, George Mason Foundation, Novartis Foundation, Rockefeller Foundation, and Thrasher Research Foundation;

- *Medical-research organizations* — Karolinska Institute, National Institutes of Health, New England Medical Center, National Vaccine Programme Office, Northfield Laboratories, Procter and Gamble, Rhone-Poulenc Rorer, and Walter Reed Army Institute for Research–USA;

- *Universities* — Johns Hopkins University, London School of Hygiene and Tropical Medicine, University of Alabama at Birmingham, University of California at Davis, University of Göteborg, University of Maryland, University of Newcastle, University of Pennsylvania, and University of Virginia; and

- *Others* — Arab Gulf Fund, Futures Group, International Oil Companies (Cairn Energy PLC, Occidental, Shell, and Unocal), John Snow Inc., Pathfinder, UCB Osmotics Ltd, and Wander AG.

Chapter 29

FILABAVI DSS, VIET NAM

*Nguyen Hoang Long,[1] Tran Thanh Do,[2] Phan Hong Van,[3] Tran Tuan Anh,[3]
and Nguyen Thi Kim Chuc[3,4]*

Site description

Physical geography of the FilaBavi DSA

FilaBavi is in Bavi District of Ha Tay Province in northern Viet Nam (Figure 29.1). The
site is 60 km west of Hanoi, at latitude 21.1°N and longitude 105.4°E. The climate is
temperate, with an average temperature of 23°C. The district covers 410 km[2] and has
lowland, highland, and mountainous areas. Altitude ranges from 20 to 1297 m above
sea level.

Figure 29.1. Location of the FilaBavi DSS site, Viet Nam (monitored population, 52 000).

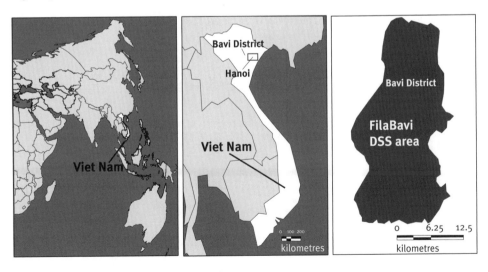

1 Health Policy Unit, Ministry of Health, Viet Nam.
2 National Institute of Nutrition, Viet Nam.
3 Health Strategy and Policy Institute, Viet Nam.
4 Hanoi Medical University, Viet Nam.

Population characteristics of the FilaBavi DSA

The whole population of Bavi District is 240 000, and the population under surveil-lance is 51 024 (11 089 households), about 21% of the district's population. The main ethnic group is the Kinh tribe, constituting 91% of the population, living mainly in lowland and midland areas. Dao people live at the foot of Bavi Mountain, and Muong people live in some communes surrounding the foot of Bavi Mountain. The predomi-nant religion is Buddhism, with 2.5% Roman Catholic. The main language is Kinh. Occupations are largely agricultural production and livestock breeding. The average annual income in 1996 was 290 kg rice (about 600 000 Vietnamese dong [VND]) (in 2001, 14618 VND = 1 United States dollar [USD]). Sixty-nine percent of the adult pop-ulation has completed primary school; 21%, secondary level; 9%, high school; and 0.5%, higher education. Illiteracy, reported at only 0.4% of the population >15 years old, varies among communes (0.1–1.1%). Women and men have equal rights. Although the government and the United Nations Children's Fund have improved water sources, sanitation remains a common problem in Viet Nam. Most of the com-munes are accessible by car.

Bavi District has 32 commune health stations (CHSs), one in each commune. Twenty-one of these CHSs are under the direct supervision of the Bavi District Health Centre, and three intercommunal polyclinics supervise and support the 11 others. The private sector is weak in Bavi District and its influence on health care is minimal: the district has only three legally licenced private pharmacies and a few private practition-ers. Son Da commune is closest to the higher level health care (3 km from the poly-clinic and 23 km from the district hospital). Khanh Thuong, Yen Bai, and Van Hoa communes are much farther from the polyclinics, especially Khanh Thuong, which has a rough road, with many hills and mountain passes. All communes are involved in the primary health-care programs, including expanded program of immunization and programs on acute respiratory infections, control of diarrheal diseases, family plan-ning, and antenatal care; 15 communes run the vitamin-A program; and 7 communes have implemented a malaria-control program. Not all communes have implemented goitre control, health education, or communication programs.

FilaBavi DSS procedures

Introduction to the FilaBavi DSS site

The overall objective of the FilaBavi DSS is to develop an epidemiological surveillance system in Bavi to

- Generate basic health data;

- Supply information for health planning;

- Serve as a background and sampling frame for specific studies, especially inter-vention studies; and

- Constitute a setting for epidemiological training of research students.

Specific objectives of the field laboratory are

- To develop an epidemiological surveillance system in a representative sample of the population in Bavi;

- To generate basic health data (for example, on fertility and mortality) for health planning;

- To provide household and individual background data, a sampling frame, and a professional field organization for specific studies to economize on resources and increase cost-effectiveness in research and research training;

- To provide a setting for epidemiological training for Vietnamese and Swedish research students; and

- To serve as an appropriate setting for intervention studies (based on findings generated by the field laboratory) and health-priority discussions with the population and relevant authorities.

In 1997, following a series of studies and the training of Vietnamese research students, the Health System Research Co-operation Programme between Viet Nam and Sweden entered its second phase, supported by the Swedish International Development Co-operation Agency (SIDA) and the Swedish Agency for Research Cooperation with Developing Countries (SAREC). In this phase, research activities have been allocated to a district where an epidemiological field laboratory is being established. Three broad research topics have been selected:

- The functions of the health-care systems (both private and public), including drug distribution and drug use;

- Sexual and reproductive health; and

- Epidemiology of health and health problems in the present rapid transition of Vietnamese society.

In 1998, a group of Vietnamese doctors, epidemiologists, and sociologists made study visits to Jojacarta, Indonesia, and Umeå, Sweden, for protocol development. Two pilot surveys were conducted at the same time, and the field laboratory began functioning in January 1999.

The FilaBavi DSS is coordinated by the Health Strategy and Policy Institute, Hanoi, Viet Nam, and IHCAR, Karolinska Institute, Stockholm, Sweden, in collaboration with Hanoi Medical School, Hanoi, and the Department of Epidemiology and Public Health, Umeå University, Umeå, Sweden. It is funded by SAREC–SIDA.

FilaBavi DSS data collection and processing

Field procedures

INITIAL CENSUS — The sampling unit is a "population unit," or "cluster," based on villages. The whole district has 352 population clusters, with a mean of 146 households each. A sample of 67 clusters (51 024 inhabitants in 11 089 households) was randomly selected in each geographical area (lowland, midland, and highland). The initial census (household baseline survey) was carried out from January to March 1999 and will be repeated every third year. The following information is collected at the household level: housing conditions, water sources, latrine, expenditures, income, agricultural land, access to nearest CHS and hospital, and economic status of the household according to the head of the hamlet. For each household member, information is collected on age, sex, ethnicity, religion, occupation, education, and marital status. Interviewees are the head of the household, normally the husband, or his wife — that is, those who know the socioeconomic status of the household and the health status of household members.

A household is defined as a person or group of people living under one roof and sharing a kitchen for at least 1 month. The exact geographical location of households was identified with GPS equipment, to generate maps of the study population and create a basis for geographic analysis of health and health-services use.

Field data collection is done by 38 professional surveyors and 6 supervisors of the FilaBavi DSS. The project has a central steering committee (7 members), a district steering committee (7 members), a scientific committee (7 members), an implementation office (7 staff), and 30 researchers and research students.

CONTINUOUS SURVEILLANCE — After the initial census, follow-up household surveys have been longitudinally carried out every 3 months. Each survey takes 3 months to complete. During these surveys, demographic and household information is updated. Baseline information has been collected on newly created households in the selected clusters. Closed and vacated households have also been recorded. Individuals in the households, newborn babies, and in- and out-migrants of the selected clusters are followed up on a quarterly basis.

In addition to pregnancy monitoring, the following information is collected in the quarterly follow-up surveys: health status and health-seeking behaviour during the 4 weeks before the interview, marital-status changes (for example, marriage, divorce, separation, widowhood), in- and out-migrations, births, and deaths. Each of these events has a separate and detailed questionnaire. All households in the 67 selected clusters have been surveyed. In almost all cases, interviewees are the people experiencing the event, except, of course, in the case of a death.

FIELD SUPERVISION AND QUALITY CONTROL — Field supervisors conduct spot checks (supervised interviews) on an approximately 5% sample of home visits per cycle. Feedback is given by the field supervisor to the interviewer. Field coordinators and researchers conduct random reinterviews on about 10 household visits each week. FilaBavi office staff review all completed questionnaires before sending them to computer-data typists. A computer validation program automatically detects inconsistencies as the typists enter the data.

Data management

Completed forms are organized in batches of 20 forms each, a batch-control sheet is dated and attached to the stack of forms, and a plastic bag is used to secure the group together.

One data manager and three data-entry clerks conduct data processing on four networked computers. The software used is a custom-designed database in Microsoft Access. A module called Bavi.mdb was developed for the first general baseline survey. Once the data entry and data cleaning were complete, all the basic data were transferred to another module called BaviSurv, and the Bavi module was closed. The BaviSurv module is now in use.

The BaviSurv software offers a built-in series of logical checks and menu-driven procedures. All forms with inconsistencies are automatically detected by the software and returned to field supervisors and surveyors for correction. All inconsistencies are recorded and discussed with fieldworkers and relevant staff, to improve the quality of data collection.

The main database system is updated after each quarterly follow-up survey. Data are regularly extracted at the request of researchers. Data can be exported to other software programs, such as Access, SPSS, EpiInfo, and Stata. Some reports, graphs, and queries are built into the FilaBavi software.

Results are disseminated in a number of ways, including monthly meetings of the FilaBavi office staff; quarterly seminars with FilaBavi staff, fieldworkers, researchers, and authorities of Bavi District Health Centre; annual workshops with collaborating institutions from Viet Nam and abroad; and international scientific publications.

FilaBavi DSS basic outputs

Demographic indicators

The FilaBavi DSA has a population of about 51 000. The age–sex composition of the area is presented in the population pyramid in Figure 29.2. The population structure is as follows: <1 year old, 1.5%; 0–4 years old, 8.3%; 5–14 years old, 22.3%; 15–64 years old, 60.1%; and ≥65 years old, 7.9%. The male–female ratio is 92.5 : 100, and the age-dependency ratio is 72 : 100. The total fertility rate is 1.83 children per woman 15–49 years old. The infant mortality rate is 31.9 per 1000 live births, and the under-five mortality ratio is 35.1 per 1000 live births. Average household size is 4.6. Males are more likely to be heads of households (77%) than females (23%). About 94.4% are literate by age 15, and 0.3% of the population is unemployed.

Table 29.1 shows the age- and sex-specific all-cause mortality at the DSS site.

Figure 29.2. Population pyramid for person–years observed at the FilaBavi DSS site, Viet Nam, 1999.

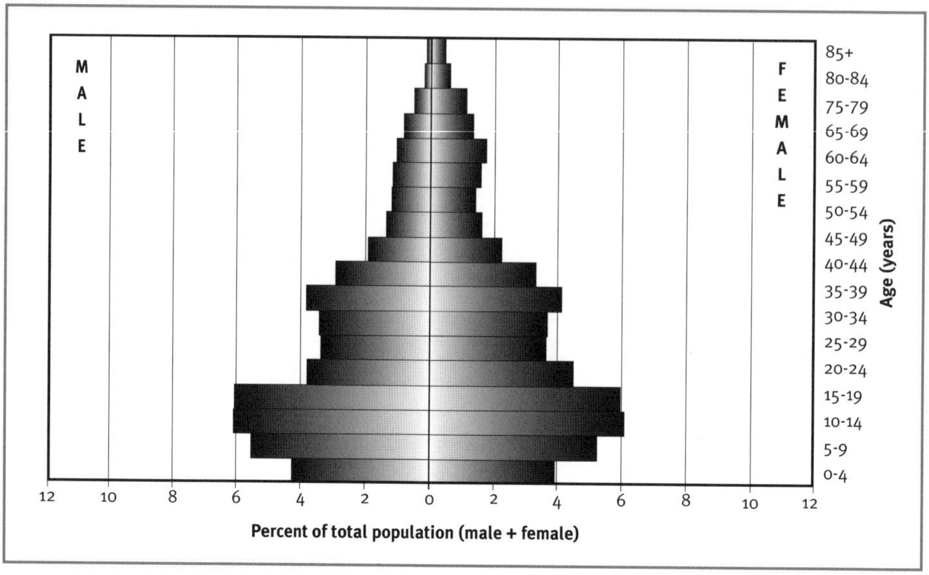

Table 29.1. Age- and sex-specific mortality at the FilaBavi DSS site, Viet Nam, 1999.

Age (years)	Deaths ($_nD_x$)		Person–years observed ($_nPY_x$)	
	Male	Female	Male	Female
<1	13	7	336	299
1–4	2	1	1532	1432
5–9	5	1	2424	2310
10–14	0	1	2671	2674
15–19	1	2	2656	2616
20–24	2	1	1660	1969
25–29	6	0	1476	1602
30–34	0	0	1490	1617
35–39	4	0	1669	1806
40–44	5	3	1285	1445
45–49	3	2	849	975
50–54	2	1	596	694
55–59	4	1	525	613
60–64	5	5	517	690
65–69	15	6	463	755
70–74	20	14	361	573
75–79	11	14	222	479
80–84	6	9	86	257
≥85	12	37	58	183

Note: $_nD_x$, observed deaths between ages x and $x+n$; $_nPY_x$, observed person–years between ages x and $x+n$.

Acknowledgments

SAREC–SIDA has provided a grant to support the FilaBavi DSS and specific studies carried out within the Health Systems Research Programme.

APPENDIX 1

WORKING EXAMPLES OF DSS FORMS

Example 1: DSS Baseline Form (Rufiji DSS)

Page ☐ out of ☐

Date of Interview ☐☐ / ☐☐ / ☐☐

Interviewer ☐☐

Village code ☐☐☐

Name of hamlet ☐☐☐☐☐☐☐☐☐☐☐

Ten cell leader ☐☐☐☐☐☐☐☐☐☐☐☐☐☐☐☐☐☐☐☐☐

Household name ☐☐☐☐☐☐☐☐☐☐☐☐☐☐☐☐☐☐☐☐

Household Number ☐☐☐

Whether sometimes living in farm house (1-Yes, 2=No) ☐

If yes where ☐☐☐☐☐☐☐☐☐☐☐☐☐☐☐☐☐☐☐☐☐

	Name	Sex	Date of birth	Present/ Absent	Mother ID	Father ID	Husband ID	Relationship to household head	Education
			/ /						
			/ /						
			/ /						
			/ /						
			/ /						
			/ /						
			/ /						
			/ /						
			/ /						
			/ /						

NB: If not applicable record *888*

Checked by ☐☐

Date ☐☐ / ☐☐ / ☐☐

Example 2: Household Registration Book (HRB) (Rufiji DSS)

Village: KIA Hamlet: SOKONI			Ten cell leader:						
Shamba 1: KORONGONI			Shamba 2:						
Head ID: KIA000500001	Household Name: I					Household #: 500			
Baseline Interview Date 12/02/99	**Round # 1** **Interview date** ..../.........../.........			**Round # 2** **Interview date** ..../.........../.........			**Round #3** **Interview date** ..../.........../.........		
	Event	Date	Notes	Event	Date	Notes	Event	Date	Notes
Member #: *1* **RLTH** *One* **Perm ID:** *KIA000500001* **Name:** **DoB:** *12/08/65* **Sex:** *M* **Father ID:** *888* **Mother ID:** *888* **Husband ID:** *888* **Education Level:** 7									
Member # *2* **RLTH** *WIF* **Perm ID:** *KIA000500002* **Name:** **DoB** *10/06/70* **Sex:** *F* **Father ID:** *888* **Mother ID:** *888* **Husband ID:** *KIA000500001* **Education Level:** 7									
Member # *3* **RLTH** *CHD* **Perm ID:** *KIA000500003* **Name:** **DoB:** *20/08/90* **Sex:** *F* **Father ID:** *KIA000500001* **Mother ID:** *KIA000500002* **Husband ID:** *888* **Education Level:** 2									

(continued)

Example 2 *(concluded)*

Member # *4* **RLTH:** OTH **Perm ID:** *KIA000500004* **Name:** **DoB:** *14/03/84* **Sex:** M **Father ID:** *888* **Mother ID:** *888* **Husband ID:** *888* **Education Level:** *6*									
Member # **RLTH** **Perm ID** **Name** **DoB** **Sex** **Father ID** **Mother ID** **Husband ID** **Education Level**									
Checked by:									
Date:									

Example 3: Pregnancy Outcome / Birth Form (Rufiji DSS)

Enumerator's initials ☐ ☐

Pregnancy outcome: ☐ ☐ ☐   Date of event ☐ ☐ ☐ ☐ ☐ ☐

(**BIR**=Birth; **ABT**=Abortion; **MIS**=Miscarriage; **STB**=Still birth)

Event reported in Round ☐ ☐

Details of the mother:

Village code: ☐ ☐ ☐

Name of Hamlet: ☐ ☐ ☐ ☐ ☐ ☐ ☐ ☐ ☐ ☐ ☐

Household Number: ☐ ☐ ☐

Mother ID: ☐ ☐ ☐ ☐ ☐ ☐ ☐ ☐ ☐ ☐ ☐

Name: ☐ ☐ ☐ ☐ ☐ ☐ ☐ ☐ ☐ ☐ ☐

Details about child:

Name ☐ ☐ ☐ ☐ ☐ ☐ ☐ ☐ ☐ ☐ ☐

Village code ☐ ☐ ☐   Sex (Male=M, Female=F) ☐

Household Number ☐ ☐ ☐   Relationship with household head: ☐

Child ID: ☐ ☐ ☐   Father ID: ☐ ☐ ☐ ☐ ☐ ☐ ☐ ☐ ☐ ☐

Checked by: ☐ ☐

Example 4: Death Registration Form (Navrongo DSS)

Basic Information

1. Fieldworker: □□□□□□□□□□□□
2. Date of interview: □□□□□□□□□□□□
3. Permanent ID: □□□□□□□□□□□□
4. Name of member: □□□□□□□□□□□□
5. Sex: □□□□□□
6. Date of death: □□□□□□□□□□□□
7. Reported by: □ 1. Field worker (FW); 2. Field Supervisor.

3. Compound Key Informant (CKI)

Certified Correct by: □□□□□□

Example 5: Marital Status Form (Butajira DSS)

Date of interview day month year □□□□□□	Do not write in this column □□□□□□
Interviewer's name	□□
Does this event include a move to a new household No Yes (Fill out a new household form)	
Does this event include a move for male No Yes (Fill out a move form also)	
Does this event include a move for the female No Yes (Fill out a move form also)	
PA for couple Bati (007) Dirama (04B) Dobena (008) Mmeskan (005) Hobe (09B) Wrib (06B) Mjarda (09A) Yeteker (06A) Bido (011) Buta 04 (K04)	

(continued)

Example 5 *(concluded)*

Couples household ☐☐☐☐☐☐	

Event   Marriage (monogamous)   1
             Marriage (polygamous)   2
             Divorce 3	

Date of interview day month year ☐☐☐☐☐☐	☐☐☐☐☐☐
Male's name	
Male's relation (in new household) ☐☐ 01=Head 21=child of head only 02=1st spouse head 22=child of 1st spouse only 03=2nd spouse head 23=child of 2nd spouse only 04=3rd spouse head 24=child of 3rd spouse only 05=4th spouse head 25=child of 4th spouse only 12=child of head and 1st spouse 31=parent of head 13=child of head and 2nd spouse 32=parent of 1st spouse 14=child of head and 3rd spouse 33=parent of 2nd spouse 15=child of head and 4th spouse 34=parent of 3rd spouse 35=parent of 4th spouse	41=other relative of head 42=other relative of 1st spouse 43=other relative of 2nd spouse 44=other relative of 3rd spouse 45=other relative of 4th spouse 46=other relative 47=adopted child 48=non relative *Second family in the household coded 51-98*
Male's marital status (following this event) ☐ 1=married (monogamous) 4=single (never married) 2=married (polygamous) 5=widower 3=divorced	
Female's name	☐☐☐☐☐☐☐
Female's relation ☐☐	
Female's old household ☐☐☐☐☐☐☐	
Female's old PA	☐☐☐
Female's marital status following the event ☐ 1=married (monogamous) 4=single (never married) 2=married (polygamous) 5=widow 3=divorced	

Example 6: VA Form: Deaths of Children from Day 31 to 5 Years (Morogoro DSS)[1]

Time at start		Hr	Mins	AM	PM

Area	Serno		Date of interview		

Interviewer

Village/branch

Name of the ten cell leader

Name of head of household

Relation of the respondent to the deceased (circle):

1-Father	2-Mother		4-Bro/Sister	
6-Other relative			7-No relation	

Lived with the deceased during his/her illness before death?

1-Yes	2-No

Name of deceased

Sex		Date of birth		
1-Male	2-Fem	Day	Month	Year

Place of death (circle)

N-Home	H-Hospital		O-Other place

Date of death	Day	Month	Year

Cause of death according to the respondent? (write exact words as given by the respondent)

History of events leading to death

_____

_____

_____

_____

_____

_____

_____

_____

_____

_____

_____

_____

_____

_____

_____

_____

_____

_____

_____

_____

_____

_____

_____

_____

"Excuse me, I will ask you some questions concerning symptoms that the deceased had/showed when s/he was ill. Some of these questions may not appear to be directly related to his/her death. Please bear with me and answer all the questions. They will help us to get clear picture of all possible symptoms that the deceased had."

(continued)

[1] Also used in Dar es Salaam DSS, Hai DSS, Ifakara DSS, and Rufiji DSS.

Example 6 *(concluded)*

Symptoms		Months Days
1.	Was the child too small at birth?	1-Y 2-N 9-D
2.	Was the child born premature?	1-Y 2-N 9-D
3-F	If yes, how many weeks or months?	—m/—w
4	Was the child breast-feeding?	1-Y 2-N 9-D
5-F	If yes, did the child stop just before death?	1-Y 2-N 9-D
6	Did s/he have fever?	___|___
7-F	Was the fever continuous (1) or on and off (2)?	1- 2- 9-D
8-F	Did s/he have convulsions?	___|___
9	Did s/he have a cough?	
10-F	If yes, was it a dry (1), productive (2) or with blood (3)?	1- 2- 3-9-D
11	Did s/he have breathing difficulties?	___|___
12	Did s/he have fast breathing?	___|___
13	Did s/he have indrawing of chest while breathing?	___|___
14	Did s/he vomit?	___|___
15	Did s/he vomit blood?	___|___
16	Did s/he have a mass in the abdomen?	___|___
17	Did s/he have abdominal distension?	___|___
18-F	Did the distension start suddenly within few days (S) or gradually as the weeks went by (G)?	1- S 2-G 9-D
19	Did s/he have diarrhoea?	___|___
20	Did s/he have bloody diarrhoea?	___|___
21	Did s/he have abdominal pain?	___|___
22	Did s/he have weight loss	___|___
23	Did s/he have mouth sores?	___|___
24	Did s/he look pale?	___|___
25	Did s/he have puffiness of the face?	___|___
26	Did s/he have swelling of the whole body?	___|___
27	Did the eye colour turn to yellow (jaundice)?	___|___
28	Did s/he have ankle swelling?	___|___
29	Did s/he have swelling of joints?	___|___
30	Did s/he have measles?	___|___
31	Did s/he have any other skin disease?	___|___
32	Was s/he unusually sleepy?	___|___
33	Did s/he have loss of consciousness?	___|___
34	Did s/he have paralysis of both legs?	___|___
35	Did s/he develop stiffness of the whole body?	___|___
36	Did s/he have neck pain?	___|___
37	Did s/he have fits?	___|___
38	Did s/he have headache?	___|___
39	Was s/he unable to pass urine?	___|___
40	Did s/he pass blood in urine?	___|___
41	Did a dog bite him/her?	___|___
42	Was s/he bitten by another animal or insect?	___|___
43-F	If yes, what type of animal/insect? (mention the name)	___|___
44	Was s/he injured in a road accident?	___|___
45	Did s/he suffer any other accidental injuries?	___|___
46	Was s/he injured intentionally by someone?	___|___

Health services used by the deceased druing his/her illness in the period leading to death

Health Service	Order	Did s/he get medicine here?		
Was given traditional medicine		1-Y	2-N	9-D
Mother gave modern medicines		1-Y	2-N	9-D
Medicine from family		1-Y	2-N	9-D
Went to traditional healer		1-Y	2-N	9-D
Village health worker		1-Y	2-N	9-D
Government dispensary		1-Y	2-N	9-D
Government Health Centre		1-Y	2-N	9-D
Government Hospital		1-Y	2-N	9-D
Government pharmacy		1-Y	2-N	9-D
Private dispensary		1-Y	2-N	9-D
Private Health Centre		1-Y	2-N	9-D
Private Hospital		1-Y	2-N	9-D
Private pharmacy		1-Y	2-N	9-D

Evidence	Summary of details
Death certificate	Cause of death
Burial permit	Cause of death
Post mortem results	Cause of death
MCH card	
Hospital prescription forms	
Treatment cards	
Hospital discharge forms	Diagnosis
Other hospital documents	
Laboratory/cytology results	
None	

The deceased was a...	
Resident in AMMP area	R
Dead body brought home for burial	M
Home-coming sick	O

Cause of death according to interviewer	
Code	

time at end	Hr	Mins	AM	PM

Example 7: In-migration Form (Navrongo DSS)

Section I

1. Basic Information

1.1 Field Worker: ☐☐

1.2 Date of Interview; ☐☐☐☐☐☐

1.3 Compound ID: ☐☐☐☐☐☐☐☐☐☐☐

1.4 Current compound name: ☐☐☐☐☐☐☐☐☐☐☐

2. Basic information on moved in person

2.1 Current member number: ☐☐☐☐☐☐☐☐☐☐☐

2.2 Permanent ID (if known): ☐☐☐☐☐☐☐☐☐☐☐

2.3 Name: ☐☐☐☐☐☐☐☐☐☐☐

2.4 Date of Migration: ☐☐☐☐☐☐

3. Reason for migration: ☐ 1. Marriage; 2. Farming; 3. Other (Specify)

4. Information on where member has moved from

4.1 Place ☐ 1. Kassena-Nankani District; 2. Within Ghana; 9. Not known

4.2 Has member ever been registered into the NDSS? ☐ 1. Yes; 2. No

(If answer to Q4.2 is YES then answer Q4.3 to Q4.5 otherwise answer Q8)

4.3 Compound name: ☐☐☐☐☐☐☐☐☐☐☐☐☐

4.4 Section: ☐☐☐☐☐☐☐☐☐☐☐

4.5 Village: ☐☐☐☐☐☐☐☐☐☐☐

Section II (To be certified by Field Supervisor in area of Migration)

5. Field supervisor: ☐☐

6. Compound ID: ☐☐☐☐☐☐☐☐☐☐☐☐

7. Permanent ID: ☐☐☐☐☐☐☐☐☐☐☐☐

(Q8 to be completed by the FW if the answer to Q4.2 was NO)

8. Detailed Information on moved in person

8.1 Sex: ☐

8.2 Date of birth: ☐☐☐☐☐☐

8.3 Mother's Permanent ID: ☐☐☐☐☐☐☐☐☐☐☐

8.4 Father's Permanent ID: ☐☐☐☐☐☐☐☐☐☐☐

8.3 Husband's Permanent ID: ☐☐☐☐☐☐☐☐☐☐☐

8.6 Number of years of formal education: ☐☐

NOTE: Thank the respondent and check your forms   Certified correct by: ☐☐

Example 8: Out-migration Form (Navrongo DSS)

Section I

1. Basic Information

1.1 Field Worker: ☐☐

1.2 Date of Interview: ☐☐☐☐☐☐

1.3 Permanent ID: ☐☐☐☐☐☐☐☐☐☐☐☐

1.4 Name: ☐☐☐☐☐☐☐☐☐☐☐

2. Moved away from

2.1 Compound ID: ☐☐☐☐☐☐☐☐☐☐☐

2.2 Date of Migration: ☐☐☐☐☐☐☐☐☐☐☐

3. Information on migration - moved away

3.1 Place ☐ 1. Kassena-Nankani District; 2. Within Ghana; 9. Not known

(If answer to Q3.1 is (1) then answer Q3.2 to Q3.4)

3.2 Compound name: ☐☐☐☐☐☐☐☐☐☐☐☐

3.3 Section: ☐☐☐☐☐☐☐☐☐☐☐☐

3.4 Village: ☐☐☐☐☐☐☐☐☐☐☐

4. Reason for migration: ☐ 1. Marriage; 2. Farming; 3. Other (Specify)

Section II (To be certified by field supervisor in area of migration

5. Field supervisor: ☐☐

6. Compound ID: ☐☐☐☐☐☐☐☐☐☐☐

APPENDIX 2

ACRONYMS AND ABBREVIATIONS

AHPP   Agincourt Health and Population Programme [South Africa]
AIDS   acquired immune deficiency syndrome
AMMP   Adult Morbidity and Mortality Project [Tanzania]
ARI   acute respiratory infection
ASCDR   age-standardized crude death rate
ASDR   age-specific death rate
ASFR   age-specific fertility rate
asl   above sea level

BCG   bacillus Calmette-Guérin
BRHP   Butajira Rural Health Programme [Ethiopia]

CD   Coale and Demeny [model life-table system]
CDC   Centers for Disease Control [United States]
CDR   crude death rate
CHFP   community health and family planning
CHN   community-health nurse
CHW   community-health worker
CHS   commune health station
CISM   Centro de Investigação em Saúde de Manhiça (Manhiça health research
            centre) [Mozambique]
CKI   community key informant
CMWRA   currently married women of reproductive age
CNRFP   Centre national de recherche et de formation sur le paludisme (National
            Center for Research and Training on Malaria) [Burkina Faso]
CRB   compound registration book
CRSN   Centre de recherche en santé de Nouna (Nouna Health Research
            Center) [Burkina Faso]

DANIDA   Danish International Development Agency [Denmark]
DFID   Department for International Development [United Kingdom]
DHS   Demographic and Health Survey
DSA   demographic surveillance area
DSS   demographic surveillance system

FRA   field research assistant

GIS   geographic information system
GPS   global positioning system
GTRP   Gwembe Tonga Research Project [Zambia]

HA   health assistant
HDSS   health and demographic surveillance system
HIV   human immuno-deficiency virus
HRB   household record book, household-registration book
HRS   household-registration system

ICD   International Classification of Diseases [WHO]
ICDDR,B   International Centre for Diarrhoeal Disease Research, Bangladesh
ID   identification
IDRC   International Development Research Centre [Canada]
IMF   International Monetary Fund
INDEPTH   International Network for the continuous Demographic Evaluation of Populations and Their Health in developing countries
IRD   Institut de recherche pour les développement (institute for development research) [formerly ORSTOM]
ITC   insecticide-treated curtain

MCH   maternal and child health
MCH–FP   Maternal Child Health and Family Planning extension projects
MRC   Medical Research Council [South Africa, United Kingdom]
MTCT   mother-to-child transmission

NHRC   Navrongo Health Research Centre [Ghana Ministry of Health]

ORP   Operations Research Project [ICDDR, Bangladesh]

PHC   primary health care

RKB   record-keeping book
RKS   record-keeping system
RSV   respiratory syncytial virus

SAREC   Swedish Agency for Research Cooperation with Developing Countries
SDC   Swiss Agency for Development and Co-operation
SHA   senior health assistant
SIDA   Swedish International Development Co-operation Agency
SNSF   Swiss National Science Foundation
SSA   sub-Saharan Africa
SSD   sum of squared differences
STI   Swiss Tropical Institute

TB   tuberculosis
TBA   traditional birth attendant

TEHIP	Tanzania Essential Health Interventions Project
TFR	total fertility rate
TWG	Technical Working Group [INDEPTH]
UN	United Nations [model life-table system]
USAID	United States Agency for International Development
VA	verbal autopsy
VAST	Vitamin-A supplementation trial [Navrongo, Ghana]
VHW	village health worker
WFS	World Fertility Survey
WHO	World Health Organization

APPENDIX 3

GLOSSARY

Age-dependency ratio The ratio of individuals in the age groups defined as dependent (<15 years old and >64 years old) to individuals in the age group defined as economically productive (15–64 years old) in a population.

Age-specific rate A rate obtained for specific age groups in a population (for example, age-specific fertility rate, death rate, marriage rate).

Age-standardized rate An adjustment of a rate designed to minimize the effects of differences in age composition when comparing rates for different populations. *See also* INDEPTH, Segi, and WHO age standards.

Birth rate The number of live births per 1000 population in a given year. Not to be confused with growth rate.

Census A canvass of a given area, resulting in enumeration of the entire population and often the compilation of other demographic, social, and economic information pertaining to that population at a specific time. *See also* survey.

Child mortality rate The number of deaths in children 1–4 years old per 1000 person–years observed in the population of children who are 1–4 years old.

Childbearing years The reproductive age span of women, assumed for statistical purposes to be 15–44 or 15–49 years.

Closed population A population with no migratory flow either in or out, so that changes in population size occur only through births and deaths.

Cohort A group of people sharing a common temporal demographic experience who are observed through time. For example, the birth cohort of 2000 is the people born in that year. There are also marriage cohorts and so forth.

Cohort analysis The observation of a cohort's demographic behaviour through life or through many periods; for example, observation of the fertility behaviour of the cohort of people born between 1970 and 1980 through their entire childbearing years. *See also* period analysis.

Completed fertility rate The number of children born per woman in a cohort of women by the end of their childbearing years.

Crude birth rate The annual number of births per 1000 population.

Crude death rate The annual number of deaths per 1000 population.

Crude rate The rate of any demographic event computed for an entire population.

Crude rate of natural increase The crude birth rate minus the crude death rate per 100 population (does not take account of migration).

$_nD_x$ The number of people dying between ages x and $x + n$.

Death rate The number of deaths per 1000 population in a given year.

Demographic surveillance system A geographically defined population, under continuous demographic monitoring, with timely production of data on all births, deaths, and migrations.

Demographic transition The historical shift of birth and death rates from high to low levels in a population. The decline of mortality usually precedes the decline in fertility, thus resulting in rapid population growth during the transition period.

Demography The scientific study of human populations, including their sizes, compositions, distributions, densities, growth, and other characteristics, as well as the causes and consequences of changes in these factors.

Doubling time The number of years required for the population of an area to double its present size given the current rate of population growth.

e_0 The life expectancy at birth (this is the number of years a child is expected to live as calculated at the time of birth).

e_x The average remaining lifetime (in years) for a person who survives to the beginning of the indicated age interval.

Geographic information system A computer-assisted information management system for geographically referenced data.

Global positioning system A public-domain system consisting of satellite-based clocks that transmit time signals to personal ground-based receivers that are then able to compute latitude, longitude, and altitude at any location with high accuracy.

INDEPTH age standard for Africa	The standard age distribution proposed by INDEPTH and based on age distributions of African populations monitored at INDEPTH demographic surveillance system sites in Africa. Used for calculating age-standardized death rates for comparative purposes in Africa.
Infant mortality rate	The number of deaths of infants <1 year old per 1000 live births in a given year (more correctly a ratio).
L_x	The number of individuals living at age x from the total number of births (radix) of the life table.
$_nL_x$	The number of person–years lived by the life-table population between ages x and $x + n$. Usually based on a cohort deriving from 100 000 live births.
Life expectancy	The average number of additional years a person could expect to live if the current mortality trends continue for the rest of that person's life. Most commonly cited as life expectancy at birth.
Life table	A tabular display of life expectancy and probability of dying at each age (or age group) for a given population, according to the age-specific death rates prevailing at that time. The life table gives an organized, complete picture of a population's mortality.
Maternal mortality ratio	The number of women who die as a result of pregnancy and childbirth complications per 100 000 live births in a given year.
Migration	The movement of people across a specified boundary for the purpose of establishing a new or semipermanent residence.
Morbidity	The frequency of disease, illness, injuries, and disabilities in a population.
Mortality	The frequency of deaths as a component of population change.
Natality	The frequency of births as a component of population change.
Natural increase (decrease)	The surplus (or deficit) of births over deaths in a population in a given time period.
Neonatal mortality rate	The number of deaths among infants <28 days old in a given year per 1000 live births in that year.
Nuptiality	The frequency, characteristics, and dissolution of marriages in a population.
Perinatal mortality rate	The number of fetal deaths after 28 weeks of pregnancy (late fetal deaths) plus the number of deaths among infants <7 days old per 1000 live births.

Period analysis   The observation of a population for a specific period. Such an analysis takes a "snapshot" of a population in a relatively short period — for example, 1 year. Most rates are derived from period data and are therefore period rates. *See also* cohort analysis.

Population pyramid   A bar chart, arranged vertically, that shows the distribution of a population by age and sex. By convention, the younger ages are at the bottom, with males on the left and females on the right.

Postneonatal mortality rate   The number of deaths of infants between 28 days and 1 year old per 1000 live births in a given year.

Prevalence rate   The number of individuals having a particular condition at a given time per 1000 population at risk.

$_nPY_x$ The number of person–years lived between ages x and x + n.

$_5q_0$ The probability that a child at birth will die before the age of 5.

$_{15}q_{60}$ The probability that a person 60 years old will die before the age of 75.

$_{45}q_{15}$ The probability that a person 15 years old will die before the age of 60.

$_nq_x$ The proportion of individuals in the cohort who are alive at age x but die before reaching the end of the age interval starting with x. This equals the probability of dying between ages x and $x + n$.

Radix   The starting number of population at birth in the cohort of a life table (usually 100 000).

Rate of natural increase   The rate at which a population increases in a given year because of a surplus of births over deaths, expressed as a percentage of the base population. Excludes migration.

Segi age standards   A standard age distribution proposed by Segi and based on the structure of Western populations. Used for calculating age-standardized death rates for comparative purposes.

Sex ratio   The number of males per 100 females in a population.

Survey   A canvass of selected individuals or households in a population, usually used to infer demographic characteristics or trends for a larger segment or all of the population. *See also* census.

T_x The number of person–years that would be lived by a cohort after the beginning of the indicated age in a life table.

Total fertility rate   The average number of children that would be born alive to a woman (or group of women) during her lifetime if she were to pass through her childbearing years conforming to the age-specific fertility rates of a given year. This rate is sometimes used to mean the number of children that women are having today.

Under-five mortality rate
The number of deaths among children <5 years old per 1000 person–years observed in the population of children who are <5 years old.

Under-five mortality ratio
The number of deaths among children from birth to 4 years old per 1000 live births in a given year. This frequently approximates the $_5q_0$ probability of death among children <5 years old more closely than does the under-five mortality rate.

Verbal autopsy
An indirect method often used by demographic surveillance systems to ascertain cause of death. Close associates of the person who died are asked questions about the symptoms, signs, and circumstances leading to death. Sometimes called a bereavement interview.

Vital events
Births, deaths, fetal deaths, marriages, and divorces.

WHO age standards
A standard global age distribution proposed by WHO. Used for calculating age-standardized death rates for comparative purposes.

APPENDIX 4

BIBLIOGRAPHY

Alem, A. 1997. Mental health in rural Ethiopia. Studies on mental distress, suicidal behaviour and use of khat and alcohol. Umeå University, Umeå, Sweden. Medical Dissertation, New Series, No. 532.

Allen, S.J.; Otoo, L.N.; Cooke, G.A.; O'Donnell, A.; Greenwood, B.M. 1990. Sensitivity of *Plasmodium falciparum* to Chlorproguanil in Gambian children after 5 years of continuous prophylaxis. Transactions of the Royal Society of Tropical Medicine and Hygiene, 143(9), 3043–3048.

Andersson, T. 2000. Survival of mothers and their offspring in 19th century Sweden and contemporary rural Ethiopia. Umeå University, Umeå, Sweden. Medical Dissertation, New Series, No. 684.

Armstrong Schellenberg, J.R.M.; Abdulla, S.; Minja, H.; Nathan, R.; Mukasa, O.; Marchant, T.; Mponda, H.; Kikumbih, N.; Lyimo, E.; Manchester, T.; Tanner, M.; Lengeler; C. 1999. KINET: a social marketing programme of treated nets and net treatment for malaria control in Tanzania, with evaluation of child health and long-term survival. Transactions of the Royal Society of Tropical Medicine and Hygiene, 93, 225–231.

Berhane, Y. 2000. Women's health and reproductive outcome in rural Ethiopia. Umeå University, Umeå, Sweden. Medical Dissertation, New Series, No. 674.

Berhane, Y.; Andersson, T.; Wall, S.; Byass, P.; Högberg, U. 2001. Aims, options and outcomes in measuring maternal mortality in developing societies. Acta Obstetrica et Gynaecologica Scandinavica. (In press.)

Berhane, Y.; Wall, S.; Kebede, D.; Emmelin, A.; Enqueselassie; F., Byass, P.; Muhe, L.; Andersson, T.; Deyessa, N.; Gossaye, Y.; Högberg, U.; Alem, A.; Dahlblom, K. 1999. Establishing an epidemiological field laboratory in rural areas — potentials for public health research and interventions: the Butajira Rural Health Programme 1987–1999. Ethiopian Journal of Health Development, 13, Special Issue, 1–47.

Binka, F.; Gyapong, M.; Amidini, A.; Kubadze, F.A.; Phillips, J.F.; Macleod, B.; Kajihara, B. 1994. English language instructions to interviewers for the demographic data component of the Navrongo demographic surveillance system. Navrongo Health Research Centre, Navrongo, Ghana. DSS Documentation Note 2.

Binka, F.N.; Indome, F.; Adjuik, M.; Williams, L. 1996. Applying GIS to assessing the child mortality impact of permethrin impregnated bednets experiment in a rural area of northern Ghana. Ghana Ministry of Health, Navrongo, Ghana.

Binka, F.N.; Nazzar, A.; Phillips, J.F. 1995. The Navrongo Community Health and Family Planning Project. Studies in Family Planning, 26(3), 121–139.

Binka, F.; Ngom, P.; Phillips, J.F.; Adazu, K.F.; MacLeod; B.B. 1999. Assessing population dynamics in a rural African society: the Navrongo demographic surveillance system. Journal of Biosocial Science, 31, 375–391.

Bledsoe, C.H.; Banja, F.; Hill, A.G. 1998. Reproductive mishaps and Western contraception: an African challenge to fertility theory. Population and Development Review, 23(3).

Bledsoe, C.H.; Hill, A.; Langerock, P.; D'Alessandro, M. 1994. Constructing natural fertility: the use of Western contraceptive technologies in rural Gambia. Population and Development Review, 20, 81–113.

Brass, W.; Coale, A.J.; Demeny, P.; Heisel, D.F.; Lorimer, F.; Romaniuk, A.; van de Walle, E. 1973. The demography of tropical Africa. Princeton University Press, Princeton, NJ, USA.

Chiang, Chin Long. 1984. The life table and its applications. Krieger, Malabar, FL, USA.

Clark, S.; Elizabeth, C.; James, L.; Scudder, T. 1995. Ten thousand Tonga: a longitudinal anthropological study from southern Zambia: 1956–1991. Population Studies, 49, 91–109.

Cleland, J.; Scott, C. 1987. The World Fertility Survey: an assessment. Oxford University Press, Oxford, UK.

Coale, A.J.; Demeny, P. 1966. Regional model life tables and stable populations. Princeton University Press, Princeton, NJ, USA.

Collinson, M.; Garenne, M.; Tollman, S.; Kahn, K.; Mokoena, O. 2000. Moving to Mkhulu: emerging patterns of migration in the new South Africa. Paper presented at the 4th African Census Analysis Project Workshop, Jan 2001, Dakar, Senegal.

Debpuur, C.; Avogo, W.; Abokyi, L.; Akuma, I.; Kondayire, F.; Nazzar, A. 2000. NHRC 1999 Panel Survey: a report of key findings. Community Health and Family Planning Project. Navrongo Health Research Centre, Navrongo, Ghana. DSS Documentation Note 43.

Diallo, D.A.; Habluetzel, A.; Cousens, S.N.; Esposito, F. 1996. Comparison of two methods of assessing child mortality in areas without comprehensive registration systems. Transactions of the Royal Society of Tropical Medicine and Hygiene, 90, 610–613.

Diop, O.; Pison, G.; Diouf, I.; Enel, C.; Lagarde, E. 2000. Incidence of HIV-1 and HIV-2 infections in a rural community in southern Senegal. AIDS, 14, 10671–10672.

D'Souza, S. 1984. Population laboratories for studying disease processes and mortality. The demographic surveillance system, Matlab. In Vallin, J.; Pollard, J.H.; Heligman, L., ed., Methodologies for the collection and analysis of mortality data. Proceedings of a seminar at Dakar, Senegal, 17–10 Jul. Ordina Editions, Liège, Belgium.

Emerson, P.M.; Lindsay, S.W.; Walraven, G.E.L.; Faal, H.; Bogh, C.; Lowe, K.; Bailey, R. 1999. Effect of fly control on trachoma and diarrhoea. The Lancet, 353, 1401–1403.

Enel, C.; Lagarde, E.; Pison, G. 1994. The evaluation of surveys of sexual behaviour: a study of couples in rural Senegal. Health Transition Review, 4 (Suppl), 111–124.

Enel, C.; Pison, G. 1992. Sexual relations in the rural area of Mlomp (Casamance, Senegal). In Dyson T., ed., Sexual behaviour and networking: anthropological and socio-cultural studies on the transmission of HIV. Derouaux Ordina Editions, Liège, Belgium. pp. 249–267.

Enel, C.; Pison, G.; Lefebvre, M. 1993. De l'accouchement traditionnel à l'accouchement moderne au Sénégal. Cahiers santé, 3, 441–446.

————— 1994. Migrations and nuptiality changes: a case study in rural Senegal. In Bledsoe, C.; Pison, G., ed., Nuptiality in sub-Saharan Africa: contemporary anthropological and demographic perspectives. Clarendon Press, Oxford University Press, Oxford, UK. pp. 92–113.

Estève, J.; Benhamou, E.; Raymond, L. 1994. Statistical methods in cancer research. Vol. IV. Descriptive epidemiology. International Agency for Research on Cancer, Lyon, France.

Garenne, M. 1997. Demographic surveillance system: concepts and methods developed in Niakhar (Senegal). Paper presented at the 23rd IUSSP General Population Conference, 11–17 Oct 1997, Beijing, PRC. International Union for the Scientific Study of Population.

Garenne, M.; Tollman, S.M.; Kahn, K. 2000. Premarital fertility in rural South Africa: a challenge to existing population policy. Studies in Family Planning, 31(1), 46–54.

Garenne, M.; Tollman, S.M.; Kahn, K.; Gear, J.S.S. 2000. Causes of death in a rural area of South Africa: an international perspective. Journal of Tropical Paediatrics, 46(3), 183–190.

Graham, W.; Brass, W.; Snow, R.W. 1989. Estimating maternal mortality: "the sisterhood method." Studies in Family Planning, 20, 17–25.

Greenwood, A.M.; Bradley, A.K.; Byass, P.; Greenwood, B.M.; Snow, R.W.; Bennett, S.; Hatib-N'jie, A.B. 1990a. Evaluation of a primary health care programme in The Gambia. I. The impact of trained traditional birth attendants on the outcome of pregnancy. Journal of Tropical Medicine and Hygiene, 93, 58–66.

———— 1990b. Evaluation of a primary health care programme in The Gambia. II. The impact on mortality and morbidity in young children. Journal of Tropical Medicine and Hygiene, 93, 87–97.

Greenwood, A.M.; Greenwood, B.M.; Bradley, A.K.; Williams, K.; Shenton, F.C.; Tulloch. S.; Byass, P.; Oldfield, F.S.J. 1987. A prospective study of the outcome of pregnancy in a rural area of The Gambia. Bulletin of the World Health Organization, 65, 635–643.

Greenwood, B.M.; Greenwood, A.M.; Smith, A.W.; Menon, A.; Bradley, A.K.; Snow, R.W.; Sisay, F.; Bennett, S.; Watkins, W.M.; N'jie, A.B. 1989. A comparative study of Lapudrine and Maloprim as chemoprophylactics against malaria in Gambian children. Transactions of the Royal Society of Tropical Medicine and Hygiene, 83, 182–188.

Greenwood, A.M.; Menendez, C.; Todd, J.; Greenwood, B.M. 1994. The distribution of birth weights in Gambian women who received malaria chemoprophylaxis during their first pregnancy and in control women. Transactions of the Royal Society of Tropical Medicine and Hygiene, 88, 311–312.

GTG (Government of The Gambia). 1981. Primary health care action plan 1981–85. Ministry of Health, Banjul, Gambia.

Habluetzel, A.; Diallo, D.A.; Esposito, F.; Lamizana, L.; Pagnoni, F.; Lengeler, C.; Traore, C.; Cousens, S.N. 1997. Do insecticide-treated curtains reduce all-cause child mortality in Burkina Faso? Tropical Medicine and International Health, 2, 855–862.

Hayes; R.; Mertens, T.; Lockett, G.; Rodrigues, L. 1989. Causes of adult deaths in developing countries: a review of data and methods. World Bank, Washington, DC. Working Paper 246.

Hill, A.G.; Hill, M.C.; Gomez, P.; Walraven, G. 1996. Report on the living standards survey conducted in the villages of the MRC main study areas, North Bank Division, Republic of The Gambia in June–July 1996. Medical Research Council, Farafenni, Gambia.

Hill, A.G.; MacLeod, W.B.; Joo, D.; Gomez, P.; Ratcliffe, A.A.; Walraven, G. 2000. Decline of mortality in children in rural Gambia: the influence of village-level primary health care. Tropical Medicine and International Health, 5, 107–118.

Hill, A.G.; MacLeod, W.B.; Sonko, S.S.T.; Walraven, G. 1998. Improvements in childhood mortality in The Gambia. The Lancet, 352, 1909.

Indome, F.; Binka, F.; MacLeod, B.; Kubaze, F.A.; Phillips, J.F. 1995. The microcomputer software component of the household registration system (HRS). User's manual, version 2.0. The Population Council, New York, NY, USA.

Kahn, K.; Tollman, S.M.; Garenne, M.; Gear, J.S.S. 1999. Who dies from what? Determining cause of death in South Africa's rural north-east. Tropical Medicine and International Health, 46. 433–441.

———— 2000. Validation and application of verbal autopsies in a rural area of South Africa. Tropical Medicine and International Health, 5(11), 824–831.

Kaufman, L.; Rousseeuw, P.J. 1990. Finding groups in data: an introduction to cluster analysis. Wiley, New York, NY, USA.

KCS (Kovach Computing Services). 1998. MVSP (Multi-Variate Statistical Package). KCS, Anglesey, Wales. Internet: http://www.kovcomp.com/mvsp/index.html

Kpedekpo, G.M.K 1982. Essentials of demographic analysis for Africa. Heinemann, London, UK.

Lagarde, E.; Enel, C.; Karim, S.; Gueye-Ndiaye, A.; Piau, J.P.; Pison, G.; Ndoye, I.; Mboup, S. 2000. Religion and protective attitudes and behaviours towards AIDS and STDs in rural Senegal. AIDS, 14, 2027–2033.

Lagarde, E.; Enel, C.; Pison, G. 1995. Reliability of reports of sexual behaviour: a study of married couples in rural West Africa. American Journal of Epidemiology, 141, 1194–1200.

Lagarde, E.; Pison, G.; Enel, C. 1996a. Knowledge, attitudes and perception of AIDS in rural Senegal: relationship to sexual behaviour and behaviour change. AIDS, 10, 327–334.

————— 1996b. A study of sexual behavioural change in rural Senegal. Journal of Acquired Immune Deficiency Syndromes and Human Retrovirology, 11, 282–287.

————— 1997. Improvement in AIDS knowledge, perceptions and behaviours over a short period in a rural community of Senegal. International Journal of STD and AIDS, 8, 681–687.

————— 1998. Risk behaviours and AIDS knowledge in a rural community of Senegal: relationship with sources of AIDS information. International Journal of Epidemiology, 27, 890–896.

Le Guenno, B.; Pison, G.; Enel, C.; Lagarde, E.; Seck, C. 1992. HIV2 seroprevalence in three rural regions of Senegal: low levels and heterogeneous distribution. Transactions of the Royal Society of Tropical Medicine and Hygiene, 86, 301–302.

Leon, D. 1986a. The microcomputer software component of the sample registration system of the MCH-FP Extension Project. User's manual, SRS version 1.1. International Centre for Diarrhoeal Disease Research, Dhaka, Bangladesh; The Population Council Regional Office for South and East Asia, Bangkok, Thailand.

————— 1986b. The microcomputer software component of the sample registration system of the MCH-FP Extension Project. Technical Manual, SRS Version 1.1. International Centre for Diarrhoeal Disease Research, Dhaka, Bangladesh; The Population Council Regional Office for South and East Asia, Bangkok, Thailand.

————— 1987. The microcomputer software concept of the sample registration system. Demonstration manual. The Population Council Regional Office for South and East Asia, Bangkok, Thailand. Unpublished.

Loslier, L. 1995. Geographical information systems (GIS) from a health perspective. *In* de Savigny, D.; Wijeyaratne, P., ed., GIS for health and the environment. Proceedings of an international workshop, 5–10 Sep 1994, Colombo, Sri Lanka. pp. 13–20.

MacLeod, B.; Leon, D.; Phillips, J.F. 1991. The household registration system: a database program generator for longitudinal studies of health status and demographic dynamics. Paper presented at the 2nd Annual Conference on Advanced Computing and Information Technologies for the Social Sciences, Athens, GA, USA.

MacLeod, W.B. 1998. Description of the Farafenni surveillance demographic surveillance system and operation of the household registration system. Medical Research Council, Farafenni, Gambia.

MathSoft Inc. 1999. S-PLUS 2000: guide to statistics. Mathsoft Inc., Seattle, WA, USA.

Menendez, C.; Kahigwa, E.; Hirt, R.; Vounatsou, P.; Aponte, J.J.; Font, F.; Acosta, C.J.; Schellenberg, D.; Galindo, C.; Kimario, J.; Urassa, H.; Brabin, B.J.; Smith, T.A.; Kitua, A.Y.; Tanner, M.; Alonso; P. 1997. Randomised placebo controlled trial of iron supplementation and malaria chemoprophylaxis for prevention of severe anaemia and malaria in Tanzanian infants. The Lancet, 350, 844–850.

Menendez, C.; Todd, J.; Alonso, P.L.; Francis, N.; Greenwood B.M. 1994. Malaria prophylaxis, infection of the placenta and birth weight in Gambian primigravidae. Journal of Tropical Medicine and Hygiene, 97, 244–248.

Menendez, C.; Todd, J.; Alonso, P.L.; Lulat, S.; Francis, N.; Greenwood, B.M. 1994. The effects of iron supplementation during pregnancy given by traditional birth attendants on the prevalence of anaemia and malaria. Transactions of the Royal Society of Tropical Medicine and Hygiene, 88, 590–593.

Menon, A.; Otoo, L.; Herbage, E.A.; Greenwood, B.M. 1990. A national survey of the prevalence of chloroquine resistant *Plasmodium falciparum* malaria in The Gambia. Transactions of the Royal Society of Tropical Medicine and Hygiene, 84, 638–640.

Menon, A.; Snow, R.W.; Byass, P.; Greenwood, B.M.; Hayes, R.J.; N'Jie, A.B.H. 1990. Sustained protection against mortality and morbidity from malaria in rural Gambian children by chemoprophylaxis given by village health workers. Transactions of the Royal Society of Tropical Medicine and Hygiene, 84, 768–772.

Mozumder, K.A.; Koenig, M.A.; Phillips, J.F.; Murad, S. 1990. The sample registration system: an innovative system for monitoring demographic dynamics, Asia–Pacific Population Journal, 5(3), 63–72.

Muhe, L. 1994. Child health and respiratory infections in Ethiopia: epidemiology for prevention and control. Umeå University, Umeå, Sweden. Medical Dissertation, New Series, No. 420.

Müller, O.; Boele van Hensbroek, M.B.; Jaffar, S.; Drakeley, C.; Okane, C.; Jorf, D.; Pinder, M.; Greenwood, B.M. 1996. A randomised trial of chloroquine, amadiaquine and pyrimethamine-sulphadoxine in Gambian children with uncomplicated malaria. Tropical Medicine and International Health, 1(1), 124–132.

Mwageni, E.; Irema, M. 1999. Demographic surveillance as a source of data for health management information systems (HMIS): experiences from the Rufiji demographic surveillance system. Paper presented at the 18th Annual Scientific Conference of the Tanzania Public Health Association, 22–25 Nov, Dodoma, Tanzania.

Newell, C. 1994. Methods and models in demography. John Wiley & Sons Ltd, London, UK.

Ngom, P.; Wontuo, P.; Wak, G.; Apaliya, G.; Nchor, S.; Nazzar, A.; Binka, F.; Macleod, B.; Phillips, J. 1999. The Navrongo demographic surveillance system: 1999 report to the Rockefeller Foundation. Documentation Note 41.

Nyan, O.A.; Walraven, G.E.L.; Banya, W.A.S.; van der Sande, M.A.B.; Ceesay, S.M.; Milligan, P.W.J.; McAdam, K.P.W.J. 2001a. Atopy, intestinal parasite infection and total serum IgE in rural and urban adult Gambian communities. Clinical & Experimental Allergy. (In press.)

—————— 2001b. Prevalence of diabetes, impaired glucose tolerance and insulin resistance traits in rural and urban communities in The Gambia. Tropical Medicine and International Health. (In press.)

Phillips, J.F.; MacLeod, B.; Leon, D. 1991. Final narrative report on grant HS 9015/GA PS 9011: developing microcomputer software for longitudinal studies of child survival. Report to the Rockefeller Foundation. Unpublished.

Phillips, J.F.; Mozumder, K.; Leon, D.; Koenig, M. 1988. The application of microcomputer database technology to longitudinal studies of survival: lessons from a field study in Bangladesh. Paper presented at the Community-based Health Research Conference, Oct 1988, Mexico City, Mexico.

Pison, G. 1980. Calculer l'âge sans le demander. Méthode d'estimation de l'âge et structure par âge des Peul Bandé (Sénégal oriental). Population, 4–5, 861–892.

—————— 1982. Dynamique d'une population traditionnelle : les Peul Bandé (Sénégal oriental). PUF, Paris, France. Cahier de l'INED, n° 99.

—————— 1985. Nouvelles méthodes de collecte dans les enquêtes à petite échelle. IUSSP International Population Conference, 5–12 Jun, Florence, Italy. International Union for the Scientific Study of Population, Liège, Belgium. Vol. 4, pp. 23–38.

Pison, G.; Desgrées du Loû, A.; Langaney, A. 1997. Bandafassi: a 25 year prospective community study in rural Senegal (1970–1995). *In* Das Gupta, M.; et al., ed., Prospective community studies in developing countries. Clarendon Press, Oxford University Press, Oxford, UK. pp. 253–275.

Pison, G.; Le Guenno, B.; Lagarde, E.; Enel, C.; Seck, C. 1993. Seasonal migration: a risk factor for HIV infection in rural Senegal. Journal of Acquired Immune Deficiency Syndromes and Human Retrovirology, 6(2), 196–200.

Pison, G.; Trape, J.F.; Lefebvre, M.; Enel, C. 1993. Rapid decline in child mortality in a rural area of Senegal. International Journal of Epidemiology, 22(1), 72–80.

Pressat, R. 1985. The dictionary of demography. Basil Blackwell, Oxford, UK.

Preston, S.H.; Heuveline, P.; Guillot, M. 2001. The life table and single decrement processes. In Demography: measuring and modeling population processes. Blackwell, Oxford, UK. pp. 38–70.

Rahman, M.; D'Souza, S. 1981. A review of findings on the impact of health intervention programmes in two rural areas of Bangladesh. In United Nations Economic Commission for Asia and the Pacific (ESCAP); World Health Organization (WHO), ed., Mortality in South and East Asia: a review of changing trends and patterns 1950–75. Report and selected papers presented at a joint ESCAP–WHO meeting, 1–5 Dec, Manila, Philippines. World Health Organization, Geneva, Switzerland.

Ratcliffe, A.A.; Hill, A.G.; Walraven, G. 2000. Separate lives, different interests: male and female reproduction in The Gambia, West Africa. Bulletin of the World Health Organization, 78, 570–579.

Sauerborn, R.; Nougtara, A.; Benzler, J.; Borchert, M.; Koob, E.; Krause, G.; Heinmueller, R.; Hien, M.; Hornung, U.; Diesfeld, H. 1996. The impact on infant mortality of improving mother's home treatment and access to health services: an intervention study in rural Burkina Faso (progess report 1994–1996). Department of Tropical Hygiene and Public Health, University of Heidelberg, Heidelberg, Germany.

Schellenberg, D.; Menendez, C.; Kahigwa, E.; Font, F.; Galindo, C.; Acosta, C.; Armstrong Schellenberg, J.R.M.; Aponte, J.J.; Kimario, J.; Urassa, H.; Mshinda, H.; Tanner, M.; Alonso, P. 1999. African children with malaria in an area of intense P. falciparum transmission: features on admission to hospital and risk factors for death. American Journal of Tropical Medicine and Hygiene, 61, 431–438.

Segi, M. 1960. Cancer mortality for selected sites in 24 countries (1950–57). Tohoku University School of Public Health, Sendai, Japan.

Shackleton S. 1998. The approach and methods used in the Agincourt Demographic and Health Study: practical guidelines and lessons. Health Systems Development Unit, Department of Community Health, University of the Witwatersrand, Acornhoek, South Africa.

Shamebo, D. 1993. Epidemiology for public health research and action in a developing society: the Butajira Rural Health Project in Ethiopia. Umeå University, Umeå, Sweden. Medical Dissertation, New Series, No. 360.

Shryock, H.S.; Siegel, J.S. 1976. The methods and materials of demography. Academic Press Inc., London, UK.

Smith, T.; Charlwood, J.D.; Kihonda, J.; Mwankusye, S.; Billingsley, P.; Meuwissen, J.; Lyimo, E.; Takken, W.; Teuscher, T.; Tanner, M. 1993. Absence of seasonal variation in malaria parasitaemia in an area of intense seasonal transmission. Acta Tropica, 54, 55–72.

StataCorp. 1997. STATA reference manual A–F. StataPress, College Station, Texas, USA.

Struyf, A.; Hubert, M. 1997. Integrating robust clustering techniques in S-PLUS. Computational Statistics and Data Analysis, 26, 17–37.

Tablin, D. 1984. Comparison of single and multi-round surveys for measuring mortality in developing countries. In Vallin, J.; Pollard, J.; Heligman, L., ed., Methodologies for the collection and analysis of mortality data. International Union for the Scientific Study of Population, Ordina Editions, Liège, Belgium.

Tanner, M.; de Savigny, D.; Mayombana, C.; Hatz, C.; Burnier, E.; Tayari, S.; Degremont, A. 1991. Morbidity and mortality at Kilombero, 1982–88. In Feachem, R.G.; Jamison, D.T., ed., Disease and mortality in sub-Saharan Africa. Oxford University Press, Oxford, UK. pp. 286–305.

Tanser, F.C. 2000. A model to equitably distribute fieldworker workload in a large, rural South African health survey. Africa Centre for Population Studies and Reproductive Health, South Africa.

Targett, G.A.T.; Drakely, C.J.; Jawara, M.; von Seidlein, L.; Coleman, R.; Deen, J.; Pinder, M.; Doherty, T; Sutherland, C.; Walraven, G.; Milligan, P. 2001. Artesunate reduces, but does not prevent, post-treatment transmission of *Plasmodium falciparum* to *Anopheles gambiae.* Journal of Infectious Diseases, 183, 1254–1259.

TBS (Tanzania Bureau of Statistics). 1994. 1988 population census: coast regional profile. Government of Tanzania, Dar es Salaam, Tanzania.

TEHIP (Tanzania Essential Health Interventions Project). 1996. Demographic surveillance workshop report. TEHIP, Dar es Salaam, Tanzania.

TMH (Tanzania Ministry of Health). 1997. Policy implications of adult morbidity and mortality: end of phase 1 report. TMH, Dar es Salaam, Tanzania.

Tollman, S.M. 1999. The Agincourt field site: evolution and current status. South African Medical Journal, 89(8), 855–857.

Tollman, S.M.; Herbst, K.; Garenne, M. 1995. The Agincourt Demographic and Health Study: phase I. Department of Community Health, University of the Witwatersrand, Johannesburg, South Africa.

Tollman, S.M.; Kahn, K.; Garenne, M.; Gear, J.S.S. 1999. Reversal in mortality trends: evidence from the Agincourt field site, South Africa, 1992–1995. AIDS, 13, 1091–1097.

Trape, J.F.; Pison, G.; Preziosi, M.P.; Enel, C.; Desgrées du Loû, A.; Delaunay, V.; Samb, B.; Lagarde, E.; Molez, J.F.; Simondon, F. 1998. Impact of chloroquine resistance on malaria mortality. Comptes rendus de l'Académie des sciences : Sciences de la vie, 321, 689–697.

United Nations. 1982. Model life tables for developing countries. United Nations, New York, NY, USA.

———— 1983. Manual X: indirect techniques for demographic estimation. UN Department of International Economic and Social Affairs, New York, NY, USA. Population Studies No. 81, ST/ESA/SER.A/81, 304 pp.

———— 1988. MortPak-Lite. Department of International Economic and Social Affairs, United Nations, New York, NY, USA.

Utomo, B.; Costello, C.; Phillips, J.F.; Budiono, T.; DasVarma, G. 1990. A general description of the Indramayu Health and Family Planning Prospective Study. Center for Child Survival, University of Indonesia, West Java, Indonesia. Unpublished.

van der Sande, M.A.B.; Ceesay, S.M.; Milligan, P.J.M.; Prentice, A.; Nyan, O.A.; Banya, W.A.S.; McAdam, K.P.W.J.; Walraven, G.E.L. 2000. Blood pressure patterns and risk factor profiles in rural and urban Gambian communities. Journal of Human Hypertension, 14: 489–496.

———— 2001. Nutritional status of adults in rural and urban Gambian communities. American Journal of Public Health. (In press.)

von Seidlein, L.; Jawara, M.; Coleman, R.; Doherty, T.; Walraven, G.; Targett, G. 2001. Parasitaemia and gametocytaemia after treatment with chloroquine, pyrimethamine/sulphadoxine, and pyrimethamine/sulphadoxine combined with artesunate in young Gambians with uncomplicated malaria. Tropical Medicine and International Health, 6, 92–98.

Walraven, G.E.L.; Nyan, O.A.; van der Sande, M.A.B.; Banya, W.A.S.; Ceesay, S.M.; Milligan, P.J.M.; McAdam, K.P.W.J. 2001. Asthma, smoking and chronic cough in rural and urban adult Gambian communities. Clinical & Experimental Allergy. (In press.)

Walraven, G.; Scherf, C.; West, B.; Edpo, G.; Paine, K.; Coleman, R.; Bailey, R.; Morison, L. 2001. The burden of reproductive-organ disease in rural women in The Gambia, West Africa. The Lancet, 357, 1161–1169.

Walraven, G.; Telfer, M.; Rowley, J.; Ronsmans, C. 2000. Maternal mortality in rural Gambia: levels, causes and contributing factors. Bulletin of the World Health Organization, 78, 603–613.

THE PUBLISHER

The International Development Research Centre (IDRC) is a public corporation created by the Parliament of Canada in 1970 to help researchers and communities in the developing world find solutions to their social, economic, and environmental problems. Support is directed toward developing an indigenous research capacity to sustain policies and technologies developing countries need to build healthier, more equitable, and more prosperous societies.

IDRC Books publishes research results and scholarly studies on global and regional issues related to sustainable and equitable development. As a specialist in development literature, IDRC Books contributes to the body of knowledge on these issues to further the cause of global understanding and equity. IDRC publications are sold through its head office in Ottawa, Canada, as well as by IDRC's agents and distributors around the world. The full catalogue is available at http://www.idrc.ca/booktique/.